From Powerless Village to Union Power Secretary

Memoirs of an IAS Officer

From Powerless Village to Union Power Secretary

P. Abraham

SURYAKUMARI ABRAHAM MEMORIAL FOUNDATION, HYDERABAD
AND
CONCEPT PUBLISHING COMPANY (P) Ltd., NEW DELHI-110059

Cataloging in Publication Data—DK
Courtesy: D.K. Agencies (P) Ltd. <docinfo@dkagencies.com>

Abraham, P. (Prathipati), 1939-
From powerless village to union power secretary : memoirs of an IAS officer / P. Abraham.
p. cm.
Includes index.
ISBN 13: 9788180695551
ISBN 10: 8180695557

1. Abraham, P. (Prathipati), 1939- 2. Civil service—India—Biography. 3. Government executives—India—Biography. I. Title.

DDC 352.630 92 22

Cover Design: Interads Advertising Pvt. Ltd.

ISBN-13: 978-81-8069-555-1
ISBN-10: 81-8069-555-7

Edition 2009

Published and Printed by
Ashok Kumar Mittal
Concept Publishing Company (P) Ltd.
A/15-16, Commercial Block, Mohan Garden
New Delhi-110059 (INDIA)

Phones : 25351460, 25351794
Fax : 091-11-25357103
Email : publishing@conceptpub.com

Dedicated to the memory of my beloved wife Suryakumari

"I will not be presumptuous enough to say that my life can be a role model for anybody; but some poor child living in an obscure place in an underprivileged social setting may find a little solace in the way my destiny has been shaped. It could perhaps help such children liberate themselves from the bondage of their illusory backwardness and hopelessness."

Dr. A.P.J. Abdul Kalam
Former President of India

PREFACE

I never dreamt, even in my wildest dreams, that one day I would even be attempting to write my *memoirs*, leave alone writing it. Indeed I quite often pinch myself, to test that it is indeed a reality and not a dream. For that matter, I had never dreamt that I would be an IAS (Indian Administrative Service) Officer. Having been born and brought up in a small non-electrified village with humble background and uneducated parents and having studied in Telugu (vernacular) medium in a village school with the assistance of hurricane lamps, loans and scholarships, it is really a dream come true to be in the IAS for a first generation educated person. When I started going to school, my father, at best, may have expected me to have the barest minimum education, which he didn't have, to get a small job at the village level, if at all I even completed my village school education. The heights I scaled must have, to say the least, shocked not only my parents but also the village and the neighbourhoods. I don't think my father ever dreamt of making me a Collector, like many, who dream about it even now, even though there are many other competitive avenues of challenging employment opportunities available for bright youngsters. The loans and scholarships were my lifeline and I would still perhaps have been in my village, as a nobody, like many with whom I played in my childhood, if these have not come my way. In the humble environment of my childhood, I did not have any access to either books or newspapers. I was fortunate in my school, college and university to have dedicated teachers, who imparted good education and character to me. I strongly believe in the existence of a Divine Power, which guides people towards their respective destinies. Thus, whatever I achieved was due to God's will and help.

Once you get into the Indian Administrative Service, people presume that you must have been born with a "*silver spoon*", with all the facilities of the best of childhood, education, guidance and advice. Unfortunately in my case, I had none of the above.

I had never seen an IAS Officer until I became one myself. There was neither a necessity nor a chance to really see an IAS Officer in flesh and blood. Events occurred one after the other in such a sequence that I could become an IAS Officer and have a successful career.

When I went to the National Academy of Administration, Mussoorie (presently, Lal Bahadur Shastri National Academy of Administration) for my training in the IAS, the entire atmosphere, with so many young IAS Officers, was very daunting and even scary. There were many who had excellent lineage claiming to be related either closely or distantly to former Presidents of India, Governors, Judges, Members of the Indian Civil Service (ICS), IAS, Professors and Senior Bureaucrats. There were some, who wrote the IAS examination in London while studying in prestigious institutions such as the London School of Economics or at Oxford and Cambridge. Many had come from the best colleges in the country, such as St. Stephens, Loyola, Presidency and Universities such as Allahabad. Most of them had studied in the English medium convents right from childhood. To hobnob with people coming from such aristocratic lineage and educational institutions and to be a part of such a distinguished group was itself a process of growing up in an environment which was totally alien, coming as I did from a first generation educated family.

After undergoing training for one year at the National Academy of Administration, Mussoorie, I was allotted to Maharashtra State. In spite of being a so-called "outsider" (conveying that I do not hail from Maharashtra), I can never ever repay what the State gave to me as an "adopted son". Maharashtra gave me everything, indeed, much more than what I deserved. As I spoke Marathi quite fluently, people used to ask me from which place in Maharashtra I hailed from. I said very proudly that I was from Bhir district, where I was Collector more than four decades back (1966–1969). People from Bhir district recognise me, as a Collector even today, for the work I had done in a backward district of the State. Many people from Bhir, who visited either Mumbai or New Delhi, call on me and my family even now.

I was, unlike many civil servants, not tossed from one job to another several times. I was lucky to get key assignments and except for two jobs which I held for over a year each, in most of the posts, I worked for nearly three years each. I was therefore very fortunate to work in just twelve jobs in over 35 years in the IAS. I was also fortunate to work in four jobs viz., Secretary, Maharashtra State Electricity Board (MSEB); Secretary, Energy Department, Government of Maharashtra; and Chairman, MSEB and Secretary, Ministry of Power, Government of India, spanning nearly fifteen years in the crucial power sector. I had the unique distinction of being the first Chairman of any State Electricity Board in the country, to have ever become the Secretary, Ministry of Power, Government of India, since Independence. Although it is not very common that a civil servant could work in so many important posts in one sector, the credit for this should go to the successive enlightened Chief Ministers of Maharashtra like Shankarrao Chavan and Sharad Pawar and the Prime Ministers of the country like P.V. Narasimha Rao, H.D. Deve Gowda, and Inder Gujral. Not only did I become Secretary, Government of India, to which position not many IAS Officers reach, but also a Constitutional Authority, as Hon'ble Member, Union Public Service Commission, New Delhi. All this had happened, in spite of not having any Godfather.

Looking back, I feel content and satisfied that in my career spanning over 35 years in the Indian Administrative Service, I held some of the most challenging positions both in the Central and the State Governments. During all these years, I made my own humble contribution for the cause of the people. Whatever little I could achieve was entirely due to the support, guidance and help I received from all those with whom I was fortunate to work, from the lowest level of employees to Prime Ministers.

There were some very eminent civil servants who wrote their *memoirs*, which were well received as chronicles of events of the time during which they served the people and the Government. Some of them are master pieces of literature. Many had worked at the highest levels in the government and were privy to many important events in the history of our country. Momentous decisions were taken during their time, which had a bearing on the lives of the people of that time. They had a lot to convey to the people through their memoirs about the events that have shaped the destiny of our country. Some civil servants have scaled greater heights even after their retirement from the civil service, while many others have just faded away. Some faced very serious problems during their career but overcame them. Some left the service in utter disgust, as the system in which they worked did not allow them to serve people in the manner in which they wanted to serve, or they were not allowed to work at all. Some were made scapegoats for the decisions taken, for which they were not responsible, basically to save the skin of some others who didn't have the courage to acknowledge and face the consequences of such decisions. Fortunately, in my entire career, I did not have to face any major problem, although I was certainly involved in many vital and crucial decisions. I did not have any unpleasant encounters with either of my bosses nor have they treated me unfairly for things for which I was not responsible.

I don't know whether my *memoirs* would be of any interest to anyone except to myself and my family, as I do not have anything which may make "spicy" reading. I therefore had great hesitation before I undertook this work. I do realise that however insignificant it may be, I made my own humble contribution as a civil servant. Hence, I thought it is worth while putting my experience in the public domain, especially because I come from rural India and from humble background. It is my intention to convey that every human being, however, insignificant he may be in the system, can still make a worth while contribution to society.

While many prefer to call the Indian Administrative Service as the "Steel Frame" of the country, there are quite a few others who emphatically state that it is neither "Indian" nor "Administrative" nor a "Service". Whatever it may be, the service undoubtedly attracted some of the best talent in the country and continues to do so even today. There were many who tried to get into the service but failed to make it and they were the ones who were even more vociferous in their criticism. The values of the service have certainly changed, but so too has the society itself. While the nature of the service has been changing from time to time, the basic objective of the service, however, has always been to serve the people and the country. I had an excellent opportunity to interact and work with the finest administrators and prominent political leaders of the country. I want to give them their due in my *memoirs,* as human beings, colleagues and bosses and the encouragement they gave me in whatever I did. I learnt a lot from them and there is more to learn.

When I wanted to attempt my *memoirs*, I realized that one had to recollect a lot, as so much had gone by over several years. I found it quite tough and taxing to recollect, as I had not kept any personal notes over the years. The few diaries I had have either been lost or thrown away, being part of unnecessary luggage to be hauled from place to place during transfers. I had to search for information from the places where I worked and also go through some published documents and materials.

It is natural for me to write substantially on the Power Sector in my *memoirs* due to my fascination for this Sector as well as the fact that I had a long innings in the realm of "Power", for about 15 years. My initiation into the power sector started in Maharashtra as Secretary, Maharashtra State Electricity Board (MSEB) (1969–1972—Fourth Five Year Plan of the country) and continued as Secretary (Energy), Government of Maharashtra (1986–1989—Seventh Five Year Plan), Chairman MSEB (1989–1991—Seventh Five Year Plan and Annual Plan) and finally as Secretary, Ministry of Power, Government of India (1994–1997—Eighth Five Year Plan) till I retired from the IAS in 1997. Even in the face of paucity of funds and a host of administrative and technological problems, it was possible to bring about phenomenal improvement in the electricity scenario in Maharashtra and to maintain the MSEB's pre-eminent position, not only as the biggest SEB in the country but also as one of the best performing SEBs in India.

When I took over as Secretary, Ministry of Power, Government of India in 1994, at the beginning of era of globalisation and liberalisation, the power sector could not remain untouched by the sweeping changes taking place in various spheres of commerce and industry. If economic growth had to be sustained, the power sector needed to grow at a commensurate pace, which was not possible in the circumstances then. There was a need for phenomenal capacity additions, strengthening and augmenting the transmission and distribution network. The SEBs, despite their yeomen role in the socio-economic transformation of the country, needed to be radically transformed so that the power sector could play a more meaningful role in sustaining the pace of economic growth. In order to achieve this, a number of measures were initiated to turn the power sector around and make it commercially viable during my tenure as Secretary, Ministry of Power, Government of India.

With more than ten years experience in Maharashtra, especially the "hands on" experience in managing the MSEB, the biggest

Electricity Board in the country, and working as Secretary, Ministry of Power, Government of India, helped me to formulate the "Common Minimum National Action Plan for Power" (CMNPP), which now forms the National Agenda for the Power Sector. It covered all the major aspects and problems in the sector and suggested short, medium and long-term measures to make the power sector a viable one.

Several significant measures, such as reforms in the distribution sector and restructuring of SEBs; establishment of Regulatory Commissions; the need to have Integrated National Energy Policy, Mega Power Policy; the competitive bidding route in awarding power projects; private sector participation in power distribution in Delhi; private sector participation in transmission, which were initiated during my tenure, are all yielding rich dividends now. Starting with Orissa, 12 more states have restructured their SEBs. The remaining states are legally obliged to do so at the earliest, under the Electricity Act, 2003. There has been considerable improvement in the performance of utilities after the restructuring. One of the major gains is the improved commercial performance and reduction of financial losses of the SEBs. The establishment of the Regulatory Commissions initiated during my period brought in much needed transparency and also contributed substantially in improving the commercial viability of the sector. The mega power policy is now being rechristened as "Ultra Mega Power Policy". Competitive bidding was able to bring down the tariffs to the consumers substantially. The Rajiv Gandhi Gramin Vidhyutikaran Yojana is a continuation of the initiatives taken earlier towards meeting the power needs of rural India. While action has been initiated in several areas, the reforms needed to be pursued vigorously. The strong and sustained political support during all phases of reforms is the key to its success. Faster pace is the essence of reforms.

I am writing in my *memoirs* only about those matters which I was involved or had the opportunity to deal with during my long public service both at the national and at the state level in Maharashtra and Andhra Pradesh. I was privy to many important decisions which had vital bearing on the development of the country.

I would like to place on record my personal gratitude to my beloved wife, late Suryakumari who suddenly left for her heavenly abode in December 2001. She was the guiding spirit and inspiration for writing my memoirs, without whose association and encouragement, I would not have scaled the heights I never dreamt of. Indeed, she was the one who suffered all the inconveniences in our life and brought up the children, while I was busy making my own career. Our family started "Suryakumari Abraham Memorial Foundation" to commemorate her memory, of which I am the Chairman. It is a socio-economic voluntary and non-profit organization, dedicated to help in the empowerment of poor, youth and women in the rural areas by providing assistance in education, computer education, medical aid, and self-employment programmes.

Indeed, my grandson Manish was the first in the family to read, by chance, the first few chapters when he came during holidays from Dubai where he was pursuing studies in Engineering from BITS Pilani, Dubai Campus, as I saved the chapters on his computer desktop which he left in Delhi. He was so excited that he read them twice the same night and appreciated the chapters so much I completed my 'Memoirs' without any second thoughts. Similarly, my granddaughter Aishwarya could not believe that I did not have any pocket money during my school days. This encouraged me further to complete the 'Memoirs'.

I also thank all other members of my family: my son-in-law, B. Sam Bob, IAS; daughter, Manjula; son, Rajesh; daughter-in-law, Vineetha and grand children Manish Priyank and Aishwarya for their unstinted support and encouragement in completing this venture. I am also grateful to Rupa Chatterjee for her valuable assistance in going through the manuscript and in helping me to bring out this book. I would like to place my appreciation for the assistance rendered by Shekhar Reddy, J.A.R. Moorthy, Anil Datta Mishra, Tarun Madan, Geeta Bajaj, Shivani Sagar, Bhupinder Rawat, Manoj Bhatt and many others who have worked tirelessly, even beyond office hours and on holidays, to assist me to complete this task in the shortest possible time. I also would like to acknowledge my debt of gratitude to a large number of friends, colleagues and well wishers who helped me in collecting information on the jobs held by me during my long career. I also would like to thank Ashok Mittal of M/s Concept Publishing Company, New Delhi, the renowned publishers in the country, for completing the assignment in the shortest possible time.

Knowing that I functioned as Member, Union Public Service Commission and recruited six batches of IAS, Indian Foreign Service officers and other All India Service Officers like the IPS, IFS and several other civil services, many ask me whether it is worth its while, like in the past, to join the civil services. What they really mean is joining 'the

IAS', as everyone who appears for the civil services examination is an aspirant for the much coveted 'IAS'.

This issue is being debated often these days as, unlike in the past, there are many competitive avenues with substantial pay packages and other incentives available today for bright and professional youngsters. Many of them especially from the urban and educated families, are chasing IIMs, IITs, Foreign Universities, multinational companies and a plethora of new economic options. I am glad that it is also a sign of expanding and excellent opportunities. The easy availability of very good jobs not requiring much of hard work and preparation is turning the people away from the IAS.

There are some who feel that the time has come to write an epitaph for the IAS. In any case, for those who hanker only for huge financial packages and the urban comfort, the IAS is certainly not meant for them. It is true that the profile of an IAS officer has undergone considerable change and a reorientation is needed in the IAS. However, there is hardly any service like the IAS, which offers an excellent opportunity to serve the *aam aadmi,* and specially those, who still live "below the poverty line" and who require to be covered in the "inclusive growth".

Many join the civil services to make a visible impact on the welfare of the *aam aadmi* and to contribute for 'public good'. Many jobs in the civil services offer immense job satisfaction and great scope for creativity. Could many who aspire to become executives in multinational corporations with huge pay packets ever gain all-round independent experience in managing the complex and complicated problems of a District and become a part of its growth and development which a young IAS officer gains? There are many such opportunities in the career of an IAS Officer where he can make a difference.

It is heartening to note that the number of aspirants from smaller towns and rural areas is increasing.

It is true that a civil servant may loose out to his corporate counterparts 'cost to company' compensation. But the biggest incentive to a civil servant is directly to be a part of the growth process of the country, actively participate in policy making and indeed have the power to make policies and implement them. He can also be a facilitator for a change which the country needs for progress. The IAS is meant for serving the general public. Those who are committed to serve the nation in the larger interest are bound to be fascinated by the IAS, whose experience is highly rewarding personally and professionally.

The primary objective in penning down my memoirs is to inspire the younger generation, to avail the opportunity to join the IAS and the other Civil Services and make major and everlasting contribution and make a difference to the cause of common man and the country.

It is indeed a fascinating and rewarding experience to have been in the Indian Administrative Service and I commend this service to all youngsters who are committed to serving the people and the country with dedication.

New Delhi **P. Abraham**

1 July 2008

CONTENTS

ONE

A VILLAGE BEGINNING

I was born and grew up in Gaddamanugu, a tiny, isolated and non-descript village situated about 5 kms from Kondapalli and 28 Kms from Vijayawada, in Krishna District, Andhra Pradesh. My father, paternal uncles, aunts, cousins and most of my other relatives were born here. The remnants of battle scars on the high mountains of Kondapalli fort for centuries served as a source of famous Kondapalli toys and handicrafts made from a special variety of wood grown in the nearby forest in various forms of animals, especially elephants, horses, camels etc. artistically painted in pleasing colours, are very famous all over the world. It is a renowned place for art, art patrons and art critics. But inexplicably I remained oblivious to its famed legacy during my early childhood, till my village school took us for a day's excursion to Kondapalli Fort. We walked to Kondapalli through the fields and climbed the mountain to reach the fort by a footpath route, as there was no road to the fort. We were told about the battles fought to protect the Kondapalli kingdom. There were several inscriptions on the stones and a dilapidated fort devoid of maintenance.

Vijayawada (earlier known as Bezwada or jocularly called as Blazewada for its excessive heat in summer) is the second biggest city and a big commercial centre in Andhra Pradesh with a major railway junction linking the South to the rest of the country. Chandrasekhar, former Union Health Minister and Population Control Specialist, once referred to "excessive heat of Vijayawada and stated famously that Vijayawada is place where hens straight away lay chickens and not the eggs due to excessive heat." It is a famous pilgrimage centre with abode of Goddess Kanakadurga temple, an education centre, located on the bank of Krishna River, is about 28 kms from my village, Gaddamanugu. Kondur, Pinapaka, Vidyanagaram and Kattubadipalem are our neighbouring villages. All these villages are on the Vijayawada-Kondapalli-Mylavaram-Tiruvuru road.

Gaddamanugu is surrounded by a thick growth of trees and high mountains with thick forest cover on the eastern and western parts. I do not remember having seen a single house from outside the village when I was small, as the entire village was covered with big trees. Most of the houses were built with mud walls with thatched roofs except for a very few houses covered with Mangalore tiles and a couple of houses with concrete floors. Adjacent to our village, there was a 'rivulet' called "Puli Vaagu" (Tiger rivulet), a little stream which flowed in the rainy seasons when the water flowed down from the nearby hills. It was said that a tiger was once washed away in the rivulet due to heavy floods caused by torrential rains, and hence the name.

DRINKING WATER PROBLEMS

A modern water supply was unheard off. There were a few wells from where people used to draw water with the help of buckets for daily use. Each community or locality had its own well and the weaker sections were not allowed to draw water from other community wells as the caste system and untouchability were very much prevalent in many places. Our village was no exception. Our village suffered greatly for lack of drinking water, as the village wells could not produce sweet water for drinking. We used to bring drinking water from a near by rivulet, Puli Vaagu. We used to drink rainwater that had fallen on the mountains and came down in the rivulet, and also water overflowing from the fields, collected in small ponds. We used to allow the muddy water to settle down in the pots and sometimes used "alum" to clear the water from impurities. During summers, the stream usually went dry. People dug small holes in the sand near the bank of the stream for springs of sweet water for drinking. During the rainy season, children, yours truly included, used to go to the Puli Vaagu for swimming.

KRISHNA RIVER

The Krishna River was about 10 kms from our village. As our village was located at a higher elevation, we had no access to river water and therefore could not utilize it for agriculture. The lands were of black cotton soil and fertile. I had seen the Krishna River only a few times in my childhood. Whenever there were flash floods, which are quite frequent in the rainy season, villages such as Ibrahimpatnam, Guntupalli, Gollapudi and Rayanapadu which are on the bank of Krishna River were often flooded and submerged. The Government hardly bothered to offer any help during such difficult times. Whenever the river submerged villages, people died in large numbers, and families suddenly became destitute. For weeks together no contact could be established with the relatives in these villages and as crops were destroyed, famine conditions loomed large over the area. Means for mere subsistence such as food and shelter became unavailable and exorbitant. My grandfather told me that once there were very heavy rains and floods and the crops were totally washed away. The rainwater stagnated in the fields for days together and as most of the villagers had nothing to eat, many died of starvation. If rains were devastating, summer was worse with excessive heat. A prolonged period of dry weather usually played havoc with the poor.

HARMONY AMONG COMMUNITIES

Ours was a small little village, with a population of about 400 people. Upper castes and other backward castes constituted the majority, followed by weaker sections. We had a few families of tribals (Erukulas) who used to rear pigs and weave baskets to earn a living. There were only a few Muslim families in our village. There was, however, no mosque. They were mostly landless like many from the weaker sections. They used to tend a few goats and sheep and lived away from the main habitation, although quite close. They used to play musical instruments during festivities, especially during marriages. There was only one family of potters, who used to meet the pottery requirements of the entire village. The noteworthy feature of our village was that there was always a tremendous amount of communal harmony, cordial relations and unity amongst the various communities. All the communities used to help each other during difficult times. If there were any disputes, they were solved amicably. There was considerable respect towards each other in the village and all communities celebrated all the festivals together with great gusto. Festivals were celebrated by *harikathas, burrakathas* and *kolatams*. There were no brahmins, goldsmiths, washermen, barbers and other artisan communities in our village, so we depended for their services on our neighboring village Kondur. Even in Kondur, there were only few brahmin families who were in great demand for their services.

Upper caste families owned a majority of the land and all of them were farmers. Most of the backward and weaker section communities were agricultural labourers, although few of them had small land holdings and also cultivated small tracks of "poramboku" (Government lands). For farming, one depended on rainwater and water stored in artificially formed ponds. Farmers used to grow mainly rainfed crops, as there were no irrigation facilities. Jowar, raagi, and sajja (millets) were the main crops. Only a few farmers cultivated some paddy during the rainy season with the assistance of artificially created ponds. Jowar remained the staple diet for all the families. Very few families in the village could eat rice regularly. In our village, milk and curd were available in abundance. One could have a hot jowar meal with chutney and curd. Gongoora (a leafy vegetable) pickle, a hot favourite of Andhraites, makes Andhra food complete by itself. Farmers were generally very rich, and a variety of cash crops were also grown, such as tobacco, chillies, tomatoes and groundnut. The village used to provide seasonal employment to many from the neighbouring villages. There were many tobacco barns for seasoning tobacco, before it was sold for manufacturing cigarettes in the neighbouring district of Guntur.

Evenings were wild and noisy in our village; I can never forget the excitement of those days in the village. I can still recollect vividly the melodious sound made by the musical bells tied on the necks of the bullocks returning from the fields and the loud and boisterous laughter of the people returning from work. Agricultural workers used to receive jowar as wages in the evening. The jowar was grounded in mortars with pestles. I remember the rhythmic beat of the pestles and the humming sounds of the people that filled the air before the food was cooked. All the family members poured hot water into small containers and bathed. Hardly any one used soap for bathing in the village. Firewood collected from the fields and nearby forests was the only fuel for heating water to bathe and for cooking. People used to collect firewood from the forest. I also used to go with my cousins to collect the firewood along with other people. Most of the people worked hard during the daytime and ate the dinner made out of millets mixed with some chutney and chilly powder.

The village was demarcated by two main streets, intersecting in the middle. While the three portions were occupied by the houses of the upper castes, the fourth portion was occupied by the weaker sections. Although the residences of weaker sections were generally located away from the main village in many places, in our village, these residences were located in the main village itself, adjoining to the upper caste location. Any one entering the village from the main entrance to the village had to pass by the side of our house, as it was the first house located in a corner of the centre of the village. In the other three corners, two corners were covered by houses of different communities and there was a Lord Sri Rama Temple in the third corner, where most of the festivities took place. There were only two provision stores in our village, one of which was just behind our house. Whenever people required some provisions not available in our village, they used to walk down to Kondur, our neighbouring village, to buy provisions, which was about a kilometer away.

VILLAGE SCHOOL

During my childhood, not many paid attention to education in our village. Hardly anyone went to High School at Kondapalli, as it was located about five kilometres away from my village, which could be reached by walking on a muddy tank bund for a kilometer and four kilometers, by walking on the road. However, our village had the best Upper Primary School upto 8th standard in the area, where children from many neighbouring villages used to come to study. Illiteracy was rampant in all the communities, more so among the backward castes and weaker sections. Most of the children were taken for work in the fields but I was fortunate to go to school from an early age.

NO ELECTRICITY

Civilized life and creature comforts were alien to our village. Very few people used to wear any foot wear. There was no electricity. There were no sanitary facilities like latrines in our village. Every one used to go to the nearby fields to answer the call of nature. No one in our village used tooth brushes and tooth paste. Most of the people used to pluck small branches of the neem trees, which were plenty in the village and used them to brush their teeth. Many used to pluck branches from the huge neem tree near our compound.

RURAL HEALTH-CARE PROVIDERS

Gaddamanugu could hardly boast of any medical facilities, so the people depended on rural health-care providers. I remember many people suffering from severe toothache came to my uncle (my father's elder brother) Rajarathnam, who knew some herbal medicine. My uncle would go to the nearby fields, whenever someone came with toothache, and pluck some green leaves from the bushes and grind them with his palms and pour the liquid in the ear, and after a few minutes he used to empty the ear by bending the head. The liquid came out with a small live germ and the toothache would disappear thereafter. Even now it is beyond my comprehension to understand the relationship between the toothache and a germ coming out of the ear. I tried my best in my childhood to get some information about the magical medical leaf, which my uncle refused to divulge lest he lose the magical touch. I doubt whether my uncle revealed this secret to any one even till his death. People also used to go to the Mission Hospital at Vidyanagaram about 3 kms from my village, which was visited by Dr. Skinner and Dr. John from the Mission Hospital Vijayawada once in a week for free examination and free medicines. The hospital was subsequently named after Dr. Skinner, a medical doctor from England. People went to Kondapalli or Vijayawada for serious ailments.

WORSHIP VILLAGE GODS

The villagers performed feasts in honour of village gods and goddesses, by sacrificing animals like sheep, goat and chicken in propitiation. People also used to install stones and wooden poles under the neem trees and worshiped 'poleramma' and 'ganganamma', two prominent village deities. These celebrations were held normally before the commencement of agricultural seasons. The entire village got into a festive look during these days and literally every one had new clothes, except the very poor. Sweets were sold on road side and those were the most enjoyable times for children. On Sri Rama Navami Day, all communities participated in the procession carrying Lord Sri Rama idol on a palanquin, dancing and singing bhajans. I still remember the melodious bhajans sung by Madala Suryanarayana with great gusto. After the festival, people distributed 'Panakam', a sweet drink prepared with jaggery and pepper, freely to all. My friend Bapaiah would take me to his sister's house during the celebrations of the festivals and I used to take part in special food festivities.

A SMALL CHURCH

There was a small church in the weaker section's locality. It was a palm leaf shed with mud walls. There was considerable influence of Christianity among the weaker sections, like many other villages in the area. Some upper caste families also believed in Christianity. Every Sunday children used to go first and spread the mats on the floor, and they continue to sing hymns till the elders joined. People used to stage dramas based on biblical stories in our village as well as at Vidyanagaram in front of packed audiences. We celebrated both Hindu and Christian festivals.

CULTURAL ACTIVITIES

Youth in those days were adept in playing Kolatum, (called 'dandiyas' in some parts of the country). Singing songs from stage plays was another favourite pastime. Some would get drunk during these festivities and prance in rhythmic movement. For entertainment, we did not have any cinema halls anywhere in a radius of 28 kms from our village, so the stage artists went from place to place and enacted mythological plays like 'Satya Harish Chandra' and 'Sri Krishna Tulabharam'. The famous artists during those days were Eelapati (whistling) Raghuramaiah, Vemuri Gaggaiah and Pisapati Narasimha Murthy, who immortalized the mythological characters and are fondly remembered even now. If a play was staged even in a far away village, people used to go there, watch it through out the night, and return in the early morning. Most of the children would go to sleep even before the first act was over. The other entertainment available in the village were puppet shows. People waited eagerly for such performances. Some affluent people from our village travelled all the way to Kondapalli on foot (5 kms) catch a train to Vijayawada to see a movie occasionally. Telugu matinee idol and evergreen hero during those days was N.T. Rama Rao (NTR), who acted as hero in more than 300 movies and later became a very popular Chief Minister of Andhra Pradesh and the architect of the National Front Government at the Centre during the 1990s. I was privileged to work with him as Commissioner of Industries when he was the Chief Minister, Andhra Pradesh. Akkineni Nageshwara Rao (ANR), popularly known as "Evergreen Hero" who played memorable and unforgettable roles, was equally popular. ANR continues to rule even now in the Tollywood (Hyderabad film world referred as such as Bombay as Bollywood) as an uncrowned king. I consider it as a privilege to claim him as my well wisher and a family friend. I met him as recently as 29 February 2008 at Hyderabad. Film heroines like Bhanumati, Savitri, Anjali Devi and Jamuna (who also became an MP) were quite popular. Whenever we went to Vijayawada, either to see a movie or for an excursion of the school, we used to walk five kms to Kondapalli and catch a train to Vijayawada. We used to carry home made food and watch three movies a day, literally running from one theatre to another, sleeping on the railway over bridge at Vijayawada Railway Station and return home the next day by following the same route. It used to be a very exciting and hectic day. I still remember once that my friend Bapaiah, another friend and I walked upto Kondapalli to catch a train to Vijayawada but having missed the train, walked all the way along the railway track upto Vijayawada (16 kms) just to see a movie! What a thrill it was to walk all the 16 kms to Vijayawada just to see a movie!

POOR COMMUNICATIONS

Communications network between villages was non existent. One never heard of happenings in other villages unless someone visited the village and gave information. There were no roads between the villages. One had to go either on foot or on cycle. During the rainy season, it was impossible to go from one village to another village as the footpath used to be very slushy. One or two persons used to get vernacular (Telugu) newspapers in our village. Some used to walk upto Kondur and gathered news from the newspapers at tea stalls. Our village Panchayat radio with a loudspeaker, which operated on the battery, was the only source providing some news and occasional entertainment through filmy songs. Appasani Kotaiah had a gramophone on which he used to play film songs loudly. As my house was very near, I used to hear the songs very clearly. Waheeda Rehman, an artist from Andhra Pradesh acted first in a Telugu movie before she became more famous nationally in Hindi films. She was an accomplished dancer even then and danced on a hit song from the film "Rojulu Marayi", which meant "the days have changed", signifying the dawn of new era after Independence, in early fifties. It was a super hit movie, which also had evergreen hero of Telugu celluloid, Akkineni Nageshwara Rao (ANR) and Savitri, as heroine. This song was played often during those days on the Radio.

VILLAGE ADMINISTRATION

The village Munsiff and Karanam (village accountant) were the uncrowned kings of the village administration. All land records with the details of survey numbers, ownership of lands, boundaries, tenants, crops grown, were available with the village Karanam. They also used to settle many disputes at the village level. The district administration depended heavily on them for any information about the village.

DEEPAWALI CELEBRATIONS

In our village, Deepawali was celebrated with great gusto for three days. As it coincides with the harvesting season, plenty of dry stems of Jowar and Bajri was available. These stems were bundled together in small quantity and lighted in the end. The children used to roam around all the streets swinging these lighted hay stacks and bringing brightness to the village.

SANKRANTI (PONGAL) FESTIVAL AND COCK FIGHTS IN THE VILLAGE

All the festivals, especially Deepawali, Christmas and Sankranti were celebrated with considerable pomp and fanfare. During the time of Sankranti (Pongal), all the villagers celebrated the festival for three days. One of the major events of the festival was the cockfight. The cockfights were usually held in the fields having big trees which offered shade for organizing cock fights. Well-bread cocks used to be brought from all the neighbouring villages to a common place and a few elders went round the fields, and selected the cocks which appeared to be equal and organized the fights in an earmarked circle. People used to bet heavily (a rupee was a big sum in the villages those days) and winners celebrated on a grand scale because of the heroic victory of the cock. Sometimes the pride and prestige of the village was at stake at these cockfights. A lot of country liquor used to flow, quite often with the connivance of the police as sale of liquor was prohibited at such public places. Similarly, there were several places in the Mela where people used to play card games, such as the popular "open and close" with heavy betting. There used to be occasional police raids on the illegal betting and gambling but it is believed that police were usually won over by the organizers. Everyone looked forward eagerly to this festival due to its festive atmosphere.

ORIGINS OF VILLAGE NAME

I always used to wonder why our village was named Gaddamanugu. Elders told me that the village had rich and fertile black cotton soil and even a small piece weighed a mound signifying that even a small piece was worth its weight in gold. Farmers were very rich and a variety of cash crops were grown such as tobacco, chillies, tomatoes and groundnut. There were many tobacco barns for seasoning tobacco, before it was sold for manufacturing cigarettes in the neighbouring district of Guntur.

These are some of the unforgettable memories of my village where I grew up. I continue to visit my village very regularly, my last visit being as late as the January, 2008, all the way from New Delhi.

TWO

EARLY EDUCATION IN THE VILLAGE

VILLAGE EDUCATION

It was on 24th January, 2007 that I saw a beautiful photo on the front page of the Deccan Chronicle (a prominent daily newspaper from Hyderabad) with a caption "Write Stuff", showing a priest helping a child to write his first alphabet on a slate as part of "Aksharabhyasam" (initiation into studies) ceremony on *saraswati pooja* day. The caption goes on to say that many children wrote their first alphabet on that day in the State. While many children have such formal initiation to schools by having regular ceremony of Aksharabhyasam with prayers on an auspicious day and time, there was no such ceremony in my case. In our village, the teachers used to go from street to street and gather children, quite often, forcibly and take them to school. Indeed in my case, it was my teacher Pilli John Sudarshanam, who took me to school and taught me my first alphabets. He came from the neighbouring village, Kondur. As our house was at the entrance of the village, John Sudarshanam would pick me first before others. My parents told me that I used to eagerly wait for him every morning, unlike many other children in the village, who used to run away from him.

THATCHED-SHED SCHOOL

Our school, an Upper Primary School, was located on the extreme side of the village on a farm land. It was only a thatched shed and with temporary partitions to separate classes. One could hear the voices of all teachers simultaneously, distracting the attention of students and teachers alike. This was the only Upper Primary School in the area and it had classes upto the 8th standard. The nearest Zilla Parishad High School was located at Kondapalli which was about 5 kilometres from our village. There were not even the basic amenities in our school. There were no benches and all the children used to squat on the floor and study, while the teachers had only stools to sit on. The Headmaster was the only privileged one to have a chair and a room. The Headmaster taught English to the students. Each teacher was assigned one class and taught all subjects. All teachers studied only upto higher grade teacher's training course. During the rainy season the thatched roof used to leak heavily and quite often all the children were bundled together in one corner. We had plenty of open space in the school for playing. Teachers used to conduct simple exercises and we also played games like Kabbadi and Kho-Kho.

Parents hardly showed any interest in sending children to the schools, as most of them were illiterate agriculturists. Instead, they took the children to work in the fields, especially from the poorer sections, as the children earned small amounts by way of wages, to add to the family income. The teachers, however, used to search the entire village and literally drag the children to the school. We used to have morning and afternoon sessions in the school. Most of the teachers came from neighbouring village Kondur, including our Headmaster, Kondur Mangeshwara Rao.

MY FAMILY

My grandparents, Muthiah and Sundaramma, had ten children, seven sons and three daughters. The eldest son was Rajarathnam and my father Sundaram was the second son. I am the only child to my parents, Sundaram and Deevenamma. All of them were uneducated, like many people in the village. They cultivated not only their own land but also used to take others land on lease for cultivation. My uncle and father, thus managed to bring up the entire family as small farmers. I was told by my father that once in a week, some foreigners used to come to the village along with some teachers who knew Telugu and made the children to write alphabets on the sand in a small school, as they never had any slates.

Our family was considered to be economically slightly better off, as we were owning some poramboku (government) lands and also cultivating others lands taken on lease. They used to cultivate jowar, millets, in addition to cash crops like groundnuts and pulses. They were all hardworking people. Like many agriculturists in the village, our family also had a pair of bullocks with necessary agricultural implements. All the children, including myself, used to assist our parents in their agriculture operations, by regularly going to the fields.

Ours was a joint family where all my uncles with their families used to stay together and cultivated the land together, till their marriages. Subsequently, they divided the household properties and agricultural land among themselves and lived separately. Both my uncle and my father, in addition to cultivation, used to buy and sell cattle and thus earned additional income to support the family. We had some milch cattle. My uncle Rajarathnam, though uneducated, was very intelligent and impartial in his dealings. Whenever there was any family or land disputes, not only in our village but also in the neighbouring villages, his intervention was sought after to mediate as an Umpire and settle the disputes. As he was impartial and never took any sides in a dispute, his decisions were considered fair by both the parties. My father, Sundaram, during the time of cultivation of tobacco, which was widely grown in our village used to supervise the work of barns used for seasoning the tobacco and he was well paid for his skills. He had to spend, literally and figuratively, sleepless nights while working on the tobacco barns, as he had to keep awake the whole night to ensure proper seasoning of tobacco leaves.

I being the only child to my parents, they brought me up with considerable care and love. If anyone took liberties on me, they never tolerated. My mother, Deevanamma was very hardworking and used to run the house very efficiently. They gave me the best within their limited means. Although they were uneducated, recognised the need for education even in those days and gave me the best education possible, which made me what I am today.

In my family, we were seven immediate cousins, including one sister. Sister was the eldest and she never went to school and got married early. My elder cousin, Prasada Rao was already in the school. While my elder cousin and myself were regular in going to school, the younger cousins would cry and run away from the house during early mornings so that they were not caught by John Sudarshanam. They preferred to go to the fields. Prasada Rao after passing the 8th standard joined the nearest High School at Kondapalli, a place about 5 kms from my village. He was the first to go to High School from my family. He went to Secondary Grade Teacher's Training School at Machilipatnam, Krishna District. He became a schoolteacher and taught in our village school and finally retired as Headmaster of a school in Vijayawada Municipal Corporation.

POWERLESS VILLAGE

There was no electricity not only in our village but also in many neighbouring villages. We could not afford lanterns. I, therefore, studied with the help of tin container lamps with wicks made out of loose cotton. My mother always used to caution me not to study till late in the night as it would affect my health. However, my father would scold my mother and told her not to prevent me from studying, as he realized the importance of education, being uneducated himself. I used to complete my home work on the same day, which was very much appreciated by my teachers.

Most of the children from my school, after completing the 8th Standard, went to the Higher Grade Teacher's Training School at Vidyanagaram, a place over 3 kms away from my village. The school was run by the Church of South India Mission. The training school had hostel facility for poor students. All the teachers teaching in the Elementary schools in the surrounding villages were trained at Vidyanagaram. Indeed, it could be said that Vidyanagaram true to its meaning in Telugu was a "Centre of Excellence in Education".

HEADMASTER KONDUR MANGESHWARA RAO

The Headmaster of our school was Kondur Mangeshwara Rao. He was very short, fat and fair. He invariably used to wear dhoti with a shawl on his shoulder. He was a terror not only to the children but to the teachers as well. He strictly believed in the philosophy of "spare the rod and spoil the child". He used to cane the children often to ensure that they were regular in attendance and studies, primarily with the objective of inculcating a sense of discipline in them. His influence had a salutary effect on the attitude and discipline of the teachers as well. He was such a strict disciplinarian that those who were not regular in studies were never spared from punishment, which included severe caning, several sit ups and standing in the last row till the end of the day. There was hardly any student who escaped the wrath of Mangeshwara Rao. I was one among the few exceptions who was not caned by him, primarily because I went to school regularly and did my homework on time. Indeed, Mangeshwara Rao used to appreciate my studies and exhorted other students to emulate me. Because of his strict discipline, there were only a few failures in the 8th Standard Public Examinations from our school. The reputation of our school, although located in a small village, spread far and wide in the district and many students from distant villages came to study there, primarily because of the commitment of Mangeshwara Rao to education. Many people who studied in our village school got employment as teachers in all the neighboring schools in our area. He was instrumental in gifting education in the area. He was a role model as a teacher. In addition, because of student hostel facility for weaker sections, many students came from far away places in the district to study in our school.

During my primary education days, English was not compulsory. It was only optional from 6th standard onwards. However, our Headmaster insisted on teaching English from early classes. He firmly believed that the English language was essential for good education and if the children learnt English in the Primary School, they would do well in future education. I liked English and the people said that I always made an attempt to speak 'broken English'. Mangeshwara Rao made me often read English lessons in the class so that others could listen. He obviously saw some merit in me and as I was very good in studies, Mangeshwara Rao gave me a double promotion from 1st standard to 3rd standard. I owe a debt of gratitude to Mangeshwara Rao, as a good foundation for my future education was laid in my village school. I would be failing in my duty if I do not acknowledge his contribution in making me what I am today.

OUR TEACHERS

There were hardly half a dozen teachers in the school, notable among them being Pajjuru Akkaiah, Kandula Gopala Rao and Gurindapalli Raghavulu. Our Mathematics Teacher Raghavulu gave tuitions for those who were weak in Mathematics. I attended his tuitions regularly. Unlike the present system of education, where children pay exorbitant tuition fees, all teachers used to take extra classes with commitment and devotion and without expecting any financial benefit from the children.

MY ASSOCIATION WITH CHILDHOOD FRIEND BAPAIAH

I had a very good friend in school, Katamneni Bapiah, who recently retired as Principal, A.N.R. College, Gudivada. Bapaiah came from Rayanapadu, a neighbouring village and stayed right from his childhood with his sister who was married in our village. We used to study together. Bapaiah's sister and brother-in-law used to treat me very kindly and were very considerate and never gave me the impression that I did not belong to their community. Their encouragement also contributed to my hard work along with Bapaiah. I used to sleep quite often in their house after late night studies, even though my house was not far off from theirs. While many children in the school used to make lot of noise and were unruly, I was generally a quiet student. I was short, thin and weak as a child and spent most of the time either with the books or with Bapaiah. I was very good in all subjects, especially in English. I found Mathematics quite tough, while Bapaiah was brilliant in Maths but not very good in English.

EIGHTH STANDARD PUBLIC EXAMINATION

One had to pass Public Examinations in the 8th Standard and the Examinations were held only at a few centres in the district. Vijayawada, which was at a distance of 28 kms from my village, was one such centre. The 8th Standard Public Examinations were conducted at Gandhi Municipal High School, Vijayawada. In order to stay in Vijayawada for a week, my father borrowed money from others to enable me to write my examinations. All the students used to stay in a community hall for the duration of the examinations, opposite the High School, adjoining Gandhi Park, Vijayawada. The teachers prepared the students for the next day's examination in the night. As it was Public Examination, which was quite tough, there used to be many failures. Once my father asked me whether I would be able to pass the examination. I seem to have told my father that "if I do not pass, nobody in the school would pass". My father often used to mention this fact to people with lot of pride. I not only passed but also stood First from my school. I secured 78 per cent marks, highest in English from my school. My Headmaster and teachers were very proud of my achievement. There were not many students who appeared for Public Examinations from my village as most of the students were from neighbouring villages. Both Bapaiah and myself passed the Public Examination in 1952. The entire coastal area of Andhra Pradesh was then a part of the Madras State and I still vividly recollect that the 8th

Standard Certificate had the emblem of Madhura Meenakshi Temple, the State Symbol.

NEW HIGH SCHOOL AT KONDUR

While I was studying in the 8th standard, fortunately for me, a Zilla Parishad High School was established at Kondur during 1951, a neighbouring village, which was just about 1 km from my village. The establishment of a High School in my neighbouring village was a God sent opportunity, particularly to me, and a turning point in my destiny. But for this High School, either I would have been sent to Higher Grade Training School at Vidyanagaram or to the High School at Kondapalli, which was a far away place. I would not know what decision would have been taken by my father, as Higher Grade Training would have given me an early job as a teacher in the village school, and thus an additional income to the family, or an admission in the High School, which would have been an expensive proposition and a long wait to start earning. As destiny would have it, my father decided to send me to Zilla Parishad High School, Kondur, for my High School education.

MY FATHER'S ENCOUNTER WITH HEADMASTER, HIGH SCHOOL

My father was overjoyed at my success for having come first in the school and felt I should pursue higher studies in the high school at any cost. He went to meet the Headmaster, M. Satyanarayana, B.A., for my admission. When my father met the Headmaster with the marksheet, the Headmaster was quite impressed and asked my father to bring me to meet him. I went along with my father who was very tall and hefty and I was literally a puny creature standing beside him. The Headmaster angrily shouted at my father and said "I asked you to bring your son; why did you come alone?" My father pointed towards me and said 'he is my son.' The Headmaster could not believe that a small child could secure such a high percentage of marks in the Public Examination and immediately gave a seat in the 9th standard. My father always narrated this incident to many people with considerable pride.

DATE OF BIRTH NOT KNOWN

My father took me to the school next day and met Prayga Hanumantha

Shastry, a teacher who was in charge of admissions in the school. While filling up of the application for admission, Shastry asked my father about my date of birth. My father did not know the date of birth, as nobody maintained the date of birth of any child in my family, as all of them were uneducated. I presumed, Shastry calculated in his mind that I should be at least sixteen years of age to get a job after passing 11th standard (SSLC) and put my date of birth as 1-7-1939. Knowing my family's financial condition, he obviously presumed the maximum I could ever study is perhaps the 11th standard and get employment. Quite often people ask me the time, date, year and star of my birth for making astrological predictions after noticing my career graph. I promptly replied that the date of birth was given to me by my teacher Shastry, who admitted me into the High School. My career went so well, Shastry gave me the best and most auspicious day, month and year! I profoundly express my gratefulness to Balakrishna Shastry, "Bala" (to friends), son of Hanumantha Shastry and a good friend of mine, who was one year senior to me in the high school, for his father giving me such an auspicious date of birth. Curiously, all my cousins were also given 1st of July of different years, fortunately, as date of births, so much so like community marriages which are celebrated on a single day, all of us could celebrate a community birth day!!

When I was scaling new heights in education and also got into the IAS, many in the village started counting my age. To my horror, I found Prayga Hanumantha Shastry put my date of birth at least about one and half years more than my actual age. I, therefore, retired earlier than my date of retirement. While many manipulate their date of births favourably, the illiteracy of my parents affected me adversely. Come to think of it if my actual date of birth was mentioned in my records, I would not have even been eligible to appear for IAS during 1961 because of underage, when I got into the IAS in my first attempt. God has his own ways of blessing those who believe in him!

HIGH SCHOOL EDUCATION

About half a dozen children used to go to the High School from my village. I used to carry a small tiffin carriage (lunch box). There was no road between the two villages and it had only a bullock cart route and a footpath through the fields. Most of us used to go barefoot. During the rainy season, we used to cross a small rivulet (Purlintha Vagu) with considerable difficulty. Whenever the stream was in floods, we used to wait till the water receded and carry our books on head and lunch box on the shoulder and cross the stream. In addition to crossing the rivulet, as Kondur and Gaddamanugu were separated by a village tank, we used to walk on muddy tank bund, and quite often slipped and fell down in mud while going to school.

The school had a long thatched shed with six separate rooms for each class and one room for the Headmaster, which was also his office. There was no compound wall and there was plenty of open space for play. I do not remember any student wearing either shoes or chappals. There were no uniforms in the school. We always wore short sleeve shirts and shorts. I had no knowledge of so-called "pocket money". Zannavarapu Venkateshwara Reddy (ZV for friends) was the first School Pupils Leader (SPL). Even in the High School, Bapaiah and myself used to be very close to each other. I used to actively participate in the debates conducted in the High School on occasions such as Gandhi Jayanthi, Independence Day and Republic Day and won prizes. During the class examinations, I used to write very lengthy answers, especially in Science. Once I was given second highest marks in the class test in a subject. When I asked the teacher, why I was given less marks, although I wrote all the points mentioned in the text book, the teacher told me that my answers were too lengthy while the reply given by the other boy, who was given highest marks was very precise. He also added that lengthy answers are appreciated and fetch good marks in the College. He almost predicted my future of going to the college which I never dreamt at that stage!

I wrote the Public Examination for the 11th standard (SSLC) in March 1955 at Gandhi Municipal High School, Vijayawada, where I had given the 8th standard public examination also. I passed with very high percentage of marks in all the subjects, which was the talk of the village and the neighbourhood. Bapaiah and myself were separated in our studies after the High School, although we continue to remain close friends even today.

MY CONTEMPORARIES FROM MY VILLAGE

While I was studying in the Elementary School at my village and High School at Kondur, Ballem Rosaiah, Gutha Venkatapathi Rao and Gutha Venkatarathnam were junior to me and were my contemporaries from my village. All of them were brilliant students and have done extremely well in their careers. Ballem Rosaiah joined Engineering College at

Kakinada and passed the B.E. (Hons.) with distinction. He was the first Engineer from my village and retired as Engineer-in-Chief, Government of Andhra Pradesh. Gutha Venkatapathi Rao also joined Engineering College, Andhra University, Waltair, and obtained a B.E. degree. He joined the Defence Research and Development Organization (DRDO), Govt. of India, and retired recently as Chief of one of the Establishments in the DRDO. Gutha Venkatarathnam, who was a cousin of Venkatapathi Rao, obtained B.Sc. and B.Ed. degrees and became a school teacher. Unfortunately, he died pre-maturely. Another person who achieved pre-eminence from my village was Nuthakki Lakshminarayana (Babu Rao), who did Engineering and joined BHEL. He resigned early and started his own industry. It was undoubtedly a golden period for my village in the educational field. Even though a few went to college from my village afterwards, none of them reached commendable heights in their careers.

THREE

HIGHER EDUCATION AND SELECTION TO THE IAS

FIRST TO GO TO THE COLLEGE FROM MY VILLAGE

This was a crucial phase of my career. A major decision was required to be taken by my father after I passed the SSLC (11th standard) either to join me for secondary grade teacher training course to get early employment, or to pursue higher studies in college. It was a difficult decision to take, as there were none to guide my father, either in the village or in the neighbouring village. Everyone who came to know my marks, suggested that I should pursue higher studies in college. It was an equally difficult decision for me too. While early employment would help my parents financially, further studies meant continued dependence on my parents to support my college education, as higher education meant higher costs. Another emotional problem was indeed the biggest, which would be to leave my parents alone in the village, as I was their only child. While it was a great dilemma for me, my father was very determined that I should pursue college studies and that he did not want any financial support from me. He was prepared to borrow money to support my studies which would be repaid slowly. My father had already started approaching people in the village to lend him money for my studies, even without my knowledge. There were many in my village who were prepared to lend money to enable me to pursue higher studies, as they all appreciated my zeal and enthusiasm for higher studies. They were indeed looking forward to sending a boy who would be first in the village to get into the portals of a college.

While there were many in my village who helped by lending money, two of them need special mention as they put lot of faith in my pursuit of higher education and in my father's ability to repay the loans. Initially, it was Jammula Kondaiah, a landlord. My father used to borrow small amounts of money from Kondaiah for my college education which he repaid in installments from his meagre earnings. Similarly, when I went to the University, as the expenses were high, my father borrowed from Gutha Venkateshwara Rao, another landlord. Although I got the scholarships throughout my college and University education, the scholarships usually came at the end of academic year. There was, therefore, a necessity to support myself with the borrowed money during the college till I got the scholarship. The scholarship normally covered the boarding, lodging and the tuition fees. At the end of each year, I used to save some money from my scholarship and pay a part of the loan while my father paid the remaining loan taken during the year from his hard earnings. I could redeem the last payment of loans, after I joined Indian Administrative Service. No amount of praise will adequately express my gratitude to these two educational lovers, apart from few others from my village, who never failed to extend their helping hand whenever I was in dire need of money to pursue my education. One had only to imagine their joy and pride when I became an IAS Officer! For my villagers, it meant, I had become a Collector!!

WGB COLLEGE, BHIMAVARAM, WEST GODAVARI

Having decided to pursue college education, the next problem was where to seek admission. The obvious place and closest to our village was Vijayawada, also called Bezwada, where there were two colleges, SSR and CVR College and Loyola College. Based on my marks I could have secured admission in either of these colleges. However, my father was very apprehensive and concerned as to how I would pursue my college education in such a big place, which was second only to Hyderabad in Andhra Pradesh and was commercial capital of the State, and where we did not know anyone. When we were debating this point, my father came to know about Nallamothu Prabhudas, who was studying in West Godavari Bhimavaram (WGB) College, Bhimavaram. Prabhudas assured my father that he would keep me in his hostel room and look after me like his own brother. On this assurance, my parents decided to send me to the WGB College, Bhimavaram.

Ever since I secured admission in the College, my parents started crying, unable to bare my separation from them, as I was their only child. My mother openly started saying that our home would be empty forever, as truly that was the beginning of the end of my life in my village, even though I spent all holidays in my village during College and University days. It was a sad day for me too, when I left my parents and my village. The entire village walked a kilometre to the bus stand at Kondur to bid good-bye to me. I could never forget that sorrowful moment.

Bhimavaram was about 150 kms away from my village. One has to commute by bus upto Vijayawada, get into a train to Gudivada and change into another train to reach Bhimavaram, which was undoubtedly a long journey that took almost a day. Prabhudas, who was one year senior to me in the college was very happy to take me under his guardianship. Prabhudas had two very good friends, N. Raja Rao from Razole and Manassey Prasad from Antarvedipalem, both from adjoining District East Godavari. We lived like brothers and thus started my college days in Bhimavaram.

The college was located outside Bhimavaram on a canal bund. It has a huge big compound. The classes were conducted in the sheds. Most of the students were from West Godavari and adjoining parts of East Godavari district except a few from neighbouring villages from Krishna District. It was a residential college except for those from Bhimavaram. The college had many hostels located at different places and could accommodate more than 600 students. I was allotted Gannabathula lodge, hardly a ten minutes walk to the college on the canal bund where we used to bathe.

I secured a seat in Intermediate in Maths, Physics and Chemistry group (MPC). As I studied in the Telugu medium, initially I found the studies, especially Maths, very difficult, as all the subjects were taught in English. My intention to take MPC group was to become an Engineer. Another popular group was Biology, Physics and Chemistry (BPC) to become a doctor. Those who could not secure admissions in these prestigious groups, opted for Arts subjects (Humanitarian Groups). I found Maths very tough, and I had no intention whatsoever to fail in Intermediate, especially as I was being supported by loans taken by my parents. After spending two weeks in MPC Group, I changed my group to two Histories and Banking (2 HB) group. Perhaps it was the first decision I had taken in my life on my own. The college conducted tutorial examinations every week in all the subjects by rotation. Often I used to get the highest marks in all the subjects and in both the years, I got the best student prize. As I got many prizes in the Annual Day Function, most of the students began recognizing me in the college. When the results of the Intermediate were declared, I got First Class in Arts and was the only First Class in the Arts in the college during the year. My parents were thrilled for the distinction I achieved in the College. When I went to seek admission to B.A. degree in the college, E. Lakshminarayana, Principal, advised me to apply for admission in B.A. (Hons), a three years Post Graduation Degree, as I obtained First class instead of studying for two years for B.A. and two years for Post Graduation. Till then I did not know the existence of three years B.A. (Hons.) Post Graduate Degree. Thus I got an opportunity to obtain a Post Graduate degree in three years which was another personal achievement in my career.

ANDHRA UNIVERSITY, WALTAIR (VISAKHAPATNAM)

I got admission in B.A. (Hons.) History in Andhra University and proceeded to Waltair, to pursue University studies. The University was located in a sprawling area with lots of cashewnut trees and very near to the lovely beach. In the evening, most of the students used to walk to the beach, play some games and enjoy the cool breeze. There were at least a dozen hostels in the University campus, each building having two to three floors. There were a couple of messes and various hostels were attached to each mess. While most of the days attendance in the mess used to be very thin, Saturdays and Sundays dinner used to be rush hour, as non-vegetarian food was served on these days.

When the list of selected candidates for B.A. (Hons.) was put on the Notice Board, many students were disappointed not to find any lady's name in the list, except one name "K. Rama" which appeared close to a lady's name. The entire class was eagerly waiting for Rama to join. One day when role call was made, a fat, short, burly looking young man said "Yes Sir". The entire class was totally disappointed. However, subsequently a very pretty young lady joined our class and she was the envy of not only our class but also for every one in the University. People used to linger around the bus stop whenever the ladies bus came from ladies hostel or departed from the University to have a glimpse of this 'University Beauty'.

The students regularly used to go to city to watch the movies. There were only two Cinema halls in Vizag. It was common to see the students climbing the hill, all the way to the University after watching the late night movies, as there were no late night buses. I used to play hockey for my hostel during Inter-Hostel Sports Meet.

I was very good in studies and used to get very high marks in most of the subjects. I still recall Prof. K. Satyanarayana, Head of the Department of Political Science, once while teaching District Administration on the role of the Collector, pointing towards me mentioned that "if Abraham was the District Collector, what could he have been done in a given situation", literally making fun of me. I blurted out unconsciously, "Sir who knows, one day I may be the District Collector", without realizing what I said. The entire class laughed. This innocent remark of mine had perhaps sown seeds to appear for the IAS Examination.

When the results for B.A. (Hons.) were declared, results of a few candidates were withheld, including mine. My father was shocked and presumed that I must have failed. I was certain that there was no question of failing, as I was getting excellent marks in all the tests conducted in the University throughout the three years. My father was reluctant to allow me to go to the University, fearing that I may not return home, if I failed. After considerable persuasion, my father reluctantly agreed to send me to the University. I met Professor Oruganti Ramachandraiah, Head of the Department of History. He informed me that my case was referred to the Vice-Chancellor for consideration whether I should be awarded First Class or declared as Highest Second Class, as the Vice-Chancellor has the powers to award First Class, for those who missed First Class narrowly. Finally, Vice-Chancellor gave me the highest second class and became a gold medalist from Andhra University, Waltair. This distinction of mine encouraged me to prepare for IAS Examinations.

MY FIRST JOB AS A TEACHER FOR A FEW DAYS

After receiving the results, I started applying for the post of Lecturer in Government colleges, as normally done by others who secured second class. While I was staying in the village, Sagam Sivarami Reddy, village Munsif, Kondur, offered to take me to meet Jalagam Vengala Rao President, Zilla Parishad, Khammam District, as he knew him well. Vengala Rao, offered immediately a job of a Teacher in Zilla Parishad High School, Gandhampalli Kothapeta. It was the first job in my career. The village was about 10 kms from Khammam and one can reach the village after travelling by train to Garla and then walking through the paddy fields for about 2 kms. It was a newly sanctioned High School in a small village with only basic minimum facilities. I could stay with one of the families in the village. I taught all the subjects to 9th standard children, as it was still not a full-fledged high school. I worked as a teacher only for a few days and left the school, as I wanted to pursue my preparations for appearing for the IAS Examinations.

FIRST VISIT TO DELHI FOR INTERVIEW

I had taken up the preparations very seriously and appeared for the written IAS examinations during October-November 1961. I cleared the written examination in my first attempt and was called for the interview on 16th March 1962. I did not visit Delhi prior to my interview, as I did not know any one in Delhi with whom I could stay during the interview. When my written results were known in the village, the post-master and a teacher of Chevuturu contacted me stating that his brother Chevuturu Rama Rao was working as an Engineer in Central Public Works Department (CPWD), New Delhi and he would write to him to accommodate me with him when I went to Delhi. It was very kind of him to offer this hospitality. When I landed in Old Delhi railway station on 12th March 1962, it was very cold and it was also drizzling. I got into an auto and I told the auto driver to take me to Moti Bagh. As it was raining heavily, I could not see much of outside area. The entire route was full of trees and gardens and looked like a forest and totally deserted. I was scared that the auto driver realizing that I was a newcomer and also did not know much of Hindi would take me for a ride. After almost 45 minutes of endless journey, he stopped outside a newly constructed Bungalow and told me that I had reached my destination. I heaved a sigh of relief and thanked the auto driver profusely. Moti Bagh at that time was still being developed. New Bungalows and roads were being constructed. The family of Rama Rao made my stay extremely comfortable and I did my interview extremely well.

IAS INTERVIEW

B.N. Jha was the Chairman, Union Public Service Commission (UPSC). The other Members, inter alia, included Hassan Zaheer and G.S. Mahajan. K.P.S. Menon, eminent Diplomat and T.N. Subhedar were the Advisors. There was only one Interview Board. The entire Commission interview the candidates for IAS.

It is difficult for me, after a lapse of more than four decades, to recollect the entire IAS interview. However, I was extensively quizzed on the "Liberation of Goa", which had taken place a few months before my interview. Referring to 2 HB subjects offered in Intermediate Examination, one of the Members of UPSC asked me whether 2 HB refers to 2 Hydrogen Bombs. When I mentioned that the 2 HB referred to 2 Histories and Banking subjects offered by me for Intermediate Examination, all the Members of the commission had a hearty laugh! The interview was quite tough and gruelling, to say the least. When I came out of the interview, I met one of the candidates appearing for the interview the next day. He told me that 'you are appearing so happy! I am sure you must have done your interview extremely well, and sure to get into IAS.' He turned out to be M.P. Khosla, another successful candidate whom I met in the Academy and he fondly recalled my first meeting with him after the interview.

After I returned to my village from Delhi, I was strolling on 20th March 1962, outside my house and listening to the news on Radio operated by battery when I came to know that the results of IAS were announced. As was the practice, the names of ten toppers were announced. In any case I did not expect to be in the first ten. I was under tremendous anxiety about my results the whole night. The next day early morning I went to the neighbouring village Kondur and saw the results in the Telugu Newspaper at a Tea stall and was happy to find my name in the successful candidates list. There was also a separate news item in the paper mentioning the names of ten successful candidates from Andhra Pradesh. The entire family was overjoyed at my success in IAS in my first attempt. The entire village celebrated my selection to IAS. The Upper Primary School in my village and Zilla Parishad, High School, Kondur, where I studied honoured me with grand functions on my selection into the IAS. The village honoured me with a grand farewell function on the eve of my departure to Mussoorie to join the IAS.

FOUR

THE MUSSOORIE ACADEMY

JOINED THE IAS

I appeared for the Indian Administrative Service (IAS) Examination (since 1979 called the Civil Services Examination), held by the Union Public Service Commission in October-November 1961. Although my performance in the written examination and the interview was very good, I had the usual pangs of anxiety about my chances of success, as it was one of the toughest competitive examinations in the country. The result of the 1961 IAS Examination was announced by the Commission at Dholpur House, New Delhi on 20 March 1962. I heard about it accidentally from the battery-operated radio of the Gram Panchayat, which was very close to my house in the village. Since I had appeared for the interview on 16th March, I did not expect that the results would be announced so soon. However, since I was in my village near Vijayawada in Andhra Pradesh, I had to wait for another twenty four hours to get to know the results, since I did not have access to any newspapers. I had to walk to the next village to see that my name had figured in the merit list of successful candidates from a Telugu newspaper at the roadside tea stall. The news of my success was hailed in my village and the surrounding areas as a great achievement. I too was thrilled, as overnight I became a celebrity and the local people had appreciative discussions about my scholastic abilities and intellectual competence. In those days, neither print nor electronic media was available in remote villages, unlike today, and therefore the selection of a village boy into an elite service, as early as 1962, went totally unnoticed, both literally and figuratively.

Foundation Course

I joined the IAS on probation on 26th May 1962 at the National Academy of Administration, Charleville, Mussoorie, Uttar Pradesh, presently called the Lal Bahadur Shastri National Academy of Administration. In 1959, when the venue of training shifted to the Academy, the old and sprawling Hotel Charleville of the British days was purchased by the Government of India and remodeled to cater to the training of not only officers of the IAS, the IFS (Indian Foreign Service), the IPS (Indian Police Service) but also a large number of other young probationers of the Central Services.

We were a large contingent of 98 IAS probationers and a substantial number of them hailed from Tamil Nadu. In addition, 12 successful candidates in the merit list joined the Indian Foreign Service (IFS) on probation. Many of the IFS probationers were ranked very high in the merit list, unlike today. The topper of the batch Krishnan Raghunath chose the Indian Foreign Service in preference to IAS. Raghunath eventually became the Foreign Secretary of India and after retirement from the service was sent to Moscow as our Ambassador there.

In our batch of 98 probationers in the IAS, Andhra Pradesh—my home State—had a surprisingly large contingent of 10 IAS probationers. This was a record of sorts, as hitherto only about one or two persons from Andhra Pradesh had qualified in the Examination.

Our batch, which had probationers from all parts of the country, came from different social and cultural backgrounds. Since we were staying in the premises of the National Academy of Administration, a spirit of camaraderie developed quickly. It was not unusual to see probationers belonging to different parts of the country walking together in small groups on the Mall in Mussoorie, one of the prettiest "Hill Stations" developed by the British.

Mrinalini—Only Lady IAS Probationer

The major disappointment of our batch was that it had only one lady probationer, Tara Bhaskar Abhyankar. However, immediately after qualifying, she got married and when she came to the Academy, she had already changed her name to Mrinalini Vijaykumar Garde. Her husband, a handsome young engineer from Bharat Heavy Electricals Limited, Bhopal, was Vijayakumar Garde. Even after all these years, I can still recall how the young hopefuls in our batch were disappointed to learn that the only lady in the batch was already married. I believe marriages among gentlemen probationers and lady probationers who meet for the first time in the Academy at Mussoorie are quite common these days, as a fairly large number of lady officers qualify every year in the Civil Services Examination. Who knows it better than me, since as Member, UPSC, I had the unique distinction of selecting six batches of young civil servants in the country.

Director—Aditya Nath Jha

Our Director in the Academy was Aditya Nath Jha of the Indian Civil Service (ICS) who belonged to the 1937 batch of the ICS. Being the son of the famous Ideologist Pandit Ganga Nath Jha, and brother of Amar Nath Jha, a scholar of English language and literature, and a former Vice-Chancellor of the University of Allahabad—Aditya Nath Jha was a great scholar himself. His command over Sanskrit language and literature was matched by his command over English language and literature. He was also very proficient in French and as he himself once narrated in the Academy, his French, both in choice of words and intonation, was that spoken in Parisienne high society.

Aditya Nath Jha was a very magnanimous person. He never gave sermons. He only exhorted the probationers that they should never forget they were now officers of the most prestigious service of the country and should serve the people with commitment and dedication. He left the probationers to learn on their own, after a well earned entry into the portals of the "Steel Frame", as the IAS was generally referred to. Aditya Nath Jha used to take only a few special class as with the probationers and his lectures, on any subject—be it public administration or any other subject of general interest—were simply delightful to hear. One learnt a lot from his lectures and wished he could take more classes. One day, some fellow probationer asked him why he was not taking more classes, as he knew such a lot on a variety of subjects. Jha replied with his usual wit that he was the captain of the ship of the training Academy and if the captain of the ship was seen to be working vigorously when the ship was afloat on the high seas, obviously an impression would be created that the ship was in danger!!

There was also a story current in the Academy that Jha, who was very tall but grossly overweight even in his youth, appeared before the interview board of the ICS. He was asked whether because of his enormous bulk, would it not be difficult for him to do horse riding, which was compulsory for the ICS trainees? Jha replied with his characteristic wit that whether the interview board felt that horse riding would be difficult for him because of his bulk or difficult for the poor horse! The interview board burst into laughter. Naturally Jha was apprehensive about the result, but when the results of the ICS examination were announced he was at the top of the merit list.

Visit to Kashmir

Our training commenced in the last week of May 1962. In the first week of June, when we had barely spent a few days at the Academy, we got the most welcome news that the Government had decided to send all of us on tour to the Kashmir valley, which would be followed by a two weeks attachment with the Indian Army. The entire group travelling in the reserved first class (for me it was the first time) compartments and air conditioned buses, sang and made merry. Kashmir was described as 'If there is a Heaven on Earth, it is this! It is this!' It was really so, so breath taking by beautiful. Those days the most popular movie was "*Jab Pyaar Kisi se Hota Hai*" starring matinee idol Dev Anand and Asha Parekh. While singing the title song, the entire group used to give special emphasis on the word HOTA, to make fun of Purna Chandra HOTA, one of the popular probationers, who retired recently as Chairman, UPSC. We enjoyed the excellent hospitality of the people and Government of Jammu and Kashmir. We met the Chief Minister Bakshi Ghulam Mohammed, who assured us that since we were the honoured guests of the Government, the lodging and boarding bills need not be settled immediately, but, after we received our salaries in Mussoorie. This announcement was a great relief, as many of us reached Mussoorie with a bare minimum of cash, as we were not aware of the immediate trip to Jammu and Kashmir. At Srinagar, we were accommodated at the Tourist Reception Centre, which was a fairly comfortable place. Every morning we used to assemble at the Tourist Reception Centre and went by bus to different places for seeing the implementation of various schemes for the socio-economic development of Kashmir. We had several memorable *shikara* rides on the Dal Lake. During our stay in Srinagar, we were invited one day for high tea by

Bakshi Ghulam Mohammed, Chief Minister of J & K. Another day we went to the Raj Bhavan overlooking the Dal Lake, where Yuvraj Karan Singhji, the Sadar-i-Riyasat of J & K, gave us sumptuous high tea at his Palace, where we could watch the supposedly best sunset view. We visited all the places of historical and tourist importance, including the snow peaks of Gulmarg and Kilanmarg, riding on ponies.

Army Attachment

The Kashmir visit was followed with a two weeks attachment with the Army in the forward areas. We were divided into small groups of three to four probationers and sent to the forward areas on the Indo-Pak border. This was my first exposure to the Army and I was attached to the Second Grenadiers, near Jammu. We were shown all the army exercises and demonstrations of arms, ammunitions and armaments. We were also given training in the use of fire arms. In the end, we performed all exercises which the officers in the armed forces were required to do while in active service. At that time I never realized that I would be a part of the armed forces services fraternity in the later part of my career, as Additional Secretary, Ministry of Defence, Government of India.

Foundation Course

We returned from the tour of Jammu and Kashmir and the Army attachment some time in early July 1962 and were joined at the Academy by about 250 probationers of the Central Services and the Indian Police Service. Our batch for the Foundation Course thus totalled almost 350 and there was a huge big crowd of young probationers being trained at one place. In our time, the Foundation Course was for about four months, and as far as possible, probationers belonging to other services shared rooms in the Academy with members of the IAS to promote fellow-feeling among the officers. There were about 350 probationers belonging to all services and as the accommodation in the old hotel Charleville where the Academy was located was not adequate, adjacent big buildings were hired by the Academy to accommodate probationers of the Foundation course.

There were many lady probationers from the Central Services who came for the Foundation Course. The first lady who was recommended for the Indian Police Service was from our batch and although Indu Lekha Passey was very keen to join the IPS, she was dissuaded from doing so and for some inexplicable reasons was persuaded to join the Indian Railway Accounts Service. It took a decade for the establishment to accept a lady IPS officer. Kiran Bedi, thus, became the first lady IPS officer in 1972.

While it was difficult to know each one of the trainee officers personally, as the duration of our training was very brief, we still managed to make plenty of friends from other services and many of us also worked together subsequently in some posts. A large number of officers from Andhra Pradesh were selected for other services as well, which made people joke that we could form an Andhra Probationers Association at Mussoorie. Subsequently, when I occupied important positions under the State Governments in Maharashtra, Andhra Pradesh and the Government of India at New Delhi, I used my old friendships to resolve many ticklish official issues by taking help from the other services, who had also come to occupy top positions in their hierarchy. After the Foundation Course was over, officers of the IFS, the IPS and the Central Services left Mussoorie to go to their respective training institutions for professional training, while the IAS Probationers stayed back for the training.

Daily Life at the Academy

At the Academy, the day for the probationers started early in the morning with either physical exercises or horse riding. If, due to heavy rains in the hills of Mussoorie from the middle of June to the end of September, riding or physical exercises could not be held in the morning, depending on the dryness of the riding ground, riding class used to be held in the afternoon.

Our classes used to begin at 10 AM on every working day and end by 1 PM. The dining hall in the Academy was large enough to accommodate for sit-down lunch of about 200 to 250 probationers at a time. Those of us who for some reason were late used to have lunch with the second batch. After lunch, there were seminars, tutorials or talks by eminent persons. In the evening, the probationers were free to go out for long walks to the town.

K. Madhava Rao, who studied with me in Andhra University, was also selected for the IAS. As I used to be very thin and under weight when I got into the service, I was quite apprehensive about whether I would get medical clearance. However, I was cleared by the obviously considerate medical board in Nizam Hospital, Hyderabad. Madhava

Rao's favourite joke about me was that the best place to find me, whatever may be the time was the dining hall, as my one point programme, after having got into the IAS, was to put on as much weight as I could at the earliest!! Purna Chandra Hota, another IAS probationer, looking at my frail figure used to joke with some of the Andhra friends that "Abraham would be either 'nedo' ('today' in Telugu) or 'repo' (tomorrow)" signifying that my days on earth were numbered!! I, however, successfully weathered the storm caused by my frail physical frame and actively participated in the morning physical exercises and compulsory horse riding, even managing to clear the riding test in the first attempt.

We had to study both criminal and civil law and the Constitution of India, in addition to Economics, Public Administration and Phonetics. The Code of Criminal Procedure, Indian Penal Code, and the Indian Evidence Act were taught by Pathak, a retired District Judge. He taught the complex provisions of Criminal Procedure and the Law of Evidence with the help of some charts, which contained drawings illustrating different provisions of the law. He was a very good teacher, who was able to make the complexities of law appear very simple. He used to make complex and complicated points of Law so interesting with several acronyms that no one missed his classes, whereas the attendance in many other classes was thin. One could recollect even after the lapse of four decades, the easy definition of 'Theft' given by Professor Pathak. He defined Theft 'as "*Madhya Pradesh Without District Magistrate*", which when expanded conveys "movable property without consent with dishonest intention moved from place to place". The absence of any of these ingredients does not amount to 'Theft'. Professor Sharma used to teach us 'linguistics' and while teaching phonetics, he used to make us repeat the correct 'phonetic sounds' and the class room used to reverberate with various sounds resulting in a great deal of mirth.

Horse Riding

A description of our outdoor training in the Academy would be incomplete without mentioning the redoubtable Nawal Singh, the horse riding instructor, who was an ex-Army man. He had a very tough and imposing look and a big moustache. The horses in the Academy were from the cavalry battalion of the Army and were very ferocious. All of them had the "Horse Sense" to know that most of us were inexperienced riders. Many of us used to spend sleepless nights before the days fixed for riding.

On the appointed day for horse riding, there used to be a competition among the probationers to rush to the riding ground, well before the start up time, so that one could select a supposedly mild horse. After a few days, I noticed that some of the probationers were carrying small packages, which I later learnt contained jaggery to feed the horses before the start up, so that the horse became mild and behaved well without throwing the rider off the saddle! There was hardly anyone of us who had not fallen at least once from horseback. We used to have several exercises on horse riding including trot, canter, gallop and hurdle crossing. Whenever the horse galloped, we used to clutch the saddle very tightly and invoke God Almighty's blessings till we dismounted from the horse. Some of the horses, particularly a huge dark horse by the name Nisha, were very sturdy animals and inspired fear in us. Nawal Singh, would of course ride Nisha and keep it under total control while performing some acrobatics on horseback. Among the fellow probationers, B.N. Yugandhar, who is now a Member of the Planning Commission and a very few others, could ride Nisha very well. Nawal Singh's famous lines when a probationer fell off his horse while riding was, "Saab, how did you dismount without orders?" He would not rush to the aid of the fallen probationer and ensured that the probationer got up from the ground all by himself and mounted the horse again to complete his riding exercises. Naval Singh's yardstick of performance of an IAS officer was measured in terms of handling the horse and he used to exhort the probationers often, "if you cannot ride a horse, how can you run a district as Collector and District Magistrate". He would come behind a horse and whip it which made it to gallop and we used to clutch the saddle very tightly and invoke God Almighty's blessings for a smooth ride.

As passing the riding test at the end of a year's training in the Academy at Mussoorie was required for confirmation in the Indian Administrative Service, all of us tried hard to learn the skills of a reasonably competent rider to get at least pass marks in the riding test. The test used to be held towards the end of the training period at the Academy, with the Director chairing the panel of judges, which included the two Deputy Directors.

During training Mrinalini Garde, the only lady probationer, fell from horseback so frequently that on the recommendation of Nawal Singh A.N. Jha exempted her from horse riding. However, she considered it infra dig to be granted such an exemption. She tried very hard and by continuous practice—during which she also fell down several times—

she passed the riding test, at the first attempt, while some gentlemen officers failed and had to go back to the Academy in subsequent years.

It would be interesting to recollect the reasoning given by Mallavarapu Venkata Siva Prasada Rao (many probationers made lot of fun of the long name) about the riding test which unfortunately he failed. During the hurdle crossing test, he crossed the hurdle, as he was thrown over the hurdle by the horse but the horse did not clear the hurdle. He vehemently argued with the instructor that he should pass the test as he crossed the hurdle and it was not his fault, if the horse did not do so. But the argument was of no avail. He had to appear the next year for the riding test. Fortunately, this time he passed.

Equitation Medal

In order to encourage competition among the probationers, an Equitation medal was instituted in the Academy for the best horse riding probationer. The judges for this medal were M.A.S. Rajan, who by then became Director, Academy and a representative from the Indian Military Academy, Dehra Dun. There were several contenders for the medal. The test comprised of trot, canter, gallop under controlled conditions, hurdle clearance and multiple hurdle clearance. Everyone expected B.N. Yugandhar, who rode "Nisha" to get the medal, but he was upstaged by G. Sundaram, the ultimate winner.

Even after so many years, I remember the remark of Nawal Singh, which he was not tired of repeating that if, we as trainees, could not control horses, we could never expect to manage a district as Collector and District Magistrate. In later years in the service, we came to realise that horse riding not only gave us physical stamina and endurance but also a sense of confidence in handling men and matters. One day while I was serving as Secretary, Ministry of Power, I was pleasantly surprised to receive Nawal Singh, who looked almost the same after 35 years. He was accompanied by his grandson and had come with a request for an electricity connection to an agricultural pump in his village. When I spoke to the Chairman, Uttar Pradesh State Electricity Board in his presence; he was quite moved by this gesture. After the electrical connection was given to the pump, he wrote a very touching letter to me.

I understand that in the Academy at Mussoorie, riding has become optional for IAS probationers on the specious ground that with the advent of the automobile, no officer was expected to do his tours and inspection on horseback. Well, it is true that no civilian now maintains a horse for performing duties and maintaining a horse has also become very expensive. But in my opinion horse riding as a part of initial training of an officer of the Administrative Service has relevance in the overall context of grooming an officer to face very difficult situations with composure and confidence.

Our physical training instructor Gaikwad, a former Army Officer, was a picture of physical fitness and used to tell all of us that the physical exercises that he asked us to do would have not only short-term but very long-term benefits. As Gaikwad hailed from Maharashtra, he also initiated me and others who were allotted to Maharashtra in learning Marathi. Gaikwad has settled down in Mussoorie after his retirement and is still physically fit and mentally alert.

ANIL KUMAR, FONDLY CALLED 'CHACHA'

We had some indoor games and many probationers used to gather during the wintry months in the billiards room. One day Anil Kumar (Chacha, as he was fondly called by all the probationers to distinguish him from another Anil Kumar, who was also old enough among the officers to be deservedly called Chacha) and Yogesh Chandra, an alumnae of Oxford, also known as "Charpi" played a game of billiards. Yogesh Chandra claimed that he was playing billiards right from his childhood, whereas, Chacha saw the billiards table for the first time in the Academy. One day Chacha defeated Yogesh Chandra, who promptly challenged him for a replay, as he alleged that Chacha had won by fluke. Chacha, who hailed from rural Uttar Pradesh, in his typical rural wit stated that "if I say that you got into IAS by fluke, would you resign and appear for the IAS examination again?". That settled the issue then and there!!!

Anil Kumar was well known for his frank repartee even in later years in service. While serving in Maharashtra, he was transferred three times in one and a half years, involving change of headquarters. The last transfer required him to move out of Bombay, where he was transferred only a few months back. He was, therefore, desperate to get his orders cancelled from Bombay. He reportedly called on the then Chief Secretary BB Paymaster, ICS (1933) to get redressal of his problems. Paymaster was a very sympathetic, considerate and highly human Chief Secretary. Paymaster, obviously, guessed the purpose of Anil Kumar's meeting with him and even before, Anil Kumar could mention his transfer, Paymaster started recounting his own experience of transfers. Once as a young officer from Sind (then part of the old Bombay province) he went to Poona on transfer. After changing trains thrice and travelling for four days, he finally reached Poona railway station, where he received orders not to take over charge at Poona ! Anil Kumar could not contain himself any longer and mentioned to the Chief Secretary, "Sir, there seems to be some misunderstanding. I sought an appointment to discuss about my problems and not to hear about your problems". Paymaster had a hearty laugh and immediately got Anil Kumar's transfer orders cancelled.

Temen Aunok, First IAS Officer from Nagaland

My roommate at the Academy was Temen Aunok the first IAS Officer from Nagaland. Temen was short, stocky and fair. He was very friendly and jovial. After we left the Academy, I did not have the opportunity to meet him again. However, when I was functioning as the Chairman, Maharashtra State Electricity Board during 1989–1991, he suddenly called me requesting for fixing up an appointment for his younger brother in the Tata Memorial Hospital, as he was suffering from cancer, I not only fixed up the appointment but also arranged a guest house for the stay of his family and also placed a vehicle at the disposal of his family for a month. Subsequently, Temen wrote a very touching letter about my hospitality and generosity which greatly helped his brother to recover from the disease and thanked me profusely for my kindness, even though we did not meet for thirty years, after our stay in the Academy, Mussoorie.

Hari's Canteen

Just outside the gate of the Academy, there was a canteen run by K. Hari. He was also running a canteen for the probationers when the IAS officers were trained at the Metcalfe House, Delhi. Hari was an institution by himself. Anyone who had entered the portals of Lal Bahadur Shastri National Academy of Administration, can never forget Hari and his canteen, located outside the entrance gate of Academy. The Stores stocked all types of stationary embossed with the service emblem, service tie, socks, handkerchiefs and a variety of books. He also supplied embossed envelopes and letter pads with which we used to correspond with friends and family members. He used to supply items on credit and promptly collected the amount due on pay day.

Bharat Darshan Tour

Our Bharat Darshan tour—a tour of about a month in December-January, when Mussoorie had a very cold weather—got cancelled for the year 1962. During the post-foundation course training, in October 1962, the nation got a rude shock, when China attacked India in the north-east sector. Since India was not prepared for the attack, we lost heavily and some of our fine officers perished while bravely facing the Chinese. The war had catastrophic consequences for India, both in terms of international standing and financially. The nation rallied round the brave heroes of our armed forces, and people belonging to all sections of society donated handsome amounts for augmenting the war effort. We therefore had a mini Bharat Darshan tour, during which we came to New Delhi. We called on Dr. Sarvepalli Radhakrishnan, President of India, the Vice-President, the Prime Minister and the Union Home Minister.

Even though the Chinese retreated quickly after inflicting defeats on our armed forces, the Government of India started a massive programme of defending the vast borders of India with China by organising local self-defence forces and other measures. We went to different border districts to help the Collectors and District Magistrates of such districts to organise Civil defence forces by mobilising the local population. I went to Gonda District in Uttar Pradesh, which was bordering Nepal, along with Jamna Lal Bajaj, V.S. Gopalakrishnan and P. Subrahmanyam. After completing district attachment, we returned to the Academy to continue our training.

Meeting with Pandit Jawaharlal Nehru

Our meeting with the then Prime Minister Pandit Jawaharlal Nehru, during our mini Bharat Darshan tour, which took place at his official residence at Teen Murti Bhavan, was a memorable experience. Our meeting was slotted at 6.30 PM but due to the visit of some foreign delegation, Panditji was late by about 20 minutes. The delay was adequately made up by Indira Gandhi, who played the perfect hostess during Panditji's absence. It was a privilege to see the young lady whose duties were primarily restricted at that time playing hostess to all the dignitaries who were calling on Pandit Jawaharlal Nehru. It was a privilege to meet Pandit Jawaharlal Nehru, our beloved first Prime Minister, who was acclaimed as one of the world's greatest statesmen. When Panditji came, he profusely apologised for the delay and wanted to know what we would like to hear from him. When one of us mentioned that the Chinese attack on India has been uppermost in our minds, Pandit Nehru suddenly looked very grim and in a sombre voice, gave us an account of how India had always treated China as a friend, as China was a newly-liberated nation and had been building up the country with a strong socio-economic base. He said that China was a communist country but in spite of our ideological differences, we were the best of friends with them—with the slogan of "Hindi-Chini Bhai Bhai" (India and Chinese are brothers). We believed in the doctrine of 'Panchsheel' and the underlying philosophy of peaceful co-existence. But we did not apprehend that China had secret ambitions of occupying some of our border areas in the North East Frontier Area (NEFA) and Ladakh. He said that he still hoped that China would see reason and settle the border dispute amicably. He, however, added that India would spare no efforts to strengthen its defence forces by getting new equipments and weapons for high-altitude warfare. He also spoke to us about the role of the civil services in building up future India. He gave us glimpses of Indian history for almost an hour and exhorted us not to lose courage at the set back suffered by the country due to the Chinese aggression. He told us that we should continue to fight for the cause of freedom, which the country achieved through non-violent means. We were all very much impressed by the patience of Pandit Jawaharlal Nehru, for having spent such a long and valuable time with young probationers, leaving aside the most important matters of the State agitating his mind. After meeting Pandit Nehru, I got the distinct impression that he had been very badly shaken by the Chinese attack and that he had aged considerably after this episode.

We also called on Lal Bahadur Shastriji, who was the Union Home Minister, who subsequently became a very endearing Prime Minister. He gave to the country the memorable slogan of "Jai Jawan–Jai Kisaan". He was very humble and extremely courteous towards us and his humility and simplicity stunned us completely.

Allotted to Maharashtra Cadre

While I was undergoing training in the Academy, the notification allotting the State cadres were received by all the probationers. I was allotted to the Maharashtra cadre. While I was disappointed that I could not get my home state of Andhra Pradesh, I was very happy that I was allotted to Maharashtra, which was a very highly industrialised and progressive state.

In April 1963—at the end of our professional training in the Academy—I left Mussoorie with very pleasant memories of my initiation into the IAS. After a brief visit to my native village, Gaddamanugu near Vijayawada in Andhra Pradesh, I left for the city of Bombay to report at the Sachivalaya, which was later renamed as Mantralaya (Secretariat of the State Government). I was posted as Supernumerary Assistant Collector, Jalgaon for the second phase of my training in the state, before confirmation into the IAS.

FIVE

TRAINING IN MAHARASHTRA

(I) SECRETARIAT TRAINING IN BOMBAY

All the IAS probationers were required to undergo training in the State Secretariat before we proceeded to the allotted districts in the State. As there was enough time before reporting at Bombay, now renamed Mumbai, most of the probationers went to their home towns before joining in the allotted states. I visited my parents for a brief period and proceeded to Bombay in May 1963. I reported at Sachivalaya, presently called Mantralaya, which had been so designated by Shankarrao B. Chavan when he was Chief Minister. The Chief Secretary at that time was N.T. Money, ICS, who was reputed to be an able administrator and a no nonsense man.

All the probationers reported to K.P. Nadkarni, Under Secretary, in the General Administration Department. Nadkarni, who belonged to the State Secretariat Service, was handling the management of the IAS cadre for quite some years. Our first experience of Sachivalaya was none too pleasant, as there was no waiting room for Nadkarni's visitors, so all of us waited in the corridor for more than half an hour to meet him, since he was supposed to brief us about our programmes. Although Nadkarni was very pleasant and courteous, he made it obvious that we should maintain cordial relation with him, as he would be dealing with our postings and transfers in the state. He had been primarily retained in that position, as he was able to maintain absolute secrecy about all the postings and transfers of IAS officers in the State. He had the full trust of successive

Chief Secretaries and managed to keep himself aloof from all the officers in the Secretariat, although many of us felt that the transfers and postings of IAS officers should be dealt with by an IAS officer, rather than be under the control of the state secretariat officers.

The Government had chalked out an elaborate programme of briefings and visits to senior officers for us. This included calling on the Chief Minister, Home Minister, Revenue Minister, Chief Secretary and other Secretaries in the Government, who took pains to explain to us the functions of the various departments.

I distinctly recall when we called on Balasaheb Desai, the Revenue Minister, who was a very powerful Minister in the Cabinet. We were introduced one by one, starting with V.S. Gopalakrishnan, S. Padmanabhan, P. Subrahnmaniam, P. Abraham and so on. Unable to contain himself, Balasaheb Desai remarked in a jocular way whether we were from the Madras cadre or the Maharashtra cadre!! There were ten officers in our batch and except Dinesh Afzalpurkar and Sharad Upasani, all were from other states.

The Secretariat training lasted for about 10 days during which period we stayed in the Magestic Hotel, Colaba. During this time, we attended the wedding of Mahesh Modi (Orissa—62), a batchmate of ours at Mumbai. We were treated lavishly for about four days, giving us an excellent opportunity to see the whole of Bombay, as the groom's honoured guests. Many years later I attended the wedding of Modi's son at Delhi, and told that I had also attended his father's wedding at Bombay, to the utter delight of the young groom!!

After successful training in Mumbai, we were sent to our respective districts to continue further training before our probation was confirmed. I proceeded to Jalgaon district, in Khandesh, as Supernumerary Assistant Collector.

(II) DISTRICT TRAINING AS SUPERNUMERARY ASSISTANT COLLECTOR, JALGAON

After completing the Secretariat training at Bombay, I reported to the Collector of Jalgaon, in May 1963, for my first posting in the state as Supernumerary Assistant Collector.

Jalgaon is the district headquarters, about 200 Kms from Bombay and is a part of the area traditionally known as Khandesh in Maharashtra. Jalgaon district is internationally famous for its bananas.

My predecessor, P.B. Rajagopalan, fondly known as "Raju" (Mah—1961), volunteered to receive me at the railway station. He, however, advised me to wear an 'IAS tie' for identification. It was the height of summer and Jalgaon being such a hot place, hardly anyone wore a tie while travelling by train, except for the ticket collector! I, however, had little alternative but to wear a service tie so that Raju could recognize me. He received me with brotherly affection, knowing that I was taking up the first assignment in my career, amidst an unknown and unfamiliar territory and people.

When we came out of the railway station, I tried to locate the Government jeep or a car that would take us into the town, but there was none. Raju hailed a 'Tonga' (a horse drawn carriage), the common mode of transport in Jalgaon, and probably in all the district headquarters at that time. My luggage consisting of a small steel trunk, (suitcases were not common in those days and in any case were prohibitively costly for a probationer), and a hold-all. He seated me on the tonga and followed on his bicycle. All that I had heard that an IAS Officer, from his very first day in the service, enjoyed the luxury of a car or jeep and many other trappings of office was dashed to the ground at the railway station itself. While travelling in the tonga, I was forced to recollect what my colleagues had joked in the Academy that all those who were allotted to Maharashtra and Gujarat should buy as many IAS ties as possible to remember that they were also IAS Officers, as all the powers and privileges enjoyed in the district as Collectors had been transferred to Zilla Parishads in Maharashtra in May 1962, the month and the year I entered into IAS.

P.K.—A Friend in Need is a Friend Indeed

Raju was staying with K. Padmanabhan IPS (1960), affectionately known as P.K. who was Assistant Superintendent of Police (ASP). He was a genial and friendly bachelor police officer, with a comfortable new bungalow adjoining the police parade ground. His bungalow was very near to the Collector's office, with plenty of police orderlies to look after the house, garden and guests like me. When we landed at P.K.'s place, he insisted that I should make myself comfortable for as long as I wished to stay with him. P.K. was so hospitable that I continued to enjoy his hospitality and house for a year, although I was allotted a flat later, until I was transferred on promotion as Assistant Collector, Panvel.

P.K., being a police officer, was mostly away on routine inspections, tours and compulsory visitations (in all cases of murders, which were not uncommon, he was required to stay in the place of crime for 3 or 4 days continuously to complete investigations). I, therefore, used to enjoy the comforts of his bungalow. As I was a permanent resident of the bungalow, most people soon thought that I was the ASP and P.K. was my house guest! P.K. had a car which he used to drive whenever we went out to watch movies and to our favourite canteen. At that time, the only place for eating out used to be the railway station canteen. Sometimes, sitting in the rear seat of the car, I used to order P.K., "Driver, take me to the railway station!" Obviously P.K. used to get cheesed off. Raju, who was posted in the same district as Assistant Collector (Prant Officer) at Amalnair (which incidentally happened to be the ancestral home of Azeem Premjee, Chairman, Wipro) used to visit Jalgaon on every conceivable pretext, making my stay there unforgettable and memorable. P.K. and Raju remain very close friends and even when we meet today, we relive our bachelor days in the district.

Normally only some districts were earmarked for training IAS officers and Jalgaon was one of them. Since Jalgaon quite often had directly recruited IAS Officers, as Collectors, their presence was of immense help for a young officer for training, as directly recruited Collectors also went through the same drill and the common background helped the training process.

When I joined at Jalgaon, W.G. Pathak, a special recruit from the army into the IAS, was the Collector. When I called on him, it was my first contact with any Collector in my life. He received me with considerable warmth, exquisite army protocol and manners and asked me to make myself as comfortable as possible. He advised me to meet him whenever I wanted and told me to follow the training regimen strictly, as this would help me in my future career.

Club Life in the District

There was a District Officers' club, literally an attachment to the Collectors huge and sprawling bungalow, located on a few acres of land with plenty of vegetation. It was very considerate of the Collector to write to me while I was at the Academy and invite me to stay in his bungalow till I got regular accommodation. However Raju felt that I would be more at home with P.K. rather than with the Collector.

Most of the District Officers, whenever they happened to be in the District headquarters, used to assemble in the club, either to play badminton, table tennis, tennis or card games. Indeed, I was initiated into tennis during those days. After a fortnight of my training, I happened to meet the District Collector at the club. It appeared that he had clearly noticed not only my irregular attendance or even absence from office but also my absence from the club and smilingly mentioned that my daily attendance in the club was compulsory! This was only to be expected because of his army background. He was very fond of the club, returning from long and arduous tours in the district on the same day, so that he could be on time in the club to play his favourite game of bridge! Dr. Kulkarni, Civil Surgeon and D.B. Sasane, Chief Executive Officer, Zilla Parishad, another promotee IAS Officer, were regulars in the club. Life in a district was incomplete without a club. Fortunately, we had an excellent group of young direct recruits in various departments. V.P. Rane, Deputy Collector, and S.V. Joshi, Asst. Conservator of Forests were also undergoing training like me and we would go to the club and to film shows in the local theatres regularly.

Both the Collectors, W.G. Pathak and subsequently John Innocent, IAS (1955) took considerable interest in my training. A detailed programme of training was designed to fully familiarise a new entrant into the service with his duties and powers, in accordance with guidelines issued by the Government from time to time. The training was exhaustive and needed attachments to the Collector and Resident Deputy Collector (PA to the Collector in some states), Assistant Collector, Mamlatar (Tahsildar in some states), Treasury Officer and down to the level of a Talathi (village level officer). It also included training in various wings of the Zilla Parishad, starting from Chief Executive Officer (normally an IAS officer junior to the Collector) of the Zilla Parishad to give a feel of the development administration at the district level. Similarly, it also included training in the police department, starting from the Superintendent of Police, to give an insight into criminal administration and maintenance of law and order in the district. The training programmes also included attachments to the District Judge and to other judicial officers, to know about the administration of criminal and civil justice.

All the revenue officers in the district, including the Collector, were required to dispose of a certain number of tenancy and revenue appeals, carry out a quota of village inspections to verify the ownerships and tenancy rights with reference to mutation registers, crop inspections and also to redress the general grievances of the villagers. Mostly the road side villages were preferred for inspection, depending on the age and enthusiasm of the officers. I observed that while some villages were inspected every year due to their easy accessibility, many were rarely visited.

The revenue officers were also required to carry out a quota of tours and night halts, including staying in the tents in interior villages, so as to enable the people to meet them and get their problems redressed. The Collector, in addition to the revenue work, was also the Chairman of a number of district level committees. He was required to attend to the visits of the VIP's and other dignitaries. Although, at one time, the Collector was required to attend on all the Ministers during their visits to the districts, it was subsequently decided that the Collector would attend only to visits by the Chief Minister, Revenue Minister and Home Minister, thereby offering considerable relief to him and giving him time to perform other important tasks in the district.

J.H. Patwardhan as Affectionate Commissioner

J.H. Patwardhan, better known as 'Janubhav' Patwardhan was Commissioner, when I joined as supernumerary Assistant Collector at Jalgaon. He hailed from the famous and cultured Patwardhan family, which had participated in the freedom struggle. He was always very considerate and used to shower fatherly affection on young probationers. Although he was very generous in extending an invitation to come on tour to visit him in Bombay whenever we were bored in the Districts during training, hardly anyone could take the liberty of breaching the training regimen, for fear of incurring the displeasure of the superiors.

Training with Natarajan

M.R. Natarajan was the Assistant Collector of Jalgaon subdivision. A very studious, hard-working and methodical officer, he discharged his duties diligently, in accordance with the directions of the Government and the District Collector. He would invariably exceed the targets for the number of inspections and tours fixed for an Assistant Collector. His wife, Prema, accompanied him on tours and he insisted that I should tour with him, so that I would get an idea of the various kinds of field work. This also gave me ample opportunity to learn about the different facets of district administration, which was of immense help in my subsequent postings. Within a short span of staying in Maharashtra, Natarajan could not only speak Marathi exceedingly well, but had also acquired excellent skills in drafting very good notes in Marathi. The Sub Divisional Magistrate also tried cases of pick-pocketing at the railway stations, which was quite a common offence. I remember that Natarajan was once going to Bhusaval to try the cases of some pick-pockets at the railway station. After he got down from the train and came out of the railway station, he noticed to his horror, that his own pocket had been picked! He always used to speak in Marathi and insisted that I learn Marathi quickly.

I used to accompany the Natarajans in their old Hindustan car and enjoyed their hospitality fully during these tours, as they made my stay as comfortable as possible. I must mention my experience in travelling in his Hindustan car, which would often stop on the roads, leaving me, Prema Natarajan and the peon to push the car for long distances till it restarted. In frustration, Natarajan often used to say that he would like to be reborn as the tyre of a Mercedes car than as an IAS Officer!

At that time, Mercedes was a dream car in India. No one could imagine at that time that it would one day be made in India. Natarajan retired as Additional Chief Secretary, Government of Maharashtra.

I went for my first tent camp in Jalgaon Taluka with Natarajan. During those days, doing tent halts was compulsory and one was required to make tent camps as per targets. It was an altogether new experience for me and the villagers would come and chat with us. It was a great education to listen to their problems and redress their grievances.

Natarajan taught me how to handle complicated revenue cases, most of which were pending finalization for a long time. As Sub Division Magistrate, Natarajan also had to dispose of routine criminal cases. Invariably the charge against the accused was that he was found loitering in suspicious circumstances and action was required in terms of Sections 107, 109 and 110 of the Criminal Procedure Code to bind him over for good behaviour and to put him in a prison for some time to keep him out of mischief.

Since the training programmes also included holding an independent charge of a tahsil for three months, I was posted as Tahsildar, Bhusaval, which was an important railway junction on Bombay-Calcutta railway line.

Attachment with District Judge

My attachment with the District Judge, Coutinho, a pious God-fearing man, who looked distinguished in his robes, was extremely useful as I learnt how to record evidence, especially in criminal cases, and how it is administered at the district level. He used to often invite me for a cup of coffee at his house in the evenings, as he and his wife were the only two occupants of the huge bungalow of the District Judge. They could not mix with the rest of the people, including officers at the District Level, as a district judge was required to deal with various types of cases, including the cases pertaining to several departments in the district. I still recall an occasion when W.G. Pathak, Collector, invited him for dinner being hosted for the various officers. The District Judge requested the Collector for a list of the invitees, obviously to verify whether anyone whose case is pending with him was also included in the list. After perusing the lists, the District Judge politely excused himself. He, however, promised to have a cup of coffee with the Collector at a mutually convenient time. This speaks volumes about the integrity and independence of the Judiciary at that time.

In later years when I became Collector, Bhir, I found the District Judge there appeared to be too keen to be invited for 'Hurda' (tender grain of jawar, before harvesting, eaten with joggery and with some fruits locally available in the field itself) parties by advocates, practicing before him!!

The training with the District Treasury Officer enabled me to understand the administration of public finance, as most of the Government transactions were done through the Treasuries in the absence of banks at many places. The Assistant Collector in the sub-division was required to inspect the treasury and the inspection had to be very thorough as it involved counting and verification of huge amounts of cash, which needed to be reconciled till the very last paise was accounted for.

Training with Ramachandran, Superintendent of Police

My training with S. Ramachandran, IPS (1956) gave me a clear picture of how the police administration functioned at the district level. Ramachandran and his wife knew some Telugu, my mother tongue, which really put me at ease in an unknown place. Ramachandran's mother was fully conversant with the language and during my frequent visits to their home, Ramachandran's mother and myself used to gossip endlessly in Telugu. My visit to their home also gave me an opportunity to play with their daughter, Chitra, who was only three years old at that time and her younger brother affectionately called 'General'. Chitra is now a senior IAS Officer in Andhra Pradesh. Ramachandran and his wife were very gentle and sociable and I enjoyed their hospitality when I accompanied him on his tours. The entire police force used to pamper me, as I happened to be close to the District Superintendent of Police.

It was mandatory for an IAS probationary officer to pass both the Revenue Examination and also the Higher Standard Proficiency Test in Marathi in order to be confirmed and earn the necessary increments in salary. I cleared both the examinations without any problem, especially the *viva voce* examination in Marathi which was normally tough. The *viva voce* examiner was very considerate, as obviously he thought that I was quite sincere in making every possible effort to try to converse in Marathi, although with difficulty.

Marriage

Ever since I was allotted to Maharashtra, my parents were quite concerned about my health and well-being. They were very keen that I should get married to an Andhra girl and settle down, as they were afraid that by staying in Maharashtra, I might get married to a Maharashtrian girl and thus be permanently separated from them, as they would not be comfortable with a daughter-in-law with whom they could not converse. They were, therefore, making frantic efforts to identify a suitable girl and finally chose Suryakumari, daughter of Vejendla Moses and Irene Moses, from Guntur. She was studying in a college at Hyderabad. V. Moses, who was District Education Officer at Nellore and Vishakhapatnam, was then working as Assistant Director of Education in the office of the Director Public Instructions, Hyderabad. After seeing Suryakumari and her family, my parents were quite impressed and decided that I should get married to her, in accordance with our custom of arranged marriages. I took leave and went on short leave to Vijayawada and was married there on 11th July 1964 at Vijayawada. One particular greetings telegram which came from "Innocent Ramachandran and Nuts Padmanabhan" Jalgaon, attracted the maximum attention, as none could understand the funny greeting, till I explained to them that the greeting was from the Collector whose name was Innocent, Superintendent of Police whose name was Ramachandran, Assistant Collector Natarajan, (whom we used to call as 'Nuts') and Assistant Superintendent of Police Padmanabhan and thus it became "Innocent Ramachandran and Nuts Padmanabhan"!!

While I was still on vacation after marriage, I received my promotion order, posting me as Assistant Collector, Panvel Subdivision, which was in Kolaba District. I went back to Jalgaon to bid goodbye to the Collector and the other officers and friends and took charge as Assistant Collector, Panvel in the first week of August 1964.

SIX

DUTIES AND RESPONSIBILITIES START IN THE DISTRICTS

(I) ASSISTANT COLLECTOR AND SUB DIVISIONAL MAGISTRATE, PANVEL, KOLABA DISTRICT

After availing of a few days leave, I joined as Assistant Collector, (Prant officer) Panvel Sub Division, Kolaba District, presently Raigad. With the headquarters at Alibagh. It adjoins Thane District. There were two subdivisions in the District, Panvel and Mahad.

Panvel, which is about 45 kms from Bombay on the Bombay-Poona National highway, can be approached only by road via Thane. Panvel subdivision comprised of Panvel, Khalapur (an upcoming industrial area at Khopoli with a few petrochemical units located on Patalganga River), Karjat, Pen, Uran, Pali and Sudhaghad tahsils. The road network was very poor and even roads to some of the tahsil towns were quite bad.

My First Independence Day Celebrations

A few days after my joining as Assistant Collector, Panvel, we had to celebrate Independence Day. Not only was it my first independent charge, but it was also the first time I was required to hoist the National flag and take the salute after joining the IAS. I was, therefore, understandably, tense. I attended to all the details of the programme many times, to ensure that nothing went amiss as it was an important National Day Function and I wanted to make it a success. My wife, Suryakumari, who joined me at Panvel after marriage, was also present on the occasion. It was her first official function as the wife of an IAS Officer. I wore a Gandhi cap (a white cap was usually referred as such) while taking the salute and the function was a grand success.

Although most of the tahsils were connected with motorable roads, it was quite difficult to tour the interior villages, where there were hardly any roads. The District is located in the Western Ghats with very thick forest cover and most of the Tahsils were hilly and very backward. During the monsoon it used to rain 'cats and dogs' and the rainwater would fill the near by creeks and then flow into the Arabian Sea.

No Official Residence

There was no earmarked accommodation for the Assistant Collector in Panvel, unlike many other places. Indeed, no IAS officer had ever been posted to the Panvel subdivision as Assistant Collector, except for S. Rajgopal, IAS (1957), who eventually retired as Cabinet Secretary to the Government of India. I had to stay in the Government guest house till I got a private bungalow in a cooperative housing society.

Maharashtra was at the forefront of democratic decentralization ever since the Maharashtra Zilla Parishads and Panchayat Samitis Act, 1962, was passed, ushering in the three-tier decentralized development administration. At the bottom was the Village Panchayat, then the Panchayat Samiti at the Tahsil, and, finally, the Zilla Parishad at the District level. In this new structure, most of the development subjects, such as agriculture, education, rural health, minor irrigation, district and village roads, along with the staff, were transferred to the Zilla Parishads and Panchayat Samitis. After the formation of the Zilla Parishads in 1962, the Block Development Officers, who had the facilities of jeeps, were allotted to the Zilla Parishads.

Tours by State Transport Buses

In those days, no government jeep was provided to the Assistant Collector. I used to go to office on a bicycle, with my *pattewalla* (a peon who wore a red band of cloth across his shoulder), cycling in front of me, almost like a present day pilot car, which clears the way for VIPs.! As we did not have a car or a government jeep, my wife and I travelled by the State Transport (ST) bus, when we went on tours in the District. We were the cynosure of all eyes, as the *pattewala* proceeded ahead to ensure there were seats so that my wife and I could sit together and if there were none, he would make sure that the seats were vacated!

I used to get files, which came daily from headquarters and cleared them under 'petro max' light while listening to the transistor radio, which was the only entertainment in those days. The most popular programme on the radio was 'Binaca Geetmala' compared by the inimitable and very famous Amin Sayani.

The salary of an Assistant Collector was paltry, to be precise rupees four hundred per month, all inclusive. Even a decent second-hand car would cost more than what one could afford. After a few months, however, I purchased a totally run down Morris Minor car, after taking a loan from the Government and spent a fortune to make it roadworthy. This old Morris Minor car, for some strange reasons, apart from stopping at will on the roads, used to stall within the sighting range of Government rest houses, so that all those who were waiting to receive the Hon'ble Assistant Collector and Sub Divisional Magistrate would, to my utter embarrassment, come along and give a helping hand in pushing the car, while my wife walked besides it!

When on tour, I made it a point to travel with all my provisions, except the fresh vegetables, which we used to buy locally. The local peon used to cook our food.

Every young IAS Officer was required to familiarise himself with Anderson's Manual on Revenue administration. Among several forms in which the revenue records at the village level were maintained, the most important form was *Saat-Baara* (7-12), in which all the details of land holdings, such as survey number, area, name of the owner/tenant and the crop sown in the land, were recorded. There was also another register called the 'Mutation register' which contained changes made in the names of the tenants and the owners from time to time. The Assistant Collector was also required to carry out annual inspection of taluka offices and conduct 'jamabandis' to assess the land revenue of the taluka. The treasury inspections were also carried out, as the banking system was not introduced in all the places; the reconciliation of the cash was invariably done to check any misappropriation of Government funds.

It was compulsory to tour for twenty one days in a month with at least ten night halts. As per the rules, the Assistant Collector was required to visit all the villages in his jurisdiction once in three years. However, this rule was observed more in breach, as the villages which were located on the road side were visited more frequently by a majority of officers rather than the inaccessible and interior villages. I made it a point to visit the inaccessible villages, and when I did, villagers used to be pleasantly surprised about my visits. They were happy that some one had bothered to visit them and listen to their grievances. After the separation of the juidiciary from the executive, the Assistant Collector, as the Sub Divisional Magistrate, could exercise only the Chapter Case powers to bind over bad characters by asking them to produce a bond for good behaviour.

One of the functions of revenue officers was the recovery of 'tagai' loans and co-operative loans, along with the land revenue. In times of drought, scarcity or lower crop yields, which were measured through crop cutting experiments called '*Anne ware*', (which determined the quantum of yield per acre), the recoveries were suspended. If the yield was less than 6 *annas* per acre, the Collector was required to declare scarcity in the village, offer remissions in revenue collections and sanction other relief. The poor farmers were sometimes unable to pay even the paltry sum of a few rupees due to failure of crops. The threats of revenue officials used to make them sell everything they had, in order to protect their honour in the villages.

Surprise Checks on Illegal Transport of Paddy

Due to shortage of food-grains in the State, the Essential Commodities Act was under enforcement preventing transport of paddy and rice from one District to another District, without valid permission from the Collector. One of the functions required to be discharged by the Assistant Collector. was to carry out surprise checks on the lorries moving towards Bombay, smuggling paddy or rice. I used to frequently carry out these surprise checks with the assistance of the police, even in the dead of night and stop the vehicles at Khopoli in the Western Ghats, on the boundary between Pune and Kolaba Districts, on the Pune-Bombay road. Although it was risky to undertake such surprise inspections at night, it was quite exciting and a new experience, as I had police protection with me. The practice of illegal gun carrying was not as prevalent at that time as it is now.

Collector as Deputy Commissioner of Industries

N.R. Lakhar, a promotee IAS officer was the Collector of the District. Once the Resident Deputy Collector (RDC), Upadhyay rang me up stating that the Deputy Commissioner of Industries would be visiting

Panvel and I should receive him and be with him during his stay in Panvel. While I was waiting at the Government guest house, the Collector had come from Alibagh, along with the RDC, but there was no trace of the Deputy Commissioner of Industries for quite sometime. After a while, I asked the RDC as to when the Deputy Commissioner of Industries was expected to reach Panvel. He mentioned, with a smile, that you were already with the Deputy Commissioner of Industries! Till then, I did not realize that the Collector was also the Deputy Commissioner of Industries. So much for the initial training!

Officiated Twice as Collector

Although I was Assistant Collector, Panvel, for over a year, I officiated as the District Collector, twice, totalling a period of nearly four months. The first time, N.R. Lakhar, Collector, went on two months leave, hoping for a transfer to the Vidarbha Region, as he hailed from the area. He was also not happy because Alibagh, the District Headquarters was a small place without any amenities. He had to rejoin in Kolaba District, as he did not succeed in getting a transfer. The second time, I held charge as Collector once again was when Lakhar was transferred. Since no new officer was appointed, I officiated for over two months. This period coincided with the Republic Day celebrations and I had to hoist the National Flag and take the salute at Alibagh, the District Headquarters. It was a proud moment for me, as my father was present on this occasion and watched me hoisting the National Flag and taking the salute as Collector of the District, on the Republic Day of India. A dream came true for my father!

Collector's Bungalow on the Beach

The Collector's bungalow at Alibagh was located along a clean, picturesque and long beautiful beach, with the sea waves of the Arabian Sea literally touching the compound wall of the bungalow. The beach attracted more attention, after the notorious smuggler Daniel Walcott landed on the beach in his beach craft! The bungalow was huge, with several rooms with high doors, built on several acres of land and surrounded by coconut trees. Every morning, the peons would bring down several coconuts, so we sipped coconut water during breakfast, but they too helped themselves very liberally! While the sound from the waves was very soothing, acting as Nature's lullaby, we were disturbed by the sound of coconuts falling down with a thud in the night due to the heavy sea breeze.

While my wife used to accompany me regularly on tours in the initial stages, later she preferred to stay behind in the huge bungalow, as she was expecting a baby. The bungalow was very big and as she was scared to stay alone, she used to sometimes read all night, even though there were security guards who patrolled the house. As our stay in the bungalow was only for a short while, since I was holding the additional charge of Collector, she did not mind enjoying the loneliness with a book, while I was away on tour.

Talyarkhan, as Guardian Minister for the District

A.J.H. Talyarkhan, Minister for Civil Supplies and Small Savings, was the guardian Minister for Kolaba District. The local politicians did not think much of Talyarkhan. He was very fond of attending functions, whenever he came to the District. He would speak in broken parsi marathi which made all his functions quite hilarious. It was a tough job to mobilize audiences for his programmes. Talyarkhan used to telephone me from Bombay very often on some flimsy grounds. The telephone connections between Bombay and Alibagh was very poor, despite the fact that both places were so close to each other, and quite often it was almost impossible to hear. Whenever the Minister made a request which was not feasible, I used to say loudly on the phone that I was not able to hear him! The Minister in disgust used to put down the receiver. Poor communications were actually helpful in fobbing off some of the unreasonable requests from Ministers.

Meeting with Film Artists

There was considerable demand for acquiring agricultural land for non-agricultural purposes, as the entire area was developing into an industrial hub. The Assistant Collector was authorized to approve the conversion of agricultural land into the non-agriculture category under the Maharashtra Land Revenue Code. Ramanand Sagar, the famous film Producer and Director, and film star Nalini Jayawant were the first people from the world of glamour to meet me as they were acquiring some land. One can still see 'Ramanand Sagar estate' while driving on Bombay-Poona road near Khopoli.

Panvel was on the main road from Bombay-Poona and about 4 kms away from Panvel, towards Bombay, there was a nice roadside restaurant serving excellent 'biryani'. My wife and I used to visit the restaurant for a meal once in a while, as there was no other restaurant in Panvel where one could have a quiet meal. On one occasion, we were happy to meet Dilip Kumar, the matinee idol, quietly dining in the restaurant without being disturbed by the crowd. Another eating place, which was very popular was Ramakant's restaurant at Khopoli known for its 'vada'. As Khopoli was at the foothills of Western Ghats, every motorist would stop at Ramakant's restaurant to warm up himself with hot 'vada'.

During one of my tours to some villages in Khalapur, on the Western Ghats, officers showed me a place on Patalganga river, where the famous song sequence of—'*Bol Radha Bol Sangam Hoga Ke Nahi*' was picturised on the semi clad Vyjayantimala, in the super hit film 'Sangam' produced, directed and acted by Raj Kapoor.

I had another encounter with filmy fraternity while travelling in a hilly and picturesque area from Khalapur to Karjat, when I saw the evergreen singing sensation and movie hero Kishore Kumar and his troupe, basking in the shade of trees on Karjat road with a ramshackle old car shooting for—'*Chalti Ka Naam Gaadi*'.

Beginning of Konkan Railway

There was no railway line in the entire Konkan area connecting Kolaba District to Ratnagiri District. This contributed substantially to the backwardness of the region, so that a substantial population had to migrate to Bombay, looking for employment opportunities. Some of them commuted regularly from their native places to Bombay, by road, which was the only mode of communication available then. There was a persistent demand from the local people for connecting Bombay to Goa, via the Konkan region, so that the backward region, which had immense potential for establishing chemical and agro based industries, could be developed.

The first step towards having a Konkan railway was taken in the early 60s, while I was functioning as Assistant Collector, Panvel. The first six kilometres railway line was laid from Mumbra railway station, a place half way between Thane and Kalyan to Panvel. The railway line was inaugurated by S.K. Patil, the then Union Railway Minister. An interesting episode occurred at Panvel railway station, the venue of inauguration of the Mumbra to Panvel line. When S.K. Patil travelled by a special coach to Panvel to inaugurate the railway line, someone from the audience asked him how could he travel on the line which he was supposed to inaugurate. In a lighter vein, S.K. Patil replied, "I travelled on the railway line to make sure that the track is safe for your travel"!!

J.H. Patwardhan, Bombay Divisional Commissioner

Since Bombay and Panvel were close, once in a while, my wife Suryakumari, referred by friends as 'Suri' and myself used to visit Bombay. I also used to attend meetings regularly in the Commissioner's office. J.H. Patwardhan was the Commissioner of Bombay Revenue Division, and had jurisdiction over six districts in the state. He was very fond of all the young IAS probationers and used to bestow paternal care on them. He knew that I did not have an official residence at Panvel and was staying in a rented accommodation, which knocked off a substantial amount out of my meagre monthly salary of Rs. four hundred.

More than once he mentioned to me that he would give me a better posting, which had an assigned house as soon as possible, although I never asked him for such a shift.

True to his word, in October 1965, I was surprised to get transfer orders, posting me as Assistant Collector, Niphad Subdivision, Nasik District. Niphad traditionally had an IAS officer as Assistant Collector. There was a nice bungalow in front of the Golf course and adjoining the Nasik club, thus making it a coveted post by many young IAS officers.

(II) ASSISTANT COLLECTOR AND SUB-DIVISIONAL MAGISTRATE, NIPHAD, NASIK DISTRICT

In October 1965, I was transferred as Assistant Collector from Panvel subdivision to Niphad subdivision in Nasik District, with headquarters at Nasik. While Panvel was part of the Konkan region, Nasik was on the threshold of the Khandesh region. Nasik is a holy place, as the river Godavari took birth at Nasikatriumbak in the District. There is also a famous 'Jyohhirlinga'. A Cantonment was established at Deolali, on the outskirts of Nasik. There was a Government Mint, Currency and Stamp Presses and a Central jail, at Nasik Road. A new MIG factory was being established at Ojhar, about 15 miles away from Nasik, to assemble MIG planes initially and manufacture them subsequently. Nasik had a good Club with an excellent but abandoned 18-hole golf course. Social life in Nasik centred mainly around the Club which had a good membership of the district officials. As my bungalow was on the golf course road, we had the luxury of vast open grounds, which we used for morning and evening walks. As our house was on the way to the Government Rest house on the Bombay road, our colleagues from the neighbouring districts, visiting Bombay by road, used to drop in and stay with us while en route to Bombay.

The climate of the district was akin to that of a hill station, as Nasik was located above the Western Ghats. Nasik District was famous for grape cultivation, while Lasalgaon was reputed to be the largest onion market in the country. Raosaheb Gaikwad of Ojhar, a pioneer cultivator of grapes of several varieties, including Thomson seedless grapes, took immense pleasure in showing his vineyards, which were visited by several national leaders. He regularly sent us baskets of grapes in the season as a token of his affection for young officers.

SNA Razvi—District Collector

I was extremely fortunate to have SNA Razvi (IAS—1950), from the erstwhile Hyderabad Civil Service as Collector. His fatherly warmth was reflected by his typical Hyderabadi culture. He was, somewhat formal in office, but extremely affectionate at home. He was an upright, efficient and a straightforward officer and highly respected by all. He encouraged officers to take decisions even in matters pertaining to maintenance of law and order. One could not have wished for a better Collector to work with. Razvi and his wife used to treat my wife, who came to Nasik with our daughter Manjula, who was a few days old baby, with a lot of affection and kindness. They still recollect the lavish spread given by my wife on my daughter Manjula's first birthday party!

Madhav Godbole, IAS (1959), was functioning as Chief Executive Officer, Zilla Parishad. Godbole was a man of principles, very hardworking and totally committed to development administration. He was liked by people for his forthrightness and absolute integrity and his dedication to work was worthy of emulation.

G.A. Sharma, Commissioner

G.A. Sharma, Commissioner, Bombay Division, was very fond of talking all the time and used to keep on lecturing, especially to the younger officers, as he thought that we did not know anything about district administration. The young officers were literally scared to go anywhere near him, lest he may inflict his *bhashan* (lecture) on them, thus earning him the nickname of 'G A S' (G.A. Sharma)!

Nasik—A good Training District

Nasik was a good district for training IAS Officers. R.C. Iyer (1964) was already under training when I joined and was later followed by V. Ranganathan (1965). While Iyer retired as Additional Chief Secretary, Ranganathan retired as Chief Secretary, Government of Maharashtra.

Iyer used to accompany me regularly on tours. He used to smoke occasionally but would purchase one cigarette at a time, ostensibly to control smoking. One habit of his, which I was forced to correct, was smoking *beedies* after borrowing from peons and drivers!! A.S. Inamdar, IPS (1964) was also under training during this period. He retired recently as Director General of Police, Maharashtra. R. Sakhalkar and S.L. Kulkarni, both directly recruited Deputy Collectors were also trainees in the District. Both of them subsequently got promoted to the IAS and both retired as Secretaries to the Government of Maharashtra.

The Niphad subdivision consisted of Niphad, Sinnar, Chandwad and Yeola tahsils. Sinnar was famous for its beedi industry, Yeola for its silk sarees and Chandwad for its big fort. Located on the Bombay-Delhi National Highway, the Niphad subdivision was not a particularly heavy subdivision, compared to two other subdivisions—Nasik and Malegaon. In addition to the revenue work, there was lot of criminal case work, primarily under Sections 107, 109 and 110 of the Criminal Procedure Code, to bind persons over for good behaviour, or to put them in prison for a few days, to keep them out of mischief. An Assistant Collector had to do at least 210 days of touring with 100 night halts during the year. We had our share of good touring in the subdivision and stayed in rest houses, especially in Pimpalgaon Baswant (a rest house in a dilapidated condition and with detached bathroom, fit for ghosts) and Chandwad.

Maintenance of Law and Order

One of the major problems in the subdivision was the maintenance of law and order during the Ganapati festival at Yeola, which had a substantial minority population. Promises to keep peace made by the community leaders during the Ganapati festival were seldom kept. Normally, the organizers planned to take out religious processions and play music in front of the mosque, precisely around the time when the 'namaaz' was being performed inside, which led to communal tensions. One could never rule out eruption of trouble at the slightest provocation and on any pretext. I had to rush at short notice on many occasions to handle law and order situations. Fortunately, we could maintain good 'bandobast' and there was no major untoward incident during my tenure.

Drought Relief Works

During the summer of 1966, Nasik District faced one of the worst draughts in the State. The Collector, Razvi, entrusted me with the scarcity relief work of the entire district, although I was only one out of the three subdivisional officers. The worst affected Tahsils were Dindori, Surgana and Baglan. Most of these talukas were in the hilly region and inhabited by scheduled tribes. Several relief works, consisting of laying down roads in the interior areas and digging of percolation tanks were also taken up, which provided employment to thousands of labourers. Several tankers were engaged for supplying drinking water to a large number of villages. It was very strenuous work but highly rewarding and gratifying experience, so much so that people used to refer to me as ***Scarcity Collector***, as I was in charge of scarcity relief works in the District.

Additional Collector, Thane

While I was functioning as Assistant Collector, Niphad Sub Division, Nasik, I was temporarily promoted as Additional Collector, Thane District, for two months, when P.B. Rajgopalan, Additional Collector, proceeded on earned leave. It was a general practice to temporarily promote the senior most Assistant Collector in the Revenue Division due for regular promotion, in such temporary vacancies.

As it was during the monsoons, not much touring could be done in Thane District except attending to some urgent work in various Tahsils and the routine revenue work.

One interesting anecdote is worthy of recollection. Every year when the new batch of IAS Officers came to Bombay for training in the state Secretariat, invariably a day's visit was planned to the Collectorate at Thane, since it is located closest to Bombay. We deputed Hmingliana, IAS (1964), who was under training, to receive the probationers of 1965 batch at the MLAs hostel in Bombay and escort them to the Thane Collectorate. Hmingliana, took an extra vehicle to bring the probationers. However, we found the probationers came in taxies and Hmingliana came much later. When we enquired as to why he did not escort the probationers, his simple explanation was that when he went to the MLAs hostel, no probationer was present at the reception! Since he felt hungry, he took his breakfast in the mess, while the probationers who failed to locate Hmingliana and after waiting for some time, finally got into taxies and came to the Collectorate!

MIG Factory at Ojhar

The Government of India, after considering various alternatives, finally settled on Ojhar village to set up a MIG fighter aircraft manufacturing plant with Russian collaboration. Nearly 4,000 acres of land was acquired and I was also the Land Acquisition Officer for this project. At that time, land acquisition for setting up industries was not at all as problematic as it is today. Compensation was based on the sale of lands in the area and hardly any disputes or court cases were filed. If at all there were any demands for higher compensation, they were settled amicably through negotiations.

First Batch of MIGs Tested

It was during this period, the first batch of MIGs were tested in flying mode. When these MIGs entered the air space in supersonic speed, they used to produce deafening and frightening sound. When they flew for the first time, the sound was so frightening, even the window panes often rattled. Most of the people in the neighbouring villages as well as in Nasik ran out of their houses and buiddings. Me and my wife with our month's old daughter, Manjula, also ran out of the house like many, not knowing what the sound is all about, till we were informed that the supersonic speed at which the MIG fighters fly, make this abnormal sound when they enter the air space. This sound indeed created a panic among the people in the area. I had to undertake visits to several villages in the area to explain the reasons for the sound and assure the general public about their safety and exhort them not to worry about the noise made by the flying MIGS.

I was present at the function to hand over the first batch of MIGs assembled at Hindustan Aeronautics Limited, Ozhar, Nasik. Air Marshal P.C. Lal, Chairman, Hindustan Aeronautics Limited (HAL) presented the first MIG to Yashwantrao Chavan, the then Union Defence Minister. There was also flying demonstration of the MIGs at the ceremony, with one of them being flown by none other than Air Chief Marshal, Arjun Singh, Chief of Air Staff, who now has the distinction of being the only 'Marshal of the Air' in the country. Being, a young IAS Officer, I genuinely felt that Air Chief Marshal, Arjun Singh, Chief of Air Staff, should not have taken the risk of flying such an assembled supersonic MIG figher. As I meet him quite often even now, in social get togethers of Air Force, I never failed to seize an opportunity to mention to him about my concerns about the Air Chief flying the assembled supersonic MIG fighter on the presentation function at Ojhar in 1966. Whenever I mention this, the Marshall of the Air Just laughs it away!

We spent a very pleasant year in Nasik and was then promoted and posted as Collector and District Magistrate, Bhir.

SEVEN

COLLECTOR AND DISTRICT MAGISTRATE, BHIR

I was expecting my promotion to the senior time scale and a posting as Chief Executive Officer (CEO), Zilla Parishad (ZP), in one of the Districts in the State, as invariably an IAS Officer on first promotion in Maharashtra, was posted as CEO, ZP. The State government had decided that every young IAS Officer should work as Chief Executive Officer of a Zilla Parishad before being posted as Collector. Indeed, S. Padmanabhan (IAS—1962), affectionately called Paddu, my batch mate, who was *inter se* senior to me, was already posted as CEO, Nasik.

I was, therefore, pleasantly surprised to receive my promotion as Collector and District Magistrate, Bhir (presently known as Beer) District in October 1966. Subsequently, I came to know that an exception was made in my case when I was posted as Collector, as I had already officiated as Collector Kolaba District, Alibag and Additional Collector, Thane District, for nearly six months on temporary promotions, while working as Assistant Collector. I presume that my good performance during that period would have clinched the decision in my favour, so I was posted directly as Collector and District Magistrate. While I was happy to be posted as Collector, I missed out on the most valuable and useful experience of development administration at the District level as nobody was ever posted as CEO after working as Collector, unless by way of punishment.

When I joined as Collector, I was only 27 years of age and was the youngest Collector in the State at that time, may be perhaps the youngest in the country. Some of my contemporaries as Collectors in Maharashtra were S.N.A. Razvi (1950), Collector, Nasik; K.V. Seshadri (1951), Collector, Pune; P.V. Nayak (1956), Collector, Nanded; S. Hate (1957), Collector Parbhani, to name a few. While congratulating me on my promotion as Collector, S.N.A. Razvi, Collector, Nasik presented me with a lantern, as it would be the most useful companion in Bhir, where there was no electricity in the entire district. Razvi, had worked as Collector, Bhir during 1956–1957 and there were few people who knew the district better than he did.

My wife Suryakumari, our 1-year-old daughter Manjula and I reached Bhir by the evening of 8th November, 1966. I took over charge on the 9th from R.M. Mudholkar, Resident Deputy Collector (RDC), who was holding charge as Collector, after P.V. Nayak, IAS (1956) my predecessor, was transferred to Nanded, after a stint of nearly two years in Bhir.

Bhir is one of the five districts in Marathwada, the others being Aurangabad, Parbhani, Nanded and Osmanabad (present Latur district was also a part of Osmanabad) of Aurangabad *Division*. These Districts became part of Maharashtra after the re-organisation of the states in 1956. Earlier, these Districts were part of the erstwhile state of Hyderabad. Bhir is bordering Aurangabad District, (which is famous for the Ajanta caves and Ellora sculptures), Parbhani, Osmanabad and Ahmadnagar Districts. Bhir District had seven Tahsils which were Bhir, Georai, Manjlegaon, Kaij, Ambejogai, Patoda and Ashti. Bhir was perhaps one of the few District headquarters which was not connected by railway line in the State. However, Parli Vaijyanath, about 90 kms from Bhir, where one of the famous Jyotirlingas was located and a pilgrimage centre, was the only railway station in the District.

LAW AND ORDER SITUATION

Prior to my joining as Collector and District Magistrate, Bhir, there was a major communal flare up and the police had to resort to firing on an unruly crowd which indulged in large-scale arson and looting. The police firing resulted in the death of two persons, which somewhat helped in bringing the situation under control. In order to maintain communal harmony in the district, the district administration had filed FIR's against the suspected hooligans and the cases were being investigated. The law and order situation was far from satisfactory when I took over as Collector, as prohibitory orders under section 144 CrPC were in force, which restricted movements of persons in the nights and the peons working at my residence were scared to go to their houses after it became dark. These conditions prevailed for quite some time and several prohibitory measures were taken from time to time to bring the law and order situation in the district under control.

DIVISIONAL COMMISSIONERS

L.N. Bongirwar, IAS (1948), an authority on agriculture, was Commissioner, Aurangabad Division, when I joined in Bhir District. He was held in very high esteem by all, including his peers in the administration and particularly by leaders of all political parties, because of his pragmatism, development orientation and helpful attitude. He was of tremendous support to young Collectors, especially in the meetings of the District Planning and Development Council, (DPDC) chaired by Minister in Charge of the District. Even though the Annual plan of the district was prepared by the Zilla Parishads, it was formally approved by the DPDC which was presided over by the Minister in-charge of the district, with the Collector as Member Secretary of the Council.

L.N. Bongirwar, who was Commissioner for about six months of my tenure, was succeeded by L.S. Sunderrajan, IAS (1949), an officer from the former Hyderabad State. He was liked by all political parties for his soft and cooperative attitude. As Sunderrajan had worked earlier as Collector, Bhir during 1959-62, everyone whose request (mostly unreasonable ones for transfers, promotions and postings) was rejected at my level used to look to Sundarrajan for redressal. He was only too happy to oblige, whether the requests were deserving or not. He was very fond of touring and liked to dine with anyone who invited him, whether desirable or not. The dinners used to be very lavish and extravagant and the guest list unusually large. As the Guest Control Orders were in force in the entire state due to scarcity of food grains, it became embarrassing for me to attend such dinners and quite often, I had to make lame excuses, even at the cost of displeasing the boss.

Although Sunderrajan enjoyed smoking, he never smoked in public. Whenever he was on tour, he would quietly tap on the shoulder of his peon, who usually sat in the front seat, as soon as he got into the station wagon. The peon would promptly hand over a cigarette pack and match box to him. He also enjoyed non-vegetarian food while on tour, although he was a strict vegetarian at home. Narayan Valluri, IAS (1966) was

Supernumerary Assistant Collector (under-training) in the district, who on an earlier occasion was witness to the Commissioner enjoying the non-vegetarian dinner hosted by me. Later, I hosted another dinner at which Sundarrajan, Mrs. Sundarrajan and Valluri were also present. On seeing Sundarrajan scrupulously avoiding non-vegetarian curries, Valluri asked me in chaste Telugu (as both of us speak Telugu), "Why is the Commissioner avoiding non vegetarian dishes today? Is it because his wife is around?" Valluri was shell shocked when Sundarrajan revealed, to Valluri's utter dismay, that he also understood Telugu well!! Valluri ran for cover thereafter.

DISTRICT TEAM

Sudhakar Dev, IPS (1959) was the District Superintendent of Police (SP) for the first few months of my tenure as Collector. I knew him well during my stint in Kolaba District, where he was SP and had an excellent rapport with him in maintaining law and order in the District. However, local politicians were not particularly happy about his handling of law and order problems in the District, so he was soon succeeded by P.S. Narayanaswami, IPS (1963). We functioned as a team, which was also not liked by the local trouble makers as we had total control in maintaining law and order in the District, even though we had our own share of worries in handling some serious communal tensions.

G.R. Devaikar, a senior IAS officer from Vidarbha, was the Chief Executive Officer (CEO), Zilla Parishad. Although he was an excellent colleague to work with and we used to tour together often, he was not quite at home in Marathwada and was keen to move to any posting in Vidarbha. He was succeeded by M.R. Kher, another officer from Vidarbha as CEO, in February 1968. Dr. Wagle used to take care of our medical needs in the district as a Civil Surgeon. Both G.R. Abhange, Executive Engineer (Irrigation) and N.K. Mahajan, Executive Engineer (PWD) were excellent officers, who also used to organise frequent social and cultural gatherings in this otherwise dull and backward district.

T. Balaraman (1963), called 'Bala' was the Assistant Collector, Bhir subdivision, and B.N. Bahadur (1965) was the Assistant Collector under-training. Normally, no IAS Officer was sent for training to Bhir, as it was considered a backward District in the State. However, as P.V. Nayak, IAS (1956), my predecessor was a senior and an able administrator, Bahadur was sent as Asst. Collector under training. When Balaraman was promoted as CEO, Parbhani, after six months of my joining as Collector, Bahadur succeeded him as Assistant Collector. Narayan Valluri (1966) joined as Supernumerary Assistant Collector in June 1967.

I still vividly recollect that whenever Bahadur went on few days casual leave to Delhi, from where he hailed, he always used to extend his stay on some flimsy grounds, as at that time he was engaged to Milan, his future wife. Once after a prolonged absence, when Bahadur finally landed up in Bhir, Balaraman and I planned a trick on him, basically to have some fun in an otherwise totally dull place. Bala, who proved to be a better English typist than other English typists in my office (I should admit that I did not know what typing was all about), typed a neat letter personally on my letterhead as Collector in my chamber asking for Bahadur's explanation for the abnormal delay in reporting for duty. This was because the Commissioner had toured the District and had noticed Bahadur's absence and had directed me to obtain his explanation and forward it to the Commissioner, with my recommendation for taking disciplinary action against Bahadur. This "letter" was placed in his room, which he was sharing with Balaraman, in the outhouse of the CEO's bungalow. When Bahadur returned from Delhi and saw this letter, he was quite shocked and was afraid that some disciplinary action might be taken for his prolonged absence. The next day when he visited my office, contrary to my general instructions to be seated till I turn my attention, I noticed Bahadur, for a change, was standing for almost ten minutes, while I was pretending to attend to some urgent state matters. Bahadur was quite apologetic for his absence and brought a written explanation, which I immediately forwarded to the Commissioner with a recommendation to issue a 'warning' not to be recorded in the Annual Confidential Reports (CR) and directed Bahadur to proceed to Aurangabad, by the evening by bus, on the same day to meet the Commissioner. Bahadur dutifully went to the bus stand, from where he was called back! On his return, he found Balaraman was also sitting with me in my chamber. We had a hilarious time making fun of Bahadur for his nervous behaviour and called the bluff. Those were the days, when I and my colleagues functioned like a happy team in an otherwise socially dull district. Whenever we meet even today, we recount several such happy incidents. Bahadur retired recently as Additional Chief Secretary, Government of Maharashtra.

One heartening feature of my tenure in Bhir was that the CEO Zilla Parishad, the Superintendent of Police and all the officers in the district worked as a team. We often toured together. This helped a great deal in our work, as only by working together could the officers withstand the pressures and pulls from politicians and prevent them from playing one against the other. During my stay in the district, however, the relationship between the officers and the politicians were very cordial.

WHO IS MOST IMPORTANT: A DISTRICT COLLECTOR OR THE CHIEF EXECUTIVE OFFICER—A DEBATE

I attended a training course in the Administrative Staff College, Government of Maharashtra at Bombay along with my several young colleague IAS, Officers like R.C. Sinha (1962), P.R. Dasgupta (1963), T. Balaraman (1963), S. Vasudevan (1964), B.N. Makhija (1964), all young IAS Officers. While all of them were the Chief Executive Officers, of various Zilla Parishads, I was the only one among them who was working as Collector and District Magistrate. We had a very lively discussion as to who among the Collector and Chief Executive Officer, the most important person in the District. It was quite difficult for me to convince my contemporaries and very good friends that Collector represents the Government at the District level and thus the most important, as all of them (were working as CEOs) made up their mind not to get convinced. It was indeed a hilarious and lively debate of young IAS Officers.

COLLECTOR'S BUNGALOW

Normally, most of the District Collectors who were considered to be the 'eyes and ears' of the Government in the District had huge big bungalows, located in a spacious area covering several acres, outside the city. When I came to Bhir, I was looking for one such bungalow. I was totally disappointed to see a very old Municipal inspection bungalow, almost in the heart of the city, being used as Collector's bungalow for several decades. It had a few rooms, which were dark, dingy and without proper ventilation. It had a single detached bathroom, located far away from the bungalow. Even the kitchen was outside the bungalow, which was quite inconvenient. Throughout the day, one kept listening to the blaring music from the nearby *paan* shop located outside the bungalow, making the radio in the Collector's house totally redundant. The road in front was full of hawkers and rickshaws. We, therefore, decided to move out. At that time, two new small bungalows were being constructed for the Executive Engineers of the PWD and Irrigation Departments, opposite the CEO's huge bungalow, in a sprawling area with several outhouses, which was once occupied by the 'Resident Representative' during the time of Nizam. While one bungalow was already occupied by the Executive Engineer, PWD, the other was almost ready and yet to be allotted. Since the Collector was the allotting authority of new residential accommodation, I allotted the bungalow to myself, although it was much too small compared to the entitlement standards fixed for the Collectors. It had two bedrooms with attached baths and a sitting-cum-dining hall with a kitchen and a small garden in front, although the house was not even fenced. As there were not many security problems during those days, I felt it was quite safe to move to the small independent bungalow, instead of staying in the old Municipal guest house in the heart of the town. I also initiated steps to have a regular bungalow for the Collector.

ARE YOU THE COLLECTOR'S SON?

Bhir District invariably had very old Collectors in the past. Within a few days of taking over as Collector and moving into the new bungalow, I was watering the plants in the garden. Ambadas, one of the oldest peons of the Collectorate, who had not seen me earlier, brought an important file to my bungalow, with strict instructions that since the file was 'Top Secret', it should be handed over only to the Collector, and if the Collector was not available in the bungalow, he should wait till he returned. When I asked the peon to hand over the file to me, he refused to do so, saying that it would be given only to the Collector and if the Collector was not available, he would wait. My persuasive efforts to take the file did not succeed, until I revealed to Ambadas that I was the Collector. Ambadas immediately fell at my feet and apologized profusely stating that he thought I was the Collector's son, confessing that in his long career as a peon he had not seen such a young Collector!! Obviously, my predecessors must have been quite old, since I was the youngest Collector in the state at the age of twenty seven.

CHIEF MINISTER'S FIRST VISIT TO THE DISTRICT

Within a few months of my joining as Collector, Bhir, General Elections for Parliament and the State Assembly took place in 1967. It was during these elections that I had the privilege of receiving Vasantrao Phulsingh

Naik, the Chief Minister, a seasoned politician and a great administrator. He was always smartly dressed in buttoned up suits and was fond of smoking his pipe.

I had spent hardly three months in the District and there was never a day without a major communal incident in the District, especially in Bhir and Ambejogai, which were Tahsil headquarters. In order to contain the communal tensions, prohibitory orders were issued several times and suspected trouble makers were detained. Communal riots had taken place at Bhir in October 1966, and the District administration had filed several FIRs against persons suspected of indulging in large-scale looting and arson. Local leaders had been clamouring for withdrawal of the FIRs, which I strongly resisted, thus making it a major area of criticism against me as a District Magistrate by the local politicians. The Chief Minister had come for canvassing in the General Elections, which was to be closely followed by the Zilla Parishad Elections. Disgruntled politicians took advantage of the first visit of the Chief Minister to the District after the riots to make complaints, stating that I was too young and immature to be a District Collector, and that I did not understand Marathi and therefore was not able to comprehend the problems of the District nor able to redress their grievances! Finally, they came to the main grievance which was that unless the cases filed against the prominent citizens in the District after the outbreak of communal riots in October 1966, were withdrawn, the Congress party would face stiff opposition during the General Elections and many Congress candidates would lose. They, therefore, requested that the Collector should be immediately transferred. All these complaints were made to the Chief Minister immediately on his arrival to the District.

The next day morning, I was called to CM's room where most of the prominent politicians were present. He mentioned about the complaints made against me and also sought my views about withdrawing the cases filed in the recent communal incidents. When I started explaining to the Chief Minister in chaste Marathi he was taken aback and asked the leaders, "Why were you complaining that the Collector does not understand Marathi when he speaks better Marathi than me?" My reply in Marathi won me the first round of the battle. I further explained to the Chief Minister that the District was communally highly sensitive and practically every other day some communal incident took place. It would be difficult for me to function effectively as District Magistrate and control the law and order situation, if I withdrew the

FIRs filed against the trouble makers. It would be advisable to await the final report of the investigations on the FIRs, and take necessary action thereafter. Under these circumstances, I would not recommend the withdrawal of the FIRs. The Chief Minister, after listening to me carefully, directed me to submit a report to the Government. S.P. Mohini, IAS (1957), Secretary to the CM, was also present during the discussions. After seeing off the Chief Minister at the guest house, as I was not required to accompany the Chief Minister during the election tours in the district, I went home and told my wife that my days of functioning as District Magistrate were, perhaps over, as the CM during the tour in the District was bound to issue my transfer orders. I alerted my wife to be prepared to move out of the District at short notice. However, I did not receive any orders while Chief Minister was in the district. As directed by the Chief Minister, I sent a detailed report to the Government reiterating that the cases should not be withdrawn and at the same time, awaited my transfer orders. However, neither any orders to withdraw the criminal cases nor any transfer orders came and I continued for almost three years as Collector and District Magistrate!

When I look back to the past years and the current prevailing situation in the country when District officers are transferred frequently after short tenures in some states, I shudder to think how many young IAS officers would be able to give a negative reply to the Chief Minister in the presence of the politicians, and get away with it and continue to work as the Collector for long time. The maturity shown by Vasantrao Naik was due to his long years experience, maturity and leadership reflected the qualities of a seasoned politician.

ELECTIONS PASSED OFF PEACEFULLY

I was the Returning Officer for the Parliament Constituency of Bhir, the only Parliamentary constituency in the District for the General Elections held in April 1967. No chances could be taken in the matter of elections. This being the first General Elections for me, I had to be very meticulous in supervising all the processes till the elections passed off peacefully. G.L. Gangakhedkar, who was the District Election Officer, was of immense help to me during the Elections. He was subsequently elevated to the IAS. The polling stations had to be physically verified, polling and counting staff mustered and trained, polling material obtained in good time and kept ready for polling station-wise for distribution. Ballot boxes had to be secured and checked and transport arrangements made for the staff and the material. Peaceful and orderly polling had to be ensured. After polling, the ballot boxes were transported to the Tahsil headquarters for counting. Ballot papers from different polling stations were mixed and re-bundled before being handed over for counting. Counting once begun, it had to continue non-stop until the results were declared. Successful conduct of elections owed a lot to the various officers working under the Collector. I used to undertake extensive tours to check the location of polling stations, secure polling material and arrange staff and transport for conducting polls and thereafter made arrangements for counting and declaration of results. The General Elections, 1967, passed off peacefully. Out of seven MLA seats, only two seats were won by the Congress.

The General Elections were followed by the second elections to the Zilla Parishads and Panchayat Samitis in 1967, which were also conducted very smoothly.

VISITS OF SHANKARRAO CHAVAN, IRRIGATION MINISTER

There were many occasions during my tenure as District Collector, when S B Chavan, then Minister (Irrigation), who hailed from Nanded District in Marathwada, visited the district. He was regarded as the undisputed leader of the region, and all other politicians from the area sought his guidance on all local issues. He always wore a dhoti and kurta with a Gandhi cap, which many politicians in Maharashtra used to wear prior to the invasion of the safari suit culture. He had a very high degree of personal integrity and commanded respect from all political parties. Whenever he visited the district, he used to invariably spend some time with the District Collector after dinner, discussing the various facets of district administration and progress of developmental activities, and more particularly, the attitude of the district politicians towards the bureaucracy, in particular with the Collector. He was an authority on all matters concerning irrigation projects. He was appreciative of sincere and upright officers, who worked with zeal and dedication for the development of the district. I was fortunate to have an excellent rapport with him and he used to be highly appreciative of my work and showered lavish praise even in public. On one occasion, when he was presiding over a public function on the procurement of jowar in the district, I spoke in Marathi in the public meeting. He was so appreciative of my Marathi that he mentioned to the audience that an officer who did not know a word of the language till a few years back could not only learn Marathi but was also addressing public meetings in Marathi! This was a true example of "National Integration" about which all of us should be proud of. What better public commendation can a young officer expect to work with more zeal and dedication from a person who not only became a very successful Chief Minister but also the Union Home Minister.

VISIT OF YASHWANTRAO CHAVAN, UNION HOME MINISTER

Another occasion worthy of recollection was the visit of Yashwantrao Chavan, Home Minister, Government of India, for an election tour of the District. After a night's stay at the Government guest house, Bhir, all the officers gathered to bid good bye, including D. Thatke, District Session's Judge. Normally, District Judges kept away from such ceremonial and formal occasions of the visit of VIPs. I was quite surprised to see Thatke. When Yashwantrao Chavan saw him, he greeted him with warmth and respect, mentioning that he and Thatke had studied together. He showered lavish praise on Thatke's brilliance, studiousness and hard work. While Thatke used to study all the time, he used to bunk classes, go to cinemas and take active interest in student union activities and politics. Thatke helped him to prepare for the examinations. While patting Thatke affectionately on his shoulder, he said with a smile, "See where Thatke is now (District Judge) and where I am (Home Minister of the Country)"! We all joined in the laughter, including Thatke.

MEETING WITH SUNIL DUTT, BOLLYWOOD SUPER STAR

While, I was functioning as Collector and District Magistrate, Bhir, we went on a short holiday to Hyderabad. We met Shashi a cousin of Suri, who was a very beautiful young girl, an excellent dancer aspiring to join the movies. She pleaded with my wife that she should be taken to Bombay and introduced to the various film personalities. We took her to Bombay and we met several prominent filmy personalities which included Ramanand Sagar, famous Director and Sunil Dutt, an outstanding actor. When I sought an appointment with Sunil Dutt as Collector, Sunil Dutt immediately gave an appointment on the very next day at his residence in Pali Hills, Bombay. When we visited his resisdence,

Nargis Dutt, his wife and another very famous heroine treated us lavishly with the snacks. I always wondered how a Super Star gave me a interview so easily. I presumed that Sunil Dutt obviously mistook me as Collector of Customs (not realizing that I was only a District Collector) as customs is one of the contacts which most of the film stars would like to have.

KOYNA EARTHQUAKE 1967

A devastating earthquake struck Koyna dam area in Satara District on the night of 10th December 1967. Although Bhir District was more than 300 kms away from the epicenter, the impact of the earthquake was felt in Bhir also. Doors started rattling, the cots started shaking, ceiling fans swinging and utensils rolled down, making a lot of sound. As it was late in the night, and we were fast asleep, we initially thought that some thief was trying to break into the house, till we realized that it was something totally unnatural and all of us rushed out of the house, including the two security constables who were sleeping in the study room of the bungalow. Since communications were poor those days, it took some time to realize the large-scale damage done in Koyna and the adjoining areas due to the earthquake. Fortunately, there was no loss of life or damage to property in the District. However, the entire Government machinery in the District was mobilized to obtain voluntary contributions in cash and kind to provide relief to the earthquake victims.

MAINTENANCE OF LAW AND ORDER

Bhir District, especially Bhir and Ambajogi Tahsils, had a sizable Muslim population. Several measures had to be taken to prevent eruption of any communal trouble and to deal with individuals acting prejudicial to the interest of maintenance of law and order. I had to frequently issue preventive detention orders under the Maintenance of Internal Security Act (MISA), against persons fomenting communal trouble. However, this was done with due care, after a judicious evaluation of all the facts presented by the police and taking into consideration the over all situation in the district. All the detention orders were upheld by the Competent Authorities. The detention of a few suspicious characters always had a salutary effect and there was no trouble once they were detained. The detainees were also set free as soon as the law and order situation showed signs of improvement.

GANESH FESTIVAL

Ganesh Chaturthi festival was celebrated with great gusto and enthusiasm for ten days in the whole of Maharashtra. The festival had assumed special significance from the time of Bal Gangadhar Tilak, who focused on mobilization of masses during the festival, while we were fighting to achieve freedom for the country, which made it a mass movement. During this festival, there were always serious problems of law and order, especially in communally sensitive places in the state, more so on the days of installation of the idol of Lord Ganesh as well as at the time of immersion. Peace committee meetings were held very frequently by me, with all the prominent people to seek their cooperation to maintain peace during the period. While idols of Lord Ganesha installed by a family or individuals were immersed on different days, depending on family traditions and convenience, the *sarvajanik* or community or public Ganeshas were immersed on the last day, when all Ganeshas were taken in huge big procession on a predetermined route in the city, fixed by the district authorities, for immersion at one or two places. Quite often, the organizers obtained the services of singing and dancing artists who dance, to the popular tunes of films, while sometimes making provocative gestures to amuse the crowds. Such processions were also taken on the streets where mosques were located. Sometimes, the prayer timings in mosques coincided with the time of the procession, giving rise to communal tensions, especially as the processions were always led with lot of music, disturbing the otherwise peaceful time of prayers. The District administration was put to severe test in persuading the procession leaders to avoid playing music when they approached the mosque. On all these ten days of celebrations, the District Magistrate and Superintendent of Police maintained utmost vigil and took all possible preventive measures to ensure that the Ganesh festival passed off peacefully. Various entertainment and musical programmes were also arranged during the nights at several places with famous artists and troupes attracting huge crowds. They took the liberty of making fun of the District officials to make the event entertaining and enjoyable.

Narayanaswami, Superintendent of Police and I used to take several measures to control the situation and ensured that there was no untoward communal flare up during the entire duration of the festival so much so that the performers at time appreciated and commended our effort at maintaining law and order, and even compared us with 'Ram' and 'Laxman' working in tandem to control the situation, and inspired the confidence of all communities during the festival. We maintained total communal harmony by our complete impartiality and equity.

FIRING IN AMBEJOGAI

While I was on tour to some interior villages in Kaij Tahsil, I suddenly received a message that there was a serious communal riot in Ambejogai, about 30 kms from Kaij. Ambejogai had always been highly communally sensitive due to the presence of a large section of minority community. Unfortunately, the regular Sub Divisional Magistrate, V.N. Karandikar, a very good officer with an excellent record in maintaining communal harmony, was on leave and additional charge was given to a Land Acquisition Officer. I had to therefore rush to Ambejogai on hearing about the riots. As Ambejogai was located in a low-lying area, I could easily see the smoke engulfing the town while traveling from Kaij. As the SDM's house happened to be on the way to the main streets of Ambejogai, I stopped at his house. I found the officiating SDM was so bewildered and shocked due to the riots that he could not even recognise the District Magistrate! I reached Ambejogai earlier than the Superintendent of Police as he had to travel longer distance from Bhir. I took full control of the situation and mobilized the entire police force available in the Tahsil headquarters, including the orderlies working in the residences of the police officers, who might have forgotten how to handle a rifle. As the situation appeared to be very grave and arson and looting was taking place on a massive scale, I had to, after giving warnings about firing, issue orders to open fire on the rioting mob. The firing resulted in the death of four people, but brought the situation under control immediately. By then, the SP also arrived on the scene and deployed the force to prevent any recurrence of trouble. As I was required to send a flash report to the Government through wireless communication system immediately, I took stock of the situation and sent a report about the loss of life of four persons in the firing and also details of rounds fired to bring the situation under control. When a further review was taken subsequently, I noticed the number of rounds fired were more than double of what was earlier reported by me to the Government, as the constables who were using the rifles did not realize how many rounds were fired and they went on firing indiscriminately due to lack of experience. Luckily, the number of persons killed was very few compared to the number of rounds fired!!

HOT SUMMER

Summer was quite unbearable in Bhir District as it was a totally dry place and without any major rivers or irrigation facilities. While the desert cooler made life comfortable in the office and house, touring, especially in summer, was quite difficult. Whenever I was on tour, I used to wrap a cloth on the head and drink plenty of water to protect myself from heat-stroke. During the tours, we could see herds of deer crossing the road, especially in Kaij and Patoda Tahsils. I would stop the jeep, enjoy the spectacular sight of the deer running and disappearing into the wilderness.

SCARCITY CONDITIONS

There was inadequate rainfall during all the three years of my stay in the District, affecting the jowar crop. The failure of rains meant large-scale unemployment of the rural agricultural labour and shortage of food grains. A large number of relief works were opened to provide employment and to prevent the exodus of the rural population to urban areas. Even then, a large number of people, especially from Ashti and Patoda Tahsils, which were drought prone, used to migrate to sugar cane growing areas in western Maharashtra for several months in search of employment. During scarcity conditions, which was almost every summer, more than a lakh of persons were provided work in various relief programmes. Most of them fell in the tribal areas of the District. The emphasis of relief operations was on creation of assets to prevent recurrence of scarcity conditions, while providing work to the rural folk. The bulk of the relief work was related to soil conservation, irrigation tanks and the construction of roads and percolation tanks. On the whole, the works were of a productive nature. Every department in the District was involved and the coordination and monitoring was done by the Collector. Drinking water was supplied through tankers to a number of scarcity affected villages. Bore-wells were dug in many places. More relief works were started, depending on the intensity of scarcity.

There also used to be frequent hail-storms which affected the standing crops. As soon as reports of damage to the standing crops were received, I would visit the affected areas immediately, along with the other District officers. The President of Zilla Parishad, Sayajirao Pandit and other local representatives also used to accompany me often during these inspections to make an assessment of the damage and to carry out the necessary relief operations.

'HURDA' PARTIES

Whenever there was a good crop of jowar and when the seeds were tender and milky, prominent agriculturists used to invite the District Officers, especially the Collector, CEO, Superintendent of Police and District Judge for 'Hurda' parties in the fields. It was essentially to celebrate the early period of the harvesting season. The fresh jowar seeds were taken out from the crop plucked from the fields and roasted in the presence of all the invitees and given for eating with jaggery and fruit. This was considered a matter of honour and pride for the agriculturists to invite many VVIPs. I also had my share of 'Hurda parties' and these occasions provided excellent opportunities to mix with a wide strata of society.

JOWAR PROCUREMENT—CASH AWARDS

Jowar, pulses and groundnuts were some of the main crops grown in the district. In view of the shortage of food grains in the state, the state government had a policy of procuring excessive food grains from each cultivator, depending on the acreage. Procurement of Jowar was one of the functions entrusted to the Revenue department in the district. As the prices fixed by the Government were very low, normally cultivators did not voluntarily bring surplus jowar to the procurement centers operated by the government. The Collector had to launch several procurement drives in the villages to persuade cultivators to sell jowar to the government and sometimes had to invoke legal provisions to forcibly procure from hoarding cultivators. Bhir district had the distinction of procuring more jowar than the targets given by the government and thus had won cash awards for two years. The award amount was spent on the developmental activities of the district.

For one such jowar procurement function organised at Ashti, we had invited Balasaheb Desai, Minister, (Revenue), an aspirant to the post of Chief Minister and reputed to be highly temperamental. He never referred to the officers by name and always addressed them by their designations. True to his reputation, he also referred to me as Mr. Collector during the conversations, while looking in the opposite direction. All the officers and even the local leaders normally were under considerable tension till his visit was over. It was a successful function, with several farmers in attendance wearing white caps. While addressing the huge gathering, it was uncharitable of him, having come as a chief guest to the district, to point out that when he looked at them, he could recollect that Western Maharashtra used to be like Bhir district several decades back, indirectly pointing out that the district was very backward. No one dared to object to such uncharitable and unnecessary comments. I felt deeply hurt that such comments were made, as it was a reflection on the people of the district.

Since Bhir District was very backward and away from major cities, I did not get too many ministerial visits except Sunderrao Solunake, Minister from the District, who used to visit the district, invariably, at every weekend.

TRANSFER TO BOMBAY

I received my transfer orders as Secretary, Maharashtra State Electricity Board (MSEB), Bombay, after functioning successfully as Collector for over two and a half years. People in Bhir were genuinely sad to see me go on transfer. Indeed, all the political leaders from various parties threatened to go to Bombay to try for cancellation of my transfer order. As the saying goes, "it is always better to go when the going is good". I managed to persuade them not to go to Bombay to get my transfer order cancelled. I was given a memorable farewell, especially by the youth who accompanied my car on motor bikes as outriders till the outskirts of Bhir. In spite of being posted in a backward District which lacked basic facilities for tours and which meant a lot of inconvenience and hardship, I fondly remember the excellent experience I gained during those formative years. Long after I left, several people from Bhir, whenever they came to Bombay, made it a point to meet me and my wife and remember our association. I left the District with a heavy heart, but with very happy memories. The experience I gained helped me substantially in my subsequent assignments.

AN IAS OFFICER SELECTED BY ME WAS COLLECTOR, BHIR, WHERE I WAS COLLECTOR 40 YEARS BACK

Long after my retirement, I had to visit Bhir, where I had worked as Collector and District Magistrate during 1966 to 1969, in my capacity as Chairman, Maharashtra State Power Generation Company

(MAHAGENCO), a Government of Maharashtra undertaking, which was carved out of the restructured MSEB. I was visiting the Parli Thermal Power Station in the District for "boiler light up" programme on 21 August 2006 by Vilasrao Deshmukh, Chief Minister, Maharashtra. When I landed at Aurangabad airport, I was surprised to be received by Piyush Singh, IAS Collector and District Magistrate, Bhir who had taken the trouble of traveling for one and half hours from District Head quarters to receive me. I never received a VVIP away from the District, when I worked as Collector and District Magistrate, as all the VVIPs were normally received by the Collector at Bhir itself. When I asked the Collector as to why he had taken so much trouble to receive me at Aurangabad, Piyush Singh informed that it was an honour to receive me at Aurangabad, as he was selected by me into IAS.

I was happy to see that an IAS officer selected by me, as Member, Union Public Service Commission (UPSC), was functioning as Collector and District Magistrate, Bhir, a place where I was the Collector myself, exactly 40 years back. After the function at Parli was over, Piyush Singh personally escorted me to the Collector's office and honoured me in the presence of all the employees of the Collectorate. It was indeed a privilege and an honour to be back in Bhir under such happy circumstances.

EIGHT

FORAY INTO THE ENERGY SECTOR

Secretary, Maharashtra State Electricity Board (MSEB)

I took over as Secretary, MSEB in May 1969 and that marked the beginning of my long innings in the Power Sector. Even at that time, the MSEB was the biggest and one of the best managed SEBs in the country which pioneered many new endeavours in the electricity sector. The three-year stint in the MSEB, provided me with an understanding of the dynamics of the electricity industry in general and the challenges, problems and finer nuances of the State power utility, in particular. The experience benefited me immensely, particularly when I returned to the power sector in subsequent years.

D.R. Pradhan, ICS (1935) was the Chairman, MSEB since 1967, after retiring as the Chief Secretary, Government of Maharashtra. I took charge as Secretary from John Innocent IAS (1955), the Collector who trained me as supernumerary Assistant Collector in Jalgaon in 1963. It had never occurred to me that one day I would succeed my Collector, who had trained me in my initial years in the IAS. Although John Innocent had been Secretary, MSEB for only one year, the Chairman seemed to have requested for a replacement and asked for a panel of IAS officers with about ten years experience in the IAS and who had worked as a District Collector for at least two years. When the General Administration Department (GAD) tried to identify officers meeting the qualitative requirements (QRs) set by the Chairman, there were hardly any who would meet the QRs, since, as a convention, most of the IAS officers were posted as CEOs, Zilla Parishads, on promotion to the Senior Time Scale. However, a few names, including mine, were sent with the confidential reports. I was the junior most among the lot, with absolutely no chance of selection. When the recommendation came from the Chairman, the GAD was surprised to find that my name was picked up by D.R. Pradhan. Knowing the no nonsense reputation of D.R. Pradhan as former Chief Secretary, nobody dared to disagree with him and I was selected as Secretary, Maharashtra State Electricity Board.

First Taste of a Posting in a Metropolis—Bombay

When I reached Bombay after the long journey from Bhir, I drove straight to the MSEB officers' quarters (presently, Soudamini) where flat 7A on the seventh floor was already allotted to me. While many who were posted for the first time in Bombay had to stay in temporary accommodation in a single room in the MLA's hostel near Sachivalaya for indefinite periods, I was lucky to move into a spacious three-bedroom flat in Soudamini, due to my posting as Secretary, MSEB. As I was posted to Bombay for the first time and joining a new post, I expected someone from the office to be present to receive me but to my horror, I found no one from the office was present in the building. Even the watchman, who had the keys of the flat, was not available, as he had gone out to buy some provisions for his family! I, therefore, had to wait for some time to get into my flat and was totally deflated by the reception in a Metropolis posting.

Since MSEB did not have enough cars, all the heads of departments who were residing at Soudamini, used to pool cars and drive to the Mercantile Bank building office of the MSEB at Flora Fountain (the present Hong Kong Bank building at Hutatma Chowk). This is a far cry from the present day where plenty of cars are available for use by the staff.

Baby Sitting for Race-Going Colleagues

The Soudamini building where I was allotted a flat on the seventh floor was located opposite Haji Ali, with a panoramic view of the sea. It also had a race course boundary on the other side, with a vantage view of the entire race course. We often used to go to the race course for morning walks. I never went for the races and also rarely watched them, although I could have watched the entire race from start to finish from my balcony. Some of my friends, however, used to come to our flat to watch the races on the race days. Some of my colleagues who were regular race goers, would leave their young children with us, so that we could look after them while they were betting and enjoying the race. While baby sitting was fun in the initial stages, we lost all the holidays, as we could not move out of the house, because of the children. My wife, a good hostess, used to lay out a spread, by the time my colleagues came to pick up the children. Even though inconvenient, this gave us an opportunity to make everlasting friendship with our colleagues.

We did not take much time to settle down in '*Soudhamini*' and to the Metropolitan life style, as fortunately Balchandra Bhagwat (IAS – 1961) (Bal – for friends) Chief Executive Officer, Maharashtra Industrial Development Corporation was also staying on the same floor in an adjoining flat. Meena Bhagwat and my wife Suri became very close friends. Their two lovely sons, Nandu and Anil, and their daughter Aparna and my daughter Manjula, being of the same age, used to play most of the time. Bals presence in the building made all the difference for our stay in Bombay.

Working with a Retired ICS Officer

D.R. Pradhan, true to his reputation, was quite a terror in the Board and even the Members of the Board enquired from his personal staff about his mood, before they ventured to enter his room. He was a hard taskmaster, stickler for rules, hardworking and honest to the core. He ensured strict compliance of his orders. I remember, Rajaram Bapu Patil was the Minister for Industries and the MSEB was a part of the Industries and Labour Department. Pradhan never listened to anyone in administering the Board, and least of all to any political leader, including the Minister. Obviously, there was no love lost between the Chairman and the Minister. Pradhan rarely attended any meetings called by the Minister. As Secretary, I invariably used to attend all the meetings with the Minister and also in the Sachivalaya, (the Secretariat had not been rechristened as Mantralaya then), along with the concerned officers of the Board. However, Pradhan had his own favourites among the officers of the Board, but they were obviously few, such as Jadhav Rao, Chief Engineer, Nagpur and V.S. Shevde, Superintendent Engineer (Planning).

L.B. Dudhane, Chief Engineer (Rural Electrification), ranked high in the list of those whom Pradhan detested! To be fair to the Chairman, L.B. Dudhane was not liked by many employees, including his senior engineer colleagues, because of his totally unorthodox methods of working and proximity to politicians. However, Dudhane was the most sought, after engineer by politicians, as he was primarily responsible for carrying out Rural Electrification, which was one of the most important functions of the SEB, covering the electrification of the villages, energisation of agricultural pumpsets and strengthening the distribution network by establishing sub-stations and transmission lines. Indeed, 80 per cent of the employees of the Board worked under his control. Quite often, those who were seeking favours for electrification of villages or establishing sub-stations or energisation of pumpsets used to directly approach Dudhane. He was only too happy to oblige, although many schemes were rejected by the Chairman and the Board, as these were outright favours!

I remember when Rajaram Bapu Patil, Minister (Industries) once sent a list of the villages recommended for electrification to the Chairman, D.R. Pradhan. He promptly replied to the Minister that the villages to be electrified during the year were already approved by the Board and communicated to the field officers and many of the villages recommended by the Minister did not figure in the list, as they did not meet the criteria fixed by the Board. The new villages suggested by the Minister were not included for electrification during that year and was kept for consideration for the next year, if they fitted into the policy guidelines finalised by the Board. I knew that the Minister would be wild. He expressed his feelings in so many words when I met him subsequently. He also remarked very clearly, 'what was the point in being a Minister-in-charge of MSEB, if a simple request for electrification of a few villages was not agreed upon by the Chairman?' The Minister, therefore, found it convenient to operate through L.B. Dudhane, Chief Engineer, who was only too willing to oblige as he was carving out a bigger role for himself—first becoming a Member and subsequently Chairman of the Board. Lo and behold, when a review of the villages electrified during the year was taken subsequently, to our utter dismay, we found that most of the villages recommended by the Minister were already electrified by L.B. Dudhane, since he could divert the material from one scheme to the other, with impunity. It was a different matter that subsequently L.B. Dudhane became Technical Member and also Chairman of the

Board. While he was Chairman, his house was raided, as he was believed to have acquired assets disproportionate to his known sources of income. He was suspended and finally cooled his heels in jail for some time! What a ignominious exit for a Chairman of such a prestigious State Electricity Board!

D.R. Pradhan, although a task master, had his own failings. He was prejudiced against engineers as a class, except for a few of his favourites. No engineer was happy to enter his room as he was certain that he would be pulled up, if not humiliated, on one ground or the other. I recollect vividly one such instance when a Superintending Engineer entered his room in my presence. He started shouting at him stating that he was fully aware of where he kept the money received from various suppliers of machinery and equipment, and also who were the suppliers visiting his house late in the evenings. I was totally embarrassed at his outburst. On one occasion, after I became more familiar with the Chairman's strong likes and dislikes, finding him in a good mood, I asked him as to why he had to shout at every engineer, as all engineers were not dishonest and corrupt. He replied, "Abraham, you want me to change my views at this late hour, after being like this for all the forty years of my career in ICS!!"

D.R. Pradhan normally used to have a tea break, all by himself between 3:30 p.m. and 4:00 p.m. After a few months of my joining as Secretary and when he started liking me, he extended a permanent invitation to me to join him every day for tea. As I was a 'teetotaller', literally and figuratively I hardly took any tea at that time, he used to get me a soft drink before the tea time. I found him totally relaxed during this period and we used to chat on various matters, including happenings in the bureaucracy. Gradually, he realised that he had to change with time and used to be a totally different person for the rest of the day, at least. He might have also become conscious that his term as Chairman was coming to an end in a few months, and perhaps I would be the last IAS officer ever working under him. He used to treat me with fatherly affection and the Pradhans were also affectionate towards to my wife and invited us often to their home for tea.

Although there was considerable pressure on him to promote Dudhane as Technical Member, he resisted all pressures and ensured that Dudhane was not promoted so long as he was the Chairman. It would be interesting to note the manner in which Dudhane was promoted even as Chief Engineer from the post of Deputy Chief Engineer, before

I joined the Board. The first part of the Board Resolution contained all the negative characteristics of Dudhane such as not being amenable to discipline, getting easily pressurised by politicians, vindictive to those who did not fall in line with his views and thus unworthy of any further promotion. However, the second part of the Resolution cryptically stated that in spite of the above, the Board decided to promote him as Chief Engineer. I could clearly see the penmanship of an ICS Officer in drafting the Resolution. A classic case of how some decisions were thrust on the Board under political pressure and more classic, the manner of recording this decision as a Board Resolution, as all Board Resolutions form a part of the permanent records of the Board.

The Board was reconstituted with effect from 1 July 1970, on the retirement of D.R. Pradhan, as Chairman. The Government very seriously considered bringing in a professional who had experience of managing a huge multinational company or a big private company. After considerable search, the authorities zeroed in on L.G. Rajyadhyaksha, Chairman, Hindustan Lever who was about to retire for appointment as Chairman, MSEB. By then, Rajyadhyaksha was fully aware of the magnitude of managing an essential public utility like the MSEB, with political and public interface. After visiting the MSEB a few times and interacting with various officers, he finally decided not to accept the offer of Chairman. Under the circumstances, S.V. Bhave, Secretary, Industries and Labour Department, who was also Member of the Board, was given the additional charge as Chairman, MSEB. Bhave, a hardworking, highly principled, upright and humane officer, continued as Chairman till April 1972. He subsequently retired as the Chief Secretary, Government of Maharashtra.

The Electricity (Supply) Act, 1948, mandated that the Maharashtra State Electricity Board shall be constituted by the Government once in three years and the Board shall have a Secretary, who will be appointed by the Government. The Secretary was not only the Head of the Department but was also privy to all the discussions and decisions taken in the Board. He was also the only conduit to correspond with the Government. This clause was primarily included to prevent persons like Dudhane from resorting to parallel channels of communication with the Government directly, while keeping the Board in total darkness.

I was appointed on deputation initially for a period of two years with a clause for further extension. When my case for extension came up for consideration in April 1971, S.V. Bhave, IAS (1949) was the

Chairman, in addition to his regular charge as Secretary, Industries and Labour Department. L.B. Dudhane, who by then had become Technical Member in the Board, opposed my extension tooth and nail. He never wanted an IAS officer to be Secretary, MSEB and wanted an employee of the Board to be appointed as Secretary, so that he could exercise control over the working of the Board. The other reason was that while L.B. Dudhane and I were Heads of the Departments, I was the first among the equals as Secretary, of the MSEB and several decisions taken by me at my level and also advice tendered by me in the Board were not in tune with Dudhane's recommendations. Having become Technical Member in the Board, he wanted a 'yes' man in my place and also wanted to show to me who was the boss. However, Bhave insisted that it was the prerogative of the Government to appoint an officer of its choice as Secretary and insisted on my continuation for another year, since the Secretary was the only Government representative in the Board and it wanted a person of its confidence to be the Secretary. The matter of my continuance was considered and adjourned by the Board a couple of times. Finally, the extension was cleared, in spite of Dudhane's opposition. But for the firm stand taken by S.V. Bhave, Dudhane would have certainly succeeded in repatriating me back to the Government.

MSEB Constituted in 1960

The Maharashtra State Electricity Board was constituted on 20 June 1960, consequent to the bifurcation of the bilingual State of Bombay into the States of Maharashtra and Gujarat on 1 May 1960. Prior to the constitution of the MSEB, the electricity schemes in the State were administered by the Bombay State Electricity Board. On bifurcation, the assets and liabilities of the Bombay State Electricity Board in the Maharashtra region passed to the Maharashtra State Electricity Board and of the Gujarat region to the Gujarat Electricity Board. The formation of the MSEB did not lead to any major change in the existing administrative set-up and the total number of employees at the commencement of the Board was about 5,085.

As per the Electricity (Supply) Act, 1948, the Electricity Board had to consist of not less than three and not more than seven members. One of these, had to be a person with experience in commercial matters and in administration, one had to be an electrical engineer and one had to be a person with experience of accounting and financial matters, preferably in an electricity supply undertaking. One of the aforementioned three members was to be appointed as the Chairman of the Board. The Maharashtra State Electricity Board when thus constituted, consisted of seven members, including the Chairman. The post of Secretary, Board was the only post mentioned specifically in the Act and he was entrusted with specific statutory functions, including recording and maintenance of Board Resolutions.

The Board, under the Electricity (Supply) Act, 1948, was charged with the duty of promoting the coordinated development of the generation, supply and distribution of electricity within the State, in the most efficient and economical manner. In conformity with the obligation cast on the Board, the Board extended supply of power to rural areas having low load densities, even though the revenue from such areas was negligible in the early years.

There were four Departments in the Board, namely, (i) Technical (all four Chief Engineers, dealing with two Distribution Grids, Generation and Planning and Coordination, were heads of the Department), (ii) Accounts (headed by Financial Advisor and Chief Accounts Officer—Y.S. Das, IA & AS (1951), (iii) General Administration (headed by the Secretary), and (iv) Stores Department (headed by the Chief Purchase Officer). The Board's Secretariat, Establishment, Labour and Industrial Relations, Vigilance and Security Departments, functioned directly under the Secretary.

Status of the MSEB

When the Board was constituted, its total generation capacity was 69 MW and the total length of transmission lines was 4,262 circuit kms, most of which was 33 kv and below. The number of towns and villages electrified was 578 and the number of pumpsets energised was 5,400, while the total number of consumers was 80,000. The total revenue of the Board was Rs. 3.20 crores and there was a deficit of Rs. 32 lakhs.

The year 1969-70, when I joined, was of special significance to the Board, as it was completing a decade of its existence. During this period, it had made considerable progress in all fields. It was also the first year of Fourth Five Year Plan (1969-74). During this decade, the generating capacity increased to 873 MW and the transmission lines to 45,090 circuit kms, of which 38,800 circuit kms were of 33 kv, 2,044 circuit kms of 66 kv, 3,126 Circuit kms of 132 kv and 1,118 circuit kms of 220 kv. The number of towns and villages electrified were 10,643 and the number of pumpsets energised were 1,59,713. Thus, there was an overall increase to the extent of about 12 times in generation and an equal increase in transmission lines, about 20 times in village electrification, and about 30 times in the energisation of pumpsets. The financial position of the Board had also improved and for the first time since its formation, the Board earned a net surplus of Rs. 80 lakhs after wiping out the accumulated losses during 1969-70.

Generation

When the Board was constituted in 1960, the total generation capacity was 69 MW. At the time of constitution of the Board, the Koyana Hydro Electric Project Stage I, which was under execution by the Government of Maharashtra, was transferred to the Board. The Board had twelve Power Stations, with a total installed capacity of 873 MW, including the Bhusaval Power Station, which came into operation in 1968-69. The Board had undertaken massive expansion plans of Generation Capacity to meet the growing requirements of power. A new Thermal Power Station of 280 MW capacity at Nasik, comprising of two sets of 140 MW capacity each, was in an advanced stage of implementation, with the first set commissioned during 1970-71. Due to this, the installed capacity of the Board increased from 873 MW to 1,178 MW and the number of power stations from 10 to 11.

Parli Power Station Commissioned

Fifteenth November 1971 marked red letter day in the history of Marathwada when the first of the two 30 MW sets of Parli Thermal Power Stations in Bhir District were commissioned, as it was the first power station in the region. The work on the installation of the second set of 30 MW was also in an advanced stage of completion. It was of special significance to me, as I had monitored the progress of this project about two years earlier as Collector, Bhir. I had no doubt that it would go a long way in furthering the development of not only Bhir District, but also the entire backward region of Marathwada. The story of this power station was that of a dream come true for the Board, as it was a bold attempt to set up a complex thermal plant with maximum indigenous efforts and expertise in a backward area.

Brisk Progress on Koradi Thermal Station

Considerable progress was made in the erection work of the 1,080 MW thermal power station at Koradi, comprising of 240 MW (2 × 120 MW) under the first stage, 240 MW (2 × 120 MW) under the second stage and 600 MW (3 × 200 MW) under the third stage. All efforts were made for the expeditious completion of the work on Koradi Thermal Power Station. I was a part of the team monitoring the implementation of the major generation projects, from concept to completion stage and also participated in the decision-making process on several key issues in the Board, which was a highly rewarding experience.

India's Entry into the Nuclear Era

The year 1969-70 was momentous for the country, as it marked India's entry into the nuclear era. The agreement for cooperation for building the first nuclear power station of 380 MW capacity with two reactors, each of 190 MW at Tarapur and also the supply of enriched uranium and financing arrangements with the Agency for International Development (AID) of the U.S. Government, was concluded in 1963. The construction work at the Tarapur project began in October 1964, after the contract was signed with General Electric Company of U.S.A. in May 1964. The project provided an opportunity for the Indian engineering community to become familiar with some of the new technologies in nuclear power. The station was dedicated to the nation on 19 January, 1970 by Prime Minister Indira Gandhi, in the presence of Vikram Sarabhai, Chairman, Atomic Energy Commission. I was present at this important historical moment at Tarapore in my capacity as Secretary, MSEB. The power generated was being shared between Maharashtra and Gujarat. Both the units with a stretched output of 2 × 210 MW, even now after about 36 years, are operating very well, providing reliable low-cost non-hydel electricity to the Western Region.

Meeting with N. Tata Rao

The Western Regional Electricity Grid was comprising the Electricity Boards of Maharashtra, Gujarat and Madhya Pradesh. The MSEB, being the largest Electricity Board in the region played a coordinating role among these Boards. The coordination meetings of these Boards were invariably held in Bombay. Being Secretary, MSEB, I used to play active role during these meetings. In one such meeting, I met for the first time, N. Tata Rao, Secretary, Madhya Pradesh Electricity Board, Jabalpur.Tata Rao was already a recognized expert in the Power Sector. Being his counterpart from Maharashtra and also hailing from the same Krishna District in Andhra Pradesh, we became very close friends and we could easily sort out many thorny power problems between Maharashtra and Madhya Pradesh. Since then, we worked very closely in the power sector.

While I was Chairman, MSEB, he happened to be the Chairman, APSEB. Even after his retirement as Chairman, APSEB his advice was always available for me while I was functioning as Union Power Secretary, as Tata Rao was regarded as *Pitamaha* of Power Sector.

Transmission Schemes

Realising the importance of having an adequate network of transmission lines and sub-stations, the Board had prepared various transmission schemes for execution during the Fourth Plan Period. A crash programme of transmission schemes was undertaken in 1969-70 to support the extensive pumpsets and village electrification programme undertaken by the Board. Several inter-State links were under execution during 1969-70, with Central Government's assistance. The Board's transmission programme for the year 1969-70 consisted of certain spillover works of the Third Five Year Plan and certain works proposed under the Fourth Five Year Plan Schemes. During the year 1969-72, 1,800 circuit kms of 66 kv and above and 7,300 circuit kms of 33 kv and below were completed and a number of sub-stations were commissioned. The total length of the Board's transmission lines of 11 kv and above increased from 41,300 circuit kms to 55,500 circuit kms and the distribution lines (below 11 kv) increased from 39,220 circuit kms to 62,244 circuit kms.

Inter-State Transmission Links

Inter-State links were encouraged by the Central Government by giving 100 per cent special assistance outside the State Plan, with a view to achieving integrated operation of power systems in the region. This would reduce the total standby generating capacity, provide emergency power supply and bulk supply from power stations set up in the coal belt, thereby reducing generation costs. The 220 kv Kolhapur–Belgaum Inter-State line was commissioned in September 1970. After intensive follow-up, the Planning Commission approved the construction of the 220 kv Satpura-Ambazari line, linking Maharashtra and Madhya Pradesh. The acceptance, in principle, for the construction of two 400 kv single circuit lines from Koradi (near Nagpur) to Kalwa (near Bombay) was received from the Government of India during 1971-72. The credit for conceiving, engineering and designing for the first 400 kv transmission line and switch-gear equipment in the country went to the MSEB. Several proposals for other Inter-State links were sent for approval to the Central Water and Power Commission, as well as the Planning Commission.

Rural Electrification

The Board relentlessly pursued the electrification of rural areas, as it was felt that the development of rural areas would not be possible without electrification of towns and villages. Before the formation of the Maharashtra State Electricity Board a decade ago, very little attention was paid to Rural Electrification. The Board served only 578 towns and villages throughout Maharashtra State up to 1960, but during the last decade, there was significant progress in the activities of Board, particularly in the field of Rural Electrification.

In Maharashtra, on an average, there were 135 villages to each town as per the 1961 Census, which indicated the magnitude of the work involved in the Rural Electrification Programme in the State. Electricity is no longer an item of luxury but has become a day to day necessity. The development of rural areas would not be possible without the facility of electricity. Until 1965, the programme of Rural Electrification was centred on lighting up rural homes and village streets. The Board had, since then, been laying stress on energisation of agricultural pumpsets and on the supply of power to agro-industries in rural areas. The impact of this was already seen in the "Green Revolution" that was being ushered in the State. There was an increase in the demand for funds for rural electrification works. Since Plan outlays made by the State Government were quite insufficient, additional finances were secured through other financing institutions like the Agricultural Finance Corporation, Agricultural Refinance Corporation and Rural Electrification Corporation. During the year 1969-70 alone, the Board had electrified 623 towns and villages, as compared to 518 villages electrified at the time of its formation in 1960.

The year 1970-71 had gone down as a record year for Rural Electrification in Maharashtra, as the Board crossed the 2 lakh mark for energising agricultural pumpsets. The Board undertook special programmes in the under-developed districts of Thane, Kolaba, Ratnagiri, Bhandara and Chanda (Chandrapur). The Board continued to electrify a maximum number of villages and energise 28,200 irrigation pumpsets and thus all 14,167 towns and villages were electrified and 2,39,915 agricultural pumpsets were energised throughout the State by March 1972, thus providing electricity access to 70 per cent of the population of Maharashtra. Due to this commendable achievement, modern amenities and the need for the growth of agro-industrial production in remote areas were met.

Maharashtra—the First State to Electrify all Towns in the State

Another feather in the cap of the MSEB was that with the electrification of Dudhani town in Sholapur District on 29th February 1972, all the towns in Maharashtra were electrified; Maharashtra had the distinction of being the first State in the country, which electrified all towns by 1972.

Pioneer in Encouraging Electricity Cooperatives

Maharashtra has been a pioneer in the cooperative movement in the country. The Mula Pravara Rural Electric Co-op Society in Ahmadnagar district is one of the five Rural Electric Co-operative Societies set up in the country with the help of USAID. The assets of MSEB in 167 villages were handed over to the society on 1 March 1971. The Board had thus taken the lead to encourage cooperatives in electricity distribution in rural areas.

Electrification of Dalit Habitations

Several areas inhabited by dalits were not provided with electricity in the state, even though the villages were electrified. The number of such hamlets or basties were about 2,700. The Government of India, through the Rural Electrification Corp. (REC), had introduced a scheme for providing loan assistance to provide electricity to such dalit basties. The Board obtained sanction for schemes for electrification of 957 dalit basties from the REC.

Mission: Electricity for My Village

While I was able to sanction electrification of several villages in Maharashtra, as Secretary, MSEB, I was deeply concerned about my own village, Gaddamanugu, in Andhra Pradesh, which was still in dark. I was determined to meet the Chairman, Andhra Pradesh State Electricity Board (APSEB) and plead for electrification in my village. However, the pressure of work was such that I could not visit Hyderabad for almost two years since I joined the MSEB. However, I managed to go on leave in May 1971 and met A. Krishnaswamy, IAS, Chairman, APSEB, in Hyderabad whom I never met before. Krishnaswamy who had a reputation of being a strict and principled officer, was quite surprised that an IAS officer, working as Secretary,

MSEB, hailed from a village in Andhra Pradesh which was not electrified. He immediately summoned the officers concerned and directed that my village should be electrified within six months under any circumstances. In the process, not only was my village electrified in December 1971 but a few other villages which were en route were also electrified. All the people from the village were greatly delighted for the sincere efforts made by me to get electricity to the village, even though I was working in Maharashtra. I was personally happy that the children from my village were no longer required to study with the help of hurricane lanterns like I had done during my childhood.

Commercial Activities

The Board continued to exchange power with Tata Power, a major private electricity licensee in the country. Similar arrangements continued with Madhya Pradesh and Goa. In keeping with the policy of the Board to take over Licenses after the expiry of License period, the Nagpur Electric Light and Power Company was taken over during 1971-72 by the Board. The number of consumers served by the Board increased from 9,50,000 in 1969-70 to 12,85,000 by 1971-72.

Financial Results

Earned Surplus for the First Time Since Inception

The revenue from sale of electricity during 1969-70 was Rs. 42 crores as compared to Rs. 34 crores in the previous year, which increased to Rs. 65 crores in 1971-72. For the first time after bifurcation in 1960 the Board made a net surplus of Rs. 1.70 crores during 1969-70, which enabled it to wipe off the accumulated deficit of Rs. 90 lakhs, leaving a net surplus of Rs. 80 lakhs. The financial position of the Board further improved and there was a net surplus of Rs. 69 lakhs during 1970-71. This was the second year in succession that the Board earned a net surplus since its formation in 1960. The per-capita electricity consumption in a country was considered to be a symbol of progress achieved by that country. The per capita consumption of power had increased to 194 units for 1970-71. The door-to-door billing system, introduced partially in Poona, was extended to all consumers in the city from May 1971. The total sales of electricity aggregated 6,090 million units, an increase of about 4 per cent over the previous year. The number of consumers increased from 8.5 lakhs to 12.8 lakhs. The concessions granted to the agricultural and agro-based industrial consumers in the scarcity affected areas of state were continued. Capital expenditure, a measly figure of Rs. 25 crore in 1969 went up to Rs. 70 crore in 1971. The fixed assets went up from Rs. 158 crore to Rs. 300 crore by 1972. There were several improvements in the performance of various power stations during my tenure and several of them received awards from the Government of India for meritorious performance in respect of PLF, availability, coal consumption, and so on.

Administrative Set-Up

The State was divided into nine Circles and each Circle was further divided into Divisions and Sub-Divisions. With the rapid expansion of the Rural Electrification programme, it was found necessary to give attention to the planning and construction of Extra High Voltage Transmission (EHTV) lines and major sub-stations. The Board was having pre-stressed cement concrete pole factories at eight places to supply poles for transmission lines and three additional factories were being established to meet the additional demand for poles. In view of the substantial increase in the number of projects and civil construction activity, an additional post of Chief Engineer (Construction and Civil) was created to be in overall charge of entire civil engineering activities of the Board during 1971-72. During 1969-70, a separate Central Stores and Purchase Organisation was also created to look after the work of store and purchases, so that the technical staff could devote their time to construction, operation and maintenance and other technical tasks. With the rapid increase in Rural Electrification, electricity connections to agricultural pumpsets and additions in transmission lines and sub-stations were taken up on a large scale. The existing Operation and Maintenance (O & M) Circles were facing difficulties in coping with the maintenance work and ensuring proper service to the numerous consumers spread over all parts of the State, due to the massive expansion plans undertaken. The total strength of the Board's employees on regular establishment in all cadres, stood at about 30,000 by 1971-72, in addition to a large number of employees on Nominal Muster Rolls (NMR).

Security and Vigilance Organisation

With a large network of big and small power installations spread over the remotest villages, the necessity of building up of a statewide security organisation was keenly felt. The Security and Vigilance Organisation was created during 1970-71 with a regular staff to curb illegal and unlawful activities.

Industrial Relations

I was *inter alia* also looking after Industrial Relations, which was an altogether new experience in such a massive public utility dealing with essential services. The Board's industrial relations with its employees and Trade Unions continued to be generally cordial, even though agitations in the shape of demonstrations, slogan-shouting, protest fasts and morchas were carried out from time to time by the recognised Unions, over the revision of pay-scales, D.A., Interim relief etc. The Unions gave strike notices and conciliation proceedings were started in February 1970. The most remarkable development in industrial relations was the emergence of a comprehensive Wage Agreement on 21st November 1970, which followed seven strike notices, and four hunger strikes etc. The result of protracted discussions between the three Federations of trade unions and the Board's authorities lasted over several months.

I had prolonged negotiations with the Unions, which culminated in a successful Wage Agreement. It provided me with a unique experience in managing industrial relations in a public utility and also came in handy in my subsequent assignment as Chairman, Maharashtra State Textile Corporation and in later years as Chairman, MSEB.

I left the Board on my transfer as Managing Director, Maharashtra State Textile Corporation, after completing my deputation of three years, although the Board wanted to continue my services further. My experience taught me, "it is always better to go (leave the organisation), when the going is good." I consider myself extremely fortunate to have worked in one of the biggest statutory Boards in the country and greatly benefited by the experience, which helped in my future assignments in the power sector.

NINE

TURN AROUND OF SICK TEXTILE INDUSTRY

Chairman and Managing Director–Maharashtra State Textile Corporation

MANAGEMENT OF TEXTILE MILLS

Industrial development in the country started primarily with the industrialisation of the then bilingual Bombay State, which was bifurcated into the states of Maharashtra and Gujarat on 1st May 1960. Industrialization in the erstwhile Bombay state started with the setting up of the textiles mills, as it was an important cotton growing area. The western location of Bombay port and an international airport with excellent financial and banking facilities gave a further impetus for its industrialization. Even today, both Maharashtra and Gujarat are considered to be the top industrial states in the country.

The textile industry, which set the pace for over all industrialization and which was highly labour intensive, had become sick for a variety of reasons, prominent among them being the inability to meet the challenges of growing competition. Thus hundreds of people were thrown out of employment and in order to provide sustenance to the poor workers, the Government, being a welfare state, reopened such mills, basically to provide employment to the displaced labour. It was decided that the Government would bring all such mills under the management of a single organization, resulting in the setting up of the Maharashtra State Textile Corporation (MSTC) in 1970.

When I joined the Maharashtra State Textile Corporation (MSTC) as Managing Director in May 1972, subsequently becoming the Chairman and Managing Director of this Government of Maharashtra Undertaking, the Corporation had the management of 20 Textile Mills in the state. The Corporation was managing 6 mills, namely, the Digvijay Mills, Bombay; Model Mills, Nagpur; Mohta Mills, Akola; Chhaganlal Mills, Chalisgaon; India United Mills (INDU—six Mills), Bombay and Aurangabad Mills, Aurangabad as *Authorised Controller*. It was also managing three mills namely New Pratap Mills, Dhulia; New Kaiser I Hind Mills, Bombay and R.B.B.A. Mills, Akola as *Chief Executive Authority* as they were taken over on lease basis from the Official Liquidator. The Corporation was also the *Chief Executive Authority* of the Government of Maharashtra for two mills, namely, Shri Shahu Chhatrapati Mills, Kolhapur and Narsinggirjee Mills, Sholapur. In addition, the Government of Maharashtra *transferred the management* of the Edward Textiles, Bombay; Pratap Mills, Amalner and Savatram Ramprasad Mills, Akola to this Corporation. The 21st Textile Mill, the Osmanshahi Mills, Nanded, had also come under the management of this Corporation from 1st May 1972, the day I joined the Corporation. Most of these Mills were sick, or were made sick by their owners, and abandoned. As thousands of people were thrown out of employment, the Government took over the management of these units not only to provide employment to the workers, but also to prevent the impact of the closures of the Mills on the economy of Maharashtra, in particular, and of the country, in general. At that time, there were also more than 100 such sick mills, under the management of the National Textile Corporation (NTC), a Government of India undertaking. However, the maximum number of such units were under the management of MSTC, a Government of Maharashtra Undertaking.

The MSTC Mills had an installed capacity of 46.18 lakh spindles, out of 179,000 lakhs in Maharashtra and 77,500 looms out of 206,000 looms in the state. It was producing about 34 crore metres of cloth and 57 lakh kgs of yarn in a year. Its annual turnover was over Rs. 90 crore and had exports of Rs. 18 crores. The total number of employees in the Corporation were 52,000, making the MSTC, the biggest corporation managing the largest number of sick textile mills in the country.

HOW I RESTARTED THE APOLLO AND SAKESRIA MILLS, BOMBAY

During 1972 and 1973, the Cooperation had taken over two more textile mills for management. The Apollo Mills, Bombay had closed down only for about two months and we were able to restart it from 14th November 1972. When I personally opened the lock of the closed Mill, the joy on the faces of workers who regained their employment was a sight to cherish forever. The Sakesria Mills, Bombay which was closed for nearly five years, was also taken over personally by me in February 1973 in the presence of happy employees. After carrying out the cleaning and maintenance operations, the mill was restarted in May 1973. With regard to the third Mill, the Jayshankar Mills, Barsi, we had approached the Official Liquidator for handing over the possession of the Mills to the Corporation in its capacity as custodian. This mill was also taken over in early 1975.

DIRECTORS

There were 11 Directors, including the Chairman on the Board of MSTC. There were four full-time Directors, three Directors who represented the workers and were themselves employees of the mills, three who were Chief Executive Officers/General Managers and one nominee of the National Textile Corporation. Thus, the Board of Directors of the MSTC provided an ideal combination of professional, administrative and labour experience.

My experience in the previous job as Secretary, MSEB came in handy in managing another Corporation with over 50,000 employees.

MEASURES TAKEN TO IMPROVE THE WORKING OF THE MILLS

The year 1971 was the worst year for the Textile Industry in view of the steep rise in the prices of cotton, without a corresponding increase in the prices of cloth. In view of such adverse conditions, even the best Textile Mills faced financial difficulties and the impact on the 'sick' Textile Mills was lethal, aggravating their already weak financial condition. The 20 'sick' Mills, under the management of the Corporation suffered a net loss of Rs. 6.36 crores, after providing for depreciation and interest liability.

MAJOR HANDICAPS FACED BY THE MILLS

Some of the major handicaps for the Mills managed by the Corporation were due to:

(A) Old and Antiquated Machinery

Old and antiquated machinery which could not give normal standard efficiency. With a view to improving the production efficiency and the profitability of the Mills on a long-term basis, a programme of renovation and modernization of the old machinery was undertaken in respect of the Mills taken over by the Government of India under the Industries (Development & Regulation) Act. The funds for modernization were provided by the Government of India and the State Government in the ratio of 51:49. These Mills were India United Mills, Bombay; Digvijay Mills, Bombay; Model Mills, Nagpur; Mohta Mills, Akola and Chhaganlal Textile Mills, Chalisgaon. However, in respect of other Mills taken over on lease, it was not possible to undertake any substantial modernisation programme, as these Mills, on termination of leases, would revert to the liquidator/previous owner. Nevertheless, essential and unavoidable renovations were carried out wherever required.

(B) Heavy Interest Liability

Another handicap, the heavy interest liability, arose out of the large amounts of loans advanced to the Mills due to the heavy losses suffered by them. Proposals for financial reconstruction were sent to the Central and State Governments for approval and were persistently followed up.

(C) Delay in the Release of Funds

The third handicap was the inordinate delay in the release of funds by the National Textile Corporation which was under the Government of India, for which a vigorous follow-up was undertaken successfully.

PROFESSIONALISATION OF MANAGEMENT

The objective of the MSTC was to professionalise the management of the mills, thus making them viable on a long-term basis. The Corporation adopted a 7-point programme for bringing about improvement in the working of the mills:

- Recruiting the best available technical persons for manning key posts.
- Purchase of good quality cotton at the most competitive rates.

- Improving production efficiency.
- Purchase of quality stores at competitive rates.
- Purchase of machinery for modernisation at competitive rates and expediting the implementation of the Modernisation Programme.
- Improving the quality of production to get better prices in the market.
- Maintaining good management and labour relations.

Some good senior technicians from the private sector were recruited for the posts of Chief Executives and General Managers for the Mills. The Corporation had started a scheme of Management Trainees for the Mills as well.

CREATION OF CENTRAL COTTON PURCHASE COMMITTEE

The Corporation implemented several measures for removing the existing deficiencies and improving the working of the Mills. A Central Cotton Purchase Committee was set up in the Corporation. This Committee conducted a weekly review of the cotton market situation, and made an inventory of cotton available with the Mills. They then laid down targets for purchase of cotton and the ceiling rates for different qualities and counts. The Mills situated in cotton growing areas were permitted to purchase their requirement of cotton and send daily cotton purchase reports to the MSTC. As a result of the above arrangements, most of the mills under the MSTC management were able to procure good quality cotton at competitive prices. Since most of the mills had built up sufficient stocks of cotton to meet their requirements for a few months during the season, we could control the cost of production.

CENTRAL PURCHASE COMMITTEE FOR MACHINERY AND STORES

A Central Purchase Committee was also set up for the purchase of machinery for modernisation as most of the mills had old and outdated machinery. A Central Store Purchase Committee was also constituted for the Bombay Group of mills for purchasing quality stores at competitive rates. The Techno Economic Cell was strengthened to provide necessary technical guidance on production planning, cotton purchase, sales, modernisation etc. I also set up a Review Sub-Committee of Directors which evaluated the monthly performance of all the Mills, while the performance of Mills located in Bombay were reviewed every fortnight at the Managers' meeting by the Chairman himself.

DEVELOPMENT OF UPCOUNTRY MARKET

The Mills were encouraged to develop upcountry sales through indenting agents in various parts of the country and also through retail stockists, instead of depending entirely on the Bombay market. Indenting agents were appointed for different areas. The Corporation had also stepped up the export market through direct sales to overseas buyers, apart from indirect exports through merchant exporters.

REPRESENTATION ON BOMBAY MILL OWNERS ASSOCIATION AND OTHER ASSOCIATIONS

The MSTC, being the biggest corporation managing the largest number of textiles mills in the country, was given representation in Bombay Mill Owners Association, Indian Cotton Mills Federation, Bombay Industries Textile Research Association and also in the Ahmedabad Textile Industries Research Association. This gave me an excellent opportunity to meet various textile magnates in the country, including Dhirubhai Ambani, Chairman, Reliance Industries. These meetings gave me an opportunity to effectively take up the various problems faced by the sick textile industry in the country, thereby obtaining many decisions favourable to the sick textile industries at the national level.

FIRST MEETING WITH DHIRUBHAI AMBANI, CHAIRMAN, RELIANCE INDUSTRIES

Being a Member of several Textile Associations, I could meet several textile magnates in the Country. During one such meeting in 1974, I had an opportunity to meet Dhirubhai Ambani, Chairman, Reliance Industries, for the first time. He was at that time successfully managing his Textile Mill at Naroda in Ahmedabad. Reliance Industries was making superior quality fabrics by using polyster fibre yarn and marketing them all over the Country under the brand name of Vimal and was undoubtedly the best branded textiles at that time. The jingle "Only Vimal" was a household name in the entire Country. Knowing that I was Chairman, MSTC, managing about 20 textile mills in

Maharashtra, Dhirubhai Ambani invited me to visit Naroda Textile Mill. Perhaps it was the beginning of the makings of Dhirubhai Ambani not only Nationally but also as an International Textile Magnate. I took the opportunity of visiting Naroda Textile Mill during my next visit to Ahmedabad. It so happened Dhirubhai Ambani was also in Ahmedabad. He conducted me to all the sections of the mill personally. Undoubtedly it was the most modern textile mill with Sultzer looms, I ever saw. At the end of the visit, he presented me with a Safari suit length. Since then I am undoubtedly one of his millions of admirers for his great vision, dynamism and creativity. I had the pleasure of meeting him and his son Mukesh Ambani, several times thereafter.

IMPROVED FINANCIAL RESULTS

Several measures contributed substantially towards improving the financial performance of the mills, resulting in the Corporation making profits for the first time during 1972-73. Apart from favourable market conditions, other factors such as providing more effective management, improvement in production efficiency, streamlining of purchase and sales procedures and maintaining good management–labour relations also helped in substantially improving the financial status of the mills. All the mills, excluding the India Limited (INDU) Group of Mills, showed a net profit of Rs. 1.35 crores after providing for depreciation, interest liability and ex-gratia payment in lieu of bonus, as against a loss of 6.36 cr. during 1971. The profitability of the mills would have been even greater had they not been working with the handicaps of an unfavourable labour ratio, abnormal interest liability and antiquated machinery. These handicaps had a greater impact on the working of the Indu Group of Mills, because of its huge size, comprising six mills. However, despite these handicaps, the Indu Group of Mills made a gross profit of Rs. 1.43 crores in the year 1973 as compared to the gross loss of Rs. 2.72 crores in the previous year.

MY FATHER'S VISIT TO THE TEXTILE MILLS

While I was working as CMD of MSTC, my father Sundaram, who had visited Bombay earlier, visited again accompanied by my uncles Rajaratnam and Dharmagnani. I took them and went around the Sakseria Textile Mill. Although a lot of cotton was grown in our village, they did not have the faintest idea of how raw cotton was finally made into cloth of different sizes, colours and designs. It provided them with an excellent opportunity to observe the different activities involved in producing textiles and the intricate procedures adopted to produce various types of cloth out of cotton produced in the villages. They were also excited to see the unskilled and semi-skilled workers working on the fast moving machinery, especially the spindles and weaving machines. They were amazed to see how many people were working under me and they felt proud to see the power and success of one of their own after he became an IAS Officer.

UTILISATION OF PROFITS

The profits generated by the mills in the year 1972 and in subsequent years brought immense benefits to the workers. The voluntary cut in the Dearness Allowances, accepted by the workers at the time of restarting the mills, was not only restored, but some were even paid arrears. This was in addition to the ex-gratia payment in lieu of bonus at the rate of 8.33 per cent which amounted to Rs. 1.37 cr. In view of the improvement in the financial position, the mills repaid an amount of Rs. 1.61 crores towards the principal amount of the loan to the Government. This was an unbelievable feat which was achieved by the MSTC, when I was at the helm of affairs.

NEW PROBLEMS

While the Mills under the MSTC had come out of the red (losses) after persistent and determined efforts, they had to face certain new problems, making it difficult for them to sustain their profitability. In the month of May 1972, the Indian Cotton Mills Federation (ICMF), Bombay, levied an Export Promotion Fee at the rate of Rs. 1.50 per spindle shift, and Re. 1 per inch of reed space per loom shift on the textile mills retrospectively from 1st January 1972. While this levy may not have had any significant impact on the affluent mills, it proved a very heavy burden on the 'sick' mills, which had a large number of spindles and looms but less production and sales turnover. I had taken up with the Government of India as well as the ICMF that while the need for collecting money for the Export Promotion Fund was acceptable, the export promotion fee should be levied on the basis of annual sales turnover of the mills, instead of being linked with the spindle shift and reed space per loom shift, as this would prove to be back-breaking for the 'sick' Textile Mills which were struggling to keep afloat.

It was unfortunate that our request was not accepted due to pressure exerted by affluent and profit-making mills. It was their clout, obviously, that mattered and not the justification for preferential treatment.

Another instance of imposition of an unfair burden on the 'sick' textile mills was in the matter of allotment of Russian cotton on the basis of spindle shift working during this period. The Russian cotton of 31/32 mm length was useful for spinning 30'/40' count group only. As most of our mills with old and outdated machinery were spinning coarse and medium counts, the Corporation mills could not utilise the Russian cotton. I took up the matter with the Government of India and the ICMF, stating that it would be more equitable if the Russian Cotton was allocated only to those mills spinning 30'/40' counts. However, this suggestion too was not accepted, because once again it was 'clout' that made a difference at the Government level, not the merits of the situation.

PAYMENT OF BONUS TO THE EMPLOYEES OF THE MILLS

Two important events affecting our Mills occurred during this period. One was the promulgation of an Ordinance providing for payment of minimum bonus of 8.33 per cent to the industrial employees. The bonus pertained to the year 1971-72, when almost all our mills under the Corporation incurred heavy losses. The State Government decided that ex-gratia payment of 8.33 per cent, in lieu of bonus, should be made to the employees of all the textile mills. We welcomed the decision as a measure of promoting good industrial relations and made payments to all the employees before Diwali.

TAKE OVER OF MILLS AS CUSTODIAN

The second important event was the promulgation of the 'Sick Textiles Undertaking (Taking Cover Management)' Ordinance 1974, for taking over the management of sick textile mills by the Government of India, with retrospective effect from 1 April 1974, of 46 textile mills in the country, although the ordinance was promulgated much later. During the year 1974-75, consequent to the enactment of the 'Sick Textile Undertakings (Nationalisation) Act, 1974', the management of 21 mills which were hitherto with the Corporation was taken over by the Subsidiaries of the National Textile Corporation, namely, National Textile Corporation (South Maharashtra) Ltd., and National Textile Corporation (Maharashtra North) Ltd. This was done with retrospective effect from 1 April 1974, even though the Government of Maharashtra insisted on running them as Joint Venture Companies. However, the Government of India had not accepted the recommendation made by the Government of Maharashtra. Narendra Tidke, Minister of Industries and Labour and myself had several rounds of discussions with the Government of India without much success. Finally, the MSTC was left with the management of only four mills, namely, Narsinggirjee Mills, Sholapur; Shri Shahu Chhatrapati Mills, Kothapur; Pratap Mills, Amalner and Vijay Manufacturing Co., Badnera in November 1974.

INDUSTRIAL RELATIONS

The Corporation had followed a policy of creating better rapport and co-operation between the management and the workers. There was not even a single instance of loss of 'man days' on account of any industrial disputes. Mill-wise Local Committees had helped in settling a number of disputes within the mills and contributed to increasing efficiency and creating better employee–employer relations. A house journal, "MSTC News Letter", was launched to disseminate information on recent developments in the industry and also to establish the Corporation's identity.

NEW ACTIVITIES

I initiated discussions to enlarge the scope of the Corporation by bringing under its fold the Maharashtra State Power Looms Corporation, Bombay; Maharashtra State Handlooms Corporation, Nagpur and Textile Corporation of Marathwada Ltd. Aurangabad, which would result in the integrated development of the textile industry in the State.

NEW TEXTILE MILLS

The Corporation decided to set up two new textile mills during the Fifth Five Year Plan (1974-79), one each in the districts of Aurangabad and Nagpur. Industrial licenses for 25,000 spindles and 300 looms each for both the projects were received from the Government of India due to my persistent efforts. Twenty-five acres of land at Chikhalthana, Aurangabad were obtained from the Maharashtra Industrial Development Corporation (MSTC) and discussions were in progress with IFC, IDBI, LIC, and UTI to raise necessary funds for setting up of the projects.

I resigned from the Board with effect from 24th September, 1975 on my appointment as Joint Secretary, Industries, Energy and Labour Department, Government of Maharashtra.

TEN

POLICY AND PLANNING OF INDUSTRIAL PROMOTION IN MAHARASHTRA

Joint Secretary, Industries Department

Maharashtra is recognized as one of the most highly industrialised states in the country, but the State Government, instead of resting on its laurels, continued to take several measures to retain its pre-eminent position in the country.

I was posted as Joint Secretary in the State Industries Department in July 1975, after my assignment as Chairman and Managing Director, Maharashtra State Textile Corporation. My immediate illustrious predecessor was Dr. Madhav Godbole, IAS (1959). Anyone who succeeded Godbole had a difficult time living up to the standards set by him. I found Godbole to be an officer of unimpeachable integrity and character, with an eye for minute details, thorough in analyzing the pros and cons of every issue and working with total dedication. He set exacting standards of efficiency and perfection for himself. He was result oriented and very objective and remained unafraid of any adverse consequences of his advice. He was a no nonsense man for friends and foes alike. While many officers stayed in 'Buena Vista' (his residence from where Mantralaya could be reached faster on foot than by car), I often saw Godbole, then and later, as Secretary (Energy) and Chairman, MSEB walking to Mantralaya like any other commoner. He was a stickler for rules. When once the Government decided to impose a ban on smoking in public places, although there were many cigarette smoking buffs in Mantralaya who vehemently protested and used to smoke clandestinely in the rest rooms, Godbole was the first to not only give up smoking in public places, but to give up smoking altogether!!

I vividly recall a Cabinet meeting presided over by Shankarrao Chavan, the then Chief Minister. Chavan held Godbole in very high esteem because of his intellectual honesty, integrity, competence and commitment. After Godbole advanced several arguments for rejecting a proposal, Shankarrao Chavan, looking towards Godbole (the literal translation of the name in Marathi means "one who speaks sweet (good)") jocularly remarked: "Godbole, speak 'sweet' at least sometimes!!" All those who were present in the cabinet meeting had a hearty laugh, including Godbole.

TIDKE—MINISTER (INDUSTRIES AND LABOUR)

I was lucky to have a mature, kind and considerate Minister (Industries and Labour) in Narendra Tidke. He used to maintain a fine balance between Industrial development and harmonious industrial relations with labour Unions. Whenever there were problems of industrial relations such as strikes and agitations, he would spend a considerable amount of time in negotiating with the Unions. Watching him negotiate with the Union leaders in order to maintain industrial development in the state was a good learning process. The high level of industrialization of the State contributed towards several agitations by the Unions and the Minister was always under considerable pressure. Whenever a note was prepared on any subject, Tidke always found that the note was either too lengthy or too short. After a while, I used to carry three sets of notes (length-wise)—long, medium and short. Depending on the request of the Minister, I used to present the desired size of the note. One day I complained to P.C. Nayak, Secretary (Industries) that a lot of time was wasted in preparing too many notes of varied sizes on the same matter. Nayak, in his typical style, stated that I should be thankful that the Minister was asking me to produce "paper notes" and not "currency notes"!!

P.C. NAYAK, SECRETARY (INDUSTRIES)

A dynamic, development-oriented and, above all, a humane person,

P. Chandrakant Nayak was Secretary (Industries). He was the first Chief Executive Officer, Maharashtra Industrial Development Corporation (MIDC). Maharashtra was the first state in the country to establish an Industrial Development Corporation, whose primary responsibility was to develop industrial estates, with all infrastructure facilities and to provide escort services to prospective entrepreneurs and industrialists. The credit for initiation of steps for the industrial development of the Thane–Belapur area, outside Bombay, certainly goes to Nayak. He made the MIDC so successful that many other states took inspiration from this successful experiment and set up Industrial Development Corporations in their states.

I still vividly recollect that when I was posted as JS (Industries), I was allotted a flat at Lands End on Malabar hill which was quite far away from Mantralaya. I was required to commute every day by BEST (public transport) bus at odd times, as I did not have a car and my job required me to spend long hours in the office. Nayak was quite concerned about my inconvenience and asked me to make a representation to allot an accommodation nearer to the Mantralaya. He took the letter personally to the Chief Secretary, D.D. Sathe and got a flat allotted in Buena Vista, which was walking distance from Mantralaya. I wish we had more such considerate officers in the service.

I still remember the advice given to me by Nayak when I joined as Joint Secretary in the department. He said in his exuberant style, "you may excercise all the powers of Secretary and even if you took a wrong decision, I would defend the same to the hilt. But don't exceed my powers. Then I would find it difficult to defend." What a sound advice from a seasoned administrator who was known to be an 'achiever'.

Similarly, when I was awarded a UNIDO (United Nations Industrial Development Organisation) fellowship for six months in Europe to study 'Promotion of Industries with special emphasis on export oriented industries' in 1976, Narendra Tidke, Industries Minister, was reluctant to spare my services for UNIDO for such a long period. It was again Nayak who persuaded the Minister by pleading that I was working day and night and also in view of recent sad demise of my mother in January 1976, I needed a break badly and should be allowed to go for foreign training under UNIDO. The Minister agreed to spare me for the UNIDO training on the condition that I would come back and work in the Ministry with him. The Minister kept the post vacant for six months till I returned from the UNIDO Fellowship. It is difficult to find such

Ministers and Secretaries who encourage and recognise the value of hardworking officers.

P.S. PALANDE—INDUSTRIES COMMISSIONER

Purushotham S. Palande, IAS (1961) was the Industries Commissioner. Palande was a simple, smiling and hardworking officer. We had excellent coordination between the Commissionerate and the Industries department in all our work. The Industries Commissioner was required to attend all the Licensing Committee meetings held in the Ministry of Industrial Development, Government of India, New Delhi, as a representative of the State Government to obtain the licenses, letter of intents and DGTD registrations to set up industries in the state, as the industrial development of the country was totally regulated. Whenever the Commissioner was unable to attend the meetings, I used to represent the State Government, although I was the only Joint Secretary in the Department. As Palande was scared of traveling by air, he used to travel by train taking almost four days to commute to and fro from Bombay to Delhi, at considerable inconvenience to himself and also spending valuable time in the train, which could have been more productively used for touring the state to promote industries. I still recollect instances where Palande went up to the airport to catch a flight to Delhi and after reaching, redeveloped cold feet and returned from the airport, leaving the Maharashtra Government unrepresented in the Licensing Committee Meetings! Subsequently, we always made air reservations for both of us, but mostly I was left to attend many Licensing Committee meetings in Delhi. I also officiated as Industries Commissioner whenever Palande went on leave, which gave me an opportunity to work in an executive job, entrusted with the promotion of Industries.

DISPERSAL OF INDUSTRIES—POLICY OF GOVERNMENT

Maharashtra State accounted for about 18 per cent of the productive capital, 19 per cent of the employment, 24 per cent of the gross value of output and 26 per cent of the value added by manufactures in the factory sector in the country. The State is, however, too diverse and industrial growth too localized, as industrial development was concentrated in only a few areas. Out of 26 districts of the State, the Planning

Commission had designated 13 districts as industrially backward, which accounted for 54 per cent of the total area and 42 per cent of the total population.

If we exclude the Bombay–Poona belt, the State is industrially as underdeveloped as many other states in the country. Concentration of industries in the Bombay–Poona region had posed a number of problems, the main one being imbalanced regional development. Nearly 86 per cent of the rural workers in the State had agriculture as a source of livelihood but agriculture being a seasonal activity, a number of agricultural workers sought other avenues of employment. It was therefore necessary for diversification of economic activity through rapid industrial development in the rural areas to provide employment opportunities. This, in fact, has been the main plank of planning for industrial development in the State.

One of the main objectives of the State's industrial planning and policy, therefore, has been to secure dispersal of industries to underdeveloped and backward areas of the State, in order to bring about economic upliftment in the rural areas, while maintaining the pre-eminence of the already developed areas. Some districts like Bhir (where I was Collector during 1966-69) and Osmanabad were declared as industrially backward areas and were qualified to receive concessions offered by financial institutions. The districts of Ratnagiri, Chandrapur and Aurangabad were declared as districts eligible for obtaining outright central subsidy equal to 15 per cent of the fixed capital investment in the new industrial units. There was, therefore, a deliberate and planned attempt by the state Government to end regional imbalance and secure a balanced growth of industries in the State.

During the Third Five-Year Plan period (1961 to 1967), industrial development programmes were formulated with a view to encouraging agro-industrial development and development of small scale industries. In the Fourth Five-Year Plan (1969 to 1974), emphasis was given for increasing non-farm employment and removing regional imbalances. These objectives were sought to be achieved through development of selected industrial areas, provision of industrial finance, scarce raw materials and marketing facilities and a package of incentives to induce entrepreneurs to start industries in the underdeveloped areas.

PROMOTION OF INDUSTRIES

The Industries Commissioner, working as the Head of the Department, was entrusted with the responsibility of promoting large, medium, small, tiny and village industries in the state; dispersal of industries to the backward areas and widening industrial development to other parts of the state. The Industries Commissioner also pursued proposals with the Government of India to secure industrial licenses, registrations etc. There were 38,600 SSI (small scale industries) units in the State, representing 11 per cent of the registered SSI units in the country. Loans were given to small scale industries at a concessional rate of interest. The Government had initiated several measures which would enable SSI units to grow at about 8 per cent per year.

INDUSTRIAL LOCATION POLICY

The most significant milestone during my tenure was the implementation of the Industrial Location Policy, which was recently prepared in the state as industrial development in Maharashtra was largely concentrated in the Bombay—Thane belt. Although considerable efforts were made to encourage dispersal of industries to the backward areas of the state, not much could be achieved. If industrial development was not allowed in Bombay, there was also no guarantee that industries would be set up in some other location in Maharashtra, especially as Gujarat, which was a competitor, was offering several incentives. In addition, as the border of Gujarat was very close to Bombay, many industries even migrated to set up units in Gujarat, taking advantage of its proximity to Bombay. It was, therefore, a question of maintaining a proper balance of incentives and disincentives in the State. Many improvements were made from time to time to overcome these problems while implementing the Industrial Location Policy, so that positive results came from the policy.

EXTENSION OF REVISED PACKAGE SCHEME OF INCENTIVES

The Package Scheme Incentives was first introduced in the State in 1964 as a positive measure to effect industrial dispersal and generate industrial investment in the developing areas of the State. It was being implemented through the State Industrial and Investment Corporation of Maharashtra (SICOM) since 1969. Under this scheme, incentives were being offered by way of sales tax refund to industrial units set up in backward areas.

The Package Scheme was revised from time to time and the Graded Package Scheme of Incentives was introduced in August 1973 to remain in operation till 31st July 1976. One of my major tasks was to get the scheme extended beyond 31st July 1976. After considerable efforts and after a series of meetings, especially with the Finance Department, the Graded Package Scheme of Incentives was extended beyond 1976 for a further period of three years, with extensive modifications. The State is now divided' into three groups (A, B and C) according to their level of industrial development. The greater the backwardness, the higher were the incentives. In selected growth centres, special capital incentives at 15 per cent of fixed assets would also be available under the new "Special Capital Incentive Scheme." The results achieved under the scheme as on 31st March 1977 was that 1,700 projects had been committed with an investment of Rs. 256 crores, with an employment potential of 42,000 persons.

FUNDS FROM DISTRICT PLANS FOR INCENTIVE SCHEME

Another major task was to obtain required funds from District Plans. The total requirement of funds during the Fifth Plan (1974 to 1979) under the Graded Incentive Scheme was Rs. 30 crores. This was a District Plan Scheme and the District Planning and Development Councils used to make very meagre provisions. It required regular liaison with the DPDCs to provide additional outlays by re-appropriation within their respective ceilings. The expenditure under this scheme was committed and the commitments already had to be met for another five to nine years, in addition to the requirements of the new scheme. An additional "on account" provision was obtained, to be adjusted against the future allocations of the DPDCs. The 'Package incentives' scheme for promoting industries was regularly reviewed, as the government was keen to promote industries in backward areas.

One serious problem which I faced, immediately after taking over as Joint Secretary in July, 1975, was related to the de-recognition of several small-scale units, which was done just before I joined and the agitation which was going on about regularisation. Verification of all records were done expeditiously from the Industries Commissioner to weed out bogus SSI units, that had come up to take advantage of quotas year-marked for SSI units. This enabled genuine units to get back all the facilities extended by the Government and financial institutions.

I was also entrusted with the work pertaining to 12 Industrial Development Corporations, including the four Regional Development Corporations set up for industrial development in the state. One of the major tasks of the Joint Secretary was to assist these Corporations in securing adequate funds from the state budget, help them to raise funds from the Banks to finance their activities and get expeditious approvals of their proposals from the Government. These Corporations were:

(1) Maharashtra Industrial Development Corporation (MIDC)

The Maharashtra Industrial Development Corporation (MIDC) was set up to develop industrial areas by providing necessary infrastructure and to make developed plots available to entrepreneurs for establishing industrial units. By the end of 1975-76, the MIDC had established 53 industrial areas, allotted 4,620 plots and 226 factories had gone into production involving a total investment of Rs. 470 crores and providing employment to 1,01,300 workers. Besides this, 642 factories were under construction.

(2) State Industrial and Investment Corporation of Maharashtra (SICOM)

SICOM played an important role in the scheme of dispersal of industries to underdeveloped areas of the State, by promoting industries in such areas. The various services offered by SICOM were (i) financial (ii) plant location, (iii) project investigation, (iv) project implementation, (v) credit guarantee scheme for medium industries, and (vi) package scheme of incentives. From the inception of the Corporation in March 1966 to 31st March 1975, 1,862 units were committed to underdeveloped areas, out of which 1,215 units had either commenced production or were under actual construction. Till the end of January 1977, SICOM succeeded in committing a total of 2,469 units to the underdeveloped areas, entailing a capital investment of Rs. 756 crores and were expected to generate 75,800 jobs. SICOM was appointed as the agent of Government for implementing the Incentive Schemes, such as the sales tax loans by way of refund of sales tax paid, rebate in electricity tariff, exemption on octroi duty and contribution towards the cost of feasibility study etc.

(3) Maharashtra State Finance Corporation (MSFC)

The Maharashtra State Finance Corporation assisted medium and small scale industries by extending term loans. The Reserve Bank of India (RBI) provided a matching share capital contribution for MSFC. It was the endeavour of the Industries Department to obtain maximum share capital contribution from the state budget, so as to obtain matching contribution with the RBI. During the Fifth Plan, the corporation obtained substantial increase in sanctions and disbursements.

(4) Maharashtra Small Scale Industries Development Corporation (MSSIDC)

I was a Director on the Board of Directors of the MSSIDC. The Maharashtra Small Scale Industries Development Corporation acted as the Agent of the State Government for distribution of scarce raw materials to the small-scale sector, especially iron and steel. In addition, it was decided that the Corporation should provide strong marketing assistance by introducing consumer marketing and undertaking activities like construction of modern warehousing facilities, opening new emporia, production centres, export of SSI products, promoting handicrafts etc. To provide infrastructural facility for small-scale industries, 69 industrial estates were established by the Corporation.

(5) Four Regional Development Corporations

The four Regional Corporations, namely, Marathwada Development Corporation; Development Corporation of Vidarbha; Development Corporation of Konkan and Western Maharashtra Development Corporation were constituted for intensive development of the various regions and to promote investment opportunities and assist development projects in the respective regions. These corporations were expected to work as overall area development corporations and not merely as industrial development Corporations. Maharashtra Scooters Ltd. (MSL) was promoted by the Western Maharashtra Development Corporation (27% shareholding) with M/s Bajaj (24%) for setting up a scooter project at Satara. I was a signatory for this agreement which I signed on behalf of the Government of Maharashtra. The Marathwada Development Corporation had set up two subsidiary companies for implementing a Dairy Project and a Leather Project in addition to promoting the Textile Corporation of Marathiwada (TEXCOM). The Development Corporation of Vidarbha was planning to set up the Tassar Silk Projects in Chandrapur and Bhandara Districts. The Development Corporation of Konkan had commissioned feasibility study for setting up salt works on the Konkan coast.

(6) Maharashtra State Textile Corporation (MSTC)

In view of the crisis in the Textile Industry resulting in the closure of textile mills and unemployment, MSTC was set up for taking over such closed mills and running them as an unemployment relief measure. As 24 textiles mills were old with outdated machinery, the Corporation was required to take up an extensive programme of modernisation and renovation of these units. A major task at the Secretariat was to obtain approvals of the proposals received from the Corporation to ensure its smooth functioning.

(7) Cooperative Processing Industries

One of the important activities in the agro-industrial development programme was the setting up of processing industries in rural areas, as these industries created employment opportunities in rural areas. Cooperative processing industries such as spinning mills, vanaspati manufacturing plants, alcohol manufacturing and biogases-based industries were promoted by the Government giving share capital assistance. Maharashtra had promoted handlooms and power loom industries on a large scale. The handloom sector had 1.85 lakh handlooms and was the largest cottage industry, while the power loom industry, with nearly 1.40 lakh powerlooms, was the largest small-scale industry in the state, providing livelihood to nearly 5 lakh persons. Every effort was made by the State Government to ensure proper functioning of this sector by extending various incentives, as most of this was in unorganized sector.

(8) Special Employment Programme to Educated Unemployed

With a view to provide gainful employment to the educated unemployed on a continuing basis, the Government of India sponsored special employment programmes by providing seed money assistance to the entrepreneurs to set up industrial enterprises. The scheme was implemented through the Regional Development Corporations, MSSIDC, and the Khadi and Village Industries Board.

DEPUTATION TO GOVERNMENT OF INDIA

While I was functioning as Joint Secretary (Industries), the Government of India had issued a circular about the availability of the post of Regional Iron and Steel Controller, Hyderabad under the Ministry of Steel. This circular was sent to all the states requesting for sponsoring officers to be spared for deputation.

Although I had found the post of Joint Secretary (Industries) very challenging and highly valuable in terms of gaining experience, I was quite inclined to take up this assignment due to my domestic problems. Both my father-in-law and mother-in-law were keeping very indifferent health in Andhra Pradesh and my wife, being their only child, was always under considerable stress as she had to be away from her parents during their difficult days. It would also give me an opportunity to be nearer to my parents, who were staying in Gaddamanugu, my native place near Vijayawada. Although they visited Bombay, they were not at all comfortable with the Bombay life style.

I, therefore, made a personal request to J.B. D'Souza, Chief Secretary to recommend my name for being appointed as Regional Iron and Steel Controller, Hyderabad. He initially thought that my request was a ploy to go on deputation to the Government of India. However, I convinced him about my domestic problems and assured him that I would be going on deputation to the Government of India, only if I was posted in Hyderabad and not anywhere else. J.B.D'Souza told me in so many words that I was doing an excellent job as Joint Secretary (Industries) and he would be very unhappy to spare my services for such an unimportant assignment at Hyderabad. He mentioned that many officers approached him for securing better assignments, whereas I was seeking a favour from him to go for an unimportant assignment! However, in view of my compelling domestic circumstances, he reluctantly agreed to spare my services for appointment as Regional Iron and Steel Controller, Hyderabad, provided I was selected for being posted at Hyderabad. Although there were many contenders for this post, especially IAS officers hailing from Andhra Pradesh and allotted to other states like me, I was finally selected by Ministry of Steel, perhaps due to my industrial experience in Maharashtra and the promotion of Iron and Steel Industries was one of the primary responsibilities entrusted to the Iron and Steel Controller.

Photo 1: The author at the time of joining the IAS in 1962.

Photo 2: Marriage Photo of the author in 1964.

Photo 3: The author as Secretary, MSEB with his wife Suryakumari congratulating Shri Merchant, son of Joint Secretary on his marriage in March, 1971.

Photo 4 : The author (extreme left) as Joint Secretary, Industries with Shri K. Brahmananda Reddy, Governor, Maharashtra in May 1977.

Photo 5: The author on his way to Olympiad, Greece in March 1976.

Photo 6: The author during his visit to Amsterdam in May 1976.

Photo 7: Mrs. Suryakumari (third from left) with her friends during the premier of 'Sholay' cinema in 1975.

Photo 8: The author (in suit) with Nobel Laureate Mother Teresa with his wife Suryakumari (on Mother's right) and daughter Manjula (on Mother's left) and son Rajesh (check shirt) with friends in 1979.

Photo 9: Family Photo of the author in 1981.

Photo 10: Abraham with his wife during their visit to New York in 1981.

Photo 11: As Commissioner of Industries and Chairman, AP Steels receiving "Productivity Award" from Shri N.T. Rama Rao, Chief Minister, Andhra Pradesh in May 1985.

Photo 12: Shri N.T. Rama Rao, Chief Minister, Andhra Pradesh releasing the "Guidelines to Entrepreneurs for setting up Industries in Andhra Pradesh" written by the author (extreme left) as Commissioner of Industries.

Photo 13: The author with his son-in-law Shri Sam Bob and daughter Manjula at the time of their marriage.

Photo 14: As Chairman, MSEB receiving the Productivity Award for Excellent Performance of the Power Stations from Shri Arif Mohd. Khan, Union Minister for Energy.

Photo 15: The author received Shiromani Vikas Award for 'Best Administrator' in 1990.

Photo 16: As Chairman, MSEB receiving Shri Sharad Pawar, Chief Minister, Maharashtra during the Foundation Stone laying ceremony of Waste Heat Recovery Plant at Uran.

Photo 17: The author in conversation with Shri Sharad Pawar, Chief Minister, Maharashtra during a function.

Photo 18: Abraham collecting a souvenir of Berlin Wall during his visit to Berlin in February 1990.

Photo 19: As Chairman, MSEB (in suit in the centre) with the World Bank team led by Mr. F. Bauer.

Photo 20: As Chairman, MSEB (red shirt) during the inspection of Khaperkheda Thermal Power Station.

Photo 21: As Chairman, MSEB (with white cap) inspecting the site for expansion of Koradi Thermal Power Station.

Photo 22: The author speaking after felicitation by Bombay Andhra Mahasabha and Gymkhana in 1990.

Photo 23: Shri N. Janardhana Reddy, Chief Minister, Andhra Pradesh at author's residence in 1991.

Photo 24: As Additional Secretary, Defence (centre) with Shri Sharad Pawar, Union Defence Minister at Siachin in 1991.

Photo 25: As Additional Secretary, Defence (second from left) with Shri Mallikarjun, MOS (Defence) during visit to Andaman and Nicobar Islands in 1993.

Photo 26: As Additional Secretary, Defence (third from left) during his visit to Somalia in April 1993.

Photo 27: As Additional Secretary, Defence (third from left) during discussion with his counterpart in Budapest, Hungary in May 1993.

Photo 28: As Additional Secretary, Defence during visit to INS Viraat with Captain Arun Prakash, who subsequently became the Chief of Indian Navy.

Photo 29: The author with Lt. Gen. Robert L.Ord, Commanding General, USARPAC, January 1994.

Photo 30: The author (fourth from left) with Shri P.V. Narasimha Rao, Prime Minister, with NRIs in Paris.

Photo 31: As Union Power Secretary with Shri N.K.P. Salve, Union Power Minister in 1995.

Photo 32: The author being felicitated at Vijayawada by Shri G. Venkat Swamy, Union Minister, Textiles and Shri Ch. Venkat Rao, Former Cabinet Minister, Andhra Pradesh on his appointment as Union Power Secretary in 1994.

ELEVEN

PROMOTION OF STEEL INDUSTRIES

Regional Iron and Steel Controller, Hyderabad Region

I joined as Regional Iron and Steel Controller, Government of India, Hyderabad on 1st September 1977. It was a good opportunity to work in a core sector industry which contributed substantially to the country's industrial and economic development. My jurisdiction as Regional Iron and Steel Controller, Hyderabad covered the states of Andhra Pradesh and Madhya Pradesh. After working for a year, I was entrusted with the additional charge of Regional Controller, Bombay Region, which comprised the States of Maharashtra, Gujarat and Goa. This continued till the end of my deputation to the Ministry of Steel, so that I had jurisdiction that covered a vast area of the country, giving me an opportunity to extensively tour Western, Central and Southern India to promote the steel industry.

Prior to May 1977, the Department of Steel and the Department of Mines functioned separately under different administrative Secretaries to the Government. Since May, 1977, both the Departments were placed under one Secretary as the administrative head. This was done to achieve a coordinated and integrated development of the steel industry, which was required for rapid industrialization and speedier attainment of the country's economic goals.

The Department of Steel had only one attached office of the Iron and Steel Controller at Calcutta under its administrative control. The Iron and Steel Controller had six regional offices at New Delhi, Kanpur,

Calcutta, Madras, Hyderabad and Bombay. This Organisation was set up initially to perform certain regulatory functions under the Iron and Steel (Control) Order, 1956. Over the years, however, the functions of the Iron and Steel Controller's office were extended to cover wider areas.

Since scarcity of various items of iron and steel continued to persist even in the mid-1970s, end use restrictions were re-imposed on all categories of iron and steel during my tenure in this sector. Anyone acquiring iron, steel, or scrap under clause 7 of the Iron and Steel (Control) Order was prohibited from using it for any other purpose than for which it was acquired. The Iron and Steel Control Organisation dealt with the violations of the provisions of the Iron and Steel (Control) order and was given authority to suspend supplies and to debar units, violating its orders.

While several functions, both regulatory and developmental, were entrusted, the following activities received my maximum attention as the Regional Controller:

- To oversee the functioning of the Stockyards of the Main Steel Producers regarding supplies of steel to the small-scale industries and house builders to whom steel was allocated.
- To coordinate with the State Directorate of Industries and Small Scale Industries Corporations.
- To monitor supplies of steel, from the Main Producer's Stock yards to the export fabricators and ensure proper utilization of imported raw materials.
- To inspect steel re-rolling mills to check proper utilization of Billets allotted by the main producers.
- To inspect and collect data on Mini Steel Plants (electric furnace units) which were given permission to install re-rolling mills.
- Review implementation of licenses issued by the Government of India.
- To conduct monthly market surveys and report the price trends of critical iron and steel items to the Government of India.

RATIONALIZATION OF RE-ROLLING INDUSTRY

I was also entrusted with the study of the steel re-rolling industry in the region to assess the status and performance of the units and to recommend a plan of rationalization of products from the integrated steel plants and the re-rollers. During this period I also regularly reviewed the status of the Electric Arc Furnace, Re-rolling Industry, Ferro Alloys, Wire Drawing, Cold Rolled and Pig Iron units and recommended measures for strengthening these sectors.

REVIVAL OF MINI STEEL PLANTS

Another major task entrusted to me was to devise measures for revival of mini steel plants. With an investment of over Rs. 150 crores spread over in 120 units in the country, the electric arc furnace industry had been languishing for some time. The Government carried out in-depth studies for the mini steel industry with the assistance of Regional Iron and Steel Controllers and took several important decisions, such as the removal of excise duty on production of ingots/rolled products; removal of import duty on melting scrap; permitted diversification into production of alloy steels and setting up of rolling facilities. As a result of these efforts and close monitoring, the production in these units had picked up substantially, which consequently improved the financial position of the sector.

LIBERALIZATION OF STEEL DISTRIBUTION

The earlier distribution policy required that all consumers, except Defence, Railways and State Small Scale Industries Development Corporations (SSIDC), could get materials directly from Steel plants in rake loads. With a view to helping a large number of consumers, the Government decided to supply hot and cold-rolled coils and sheets to actual users from August 1977. A similar relaxation was also made in respect of rake load supplies of pig iron directly from the plants. Earlier, all the small-scale industrial units had to obtain their requirements mainly through the SSIDCS. An important change introduced was that small-scale units, whose off-take in the past had been 200 tonnes in a quarter, were permitted to obtain supplies directly from the steel plants' stockyards. I also monitored supplies to SSIDCs by the main producers, with a view to ensuring that the SSIDCs were helped to meet the requirements of small-scale units. This arrangement ensured regular supply to small-scale industrial units of even those categories of steel which were in short supply. The Iron and Steel organization was entrusted with the responsibility of surveillance in the utilization of steel materials to prevent misuse of supplies to them.

DISTRIBUTION

Domestic supplies were augmented by imports both for buffer stocks and also against specific demands of consumers, in addition to direct imports by actual users. The distribution policy was constantly reviewed to ensure that the requirements of the priority sectors such as defense, railways and power projects were fully met. Requirements of small house builders, colleges, schools and hospitals received adequate attention. Rural distribution centers continued to function and end use restrictions continued on all categories of iron and steel. A large number of inspections were carried out by me during this period to check misutilisation of iron and steel materials. Between 1977 and 1980, as many as 3,400 inspections were carried out to check misutilisation in the Hyderabad region alone, while about 850 units were suspended from receiving raw material and about 350 units were debarred from receiving raw material from the stockyards.

SPONGE IRON PLANT AT KOTHAGUDEM

The production of steel, other than through the conventional blast furnace route, has assumed national importance, in view of the limited resources of coking coal in the country. Sponge Iron India Limited, a Public Sector company, was formed to establish such a plant with UNDP/ UNIDO assistance, with a capacity of 30,000 tonnes of sponge iron annually, using non-coking coal at Palavancha, Khammam District, Andhra Pradesh. I was closely associated with monitoring the setting up of this project. The plant was formally inaugurated by the Vice-President of India on the 31st December 1980. This marked a major break through in enabling the production of steel using non-coking coal, of which India had abundant resources.

OFFICIATED AS IRON AND STEEL CONTROLLER, CALCUTTA

I had the opportunity of working as Iron and Steel Controller, Government of India, Calcutta, having jurisdiction over the entire country for about three months in 1981, as the incumbant, P.K. Sarkar, IAS (1959, West Bengal), went on leave. It was during this period that I did a considerable amount of planning with the main producers to supply Iron and Steel material, in substantial quantities, for infrastructure development in Delhi for the Asian Games of 1982.

VISHAKHAPATNAM STEEL PLANT

A proposal to set up an Integrated Steel Plant at Vishakapatnam was pending with the Government of India for a long time and the people of Andhra Pradesh were quite agitated about the delay, as it was a long pending demand of the State. Further, a steel plant there would utilize the natural minerals available in the region. Although several promises were made in the past by the Government of India to set up the steel project, nothing much had happened. One of the major constraints holding back the setting up of the steel plant was the heavy congestion at Vizag port, due to which import of raw materials and export of finished steel was not possible. While Biju Patnaik, the former dynamic Chief Minister of Orissa and a great visionary, was the Union Minister of Steel in the Janata Party Government, he visited Vishakhapatnam in 1979. He went around the Vizag Port area personally and made an on the spot assessment about the feasibility of setting up a steel plant. As Regional Iron and Steel Controller, Hyderabad, I had the privilege of accompanying Biju Patnaik in a specially commissioned naval boat and went around the area near Gangavaram, south of Vizag on the East Coast. After satisfying himself that a port could be developed at Gangavaram, he announced the proposal to set up the Steel plant at Vizag. Accordingly an integrated Vizag steel plant was set up, which totally transformed the entire area. In close proximity of the Vizag steel plant, the National Thermal Power Corporation (NTPC) had already set up a 1,000 Mw capacity coal based Thermal Power Station, at Simhadri. Several other industries thus came up and contributed substantially to the overall economic development of the area.

MEETING MOTHER TERESSA

While I was officiating as Iron and Steel Controller, Calcutta, it was a golden opportunity for me and my family to fulfil the long cherished dream of meeting Mother Teresa. We went to the Missionaries of Charities to meet Mother Teresa after an appointment. We were all waiting eagerly to meet her. When all of his sudden a fragile and thin looking lady in the typical uniform of a nun came in. She was so unbelievably simple and ordinary, we did not recognise her for a while, although she was well recognized for her commitment to help the poorest of the poor and sick and lonely in the entire world. We felt quite ashamed that we did not recognise such a well-known Philanthropist and a Nobel Prize Winner whom we had seen in several photographs. She was humility and simplicity personified and prayed specially for all of us. It was a dream come true. Since then, every time I visited Kolkata I never fail to visit the Missionaries of Charities.

MAJOR BEREAVEMENTS IN THE FAMILY

Although the objective in accepting an assignment in Hyderabad was to be with the family, unfortunately, within a few months of my posting there, my father-in-law, Vijendla Moses who had been ailing, passed away in January 1978. After a year, my mother-in-law Irene Moses also passed away. While the loss was irreparable, my wife and I had the satisfaction of having been with them during their last days.

DEPUTATION TO THE GOVERNMENT OF ANDHRA PRADESH

While working at Hyderabad, I was empanelled in the first list of Joint Secretaries from the 1962 batch. This period coincided with the change of Government at the national level, following the 1980 Lok Sabha elections. In the new power equation, the Government headed by Indira Gandhi was keen to bring back many key officers who had worked with her, and who had been repatriated to their respective states by the previous Government. Based on my experience, my name was sent to the Ministries of Industry, Commerce, Steel and Power, all very coveted Ministries in Government of India. The competition was very intense. Even though I was already on the establishment of Ministry of Steel, I could not be selected in the Ministry, despite the fact that there were clear vacancies. On the contrary, officers who had no experience in these Ministries were brought from different states and posted in these Ministries because of their close connections in Delhi. Indeed, I was getting frustrated, as many of my batch mates, who happened to be in Delhi, were already functioning as Joint Secretaries. After several rounds of circulation to Economic Ministries, my name was sent to the Ministry of Justice for being appointed as Joint Secretary. I felt that in spite of having rich experience in many economic ministries in the state, and in the Ministry of Steel in the Government of India, sending my name to the Ministry of Justice was quite an injustice to me!! I then approached P. Venkatasubbaiah, who was Minister of State (Personnel) in the Ministry of Home, not to consider my name for any Joint Secretary posting in the Government of India and instead requested him to help me to go on deputation to the Government of Andhra Pradesh. He was kind enough to accede to my request. I, therefore, went to the Government of Andhra Pradesh on deputation, instead of becoming a Joint Secretary in Government of India, which was a great disappointment.

TWELVE

PROMOTION OF NRI INVESTMENTS IN ANDHRA PRADESH

Vice Chairman and Managing Director, ANRICH

The Government of Andhra Pradesh was the first state to recognize the necessity of inviting and integrating Non-Resident Indians, especially those hailing from Andhra Pradesh with the development of the state. Many qualified doctors and engineers from Andhra Pradesh initially went for higher studies to countries such as the U.S.A. and the U.K. and later settled down there. Most of them were from high income earning groups in their respective countries and such NRIs also looked forward to re-establishing cultural, social and family linkages with their homeland. In addition, investment opportunities in the country, and particularly in Andhra Pradesh, had become very attractive. The Government of Andhra Pradesh had taken several initiatives to attract investments in the state. New opportunities for employment of technical, skilled and semi-skilled workers had improved substantially in the Middle East countries, but many of those who wanted to work there required assistance in securing employment so that they were not exploited by unscrupulous agents. The Government of Andhra Pradesh therefore felt that an effective organisation to further the interests of the NRIs and liaise with various authorities in the country and abroad was necessary. Under these circumstances, the State Government constituted a separate

Corporation, called Andhra Pradesh State Non-Resident Indian Investment Corporation Ltd (APSNRIICL) in March 1981.

While E.V. Rami Reddy, IAS (Retired) was the Chairman, I was appointed as the first Vice-Chairman and Managing Director of the Corporation, when I went on deputation to the Government of Andhra Pradesh. T. Anjaiah was the Chief Minister. I joined the Corporation in September 1981. As the acronym for the Corporation appeared to be too lengthy and too cumbersome to pronounce, my first task was to choose an acronym appropriate to the objectives and functions of the Corporation. I, therefore, coined the acronym "**A** (Andhra Pradesh) **NRI C** (Corporation) **H** (Hyderabad)" ANRICH, which was greatly appreciated, as it jelled well with the objectives of the Corporation to enrich the NRIs.

The Corporation was established with the twin objectives of mobilizing investments from Non-Resident Indians for investing in industries, medical care centers, trade and commercial complexes, business activities and housing projects all of which would enhance the economic and industrial development of the State. It also aimed to secure gainful employment for technical, skilled and semi-skilled personnel abroad, mostly in the Middle East countries. The government released special funds under the Special Employment Scheme for providing financial assistance to skilled and semi-skilled personnel for securing employment in the Gulf and Middle East countries by way of loan assistance. It was during this period that employment opportunities were thrown open to the NRI's in a big way in the Middle East, notably in the U.A.E. and Kuwait, especially for the skilled and semi-skilled categories of workers. Thus, ANRICH actively participated in securing suitable employment for a large number of persons in the Middle East countries.

SEPARATE INDUSTRIAL ESTATE FOR NRIs

Several proposals were received from NRIs, mostly from the U.K. and the U.S.A., to make investments for setting up of industrial units. They were required to go to several Corporations to tie-up infrastructure facilities and to secure financial assistance. It was considered necessary to develop separate industrial estates for allotment of plots so that Non-Resident Indians (NRIs) did not have to wait in the queues along with the other entrepreneurs. ANRICH, with concerted efforts, identified and secured about 200 acres of land from the Government in Bolaram,

Medak district and the steps were initiated to develop this land as an exclusive industrial area for Non-Resident Indians. Several projects such as Bimetallic Steel and Alloys Limited (Rs. 8 crores); San Napkins Private Limited (Rs. 30 crores); Indo-Japan Watch Complex (Rs. 1.30 crores) and Microsense Private Limited (Rs. 21 lakhs) were allotted land in the area. Necessary licenses, clearances and financial tie-ups with the financial institutions were secured for starting these projects. ANRICH prepared an action plan to ground at least 10 more sophisticated industrial projects in the separate industrial area being developed in Bolaram, Medak District and provided a single window service to such units.

ALLOTMENT OF LAND FOR APOLLO HOSPITALS, HYDERABAD

The Corporation had also made concerted efforts to induce doctors from the United States to establish sophisticated Medical Care Centres at Hyderabad. As a part of this initiative, several doctors and groups of doctors had come forward to set up sophisticated hospitals in Andhra Pradesh. One such group was Apollo hospitals, who were allotted 30 acres of land by the Government in Jubilee Hills, Hyderabad. This was the second project set up by Apollo hospitals in India. Ever since, they have been doing yeomen service to the people, not only from Andhra Pradesh but also from several countries, including the Middle East countries. The Apollo group has since established several hospitals in the country and also in our neighbouring countries.

VISIT TO U.K., U.S.A. AND CANADA

As ANRICH created substantial interest among the professional NRIs located in U.K., U.S.A., Canada and other developed countries, a large number of NRIs started visiting Andhra Pradesh, looking for investment opportunities. In order to actively propagate the various measures taken in Andhra Pradesh, the government decided to send a delegation consisting of the Chairman and the Vice-Chairman and Managing Director to visit foreign countries. Accordingly, E.V. Rami Reddy and I undertook an extensive tour to U.K., U.S.A. and Canada and visited several cities and addressed meetings of NRIs, mostly from the Andhra Pradesh, with a view to encourage them to invest in Andhra Pradesh in various projects. My wife, Suryakumari accompanied me during this tour, which happened to be her first foreign trip.

Several such initiatives taken by the ANRICH brought substantial investments to Andhra Pradesh. After seeing the results, other states emulated the experience of Andhra Pradesh and have constituted such exclusive Corporations for NRIs. While I was planning several initiatives in this direction, I was transferred after a stint of only a few months, as Secretary, Municipal Administration, Housing and Urban Development Department (MH & UD) in April 1982.

THIRTEEN

MANAGING URBAN INFRASTRUCTURE IN ANDHRA PRADESH

Secretary, Municipal Administration, Urban Development and Housing Department

Before I took over as Secretary, Municipal Corporation, Housing and Urban Development (MH & UD) Department, there were two Secretaries in the department, one dealing with Municipal Administration and Urban Development, while the other dealt with the Housing department. All the three wings dealing with civic matters, important issues of urban growth and related problems, basic amenities and the important urban infrastructure of housing were combined into one department when I assumed charge as Secretary in April 1982. Sarojini Pulla Reddy, a highly cultured and very dynamic lady, greatly committed to improving urban infrastructure, was the concerned Minister. Bhavanam Venkatram was the Chief Minister and subsequently succeeded by Kotla Viyabhaskar Reddy.

The posting as Secretary, MH & UD gave me an opportunity to understand the problems of growing urbanization in the country. Municipal Administration and Urban Development aimed at tackling the formidable problems resulting from population increase, industrialization, inadequate urban services and facilities, growth of slums and environmental pollution. Industrial development had not been dovetailed with urban growth and town planning. It had, therefore, become necessary to provide larger outlays for urban development programmes for ameliorating the conditions of the slum dwellers and implementation of comprehensive area development for housing and slum improvement. Moreover, provision of amenities like water supply, sanitation, drainage, roads, street lighting and schools needed to be looked into, although the municipalities were looking after these functions in their respective areas.

There were three Municipal Corporations, 82 Municipalities, 7 selection Grade Municipalities, 11 special grade municipalities, 13 first grade municipalities, 24 second grade municipalities and 29 third grade municipalities in Andhra Pradesh. These categories were primarily based on the population. In all the Municipalities and the Vijayawada and the Visakhapatnam Municipal Corporations, elected Councils were functioning. The elections to the Municipal Corporation of Hyderabad were proposed to be held before June 1984. The Director, Municipal Administration, was the head of the Organization, functioning under the administrative control of the Secretary, Municipal Administration. These municipalities were managing 1,287 elementary schools and 126 secondary schools. Thirty municipalities were maintaining hospitals and dispensaries, while 75 municipalities were maintaining 'Protected Water Supply' schemes. Under environmental improvement schemes, the government sanctioned 100 per cent grant-in-aid for provision of amenities to the public. The Special Nutrition Programme in urban slum areas was in operation in five Municipal towns. The 'Ready to Eat' Processed Food factory, Hyderabad, supplied food to infant beneficiaries, pregnant women and also for women coming from economically weaker sections.

URBAN DEVELOPMENT AND TOWN AND COUNTRY PLANNING

One of the important wings in Municipal Administration was the Town and Country Planning Department, charged with the preparation of Master Plans for Towns. Any development can be achieved only through proper planning and strict enforcement of the planning regulations. In order to have uniform planning tools throughout the State, Andhra Pradesh (Andhra Area) Town Planning Act, 1920, was extended to the Telangana Region with effect from 10 June 1981. There was also a Chief City Planner, working exclusively for the Municipal Corporation of Hyderabad.

While master plans for three Municipal Corporations, namely, Hyderbad, Visakhapatnam and Vijayawada and for 19 Municipalities were already prepared, during my tenure the government sanctioned Master Plans for another 22 Municipalities. The Government also directed the Town and Country Planning Department to prepare Master Plans for another 43 Municipal Towns.

SLUM IMPROVEMENT PROGRAMMES

The Environmental Improvement Scheme envisaged provision of civic amenities like water supply, sewers, storm water drains, latrines, widening and paving of existing lanes and street lighting in the slum areas, mostly inhabited by the weaker sections of the community who lived in an unhygienic environment. I ensured at the time of preparation of the annual budget that a substantial provision was earmarked exclusively for the benefit of weaker sections, under the 'special component plan' in about 80 municipalities. Under the Weaker Sections Housing Scheme, 30,000 urban houses were taken up in the first phase programme during 1982-83.

INTEGRATED DEVELOPMENT OF SMALL AND MEDIUM TOWNS

Urban population was increasing at a high rate due to migration of people primarily in search of employment. As a result, the small and medium towns were shrinking. If this trend was allowed to continue, cities will be over-populated, which in turn cannot provide the basic civic facilities, as they were not planned to receive such a large influx of people. The thrust was, therefore, on bringing about an Integrated Development of Small and Medium Towns, by providing infrastructural and other facilities, in order to discourage migration to the larger cities. Keeping this in view, the Government of India, under the centrally sponsored scheme, was providing central assistance of up to 50 per cent of the cost, with matching assistance by way of loans and grants by the State Government. This scheme would cover small towns with a population of one lakh and below. We concentrated all our efforts on preparing a large number of infrastructural schemes and to get approval for them from the Government of India. Several towns were granted assistance under this scheme.

STATE PUBLIC HEALTH AND MUNICIPAL ENGINEERING DEPARTMENT

The Public Health and Municipal Engineering Department, which was under the administrative control of the department, was headed by a Chief Engineer. His functions, inter alia, included investigation, design and execution of water supply and sewerage schemes and roads and buildings of all the Corporations and Municipalities in the State. Several schemes were undertaken to supply safe drinking water.

MUNICIPAL CORPORATION OF HYDERABAD, (MCH)

The MCH did not have an elected body as it was under the administrative control of Special Officers. During my tenure, C. Arjun Rao, A.V.S. Reddy and P.C. Parakh, all of them very dynamic officers, and functioned as Special Officers. They spared no efforts to improve urban infrastructure. The objective of the Twin Cities Improvement Scheme during the Sixth Five Year Plan (1980-85) was to develop and strengthen the roads, to handle the increase in traffic and to improve and enhance storm water drainage and sewerage facilities. It was also to provide better quality street lighting.

Road Widening Schemes

The roads in the twin cities of Hyderabad and Secunderabad were developed during pre-Independence days and were totally inadequate to cater to the growing number of vehicles in the city. Hence, a development plan was prepared for the widening of almost all important roads, formation of ring roads and new roads. Since 1981, the Municipal Corporation of Hyderabad had taken up the task of widening of a hundred of the most important roads in the Twin Cities and this work was given further impetus during my tenure. It was C. Arjun Rao, Special Officer with his dynamism and foresight, who look up the road widening program in a 'Mission Mode', for the first time and achieved spectacular success in spite of considerable resistance from the affected people.

The Corporation had also taken up several slum improvement schemes to provide better civic amenities like water supply, electricity, drainage, roads, community halls and public conveniences.

Visakhapatnam Municipal Corporation

The city was fast growing into a teaming metropolis due to the location of various major public sector industries and commencement of the work relating to a major integrated Steel Plant. In order to meet the growing water requirements, the augmentation scheme to supply more drinking water to the city was taken up, in addition to obtaining additional water from the Raiwada Reservoir by the end of 1983.

Environmental Improvement and Weaker Sections Self-Help Housing Programme

There were 80 slums existing in the city and the Corporation had provided basic civic amenities like water supply, street lighting roads, community halls and houses for the weaker sections in only 20 slum areas under the Environmental Improvement Scheme. I had sanctioned similar activities in an additional 45 slum areas during the year. The Government also accorded administrative approval for taking up several development works during 1982 such as widening the main road from Sitammadhara to National Highway 5 Road; construction of a shopping complex and construction of park by the side of the beach road.

The Corporation took up the implementation of the Weaker Section Housing Programme and several other programmes aimed at improving the social and economic conditions of the slum dwellers. In recognition of the excellent work done by the Corporation, under a dynamic young IAS Officer, S.V. Prasad, as Municipal Commissioner, the UNICEF sanctioned four projects meeting the entire expenditure for these projects.

VIJAYAWADA MUNICIPAL CORPORATION

Vijayawada, which was the second biggest city, had grown immensely as a commercial center. Hence there was a need to step up the infrastructural facilities. It was also the hub of several premier educational institutions. Many schemes were initiated to meet the growing needs of the city.

Water Supply and Drainage Schemes

The construction of an additional 16 MGD Schemes was taken up to augment the water supply position of the city. The remodeling of the water supply distribution system and also additional water supply lines to cover the uncovered areas was undertaken. The underground drainage system to the eastern part of the city was completed and the work in other parts of the city was taken up during the year. After obtaining the Government of India's approval for "waste disposal," a Mechanical Compost Plant was set up, which was completed in December 1983. Under the Environmental Improvement Scheme, the improvement of seven slum areas was undertaken, in addition to providing modern street lighting, construction of shopping and commercial complexes and markets.

The resources of the Municipalities and Municipal Corporations were not sufficient to cope with the ever increasing expenditure on civic amenities required to be provided to the urban population. The Government, therefore, had constituted an official committee in April 1982, while I was Secretary, for suggesting ways and means to augment the revenue of these institutions, including devolution of state funds.

On the basis of recommendations of the Committee, the Government issued orders relieving the Municipalities from the burden of repayment of loans. It was hoped that all the Corporations and Municipalities would work hard to improve their finances and provide more amenities to the citizens.

The period of 1981–91 was declared as "International Drinking Water Supply and Sanitation Decade". The programme envisaged, *inter alia*, 100 per cent coverage of urban population in all Class I Cities (i.e., population above 1,00,000 as per 1971 census) with complete sewerage and an overall coverage of 80 per cent of the urban population. It was proposed to provide sanitary water and seal latrines in all house holds in towns where it was not possible to provide underground sewerage.

Elimination of Scavenging

A centrally sponsored scheme for elimination of scavenging by providing alternative avocations to scavengers and conversion of all existing dry latrines into water flush latrines was taken up in Warangal and Eluru towns, so that these towns could serve as models. The Government accorded administrative sanction to the 'Low Cost Sanitation' scheme for other towns also. All the Municipalities and Municipal Corporations were advised to set aside in their budgets, funds for the development of Scheduled Castes, Scheduled Tribes and Women and Children at 15 per cent, 4 per cent and 5 per cent of the funds, respectively. It was ensured that such provisions were made and also spent on the schemes meant for them.

HOUSING

Food, clothing and shelter are the basic necessities of human life. The problem of housing, as a result of urbanization and growth of big industry in and around urban areas, had become very acute, with the demand considerably outstripping the supply. Housing, therefore, plays an important role in bridging the socio-economic gulf. The Government was coordinating the activities of various public housing agencies in the State, with a view to securing the benefits predominantly to the weaker sections of society. While the social purpose of the low income and economically weaker sections is sought to be secured partly through plan funds and partly through the funds available from the Housing and Urban Development Corporation (HUDCO), the middle income sector is catered through Integrated Housing Scheme, financed by HUDCO.

Subsidized Industrial Housing Scheme

The Government has been bestowing special attention to the housing needs of industrial workers. The 'Integrated Subsidized Housing for Industrial Workers' was the principal instrument for providing housing facilities in the factories. It was decided to transfer the tenements constructed under the scheme at several places in the industrial workers cooperative societies, to the existing occupants on a hire purchase basis.

Andhra Pradesh Housing Board

The Andhra Pradesh Housing Board, the premier housing agency of the State, was constituted on 1 July 1960 and initially confined its activities to the twin cities only. However, since 1970, the Board's activities were gradually extended to cover all the districts of the State. The schemes undertaken by the Board were broadly categorized as: (a) The integrated/composite housing scheme, (b) commercial complexes, (c) low cost housing schemes, (d) sale of developed plots etc. The Board had so far constructed over 22,000 tenements, of which 75 per cent were for the economically weaker sections and low income groups. Another 20,258 tenements of all groups were approved and were at various stages of construction, which were expected to be completed by 1983-84. I also got additional 27 schemes sanctioned during 1982-83 from HUDCO.

Housing Under Special Component Plan

The Government approved the proposal from the Andhra Pradesh Housing Board for construction of 4,200 Economically Weaker Section's (EWS) houses exclusively for scheduled castes under the 'special component plan' in 12 Districts and for Scheduled Tribes under 'tribal sub plan' in 9 Districts. In addition, 426 houses constructed under HIG, MIG and LIG houses, which were completed, were also handed over to NGO's Cooperative House Building Societies. More such schemes were undertaken in big cities like Vijayawada and Guntur during this period.

SATELLITE TOWNSHIP

Hyderabad, which until recently had enjoyed a comparatively low pattern of land prices, has now entered into a spiral of very high prices, just as in cities like Bombay and Bangalore. The city desperately needed lung space to reduce the congestion by developing Satellite Townships in industrial belts like Kukatpally. The Board, therefore, had acquired lands at Kukatpally in Ranga Reddy District. The Board was directed to identify lands in all the 23 districts to set up such satellite townships. Some land had already been taken in its possession.

IRREGULARITIES IN THE HOUSING BOARD

It was during this period, a major case of irregularities surfaced in the functioning of the Andhra Pradesh Housing Board. Several allegations were made in the media about the malpractices at the time of acquisition of the land. Similar allegations were made during the discussions on the floor of the State Assembly. I was appointed as the Enquiry Officer. It was during the discussions in the Assembly, I had an opportunity to observe for the first time (having recently come to deputation to the Government of Andhra Pradesh) the oratory skills, both in English and in Telugu, of two young promising politicians, viz. M. Venkaiah Naidu, who later became a Union Cabinet Minister and also the President, Bharatiya Janata Party (BJP) and S. Jaipal Reddy, who is presently a Union Cabinet Minister. Both distinguished themselves as outstanding Parliamentarians.

URBAN DEVELOPMENT

The Government notified five development areas under the Andhra Pradesh Urban Areas (Development) Act, 1975 for the purpose of overall development of the areas in accordance with Master Plans. The Government also constituted the Hyderabad Urban Development Authority (HUDA), Visakhapatnam Urban Development Authority (VUDA) and Kakateeya Urban Development Authority. The objectives of all the Urban Development Authorities were to promote and secure the development of all areas according to the Master Plan and Zonal Development plans; to control the use of land for various purposes by acquisition, development and disposal of land; to carry out developmental works such as roads, buildings, water supply, sewerage and other schemes so as to provide the infrastructural facilities.

Master Plan for Hyderabad

As a first step to regulate the growth of the city, HUDA prepared a Master Plan for both Municipal and Non-Municipal areas, providing for the physical framework of land use pattern over a period of 20–25 years indicating the future growth of the city. To prepare and conserve the architectural character of historically important buildings in the city, HUDA was entrusted with a study, expected to be completed by March, 1984.

The government constituted a Traffic Study Committee in October 1982 to study and prepare a Comprehensive Traffic and Transportation Plan for the twin cities of Hyderabad and Secunderabad, which would be completed in a period of two years. HUDA was also directed to prepare detailed Zonal Development Plans for the overall development of neighbouring towns like Ramachandrapuram. The Authority had taken up the construction of big commercial complexes at Tarnaka and Maitrivanam. The Authority had also taken up slum re-development programme since its inception. In order to meet the shortage of housing, the Authority was directed to construct 10,000 houses per annum and had initiated necessary steps in this direction. Apart for the planning work, the Authority was also concerned with the formation of Inner Ring Road and Outer Ring Road.

Buddha Poornima Project—The Necklace Road

Another important programme undertaken was the Buddha Poornima Project. It planned to develop the shores of the Hussain Sagar Lake and other areas, provide parks, facilities for water sports and other recreational and cultural activities, aforestation, bird sanctuaries as well as tourist and commercial complexes. This was to be achieved by providing a necklace road around the lake. The total cost of the project was about Rs. 110 crores. An amount of Rs. 1 crore was released by me during 1982-83 to HUDA to proceed with the work. Charles Correa, an internationally renowned urban planner and architect of Bombay, was appointed as consultant. The acquisition of land was in progress.

Quli Qutub Shah Urban Development Authority

While I was Secretary, a detailed examination of the area covered by HUDA was undertaken. It was considered necessary to constitute a separate development Authority for the old city of Hyderabad to preserve its historic heritage. While I was Secretary, the Government constituted the Quli Qutub Shah Urban Development Authority with effect from 2 August 1982 for the development of the Old City. The aims and objective of the Authority were to plan and promote the development of the Old City, including its renewal with emphasis on provision of better civic amenities, including communication, electricity, water supply, drainage, housing and also provision of more educational, recreational and market facilities. The Authority was directed to prepare plans to undertake various activities.

Visakhapatnam Urban Development Authority (VUDA)

VUDA was constituted in June 1978. The VUDA had formulated Urban and Rural Housing Schemes, with financial assistance of commercial Banks and HUDCO. One thousand sixty houses for 'economically weaker sections' were sanctioned during my time and were under construction to provide permanent shelter to the weaker sections.

The master plan for Visakhapatnam Town was prepared 15 years ago. In order to revise the plan to meet the growing needs, land use surveys were directed to be conducted for preparation of physical plans. Zonal Development Plans were also under preparation. The Authority had taken up construction of Commercial Complexes at Vizianagaram during the year 1982-83 and the works were nearing completion. In order to relieve the traffic congestion, 33 road widening schemes were taken up and 15 schemes were already implemented, while others were under progress in Visakhapatnam. It was also decided to prepare ecological conservation and Beach Front Development Scheme, including tourism for the areas from Visakhapatnam to Bheemunipatnam, along the beach road of about 20 kms. In October 1982, the Government entrusted the work for preparation of a scheme to a consultant. The Authority had already acquired land in the Beach Front, to develop a Bay-view Recreational Complex.

Vijayawada-Guntur-Tenali Urban Development Authority

The Authority was constituted during 1982, when I was Secretary of the Department. The development area under this Authority included the Municipal Corporation of Vijayawada, the Municipalities of Guntur, Tenali and Mangalagiri, besides 158 Gram Panchayats. There were sanctioned Master Plans for the urban area of Vijayawada, Guntur and Tenali. However, the Authority was directed to prepare the Master Plan for the entire urban region. The Zonal development plans for the growing vicinity areas was also under preparation. It was initially proposed to take up widening of existing roads and formation of newly proposed roads as per the Master Plans of Vijayawada-Guntur-Tenali area.

Kakatiya Urban Development Authority

This Authority was constituted with effect from 1-2-1982, with a view to promoting orderly development of areas comprising of 144 villages in Warangal District and 27 villages in Karimnagar District besides Warangal Town. The Master Plan for the entire area was under preparation and was expected to be completed by the end of 1983-84.

Tirupati Urban Development Authority

The Government constituted the Tirupati Urban Development Authority consisting of Tirupati and 89 villages in August 1982. The Authority proposed to undertake several works in the area. A master plan for developing the entire area and simultaneously the zonal development plans were under preparation.

Several measures were initiated in urban planning and development with a view to addressing basic problems being faced by the Municipalities in terms of population growth, slums, road congestions and lack of other infrastructure facilities in the urban areas. Area development plans and Zonal development plans were under preparation in most of the urban areas. I felt that there was considerable scope to take up several activities which would go a long way in helping the weaker sections, who were the worst sufferers in the urban areas, primarily due to lack of housing facilities.

While I was getting ready to initiate more urban infrastructural programmes, I was transferred from the Department, as Vice-Chairman and Managing Director of Andhra Pradesh Mining Corporation, Hyderabad. I had hardly worked in the Corporation for a few months, when I was transferred as Commissioner of Industries, Government of Andhra Pradesh.

FOURTEEN

INDUSTRIAL PROMOTION IN ANDHRA PRADESH

Commissioner of Industries, Andhra Pradesh

Andhra Pradesh had been emerging as an important industrial destination in the country. It had abundant natural resources, technical manpower and surplus electricity and above all, an enlightened political leadership which strongly believed in industrializing the state. The industries department, which was entrusted with the responsibility for planning and execution of various developmental programmes relating to the industrial development of the state, had embarked on a massive industrial development programme in the state. The Department was responsible for the implementation of various extension programmes, which were primarily aimed at accelerating the pace of industrial development, with special emphasis on the promotion of large, medium, and small-scale industries. The Department was also paying special attention to selected artisan-oriented sectors like handicrafts, industrial cooperatives and coir industries, thereby leading to an appreciable growth in all fields relating to industrial development.

When I was appointed as Commissioner of Industries, Government of Andhra Pradesh in October 1983, T.L. Sankar, IAS (1957) was the Principal Secretary, Industries Department. While working as Regional Iron and Steel Controller, at Hyderabad, I had close interaction with Sankar, regarding the development of Iron and Steel Industries in the state. I had also worked with him closely after the 'super cyclone of

1977' in restoring and rehabilitating those industries which had been badly affected by the super cyclone.

WORKING WITH N.T. RAMA RAO

My appointment as Commissioner Industries gave me an excellent opportunity to work closely with NT Rama Rao, who had become Chief Minister after the State Assembly Elections held in 1983. NT Rama Rao retained the portfolio of the Industries Development with him. NT Rama Rao, who was a super hero of Telegu Cinema, had brought in new dynamism to the entire administration. He believed in the rapid industrialisation of the state, so that it would provide much needed employment to the rural youth. Thus, he spared no efforts in promoting industrial development. He also encouraged honest and hardworking officers, who were committed to the development of the state. NT Rama Rao, by habit, was a very early riser and used to be ready for work as early as 5.00 in the morning. He obviously believed that every officer must also be an early riser. If there was any telephone call at such an unearthly hour, as I was a late riser, one could be almost certain that it was from the CM's residence and invariably one would be required to immediately present oneself at his residence in the Abids area of Hyderabad.

Sankar had wide experience in the energy and industrial promotion sectors, having worked at senior positions both at the state and national levels. He was an internationally acknowledged energy expert. It was a great learning experience to work with such an eminent personality, who always encouraged sincere officers. I continued my close association with Sankar, even after I returned to my parent cadre Maharashtra, especially during the period when I was Chairman, MSEB, while Sankar was Chairman, APSEB. Our association continued even, subsequently, when I was Secretary, Ministry of Power, Government of India, as he has been truly a "friend, philosopher and guide" to me. Sankar was succeeded subsequently as Principal Secretary by Sushil Kumar, IAS (1957), another outstanding officer.

The Commissioner of Industries heads the Commissionarate of Industries, which is the main field organisation of the Industries Department. As Head of Department, he was assisted by two Additional Directors and subject matter specialists as Joint Directors and other officers. At the district level, the District Industries Centre

(DIC) was headed by a General Manager in the cadre of Joint Director, assisted by Functional Managers and other field staff.

When I assumed charge as Commissioner of Industries, the State had about 388 large and medium scale units, with a total capital investment of Rs. 1950 crores, providing an employment to 3.50 lakh persons. In addition, the investments in the pipeline amounted to about Rs. 6873 crores. The setting up of the Vishakhapatnam Steel Plant was already on the anvil. There were 518 Industrial licenses, Letters of Intent and Registrations for setting up large and medium scale industries, approved by the Government of India. These Licences were at various stages of implementation and were expected to create employment opportunities for about 1.5 lakh persons. These clearances covered chemical, heavy engineering, electrical, electronics, agro-based and mineral based Industries.

LARGE AND MEDIUM SCALE INDUSTRIES

Due to the concerted efforts made by the Industries Department, as against 388 large and medium units in 1982-83, there were 462 large and medium scale industries in the state with a capital investment of Rs 2165 crores, providing employment to 3.50 lakhs persons as on 31 March 1985. During 1985-86, another 40 new large- and medium-scale industries with a capital investment of Rs. 1077 crores providing employment to 5633 persons, had gone into production. Another 274 medium and large scale industrial projects were at various stages of implementation. I attended all the Licensing Committee meetings in the Ministry of Industrial Development to obtain licenses for the proposed industrial units in Andhra Pradesh, in preference to the claims of other competing states.

SMALL SCALE AND VILLAGE INDUSTRIES

The State Government was actively engaged in the promotion of small scale, cottage and village industries. During 1984-85, 5,200 units with an investment of Rs. 71 crores providing employment to 46,800 persons, were promoted. There were 48,862 Small Scale Industries (SSI) units as on 31 March 1985 with an investment of Rs. 657 crores, providing employment to 4.8 lakhs persons. I was instrumental in preparing an Action Plan during 1985-86 for setting up of about 50,000 Small Scale

Industrial Units in the next five years, with an investment of Rs. 733 crores, which would provide employment to 5.50 lakhs persons. There was still vast potential for further development in the areas of drugs, pharmaceuticals, dyes, paints, salt and salt-based chemicals, processing of fruits and vegetables and a wide range of engineering industries.

CEMENT INDUSTRY

The State continued to make concerted efforts for maximum exploitation of mineral resources. There were of 13 cement plants in the state. Further, as many as 10 major cement plants, 8 mini-cement plants and 3 micro-cement plants, were in the pipeline and when put up, the overall capacity in the state would be reaching 102 lakh tonnes per annum. Various steps were taken and financial assistance was given for early commissioning of these projects.

DISTRICT INDUSTRIES CENTRES

The Government established "District Industries Centres" (DIC) in all the 22 districts of the State, to provide all services under a 'single window' and support at pre-investment and post-investment stages of small and cottage industries. Further, 'Growth Centres' at the rate of one in each District had been set up during my time to accelerate industrial growth. Since the formation of DICs in the State, the growth rate of small and tiny sector units registered a steady rise. In the area of rural industrialization, the Department, through the DICs, undertook several programmes like identifying and motivating the entrepreneurs to start new industries through 'entrepreneurial training campaigns', training of artisans, assisting artisans and tiny sector units, through grants and loans etc.

RURAL ARTISAN COMPLEXES

Another important programme taken up during my tenure for artisan development was the "Establishment of Rural Artisan Complexes", a new concept of providing a package of services to the artisans like training in improved tools, providing work sheds and working capital to the artisans. These Artisan complexes were set up in each Panchayat Samiti and as many as 361 complexes, were set up by end of March 1986 in the rural areas. Under this scheme, a large number of small and tiny sector units were promoted, providing employment opportunities for thousands of people. Several artisans were trained and financial assistance was given to set up tiny sector units. Several development activities and extension programmes were undertaken during the period, such as incentives for industrial promotion; loans under the state incentive scheme; incentives for SCs and STs under Special Component Plan (SCP) and incentives for tribal entrepreneurs under Tribal Sub Plan (TSP) were extended liberally for entrepreneurs.

INCENTIVES FOR INDUSTRIAL PROMOTION

Central Investment Subsidy Scheme

The Commissioner of Industries is the nodal agency for administering the Central Investment Subsidy Scheme at the State level. In order to give a fillip to rural industrialization and to help dispersal of the industries to the rural and semi-urban areas, the Government of India and the State Government offered several subsides and incentives to the industries set up in the backward areas of the State. Under the revised incentives scheme, which came into operation from 1 April 1984, 118 blocks in the state were brought under central subsidy scheme. The industries coming up in these blocks were eligible for investment subsidy, confessional finance from Central financial institutions and tax-rebates. One of the major tasks of the Commissioner of Industries was to obtain maximum disbursements under the Central Subsidy Scheme.

While the procedures prescribed to obtain these incentives were laborious, with any delay in the release of funds adversely affecting the functioning of the unit for lack of adequate financial resources, I visited Delhi frequently and followed up with the Ministry of Industrial Development for the release of the central subsidy. We obtained Rs. 949 lakhs for various projects during 1985-86.

State Incentives for Industrial Promotion

The State Government also offered new package of incentives to industries coming up in 20 Growth Centres in 7 districts (Vizianagaram, Visakhapatnam, East Godavari and West Godavari, Krishna, Guntur and Rangareddy), which were eligible for state incentives like land and investment subsidy, power tariff concessions, water rebate and deferment of sales tax, depending on the investment level and location. In addition,

Srikakulam, Anantapur and Adilabad were declared as 'Intensive Industrial Development areas', where a higher package of incentives were offered. An amount of Rs. 397.00 lakhs was disbursed under the State Incentives Scheme during 1985-86 to various large, medium and small scale industries.

Andhra Pradesh Assistance Centre for Entrepreneurs (APACE)

The APACE was established in 1983 under the administrative control and supervision of the Commissioner of Industries, to help entrepreneurs in obtaining quick clearances, approvals, sanctions and implementing their projects expeditiously. The APACE had extended assistance to as many as 890 entrepreneurs till the end of 1985-86.

ENTREPRENEURIAL DEVELOPMENT PROGRAMMES

There were concerted efforts all over the country for entrepreneurial development programmes to persuade entrepreneurs, especially the educated unemployed, to set up their own industries. Several incentives were given for such persons setting up their own industrial units. One of the jobs entrusted to the Commissioner of Industries was to organise as many entrepreneurial developmental workshops as possible all over the state, which encouraged several entrepreneurs in the state to set up industries. The Government of India adopted a policy of 'promoting self employment scheme' as a strategy to alleviate the problem of unemployment. Unemployed engineers and qualified technicians were given priority. Similarly, educated unemployed from families having no source of income were given preference over others. We conducted several entrepreneurial development campaigns and special employment drives in the districts to motivate the educated unemployed to take up various self-employment ventures.

INDUSTRIAL COOPERATIVES

The department had administrative control over all the Industrial Cooperatives functioning in the State. In order to help raise the income levels of rural artisans and craftsmen working in the decentralised sector, the department had been promoting industrial cooperative societies. They were assisted through schemes like equity participation, subsidies, share capital loans, allotment of work sheds etc.

HANDICRAFTS

In order to help the artisans engaged in various trades, the State Government had set up a separate Handicrafts Development Corporation for providing necessary inputs, suitable designs, training facilities and marketing assistance. I regularly monitored the progress made in this connection.

DEVELOPMENT OF SALT INDUSTRY

As Andhra Pradesh had a vast coastline, an extent of over 1,03,700 acres of saline land suitable for salt cultivation in the State had been identified. Incentives were provided to bring the entire area under salt cultivation. With the entire area being put to use, the salt production in the State was expected to reach a figure of 18 lakh tonnes per annum by the end of 1987.

RAW MATERIAL AND MARKETING ASSISTANCE TO SSI SECTOR

The department provided necessary assistance to the SSI units in procuring the raw materials required by them. All the scarce raw materials were channelised through public sector corporations and imported raw materials were also made available to SSI units by recommending their actual requirements to the concerned authorities for imports.

The department was also providing marketing support required by the SSI and tiny sector units. Government made it compulsory for all the Government departments and the Corporations to give purchase and price preference to local small-scale industries in regard to all purchases made by them. For this purpose, the Government constituted a Purchase Review Committee with Chief Secretary as its Chairman and Commissioner of Industries as Member Secretary for this purpose. The State Government had reserved 384 items/products for exclusive purchase from the SSI sector and the Commissioner of Industries was assisting in marketing these products. In addition, the department participated in various industrial exhibitions within and outside the State.

DEVELOPMENT OF PRODUCTION-CUM-TRAINING CENTRE

Emphasis was given for the development of production-cum-training. Several centres had started imparting training for artisans to upgrade their skills and technologies to suit modern market requirements. Since the small-scale industries and tiny units cannot afford to have their own testing equipment, the Government set up the much needed testing laboratories to facilitate proper testing.

GRAMODAYA PROGRAMME

Under the Gramodaya Programme, women and technically trained personnel were eligible for a composite loan not exceeding Rs. 25,000/- with a subsidy component of 25 per cent. Under this programme, one educated unemployed person in each village of the state was being assisted for starting self-employment ventures, such as tiny industries, business or services. As against the target of 17,300 candidates for the year 1985-86, 22,891 candidates were selected and an amount of Rs 10.42 crores was released to 7,806 to self-employed persons.

COIR INDUSTRY

Andhra Pradesh is rich in the production of coconut and stands fourth in the country. 30,700 artisans in East and West Godavari and Srikakulam districts depended on coconuts. A comprehensive integrated coir development plan was prepared by me to develop the coir industry. 12 coir co-operatives were organized. Several coir workers were trained under Training under Self Employment (TRYSEM) Programme.

ELECTRICALS AND ELECTRONICS

During the period, 34 units were issued eligibility certificate for import of capital goods and raw materials. Production programme approvals for 149 units for setting up Electronic Industries were given. Approvals were obtained from the Development Commissioner (SSI), New Delhi for 39 units for the manufacture of colour T.V. Receivers etc.

INDUSTRIAL PROMOTION CORPORATIONS

The Government of Andhra Pradesh established several Industrial

Promotion Corporation in the state. As Commissioner of Industries, I was also ***Director on the major State Public Sector Undertakings***, which has been entrusted with the task of promotion of industries in the State.

ANDHRA PRADESH INDUSTRIAL DEVELOPMENT CORPORATION LIMITED (APIDC), HYDERABAD

The Corporation was established in 1960 for promoting large and medium industries in the State, with the objective of identifying and promoting entrepreneurial talent; to provide concrete plans for the exploitation and use of the raw material resources available in the state; and to function as an extended arm of the national level Industrial Development Financial Institutions, such as IDBI, IFCI, and integrate all industrial development activities within the State. The development of backward areas of the State was one of the main objectives of the Corporation. Out of the 115 units recently promoted, about 77 per cent of industries were slated to come up in identified backward areas.

ANDHRA PRADESH STATE FINANCIAL CORPORATION (APSFC)

The Andhra Pradesh State Financial Corporation came into existence on 1st November 1956. It has greatly furthered the cause of industrialization and is a pioneer 'term lending institution' in the State. The Corporation had designed a number of innovative schemes to suit the specific requirements of technocrat entrepreneurs, entrepreneurs under various self-employment programmes, village artisans, to eradicate regional imbalances and provide gainful employment opportunities. A.P.S.F.C. retained the coveted no. 1 position among all the SFCs in the country for the Fourth Year in succession during 1985-86, in all areas of operation, namely, sanctions, disbursement and recovery of loans. This, indeed, was a remarkable achievement considering the level of industrial development in certain other States in the country. In line with the policy objectives of the Government, the bulk of the assistance was provided to the backward areas of the State. The Corporation has crossed Rs. 760 crores in sanctions and Rs. 470 crores in disbursements of loans in the State.

ANDHRA PRADESH SMALL SCALE INDUSTRIAL DEVELOPMENT CORPORATION LTD. (APSSIDC)

The Corporation was established in 1961 with the object of aiding, assisting, financing, and promoting the interests of small-scale industries in the State. The Corporation's activities covered promotion of new units, especially in plastic, agro-based industries and drugs and pharmaceuticals; procurement and distribution of raw materials; providing marketing assistance and industrial escort services and promotion of ancillary industries for the major public sector undertakings. The Corporation was marketing SSI products to Government Departments, Undertakings and local bodies, municipalities etc. The Government of Andhra Pradesh nominated the Corporation as the Sole Selling Agency for supply of several items commonly required by number of Government Departments such as steel furniture, electrical fittings, air coolers etc. These items were procured after inviting tenders by a Committee with the Commissioner of Industries as Chairman.

ANDHRA PRADESH INDUSTRIAL INFRASTRUCTURE CORPORATION LIMITED, (APIIC)

The Corporation was established in 1973 to create a sound industrial infrastructure base in the State by providing developed land, built-in sheds, water, power and other facilities. Dr. Bhanu Prasad Committee recommended establishment of 69 Industrial estates, Autonagars, Industrial townships etc., with an investment of Rs. 152 crores, involving the acquisition of 10,730 acres and construction of 546 sheds and 600 houses during the Seventh Five Year plan (1985-90). The Corporation had undertaken several activities such as identification of potential growth centers, acquisition of land for setting up of Industrial Estates (IE) and Industrial Development Areas (IDA); allotment of developed plots and built-in sheds, provision of housing for industrial workers and provided other necessary infrastructure facilities.

KONDAPALLI INDUSTRIAL ESTATE

Kondapalli industrial Estate, nearer to my native place, was developed while I was Commissioner of Industries. Initially, there was not much response to set up industries in the Estate. However, I pursuaded Lanco group to set up its 368 MW gas-based power station at Kondapalli Industrial Estate, while I was Secretary, Ministry of Power, Government of India, in view of availability of land, water, railway line and other infrastructure facilities. Lanco is planning to double its capacity at the existing site. The estate is so successful, there is no land available for any new industries.

CAMPAIGNS FOR PROMOTING INDUSTRIAL DEVELOPMENT

Andhra Pradesh enjoyed a very comfortable power situation compared to many other states in the country. It also had the ideal thermal and hydropower generation mix of 50:50 per cent. It was common for many states to go to the other states and highlight the opportunities available in their state for setting up industries. We always claimed that one of the best advantages the state could provide for industrial growth was adequate availability of electricity. I organized and coordinated extensive tours to Bangalore, Bombay and Calcutta to invite entrepreneurs to set up industries in Andhra Pradesh, with a team of Chief Executives of State Industrial Promotion Corporations and Dr. N. Tata Rao, Chairman, Andhra Pradesh State Electricity Board (APSEB). It was a 'permanent Invitee' for all the Board meetings of APSEB to further the growth of industrial promotion.

GOVERNOR'S ADVICE

Shankar Dayal Sharma, the then Governor of Andhra Pradesh, who was subsequently elevated to the position of President of India, was the chief guest in one such industrial promotional programme at Hyderabad. While highlighting the various facilities available in the state, I graphically described about the availability of adequate power, which was very well appreciated by the audience. Shankar Dayal Sharma, in his speech very smilingly ticked off the Industries Department stating that the availability of surplus power denotes inadequate work done by the Industries Department over a period of time in not promoting the industrial growth in the state. Looking towards me, he said that he was happy to know that the Industries Commissioner had now planned several campaigns for promoting industries in the state. His remarks drove home the point that concerted efforts were required to be undertaken on a continuous basis to increase industrial growth and development in the state.

DHIRUBHAI AMBANI MEETING WITH THE CHIEF MINISTER

We identified several major industrial houses in the country that needed to be escorted to set up industries in the state. One such well-known industrial house was Reliance, which did not make any investments in the state till then. As I knew Dhirubhai Ambani, Chairman, Reliance Industries, during my earlier stints in Maharashtra, I could persuade him to visit Hyderabad and meet Chief Minister N T Rama Rao, who was also holding charge of the Industries Department. Accordingly, a breakfast meeting was fixed at 6.30 am with N.T. Rama Rao. One of the major projects suggested during the breakfast meeting was Mangalagiri Tyre Project in Guntur District, which N.T. Rama Rao vowed to start in his Election Manifesto in 1983, while successfully launching the Telugu Desam Party (TDP). Dhirubhai Ambani, while expressing his readiness to invest in Andhra Pradesh, politely mentioned that he would be interested in a project whose cost was at least Rs. 100 crore and above and not in Mangalagiri Tyre Project whose cost was only Rs. 40 crore. Unfortunately, Andhra Pradesh did not have a project whose cost was more than Rs. 100 crore at that point of time!! Investors these days talk of nothing less than multiples of thousands of crore!! Mukesh Ambani his eldest son of Reliance Industries now talks only in investments of several multiples of billions of $.

BOOK ON "GUIDELINES FOR SETTING UP SMALL SCALE INDUSTRIES IN ANDHRA PRADESH"

One of the major constraints in setting up industries, especially by the educated unemployed, young graduates and the first generation entrepreneurs, was lack of adequate clarity on the procedures and formalities to be completed to set up an industry. They also did not have proper knowledge of the existing potential in various sectors. There were a plethora of guidelines and circulars issued both by the Government of India as well as the State Government without much clarity, which at times were even contradictory. I brought out a booklet titled as "Guidelines for setting up of Small Scale Industries in Andhra Pradesh", which exhaustively detailed the potential sectors, various incentives provided by the Centre and the State to set up the industries, growth centres, APIIC industrial estates, prescribed proformas for applying and also availing of the incentives. The booklet was released by N T Rama Rao, Chief Minister with considerable fanfare on and was very much appreciated by the entrepreneurs.

MARRIAGE OF MY DAUGHTER

While I was functioning as Commissioner of Industries, we received several proposals for my daughter Manjula's marriage. As she was only nineteen years old and in the final year of B.Sc., we were not keen about her marriage. However, we received a proposal from a very highly respected family of Busi from Guntur. Busi Sam Bob joined the IAS in 1983 and was undergoing training at the Lal Bahadur Shastri Academy of Administration, Mussoorie. As it was a very good proposal, we had to convince my daughter for an early wedding, on the assurance that she could continue her studies even after marriage. The marriage was celebrated on 15th May 1986. Thus Busi Sam Bob became a new member of our family.

CHAIRMAN, ANDHRA PRADESH STEELS LIMITED (AP STEELS)

AP Steels, A Sick Unit makes History

While functioning as Commissioner of Industries, I was also given additional charge as Chairman and Managing Director, Andhra Pradesh Steels Ltd., Palavancha, Khammam District, a public sector unit of the Government of Andhra Pradesh, as I earlier worked as Regional Iron and Steel Controller, Government of India and had experience of the steel industry.

Andhra Pradesh Steel, located in a backward area based on arc furnace (electrical) steel making facility and continuous casting machines for production of steel billets, was commissioned in 1977 with an outlay of Rs. 29 crore and annual production capacity of 47,000 metric tonnes of mild steel and high carbon billets. Since the commencement of commercial production in 1977, it had been incurring losses and accumulated losses of over Rs. 7.50 crore till 1983-84. In view of the huge losses suffered by it, the State Government, the Industrial Development Bank of India (IDBI) and other Financial Institutions decided to sell the unit to a private party in 1983. It shocked the employees and the matter was raised in the Assembly, with the Opposition demanding that it should not be sold. It was at this stage that the Government decided to make one more attempt to revive the unit and I was entrusted with the additional charge of A P steels.

I had initiated a number of measures to tone up the production performance, set targets for higher production, promote better discipline among the employees and improve profitability, procurement of various inputs at the most competitive prices, effect economy in the consumption of various inputs, introduced new marketing strategies, and marketed its products at the best possible prices.

The company, which had huge accumulated losses of Rs. 7.5 crore and had been written off as an unviable unit, showed creditable improvement in all fields of its operations since 1984-85. The gross turn over of the company increased from Rs. 18 crore in 1983-84 to Rs. 22.5 crore during 1984-85, indicating an increase of 25 per cent. It further increased to Rs. 25 crore by March 1986. The company had a record output of 4772 metric tonnes in December 1985, the highest so far. We used more than 30 per cent of the raw material from Sponge Iron factory and imported 16,000 metric tonnes of scrap from USA as raw material for the first time, due to shortage of indigenous scrap. The steel billets manufactured by the company were supplied to 225 parties in India including the Telugu Ganga Project, Tamil Nadu Steel, APSEB and Engineers India Limited.

Not only did the productivity of the unit show remarkable improvement, but the unit was able to wipe off accumulated losses incurred by it, and in a short period it also started making profits. Not only had it turned the corner but it had also made a net profit of Rs. 1.50 crores during the year 1984-85 and nearly Rs. 3 crores during 1985-86. During 1984-85 the company has repaid Rs. 4 crores towards complete liquidation of interest arrears since its inception and part payment of term loans to all the Banks and Financial Institutions. It was decided to set up a Re-rolling unit to put the AP Steel on a sound footing on long-term basis. No sick unit of this size in the country had repaid Rs. 4 crores to the Financial Institutions in one year from its own internal resources. Wholehearted cooperation from both workers and staff had contributed to its success story. The company located in backward area of Khammam district had set an example for many sick units to go into profits through unity and discipline among employees and workers.

AP Steels wins Productivity Award

The Company, which was sick, hit the national headlines when I received the 'Productivity Award' from the Chief Minister N.T. Rama Rao on 1st May 1985. It was during this function that I met G. Mallikarjuna Rao, the present Chairman, GMR Group, who also received a 'Productivity Award' for one of his Companies. Since then, GMR Group has grown into an internationally reputed major infrastructure and power development company.

REPATRIATION TO MAHARASHTRA

While working as Commissioner of Industries, my initial deputation period of three years to Andhra Pradesh came to an end. NT Rama Rao was so impressed by my work, that he had taken up personally for extension of my deputation for two more years, which was granted by the Government of India. While requesting the Government of India for further extension of my deputation to Andhra Pradesh and appreciating the outstanding work done by me as Commissioner of Industries, he had also praised my work as Chairman and Managing Director, Andhra Pradesh Steels. He wrote, "Abraham has done commendable work in reviving the sick Government Company, AP Steels. It has not only turned the corner but has also made a net profit of Rs. 1.50 crore during the year 1984-85, and nearly Rs. 3 crores during 1985-86. In order to consolidate the improvements and to ensure that the Unit becomes viable on a permanent basis, Government decided to set up a Re-rolling Unit immediately. Shri Abraham is taking necessary follow up action to establish this Re-rolling Unit expeditiously. At this juncture, it is extremely essential to have the services of Abraham in the State for some more time so that this sick Unit could be fully revived. I would request the Government of India to extend his deputation for a further period of at least one year in public interest as a special case".

However, Government of India did not agree to a further extension and I reverted back to Maharashtra.

My deputation to the Government of Andhra Pradesh had given me an unforgettable and a rare experience in promoting industrial growth in my home State of Andhra Pradesh.

FIFTEEN

POLICY AND PLANNING FOR POWER IN MAHARASHTRA

Secretary, Energy Department

I returned to my parent cadre, Maharashtra, on completing my deputation to the Government of Andhra Pradesh at Hyderabad. I was posted in two Departments as Secretary, Energy and Environment. After joining in May 1986, I called on B.G. Deshmukh (IAS 1951), who was Chief Secretary. He mentioned that when my name came for being posted as Secretary in the Maharashtra government, several departments came up for consideration. The final choice for Secretary-Energy Department was made by S.B. Chavan, the Chief Minister himself, who mentioned that he knew me. He must have remembered that I had worked earlier as Collector, Bhir District and Secretary, MSEB, therefore, I would be the obvious choice for being posted as Secretary, Energy Department because of my earlier experience and good track record. The Chief Secretary was amazed that the Chief Minister remembered me so well, even though I had been away on deputation from the state for nine years. Such appreciative words of recognition from the Chief Minister made one to function with redoubled energy and dedication.

It goes to the credit of successive governments of Maharashtra that they recognised the importance of the power sector, *which was essential* for the all-round development of the state. Successive Chief Ministers had initiated several measures in this direction. In order to maintain the pre-eminent position of the state in the power sector at the national level, new generation, transmission and distribution schemes were sanctioned from time to time. A substantial amount of funds from the state budget was set aside for the power sector. There was rapid energisation of a substantial number of agricultural pumps in the state and rural electrification was taken up on a priority basis. Shankarrao Chavan continued the same tradition more rigorously, ensuring regular follow ups at the national level to get sanctions for new projects. He never spared any efforts to ensure that the MSEB functioned as a premier organisation in the country.

SUBRAMANIAN—ENERGY MINISTER

Dr. V. Subramanian was the Minister, Energy and Environment. He was a special recruit into the IAS and enjoyed a reputation for impeccable integrity, honesty and hard work. He was a renowned specialist in cooperative matters. He was also honourary President of Shanmugananda Society, which runs a cultural centre for staging art and cultural events with special emphasis on South-Indian performances. After retiring from the IAS, he plunged into active politics and successfully contested elections several times, thus becoming a Minister in the Maharashtra Government. It was a privilege to work with him, as he brought his immense knowledge, experience and integrity to bear on the development of the energy sector in the state. Dr. Subramanian took his job very seriously. Many Ministers, while being briefed for answering questions in the legislature, would be content with preparing themselves for up to the first ten questions or so, but not Dr. Subramanian. He would insist on being briefed up to the very last question numbering even beyond twenty. It was very interesting and instructive to listen to his studious responses, full of pertinent anecdotes and asides, even when he was dealing with this or other charges like Urban Development and Housing.

SUDHAKARRAO NAIK—MINISTER ENERGY

Subsequently, Sudhakarrao Naik became the Minister, Energy. Being a seasoned administrator, Sudhakarrao Naik strived hard to obtain maximum funds both from the State budget and from the Government of India to put the power sector on a strong footing in the state. He took periodical reviews to quickly implement the various programmes of the MSEB, especially the speedy implementation of generation projects. I recall that when Sudhakarrao Naik became Minister (Energy), I escorted him to his new chambers. As soon as he entered, the first thing he noticed was the "smoking is prohibited" board. Even before he was seated, his first orders in the Department were to remove the sign board. He lit his pipe (as he was fond of smoking a pipe) and only then, occupied the chair! Sudhakarrao Naik was succeeded by Dr. Padamsingh Patil and Datta Meghe, both of whom vigorously followed up the programmes of the Board, so as to maintain the supremacy of the state in the power sector in the country.

SRIKANTH JICHKAR—DYNAMIC YOUNG MOS

Dr. Subramanian was ably assisted by Dr. Srikanth Jichkar, as Minister of State (MoS) Energy. Dr. Jichkar was hardly thirty years of age when he became the Minister of State. He was an MBBS doctor but had a penchant of acquiring Degrees by the dozen in subjects as varied as astronomy, astrology, public administration, economics, history, philosophy, and so on. If one has to list the Degrees he acquired, it would run into a couple of pages.

As Jichkar had a fascination for the Civil Services, he wrote the Civil Services Examinations and was selected in the first attempt into the Indian Police Service (IPS). After joining the service for a few days, he resigned and appeared for the IAS next year and was selected, but before the results were declared, he joined politics and became a Member of the Legislative Council (MLC). When the results were declared, he was recommended for appointment in the IAS. He was in a great dilemma whether to join the IAS or to continue in politics as MLC. It was commonly believed that he requested the Department of Personnel and Training (DOPT), Government of India to give him a year's time before he could decide whether he should continue in politics or join the IAS. It is said that a reply came very promptly from a Section Officer, Department of Personnel and Training (DOPT) that "IAS is meant for people who take decisions and if you are unable to decide, you would do well to continue to be in politics!!" Dr. Jichkar wisely opted to stay in politics and became a Minister of State within a few months.

I had the proud privilege of working with such an enlightened young Minister, who was full of vigour and enthusiasm. Dr. Jichkar was highly talented and intelligent and believed in acquiring as much knowledge as possible, on every possible subject on earth. He was a good orator in English, Marathi and Hindi and could argue with confidence, quoting voluminous information, full of facts and figures on any subject. His analytical discourses on the country's annual budgets were next only to those of such eminent personalities like Nani Palkhiwala. He was also an avid photographer. He published several books, including one with photographs taken by him. He was also an excellent cook and took immense pleasure in inviting officers to his home and treat them with delicacies cooked by him. Above all, he was a great human being. He was and is a great inspiration and a role model to the youth. He was for long the most eligible bachelor, and indeed the story goes that the Chief Minister Babasaheb Bhosle wanted him to marry his daughter and therefore made him a Minister of State, with the charge of nearly a dozen departments, including Finance, Planning and General Administration. During Bhosle's time, Dr. Jichkar was dubbed, and not without reasons, the de facto CM! However, Dr. Jichkar remained a bachelor for quite some time.

His passion for acquiring Degrees could be gauged from the fact that once during the Assembly Session in Nagpur, he mentioned to me that I should persuade the Minister of Energy to answer the questions in the Assembly in one afternoon, on his behalf, as he had to appear for University examination for acquiring his next degree!!

Dr. Jichkar having joined politics was like a KTP or "Keen Type Probationer" (KTP is a popular word in National Academy of Administration, Mussoorie) and used to study all matters in great detail. He made very useful contributions to the energy sector, especially in the management of the MSEB. As Dr. Jichkar hailed from Nagpur, he used to visit the city very frequently and take the Board's employees to task for their lapses, often antagonizing them. They retaliated, at times, by managing to cut the power supply for his functions and to his house, making his blood pressure rise by a few notches. However, he used to take such sabotage in his stride as an occupational hazard.

Dr. Jichkar was a very polite and friendly person. He was an extrovert and optimist, undaunted by the many setbacks that he had to face during his short career. Afflicted by cancer in the early 2000's, he conquered the ailment with extraordinary will power and courage all the way through super-specialty hospitals in the U.S.A. Jealous internal party subversions plagued him throughout, resulting in his defeats in the Parliamentary polls from Bhandara constituency earlier, and from Ramtek in 2004, both by very narrow margins. Never daunted by defeat, Dr. Jichkar went ahead with his public functions. While being driven back to Nagpur from Amravati after one such programme in early June 2004, he met with a ghastly accident, leaving his friends and admirers like me and my Joint Secretary Arun Patankar in inconsolable grief.

I was ably assisted by Arun Patankar, IAS, as Joint Secretary in the department, who subsequently retired at Secretary to the State Government. Arun, an outstanding officer was selected into IAS from the State quota. He had total mastery over English and could articulate brilliantly, using his command in English to perfection in his notings even on intricate and complex matters. He had great analytical ability and his examination of issues in the MSEB were very thorough and unambiguous. He was a great asset to the Department and I was immensely benefited by his services.

The Energy Wing of the Industries, Energy and Labour Departments, were headed by the Secretary (Energy), which meant dealing with the working with the Maharashtra State Electricity Board, other electricity supply licensees, such as the Tata Electric Company (TEC), Bombay Electric Supply and Transport (BEST) and the Bombay Suburban Electric Supply Company (BSES). All these companies distributed power in Bombay and therefore coordination on matters pertaining to these organizations on generation, transmission and distribution of power was essential. The Department also dealt with formulation and implementation of the state energy policy, preparation of annual and five year plans and monitoring and coordinating of work of all organizations. It also dealt with the Maharashtra Energy Development Agency which was entrusted with the promotion of non-conventional energy sources. As Secretary (Energy), I supervised the work of the Chief Engineer (Electrical). Extensive studies were undertaken to explore the possibilities of Energy Conservation in Industry.

SUBSTANTIAL INVESTMENTS IN POWER SECTOR

Considering the importance of the Power Sector in accelerating agricultural and industrial promotion and socio-economic development, the State Government accorded high priority to power development programmes. An outlay of Rs. 3,050 crores was provided in the Seventh Plan (1985-90) for the Power Sector, which worked to 29 per cent of the total approved outlay of the Seventh Five Year Plan for the State.

EFFORTS TO MOBILIZE ADDITIONAL FUNDS

As the Power Sector was highly capital intensive with long gestation periods for projects before their completion, I continued to plead for additional allocation of funds in the Budget for this sector. However, it was always a tough task to convince the Finance Department, which was then headed by Madhav Godbole, Principal Secretary, Finance Department, who was strict in managing the scarce financial resources of the state. Although Godbole was generally considerate to the needs of the power sector for additional allocation, as he earlier functioned as Chairman, MSEB, the competing demands from various departments did not permit him to make all the additional allocations needed for it. I was once making a presentation to the state Cabinet at Nagpur when the Assembly was in session for allocation of additional funds, as there was a big gap between demand and supply of power, resulting in load shedding, low voltage, frequent interruptions and breakdowns. Any delay in investments would seriously affect the development of the sector, and consequently the state, in the long run. Godbole vehemently opposed any additional allocation due to paucity of funds, in the Cabinet meeting. But as luck would have it, there was a power failure when the discussion was going on in the Cabinet. I mentioned that unless additional provisions were made, the power situation was going to be similar in the entire state. S B Chavan, Chief Minister, smilingly mentioned, "I know Abraham that you have organized the interruption of power to prove your point. In spite of that, the Cabinet approves your proposals for additional funds!" The Chief Minister was fully aware of the requirements of funds for such a vital sector, which would be amply demonstrated by his appreciation of the needs of the power sector in the development of the state.

Ways and means were devised to improve the internal resources of the MSEB to earn 3 per cent return on capital as envisaged in the Electricity Supply Act. A detailed review was done to explore the possibilities for raising resources and the approval of the State Government for these proposals were obtained.

GENERATION

At the beginning of the Sixth Plan in 1980, the installed capacity in the state was 3,316 MW and it was targeted to add 3,345 MW capacity, thus raising the total capacity at the end of Sixth Plan (1980-85) to 6,661 MW. However, a total capacity of 2,762 MW was added during the period, bringing the total installed capacity at the end of Sixth Plan to 6,078 MW, comprising 1,293 MW (21 per cent) from Hydro Projects, 4,385 MW (72 per cent) from Thermal Projects and 400 MW from others (7 per cent) (160 MW from Tarapur Atomic project and 240 MW from Gas Turbine Units). During the Seventh Plan period (1985-90), it was targeted to add 2,337 MW generation capacity, taking the capacity to 8,415 MW by the end of Seventh Plan. During 1985-86, an additional capacity of 862 MW was added. The MSEB was operating 8 Hydro, 7 Thermal and one Gas Turbine Power Stations. Although it was generally accepted that the MSEB was one of the better managed State Electricity Boards in the country, there was still vast scope for improvement in Generation, Transmission, Distribution and Inventory control. I used to periodically review and monitor the major critical parameters of its functioning so that the performance of the MSEB could be improved. I reviewed the implementation of generation projects so as to ensure the completion of the projects on schedule. The Government had submitted several new projects to the CEA and Planning Commission for their approval, namely, Kharperkheda TPS extn. Unit 3 and 4 (2 × 210 MW); feasibility report for Parli 'C' station (2 × 210 MW); feasibility reports for Gas Turbine Extension (900 MW); Chandrapur Unit 7 (1 × 500 MW); Ujani I (2 × 500 MW); Bhusaval B. (Hatnur) (3 × 500 MW); feasibility report for Dabhol I and II (2 × 210 MW, 3 × 210 MW); project Report for Umred TPS (2 × 210 MW); Waste Heat Recovery Plant (3 × 120 MW). The 5th unit of 210 MW at Parli was commissioned during 1987-88 and 500 villages were electrified and 60,000 pump-sets were energised during 1987-88. The State Government requested Government of India to set up a Super Thermal Power Station (1 × 500 MW) in Chandrapur.

I used to pursue the proposals to obtain necessary clearances for these projects from the Central Electricity authority (CEA) and Planning Commission and various organizations of the Government of India. The Thermal Stations were functioning with precariously low stocks of coal. I followed up with the Ministry of Energy, Department of Coal, Coal India Ltd. and Western Coal Fields to ensure that the generation did not suffer from inadequate supply of coal.

TRANSMISSION

Transmission lines, along with associated substations, form an essential link between power stations and load centres and had a vital role to play in the integrated operation of the power systems. Maharashtra had one of the largest power transmission systems in the country and the MSEB had been planning and implementing several schemes of the various voltages from 33 kv to 400 kv. Periodical reviews were taken to assess the progress of the schemes and to coordinate with other Departments of the State, for early completion of these schemes.

IMPLEMENTATION OF THE 20-POINT PROGRAMME

As per point 19 of New 20-Point Programme, 1986, of the Government of India, it was necessary to provide energy for the villagers; expand the supply of electricity for productive use in villages; develop alternative sources of energy, particularly bio-gas; and promote integrated area specific programme for rural energy. Periodical reviews were taken to ensure that both the MSEB and MEDA achieved the targets required under the 20-Point Programme.

RURAL ELECTRIFICATION

In Maharashtra, out of 39,354 inhabited villages (as per 1981 Census), 34,068 towns and villages were electrified and 10,15,855 pumps were energised as on 31st March 1986. During 1986-87, 1987-88 and 1988-89, it was targeted to electrify 500 villages and to energise 60,000 pumps each year. All targets were more than achieved. An outlay of Rs. 22 crores was provided for the removal of regional imbalances and was utilized for accelerating the pace of electrification of villages and energisation of additional pump sets in the districts.

SPECIAL COMPONENT PLAN FOR DALIT BASTIES

The special component plan basically covered electrification of dalit basties and provided free domestic connections to the scheduled castes and neo-Buddhists. As a policy, whenever a gaothan was electrified, dalit basties in the villages were also taken up for electrification. Upto the end of March 1986, 27,852 Dalit basties were electrified in the state. During the year 1986-87, 1987-88 and 1988-89 it was targeted to electrify 800 harijan basties each and the same was overachieved.

FREE DOMESTIC CONNECTIONS

MSEB has been implementing a special programme of giving free domestic connections to the scheduled castes, scheduled tribes, vimukta jatis and neo-Buddhists from 2nd October 1976. Up to the end of March 1986, about 4,12,846 connections were given. It was targeted to give additional 20,000 connections to the scheduled castes and neo-Buddhist during 1986-87, 1987-88 and 1988-89 and the Board exceeded these targets.

TRIBAL SUB-PLAN

Special emphasis was given for electrification of tribal villages. There are 6,534 villages, including 491 uninhabited villages in the Tribal Sub-Plan area, out of which 4,641 tribal villages were electrified upto March 1986. The number of pump sets energized in the tribal areas was 39,920 till end of March 1986. During the years 1986-87, 1987-88 and 1988-89, it was targeted to electrify 200 tribal villages and energise1500 pump sets in the Tribal Sub-Plan area each year and the same was achieved

DEVELOPMENT OF NON-CONVENTIONAL AND RENEWABLE SOURCES OF ENERGY

Development of non-conventional and renewable sources of energy was given high priority by the Government of India and was a part of the 20-point Programme. With a view to having a coordinated approach and institutional support, the State Government established an independent agency named Maharashtra Energy Development Agency (MEDA) in July 1985. The role of the Agency was to plan, coordinate, supervise, monitor and evaluate various non-conventional energy schemes. Efforts were made to obtain maximum financial assistance from the Government of India, by proposing specific projects relating to wind energy, solar energy, biogas, biomass and urja gram. As the Agency was in a formative stage, it was necessary to give continuous guidance and advice, so that it could be an effective instrument for promoting and developing Non-conventional Renewable Sources of Energy.

A project on setting up a wind farm for power generation at Deogad, District Sindhudurg, was approved by the Government of India, while 17 major projects were sanctioned for installation of large bio-gas plants. The Centrally Sponsored Scheme, "National Project on Demonstration of Improved Chulha", was launched throughout the country from February 1984, with the aim of using these improved chulhas in place of conventional chulhas, thus making the entire village smokeless. Intensive efforts were made to promote improved chullahs in the State.

Several measures were devised to improve the internal resources of the MSEB to earn 3 per cent return on capital as envisaged in the Electricity (Supply) Act, 1948. A detailed review was done to explore the possibilities for raising resources and obtain the approval of the State Government. The tariff revision proposals submitted by the MSEB were got approved from the Cabinet to augment resources of MSEB.

ESTABLISHMENT OF PRIVATE GENERATION PROJECT BY BSES

I played a major role in establishment of private power project by BSES. The Bombay Suburban Electric Supply Limited (BSES), the present Reliance Energy Limited (REL), was granted, a Bombay Suburban Electric Licence 1926 under Indian Electricity Act, 1910, to supply electrical energy to suburban area covering 384 sq km in Bombay. The License was granted for a period of 50 years. The first extension of 10 years was granted in the year 1976 and the Licence was to expire by 1986. There were several complaints from the consumers in the licensed area about inadequate and poor quality of supply of power. There was also a demand to revoke the licence and entrust the area to the MSEB, which was the main supplier of electricity in the entire state, excluding the suburban area supplied by BSES and some areas supplied by Bombay Electric Supply and Transport Limited (BEST) and a few consumers of Tata Electricity Company (TEC) in Bombay. The Government of Maharashtra also felt that there was a need for augmentation of electric supply in the state, and especially to Bombay, to ensure uninterrupted power supply. TEC was already given permission to expand generation capacity at Bombay and it was therefore considered essential that BSES should also have its own generation capacity, if they wanted to continue in power distribution. The licence of the BSES was extended in 1976 on the condition that it would create its own generation capacity to supply to its consumers. This matter of whether to extend or to cancel the license was discussed in several Cabinet meetings, and the Government forced the BSES to implement a generation project, failing which the license would be cancelled. As BSES finally agreed to implement a generation project, it was decided to insert "Clause A—Area of compulsory supply—compulsory works" in its License specifying that the Licensee shall on or before 2nd December 1986 should take adequate steps to the satisfaction of the state government to establish and commission a generation station of 500 MW capacity in Maharashtra and it should commence work for installation of generation station on or before June 1987 and take necessary steps for early commissioning of the project. It would be the responsibility of the Licensee to raise the required resources to set up the project. If the state government was convinced that the Licensee was not able to carry out the work to its satisfaction, the License would be revoked. The option for revocation of the License was to be exercised by the Government in June 1988. These conditions required regular follow-up with the Licensee and keeping the Cabinet informed. A monitoring Committee was appointed under my chairmanship to watch the progress made by the BSES and report to the Government from time to time. Periodical reviews were taken to ensure proper implementation of the project. As the Licensee finally set up a 500 MW power station at Dahanu, in compliance with the License conditions, the Government amended the License on 30th

May 1992, extending the License period till 15th August 2011. This was the beginning of the entry of the private sector in the power generation, which was launched at the national level in 1992. Similarly, assistance was given to the M/s. Tatas, whenever required, so that they could implement their sixth unit at Bombay.

After nearly 3 years in the Energy Department, I took over as Chairman, MSEB on 1 February 1989 and continued my association with the power sector.

SIXTEEN

ENVIRONMENT MANAGEMENT OF MAHARASHTRA

Secretary, Environment Department

Maharashtra is a highly industrialized state, but the enormous industrial growth brought in its wake several problems, the most important of which were water and air pollution. As industrial pollution had a deleterious effect on human and animal health, Maharashtra became the first State Government in the country to fully realize and recognize the importance of environmental protection and initiated several legal and administrative measures to preserve the environment by enacting Water Pollution Control Act, 1969. This Act, although it predominantly dealt with control of water pollution, also dealt partially with the problem of air pollution. Taking into consideration the dire need to prevent and preserve the environment, the State Government created the Environment Department for the first time in late 1985. I was appointed as Secretary, Environment Department in May 1986, holding the charge concurrently with Secretary, Energy Department, Government of Maharashtra.

Some of the functions entrusted to the Environment Department were the formulation and implementation of the State's environment policy, monitoring the work of the Maharashtra Pollution Control Board (MPCB), supervising the implementation of Environmental Protection Act, 1986, effective servicing of several Environmental Committees under the

Chairmanship of the Governor and Chief Secretary, granting environmental clearance to developmental projects after assessing the pollution potential and taking the required mitigating measures. In addition, I had to promptly dispose of those cases requiring environmental clearance as the Secretary was the Chairman, State Appraisal Committee. Obtaining environmental clearance for projects from the Government of India undertaking, massive environmental awareness campaigns, monitoring air quality, implementing the standards fixed for automobile emissions through the State Transport Department were also part of my duties as Secretary, Environment. This Department also worked closely with the Non-Governmental Organizations (NGOs).

The Government of Maharashtra established the Maharashtra Pollution Control Board (MPCB) as early as 1970. The Government of India legislated the Water (Prevention and Control) of Pollution Act in 1974. The Government of Maharashtra subsequently adopted the same as the Water (Prevention and Control) of Pollution Act, 1974, the Water Cess (Prevention and Control of Pollution) Act, 1977, and Air (Prevention and Control of Pollution) Act, 1981. The Board had notified the entire state as 'water pollution protection area'. Hence no new industry could be established nor expanded without the permission of the MPCB. The MPCB also prescribed the quality of the treated effluent and suggested the appropriate disposal arrangement. No permission to establish any new industry was granted, unless a 'No Objection Certificate' was obtained from MPCB, in order to control water pollution created by the industries. The Board had covered 6,900 industries by way of grant of 'consents' and prescribing norms for 'pollution control'.

Taking into consideration the expanding activities of the Board to control pollution of water and air, and in view of the growing importance of pollution control and environmental improvement, efforts were made to substantially increase the budget provisions. An outlay of Rs. 50 lakhs was provided during 1986-87 as against Rs. 20 lakhs provided in the previous year and the outlay was further increased to Rs. 65 lakhs during 1987-88. It was also proposed to increase the number of regional offices of MPCB in the State.

AIR POLLUTION CONTROL ACTIVITIES

It was decided to continue the Air Pollution Control Office and Laboratory at Belapur, Navi Mumbai. It was also decided to create new offices at Pune and Tarapur to take up air survey and air quality monitoring activities, to create flying squads for checking the leakages of gas by industries and to create vigilance squads for checking vehicular pollution.

Environmental Safety Committee

After the major calamity at Bhopal due to the leakage of poisonous methyl isocyanides gas from M/s. Union Carbide, there was tremendous environmental awareness and activism generated in the State, which had a high concentration of chemical industries. The Government constituted an "Environmental Safety Committee" under the Chairmanship of R.K. Garg from Bhabha Atomic Research Centre, Mumbai, to identify chemicals which were hazardous, highly toxic or explosive in nature and to check the existing safety measures and arrangements made for storage and handling of such hazardous chemicals, in addition to verifying whether the present safety and pollution control measures implemented by the firms were adequate. The Committee visited 52 major chemical industries in the state and made 468 recommendations. A "Standing Monitoring Committee" was appointed under the chairmanship of Dr. V.V. Kale, Additional Director of Industries, Mumbai, to ensure the compliance of the recommendations made by the "Environmental Safety Committee".

Krishna River Clean Up Programme

The Krishna river is one of the major rivers in India and its basin is the fourth largest river system in India, measuring 2, 59,000 sq. kms. The Krishna river flows through the states of Maharashtra, Karnataka and Andhra Pradesh, so the State Pollution Control Boards of these three states prepared comprehensive reports on the quality of the Krishna river waters, and the activities in the catchment area leading to pollution. A 'Joint Krishna River Clean Up Programme' was prepared by the State Pollution Control Boards of these three States. After a series of meetings at Bombay, Hyderabad and Bangalore, the Krishna river clean up Programme was prepared and sent to the Central Government for taking it up as a national programme along the lines of the Ganga Action Plan.

Declaration of Air Pollution Prevention Area

As per the provisions of the Air (Prevention and Control of Pollution)

Act, 1981, initially a few areas were declared as 'Air Pollution Prevention Areas' under the Act. Bombay Metropolitan Regional Development Authority (BMRDA), MIDC areas at Tarapur in Thane District and Roha in Kolaba District were declared as 'Air Pollution Control Areas' during 1983. Patalganga area in Kolaba District was brought under the Act during November 1986.

Vehicular Pollution

In accordance with the Bombay Motor Vehicles Amendment Rules, 1984, emission standards for petrol and diesel driven vehicles were introduced. These Rules were enforced from 1-5-1986 in the entire State, requiring all vehicles to obtain "Pollution Under Control" certificate every quarter. In order to implement these rules, a continuous follow up was done with vehicle manufacturers for self-certification schemes, as well as for carrying out improvements in vehicle designs for meeting the pollution standards. A mass education programme was also launched through advertisements and press conferences to increase public awareness on the matter.

BHATSA RIVER NOTIFICATION

The Bhatsa river is one of the major sources of water supply for Bombay. While sanctioning financial aid for the Bhatsa project, the World Bank laid down stringent conditions about pollution control measures to be taken by Government of Maharashtra. Due to availability of attractive industrial infrastructure like highways, railways, water, land and labour, the Bhatsa river basin was a preferred location for industrial development. It was, therefore, considered necessary to restrict industrial development in the catchment area of the Bhatsa river. A committee was appointed under the Chairmanship of Dr. A.K. Ganguli of BARC in 1986, which recommended the shifting of existing industries in the non-conforming area. A Committee under the Chairmanship of Dr. Chandaliya, UDCT, Mumbai was appointed to examine the pollution aspects of the existing units located in Bhatsa river basin. After taking into consideration the Ganguli and Chandaliya Committee Reports, the Government of Maharashtra imposed a ban on the industrial development in the vicinity of the river up to 3 kms from the river on both sides. Further, only small-scale non-polluting industries were allowed beyond the 3 kms but up to 5 kms belt on both sides of river. This decision helped the

Government to maintain the quality of the water supply of Mumbai Metropolitan city.

CLEARANCE OF POWER PROJECT OF BSES DAHANU

After the Bhopal tragedy, environment concerns were paramount in the public mind. Several Non-Governmental Organizations started working as environmental activist groups. A 500 MW coal based Thermal Power Plant was proposed to be set up at Dahanu, by the Bombay Suburban Electricity Supply (BSES) Company, to strengthen the power supply position to Bombay. Several environmental NGOs opposed this project. I had to hold a number of meetings with the environmental groups and the project proponents. Ultimately, environmental clearance was issued to the project by Ministry of Environment and Forests, Government of India, on the recommendations of the State Government, prescribing very strict environmental conditions. Flue Gas De-sulphurization (FGD) unit was one of the major conditions imposed in the environmental clearance. No other power plant in India at that time was required to provide such a pollution control system except for one unit of M/s. Tata Power Co. which was located in Bombay Metropolitan city.

As the Department was new, several administrative measures were taken to establish the department on a sound footing, which made working in it a highly rewarding experience.

SEVENTEEN

THE GLORY THAT WAS MSEB

Chairman, Maharashtra State Electricity Board (MSEB)

I was on tour to Delhi in the third week of January 1989 to participate in the Annual Plan discussions with Sharad Pawar, Chief Minister, Maharashtra and Sudhakarrao Naik, Minister (Energy). Sharad Pawar called me to his chamber in the Maharashtra Sadan, New Delhi and told me that he had decided to appoint me as Chairman, Maharashtra State Electricity Board, (MSEB), when the post was about to fall vacant on 1 February 1989. He also mentioned that he had discussed the matter with Sudhakarrao Naik, Minister (Energy) in the morning, in the presence of the Chief Secretary, K.G. Paranjpe and Principal Secretary (Finance) Madhav Godbole. Sudhakarrao Naik told him that he was himself planning to discuss the matter of my becoming Chairman, MSEB and he whole-heartedly welcomed my posting. He also mentioned that both Paranjpe and Godbole, who had earlier functioned as Chairman, MSEB, strongly supported my appointment to this post.

Sharad Pawar told me that the Board was presently going through a very difficult phase, with several problems such as power shortages, low voltage, interruptions, breakdowns, consumer complaints and managerial problems. Obviously, he was looking for an officer who could not only handle the matter firmly, but he should also be a person of absolute honesty and integrity. Sharad Pawar was confident that with my earlier background as Secretary, MSEB and experience as Secretary, Energy, I would be able to manage the Board efficiently and put it on a sound footing. The Chief Minister assured me of full freedom and total independence to enable me to show results and restore the Board to its past glory. Although I was delighted at the news, I was fully aware of the problems of the power sector in general, and MSEB in particular, having worked in the MSEB as Secretary, during 1969-72 and also as Secretary (Energy) from 1986-89. I had a deep insight in the working of the power sector. I was also conscious about the Chief Minister's concerns about the functioning of the Board during my tenure as Secretary (Energy), as he used to openly express his dissatisfaction about its functioning, and the complaints he was receiving from several quarters.

WORKING WITH SHARAD PAWAR, CHIEF MINISTER

Earlier, I never had an occasion to meet and interact with Sharad Pawar, when he was Minister (Agriculture) during 1974, while I was working as Joint Secretary (Industries) during 1975-77. When he became the Chief Minister for the first time in 1978, in the Progressive Democratic Front Government, I was away on central deputation as Regional Iron and Steel Controller, Hyderabad. He became the Chief Minister for the second time on 26th June 1988, when I was Secretary (Energy). All the Secretaries to the Government were required to call on the new Chief Minister and brief him about the functioning of their respective departments. When I called on him at the Sahyadri Guest House in Malabar hills and introduced myself, his reaction indeed amazed me. "You do not have to introduce yourself, as I have been watching your performance from outside the Government". said the Chief Minister. From the discussions that followed, I realized that Sharad Pawar had complete information about the functioning of the Energy Department, even though he was not in the Government.

Sharad Pawar hails from a farming family of Baramati in Pune District of Maharashtra. He started early in politics and became a Member, State Legislative Assembly, at the young age of 27 and joined the State Cabinet five years later. He became the Chief Minister of Maharashtra in 1978 at the age of 38, and that made him the youngest Chief Minister in the country. He carried the mantle of the Chief Minister of the State four times and proved to be an able administrator. During these years, Sharad Pawar spared no efforts to make Maharashtra the leading industrial hub in the country. Since he hailed from a farming family with a rural background, he realized the importance of the power sector for overall rapid economic development of the state, with particular focus on rural and agricultural development. He also believed in India becoming the South Asian and Pacific hub for the sunrise sectors of software production, telecommunications, bio-technology and information technology. He always believed that abundant availability of power at proper voltage and at affordable prices would help the state to develop.

I joined as Chairman, MSEB on 1st February 1989. The job of the Chairman, MSEB was acknowledged as highly taxing, thankless and extremely difficult, especially for an IAS officer who was considered as an 'outsider' by many employees of the Board. There was strong resistance by those who were aspiring to be the Chairman of the Board, since the post was generally held by officers from the technical stream of the Board for about 15 years, except for two years during 1976-78, when Madhav Godbole, IAS (1959) was Chairman, MSEB. Godbole, an outstanding officer from Maharashtra, known for his commitment, hard work, integrity and impartiality on all matters, had a bitter experience leading to his sudden exit from the Board. Contrary to my initial apprehensions, I had, fortunately, established an excellent rapport with all sections of employees in a very short time, as I worked with them closely as Secretary, MSEB two decades back.

Despite the fact that MSEB was the biggest and one of the best managed State Electricity Boards in the country, if not the best, it was commonly mentioned in a lighter vein, that MSEB stood for 'Monday to Sunday Electricity Bandh'. There were similar acronyms for other Electricity Boards also such as "Gupchup Electricity Bandh" for Gujarat Electricity Board (GEB) and "Maha Pasand Electricity Bandh" for "Madhya Pradesh Electricity Board"!

Maharashtra had, for long, remained the leading state in the country in the field of power generation, transmission and distribution, with an investment of about Rs. 6800 crores, the highest investment by any Board in the country. In spite of such heavy investment, it was difficult to meet the growing demand for power, with inadequate power supply leading to large-scale power cuts, especially during summer. The Board had invested nearly 60 per cent of the Sixth and Seventh Five-Year Plan outlays in establishing generation capacities and only the balance amount was spent for extending and strengthening the transmission and distribution network. As a result, adequate funds were not available for augmenting the transmission and distribution system. The Board therefore decided to give more emphasis to T & D and system improvement programmes to improve consumer services. To meet the growing demand, the Board had adopted several measures, including addition to generation capacity, renovation and modernization of existing plants, improvement in various generation efficiency parameters such as plant load factor, improvement in the availability factor etc.

MANAGING THE SHORTAGES

In spite of huge investments in the sector, the power shortages, low voltage, breakdowns, and transformer failures were regular problems in Maharashtra, which were the result of very low investments in the areas of transmission and distribution sectors for several years. The Board became the target of constant criticism due to unsustainable power cuts. The power industry was highly capital intensive with long gestation periods for setting up any new generation projects and in the short run, one could only manage the shortages, with least inconvenience to various categories of consumers. These problems were further aggravated whenever there were bad monsoons, resulting in less hydro power generation, leading to imposition of power cuts on all consumers, including essential consumers, in varying degree. Bad monsoons also resulted in scarcity conditions, which increased the demand for more power.

Talking about scarcity conditions due to shortage of rainfall, I recall, V. Ranganathan (IAS—65), who was Secretary (Relief) for several years and subsequently retired as Chief Secretary to the State Government. He was very knowledgeable about how to deal with scarcity matters, as he had been holding charge for several years. The joke in the corridors of Mantralaya was that as long as Ranganathan continued as Secretary (Relief), the scarcity conditions in Maharashtra would never end and the best way to get relief from the scarcity was to shift Ranganathan from the post of Secretary (Relief)!

GENERATION CAPACITY AUGMENTATION

The MSEB had an installed capacity of 6346 MW, the highest among all State Electricity Boards at the end of 1988-89, which increased to 7503 MW by the end of 1991-92. One of the first tasks after joining as Chairman on 1st February 1989 was to review the progress of generation projects, targeted for commissioning during the Seventh Five Year Plan ending in 1989-90. One of the priority tasks which needed considerable follow-up work was the scheduled synchronization of the first extension unit of 210 MW at Khaperkheda Thermal Station which was due for commissioning before 31-3-1989. The MSEB had the reputation of ensuring the commissioning of projects, according to the targets. I had to make frequent visits in February and March to Khaperkheda to hold intensive reviews with BHEL, the suppliers of equipment, to expedite the completion of critical works. Thus it was ensured that the first unit of Khaparkheda was synchronized by 26th March 1989. During the year 1989-90, the Khaparkheda extn. Unit 2 (210 MW) was also synchronized.

During the Seventh Five Year Plan (1985-90), it was planned to add 2377 MW in the state generation capacity, including 1482 MW by the Board. The planned addition to the generation capacity of 500 MW was also achieved during 1990-91. By commissioning all the targeted projects, both by the Board and M/s Tata, the state was able to achieve the target of 2337 MW during the Seventh Five Year Plan, thus reaching an installed capacity of 8368 MW.

I also pursued vigorously the generation projects proposed to be added beyond the Seventh Plan, which were at various stages of implementation, such as:

(i) Chandrapur units 5 and 6 (500 MW each) planned to be commissioned by 1990-91 and 1991-92, respectively.

(ii) The works on Waste Heat Recovery Plant units I and II (120 MW each) at Uran gas power station which were commenced in the year 1990-91, with the assistance of bilateral credit from West Germany.

(iii) The Planning Commission approvals were obtained for Uran Waste Heat Recovery Unit 3 (120 MW) and Khaparkheda extn. Units 3 and 4 Stage II (2 × 210 MW) and action was taken to start the work expeditiously.

(iv) Techno-economic clearance was obtained from the Central Electricity Authority's for setting up the Chandrapur Unit 7 (500 MW), and the investment decision from the Planning Commission and the environmental clearance were being pursued.

FIRST 500 MW UNIT OF SEB COMMISSIONED

The credit for commissioning the first 500 MW unit by any State Electricity Board in the country went to the MSEB, when it commissioned the 500 MW unit at Chandrapur Thermal Power in Station in March 1991. The unit was synchronized in a record period of 40 months. The next unit of 500 MW was in an advanced stage of construction and was commissioned during March 1992. The third unit of 500 MW for the Chandrapur Thermal Power Station was also posed to World Bank for financial assistance, as the World Bank was already providing financial assistance for the first two 500 MW units at Chandrapur. Due to the timely steps taken by the Board to increase generation capacity, the peak demand of a maximum 6,828 MW during the year 1991-92, compared to a peak demand of 5883 during 1989-90, could be met.

IMPROVEMENT IN PERFORMANCE OF GENERATION PROJECTS

There was substantial improvement in all performance parameters of the Board during this period. Generation during the 1989-90 was higher to that of 1988-89 by 12 per cent. The PLF of 59 per cent showed an improvement of about 5 per cent as compared to the previous year. *This is the highest PLF achieved in the Board till then.* Highest peak demand of 6828 MW was satisfactorily met by the Board and the generation targets fixed by the Planning Commission and Central Electricity Authority were exceeded. The average availability factor of all the thermal power stations was about 75 per cent in 1990-91 as against 72 per cent in the previous year.

TASK FORCE FOR IMPROVING PLANT PERFORMANCE (KUKDE COMMITTEE)

As there was considerable scope for improvement in the performance of generating units at various thermal power stations, a Task Force headed by Kukde, Chief Engineer, who was one of our best engineers, was constituted for recommending short and long term measures for better performance. The Task Force prepared a comprehensive report for Koradi, Chandrapur, Parli, Bhusaval and Nasik Thermal Power Stations and recommended Renovation and Modernization by retrofitting new equipment which were of better design and superior performance. Suggestions were made for short and long term measures which would improve the performance. Based on these recommendations, the Board prepared several R & M schemes for these power stations to be implemented during the Eighth Five Year Plan. In addition, the Board also appointed Parthasarathy, an outside Expert, who retired as Member, Andhra Pradesh SEB (who subsequently became Chairman, APSEB), for giving suggestions for improving performance of all the generation units in the Board. Appropriate action was initiated on the basis of these recommendations.

MOBILIZATION OF FUNDS

One of the major tasks for the Chairman was to convince the Government about the need to make substantial investments every year, as the entire sector was dependent on Government funds and meagre internal resources of the Board, due to unremunerative tariffs. Maharashtra was fortunate to have Sharad Pawar as Chief Minister, as he was committed to improving the power supply position in the State and was very keen to improve the performance of the MSEB, as he fully recognized the importance of electricity for the overall development of the state. Since he gave whole-hearted support in this regard, finance was never a problem to undertake new projects.

Maharashtra was also fortunate to have Sushilkumar Shinde as Finance Minister, who had the unique distinction of being the Finance Minister of the State for more than nine years. He too was committed to ensuring that Maharashtra continued to remain at the forefront as the industrial and economic hub of the country. Whenever I approached him for more funds for the energy sector, he always smilingly obliged.

EFFORTS TO OBTAIN EXTERNAL AID

Biggest World Bank Loan for a State Project

I led a delegation to the World Bank to negotiate a loan of U.S. $400 million (about Rs. 680 crores) for the Koyana Hydro Electric project stage IV and transmission and distribution schemes in Washington in April 1989 and succeeded in obtaining the amount after tough negotiations. *This was the biggest loan sanctioned to any single State project in the country by the World Bank till then.*

Chandrapur 5, 6 and 7 Units of 500 MW Each

The Board had been tapping multilateral funding agencies like the World Bank (WB) and Asian Development Bank (ADB) due to paucity of funds from the State Budget. In view of the excellent performance of the Board, the World Bank had sanctioned a loan of $ 300 million for Chandrapur units 5 and 6 of 500 MW each. The work on both these units were in full swing and Unit 5 was synchronised in March 1991 while I was the Chairman. Unit 6 was commissioned in September 1991, just after I relinquished charge. The Board's persistent efforts to add more generation capacity paid dividends in getting the approval of the Planning Commission in February 1991, for implementation of the Chandrapur unit 7 of 500 MW capacity. The Board persuaded the Government of India to obtain the Second Maharashtra Power Project Loan from the World Bank. I visited the World Bank, Washington several times to mobilize additional loans for the MSEBs.

German Credit for Uran Project

The West German Government had sanctioned a mixed credit loan of DM 198 Million (Rs. 198 crores) for 2 × 120 MW capacity Waste Heat Recovery units being installed at Uran. I had also taken up the matter with KFW, the German Bank for an additional loan of DM 112 Million (Rs. 112 crores). I visited KFW, Germany twice with a team of experts and convinced the KFW for the additional loan. The German Government had advanced bilateral credit of DM 310 Million (Rs. 372 crores) for the Uran Waste Heat Recovery units of 2 × 120 MW capacity during 1990-91. The MSEB had placed a turn key contract on M/s Siemens, Germany, for the supply of the plant and equipment for DM 290 million (Rs. 340 crores) and on M/s Siemens India Ltd. for supply of the indigenous portion for Rs. 79 crores. The project was under implementation when I left the Board.

Renovation and Modernisation of Thermal Projects

Even though the MSEB power stations have been giving better Plant Load Factor (PLF) than the national average PLF and also better than many SEB's, there was still considerable scope for improving not only the PLF but also other performance parameters, as some of the units had become old and were in need of Renovation and Modernisation (R & M). Intensive efforts were made to complete Phase—I R & M programme meant for old thermal generating units at Koradi, Bhusaval, Nasik and Paras Thermal Power Stations. The Board also submitted R & M schemes estimated at a cost of about Rs. 200 crores under Phase—II R & M programme to be implemented during the Eighth Five Year plan, which were approved by the Central Electricity Authority and Planning Commission. The schemes were partly financed from a savings of Rs. 68.00 crores from the World Bank loan of Chandrapur and partly from the Power Finance Corporation.

Private Sector Participation

I was keen to encourage power generation in the private sector, as Government funds alone would not be adequate to create additional generation capacity in the State. The Tata Electric Supply Company (TEC) and the Bombay Suburban Electric Supply Company (BSES) (now Reliance Energy Ltd), two private sector companies, were already in the power sector in Maharashtra. The TEC were into both generation and distribution in Bombay for a long time, but the main distribution network was with the BSES in the suburbs and the Bombay Electric Supply and Transport Undertaking (BEST), in the main metropolitan area. It was felt that by encouraging the TEC to expand their generation capacity and BSES to establish its own generation capacity, the state could get the much needed additional generation capacity, without adversely affecting the MSEB. TEC were given a license for putting up a pumped storage hydro-project and an additional 500 MW thermal project at Trombay (Bombay). The license of BSES was also extended to enable the company to implement its 500 MW generation project.

While the Government of India was seriously considering the opening of power generation to the private sector, the Board, in order to mobilize additional funds, proposed to the Government of Maharashtra to invite the private sector participation in the proposed new projects. Accordingly, in September 1990, the Government of Maharashtra offered the Khaparkheda Thermal Project (2 × 210 MW—estimated to cost Rs. 750 crores) and Nagothane Gas based Combined Cycle Gas Turbine Project (820 MW—estimated to cost Rs. 900 crores) for private sector participation. Pre-qualification bids from prospective entrepreneurs were invited in November 1990 and were under examination with the Government of Maharashtra, when I demitted the Office of Chairman, MSEB.

National Productivity Awards for Thermal Power Stations

It had become routine for the MSEB power stations to obtain the meritorious cash awards from the Government of India, year after year due to the excellent overall performance of its power stations. Chandrapur during 1989 and 1990; Koradi in 1989 and 1990; Bhusaval in 1989, 1990 and 1991 and Nasik in 1991 received meritorious productivity awards for their performance for individual Power Stations. I received these awards personally during the Conference of Energy Ministers held during 1989 and 1990. History repeated itself during 1991 and thereafter.

TRANSMISSION SCHEMES

Emphasis on Extra High Voltage Transmission Schemes

HVDC Link between Chandrapur and Padghe (Bombay)

The Board had envisaged construction of a + 500 KV, 1500 MW High Voltage Direct Current (HVDC) transmission link between Chandrapur Thermal Power Station and Padghe near Bombay over a distance of around 700 km. This link was required for evacuation of power generated at Chandrapur Power Station as well as Maharashtra's share of power from NTPC's Thermal Power Station at Korba in Madhya Pradesh, which would be delivered at Chandrapur. Due to concerted follow-up, the project was given techno-economic clearance by the Central Electricity Authority and Planning Commission. The NTPC and Hydro Quebec International, Canada were appointed as consultants for preparation of technical specifications for the project.

Efforts were on to have financial tie-up, so that construction of the link could be taken up immediately.

400 Kv Transmission Schemes

The Board constructed and commissioned 1645 ckt. km. of 400 kv transmission lines from Koradi to Kalwa and from Koradi to Chandrapur along with associated 400 kv substations. The Board also undertook work on 400 kv Chandrapur–Parli–Lonikand–Bombay Double Circuit scheme, so that there would be a parallel line for evacuation of power from Chandrapur.

Strengthening Distribution Network

The peak demand reached during the year 1990–91 was 6448 MW, an increase of 10 per cent over the previous year's peak demand of 5883 MW. This demand was satisfactorily met by the Board. To meet this continuously increasing demand of power, the Board had been continuously making investments in Generation, Transmission and Distribution schemes. With a view to further strengthen the transmission and distribution network and thereby improve the quality of electricity supply, the Board had taken up an ambitious programme of laying transmission lines and commissioning EHV substations. During the year 1990-91, the MSEB had commissioned, 1,142 circuit km. of 400 kv lines, an increase of 100 per cent during the year, taking the total of 400 kv lines to 2,188 ckt. km; 21 EHV substations with a total transformation capacity of 812 MVA; and augmentation by 832 MVA of transformation capacity of existing EHV substations. For financing these major capital works, the Board had obtained funds from the World Bank—$170 Million (Rs. 290 crores), Power Finance Corporation and other sources.

During the year 1991-92, the Board installed and commissioned 379 ckt. km of 400 kv transmission lines and 617 ckt. km. of EHV, other than 400 KV transmission lines. It also installed and commissioned 16 new EHV substations with additional transformation capacity of 394 MVA. In addition to this, 1000 MVA were added by way of augmenting the capacities of the existing EHV substations. With these measures, the Board could strengthen the distribution network, improve the quality of supply and reduce the problems of low voltages in several pockets of the state. All these programmes were implemented through generation of internal resources, Plan Funds, open market borrowings, loans from the R.E.C., P.F.C., NABARD, UTI, HDFC and other financial institutions, including the World Bank.

138 New 33 Kv Substations in a Year—A Record for Any State

With a view to overcoming the endemic problem of low voltage in various pockets of the state and improve the quality of supply, the Board undertook and implemented an ambitious programme of strengthening the distribution network. During 1990-91, a total of 138 new 33 kv sub-stations were set up compared to a mere 32 added in 1987-88, 46 in 1988-89 and 60 substations in 1989-90, which was equal to the number of substations commissioned during the previous three years. It was a record for any SEB in the country. In addition to commissioning the maximum number of 33 kv substations and EHV substations, augmentation of transformer capacities of 68 existing substations was undertaken. The Board also constructed and commissioned 1,548.47 circuit kms of 33/22 kv subtransmission lines during 1990-91, which was more than twice the work done during 1989-90. A remote controlled 33/11 kv substation at Naigaon in Nasik District was set up and after watching its performance, many more unmanned 33/11 kv substations were started.

Mobilization of Resources for Transmission Schemes

Resource constraint is a major bottleneck in timely completion of transmission and distribution projects of vital importance. Special sustained efforts were, therefore, made to bridge the gap between available resources and requirements. Important achievements in this direction were as followed:

World Bank Finance

The World Bank has sanctioned a loan of 400 million Dollars (about Rs. 680 crore) for the Koyana Hydro Electric Project stage IV and Transmission and Distribution scheme under Maharashtra Power Project. This was one of the largest loans sanctioned by the World Bank to any state project in India. Some transmission schemes from the first three years programme of Eighth Five Year Plan were selected for execution under this loan. During 1990-91, the Board succeeded in securing an additional loan of Rs. 290 crores for Transmission schemes from the World Bank.

Power Finance Corporation (PFC)

During 1989-90, the MSEB secured PFC assistance of Rs. 42 crores for the 400 kv double circuit Chandrapur—Parli—Lonikand—Padghe—Kalwa Project. The Project was made operational in March 1991.

Rural Electrification

100 Per cent Village Electrification

31st March 1989 was a day of special significance for me, as I knew the importance of village electrification, having studied in a village with the help of hurricane lamp, due to the lack of electricity. It was also a red letter day for the State of Maharashtra, and the MSEB in particular, as the Board had achieved 100 per cent village electrification. During the year, a record number of 1,236 villages were electrified. Thus the total number of inhabited villages and towns electrified as on 31-03-1989 were 39,413 out of 39,661 inhabited villages and towns in the state. The remaining 248 villages were under submergence and were uninhabited.

Highest Number of Pumps Energized in Any State

The Board energized a record number of 1,52,803 agricultural pump sets of which 52,000 pumps were energized during the first 2 months of my tenure as Chairman, in 1988-89, which was the highest number of pumps energized by any Electricity Board in any year. The Board energized a total of 5,67,000 agricultural pumps during the Seventh Five-Year Plan period against the target of 2,93,000. The Board had also energized 3, 00,000 agricultural pump sets during 1989-90, 1990-91 and 1991-92 as against a target of 2,00,000 pump sets. The total numbers of agricultural pumps energised in the State had gone up to 17,03,161 as on 31 March 1992, which was the highest in the country for any state. The Board continued its efforts towards reaching electricity to more and more consumers throughout the state and concessions extended to various sections like agriculturists, weaker sections and power looms were continued.

Reduction in T & D Losses

Transmission and distribution losses in Maharashtra were lower compared to the losses in other states and the All India average. The Board made every effort to minimize the losses further. In order to reduce the losses and give uninterrupted power supply with proper voltage, many 'system improvement schemes', numbering over 170 for rural and urban areas were implemented, including a programme of commissioning of 1,086 MVAR shunt capacitors at a cost of over Rs. 46 crores. The Board sanctioned 5 Urban Renovation schemes for Rs. 210 crores and sent them to the World Bank for financial assistance. The Board submitted 'Integrated System Improvement Projects' for seven districts in Maharashtra at a cost of about Rs. 250 crores to the REC for availing the financial assistance under Japanese and Asian Development Bank credit. During 1990-91, 50 schemes for conservation of energy were submitted to the R.E.C. for financial assistance. A special drive was launched for combating low voltages in the system.

Urja Mitra

A forum for redressal of consumer grievances, "Urja Mitra", was launched at Zonal, Circle and Divisional levels during 1990-91. The formation of this forum was very much appreciated by the consumers and several consumer grievances were redressed at the field level.

Special Action Plans for Tribal Districts

For rapid development of Gadchiroli District and some relatively underdeveloped areas of Chandrapur District, 'Special Action Plans' were successfully implemented by the Board. Similar Action Plans were implemented in Nanded, Dhule, Bhandara and Yeotmal Districts. Due to implementation of these special Action plans, all villages in these underdeveloped areas were electrified and programmes for energisation of agricultural pump sets were given a boost.

Electrification of Dalit Basties

Although the Board, as a matter of policy, invariably covered the electrification of Dalit Basti's, while sanctioning the electrification of the Gaothan (village inhabited area), efforts were intensified to take up the electrification of Dalit Basties and Wadis on a large scale. A total of 2,845 Dalit Basties were electrified during the period bringing the cumulative number of Dalit Basties electrified in the state to 33,440 as on 31 March 1991. The Board continued its policy of giving very high priority for electrification of Dalit Basties.

All Tribal Villages in the State Electrified

There are 6,043 inhabited tribal villages in the state. During the year 1989-90, the MSEB electrified a record number of 708 tribal villages bringing the total number of tribal inhabited villages electrified to 5,965. The remaining 78 tribal villages were either under submergence or were uninhabited. Thus, electricity reached all inhabited tribal villages in the state, achieving another landmark in the electrification programme. The MSEB also energised 5,677 agricultural pump sets in tribal areas during 1988-89, 5,702 pump sets during 1989-90 and 4,909 pump sets during 1990-91, bringing the cumulative number to 63,913.

Domestic Connections to Weaker Sections

Since 2nd October 1976, the Board was giving domestic connections without charging any service connection charges to weaker sections of society, namely, (1) Scheduled Castes, (2) Nav-Buddhists, (3) Scheduled Tribes, (4) Nomedic Tribes and (5) Vimukta Jatis. During 1989-90, a total of 62,354 connections and during 1990-91, a total of 60,079 connections were released. Thus a total of 6,44,414 connections had been released to the weaker sections so far.

Kutir Jyoti

Under 'Kutir Jyoti', a new programme launched by the Government of India for release of single point domestic connection to families 'below the poverty line' in rural areas, the Board released 22,300 connections with the help of REC during 1989-90. The cumulative total of connections under this programme including 30,600 connections released during 1990-91 was 52,900.

Encouragement to Non-Conventional Sources of Energy

The Board had established, on experimental basis, a Wind Farm at Deogarh in Sindhudurg District, with the assistance of the Government of India. The project, which was initially commissioned in 1986 with 10 Wind Mills, was further extended by installation of 10 more Wind Mill units during the year 1989-90. Under the DANISH AID programme, a Wind Electric Generator of 90 kW capacity was also commissioned during 1989-90 at Dahanu in Thane District.

Restoration Work after Flood Damage on 23 July 1989

During the night of 23 July 1989, heavy rains accompanied by gusty winds lashed most parts of Maharashtra, particularly affecting the Konkan area, resulting in uprooting of trees, flooding of rivers and causing land-slides and heavy damage to the electrical installations in 5,210 villages, thus plunging the area into darkness. Steps were taken on a war footing to restore the installations and supply of power. I had personally visited Raigadh District and supervised the restoration work. Four additional sub-divisions were diverted to the worst affected areas of Raigadh district. Massive diversion of men and material including poles, transformers, LT distribution boxes etc. was undertaken and restoration work was given the highest priority. Due to strenuous efforts of dedicated staff, restoration of normalcy in most of the villages was done in a record time. Supply to all the villages was restored within two days by working round the clock on a war footing, inspite of the fact that in Thane and Raigadh districts, work was done by carrying material on head-loads across the creeks. The speedy restoration had received public appreciation and Sharad Pawar, the then Chief Minister, complimented the Board in general, and the Chairman in particular, for the excellent work done. In view of the unprecedented floods in the state, all the employees voluntarily contributed a day's salary to the Chief Minister's Flood Relief Fund and a cheque of Rs. 1 crore was handed over by me to Sharad Pawar, Chief Minister.

Thrust to Improve Consumer Orientation

One of the major areas of concern was the regular complaints that the Board's officers hardly paid any attention to consumer complaints. These complaints related to wrong billing, excessive billing, delays in the issue of bills, failure to attend fuse calls and so on. Through a series of measures, I managed to convince the officers of the need for prompt redressal of the grievances of consumers and also to promptly follow up all complaints, especially those reported in the media. Keeping in view the aim of improving the services to the consumers, there was a shift in emphasis to T & D and System Improvement Programmes from generation projects.

Computerization of Billing

The Board had over 20 lakh 'low tension' consumers and over 7,000 high tension consumers. The Board had installed main frame computers at Bombay, Pune, Nagpur, Aurangabad and Kolhapur and more computers were proposed to be set up at other centres as well. The computerization of billing and accounting system was extended to over 4.60 lakh consumers during 1988-89, covering about 22.60 lakh by March 1989. All the 7,000 H.T. consumers were covered under computerized billing resulting in an increase in monthly revenue from H.T. consumers. The Board had also decided to increase the pace of computerization of billing in order to ensure early computerization of the entire billing system. The Board initiated measures for computerisation of personnel information system. This system covered 15,000 employees in the statewise seniority and all employees in the Head Office and would soon cover all employees of Board. It was also decided to introduce computerization in various activities of the Board and Consultants were appointed for the same. Computer training programmes were taken up regularly for training the employees. During 1989-90, the Board launched 'Quality Circles' in Pune and Kolhapur zones in the distribution side and at Parli Thermal Power Station on the Generation side. The scheme would be extended to the entire state in due course. Importance was given for training at various levels to optimize on human resource development. These measures substantially contributed to increasing the revenue from Rs. 1,972 crores in 1988-89 to Rs. 3,400 crores in 1990-91 and the highest revenue collection of 90 per cent out of assessment for the year.

WAGE REVISION SETTLEMENT

Cordial Industrial Relations

It was essential to involve all the employees of the Board to improve its performance. A comprehensive review of delegation of powers in all matters including technical, financial and administrative was done and more powers were delegated to all officers for better involvement, supervision, control and co-ordination. A number of improvements were also introduced in personnel polices and to redress genuine employee grievances, so that all continued to be committed to improve the Board's performance. Regular and frequent meetings with employee's organisation were done at different levels for redressal of their grievances and for maintaining harmonious relations and industrial peace.

The revision of pay scales of MSEB employees was due in 1990-91. In the initial stages, the Board had granted an amount equivalent to 21 days salary as interim advance, adjustable against arrears of pay fixation, at the time of revision of pay scales. There was no interruption either in generation or distribution during the period of negotiations. Industrial relations during the year continued to be cordial and dedicated efforts by the staff of the Board continued to maintain the premier position of the Board in the country.

The negotiations with Employees Unions in the past used to take place in the Mantralaya with Minister (Energy) and finalized by the Chief Minister. I was fortunate to have Sudhakarrao Naik, a pipe smoking and smartly attired politician with pragmatic approach as Minister (Energy). I also had a very dynamic Chief Minister in Sharad Pawar, who fully recognized the importance of the Board and gave me the freedom to negotiate and finalize the package. However, I kept the Government fully informed about the progress of negotiations and used to get a further mandate whenever the negotiations were getting stalled, especially on the overall financial package. Quite often during the negotiations, I found a big gap between the demands of the Unions and the package offered by me. At one stage, the Unions, out of desperation, threatened to negotiate directly with Shard Pawar. Indeed, they took an appointment with the Chief Minister, who I believe, had offered them a nice cup of tea but refused to talk anything about wage revision. He directed them to resume negotiations with the Chairman who had been authorized to negotiate and finalize the package. All the Union representatives restarted negotiations with me, having realized the futility of escalating negotiations at Government level. This development, in fact, also enhanced my own standing and respect with the Unions and the discussions were carried out continuously for days together till the wage revision was concluded at the Chairman's level itself. This contributed in improving the morale of the Board's employees and they realized that the Chairman was the right person for redressal of their grievances and that no purpose would be served by approaching the political bosses.

The negotiations continued for a long time. I am happy to recollect that on 29th January 1990 we decided to have continuous negotiations without a break till a final settlement was reached, irrespective of the time taken. There were always consultations among the Unions who took a short break, moved to the adjoining hall and coming back to resume negotiations. At one stage, we all felt that we were reaching the end of the negotiations and a final settlement would be reached by around

8 o'clock in the evening. However, the negotiations were prolonged endlessly. Then we realized that there were no restaurants open at that time to get us some food. So I rang up my wife to make as many 'rotis' as possible and dal. She was gracious enough to send these around midnight. We all had a simple but hot 'dal-roti' 'dinner' and the employees were very happy that the Chairman's wife could organize a simple but tasty meal for them even at midnight. The negotiations continued and at one point of time when I came out of my chambers to refresh myself, I found one of the highly respected and senior Union leaders resting in deep sleep on a bench out of tiredness. He was none other than venerable A.B. Bardhan, present General Secretary of the Communist Party of India (CPI). I had the good fortune in negotiating with enlightened and understanding Union leaders like A.B. Bardhan, A.M. Sathye and others, from whom I could learn the skills of negotiations, without losing my cool. The revision of pay scales concluded successfully on 29 January 1990 without any disruptions during the prolonged discussions for months. Nearly 1,15,000 regular employees and about 20,000 employees on nominal muster roll (NMR) were benefited by the wage settlement. It was a win-win settlement for all the stakeholders of the Board.

WELFARE ACTIVITIES, SPORTS AND CULTURAL ACTIVITIES

A 'Gym' in Board's Office

Among the several firsts achieved by the Board, I started first time a 'Gym' in the Board's office, for physical exercise and relaxation, for the tension filled employees of the Board. This idea of a 'Gym' was borrowed from the World Bank, when I observed during several visits to the Bank that many of the employees, during the lunch break, were either in the 'Gym or on the street jogging. The 'Gym' had become hugely popular after office hours. The staff welfare fund committee, constituted for recreation of the employees, sanctioned incentives for participation in drama competitions; awarded cash prizes; scholarships and special cash prizes to the wards of employees for securing higher percentage of marks in the examinations. The Board sanctioned grants to the staff sports and recreation clubs with a view to encouraging sports and recreational activities amongst the employees. The Board's teams participated in the sports events like athletics, cricket and bridge, sponsored by the All India Electricity Sports Control Board tournaments.

Human Resource Development Plan

The need for training at various levels in the Board had a bearing on human and material resources. The Board had launched the preparation of a detailed Human Resource Development plan, which would cover all aspects of training, manpower development and career planning with the help of consultants from the World Bank and other agencies.

FINANCIAL RESULTS

Fixed Assets

The Board's fixed assets including work in progress was of the order of Rs 6,715 crore at the end of 1988-89. As per the provisions of the Electricity (Supply) Act, 1948, the Board was required to achieve a minimum of 3 per cent return each year and the Board had always earned a positive return and earned above 3 per cent, while many Boards in the country were in negative ROR. The Government of Maharashtra had invested about 30 per cent of the State's overall plan in the power sector during the Eighth Plan, although it used to be higher earlier and was reduced due to competing demands from other sectors. The Board revised tariffs in May, 1990, to generate more resources for undertaking various schemes. The revenue of the Board, excluding R.E. Subsidy was Rs. 2,998 crores.

Action Plans for Various Sectors

With a view to making the organisation more consumer oriented and to meet the rising expectations of the consumers also to give a sense of commitment and participation in maintaining the lead as the premier Board in the country, Action Plans in Generation, Transmission and Distribution, Finance, Stores Management, Civil Construction, General Administration and Vigilance and Security were drawn up during 1990-91 and vigorously implemented.

Generation

- Increase Plant Load Factor (PLF)
- Improve Plant Availability by regular preventive maintenance and speedy restoration in case of breakdowns.
- Reduction in auxiliary consumption, fuel consumption, lubricants, stores and over time.
- Energy Conservation.

Transmission and Distribution

- Image Building by better service to consumer.
- Completion of targeted transmission lines and substations and installation of capacities.
- Ensure proper and regular meter reading and billing and collection to augment revenues.
- Proper inventory management.
- Reduce revenue arrears.
- Prevent theft of Energy.
- Control cost and effect economy.

Accounts and Finance

Improvements in this very important area were sought to be brought about by:

- Streamlining and implementing—Meter Reading, Billing and Collection Procedures; Prompt redressal of billing complaints and prompt recovery of arrears.
- Improving and expanding the computerized Billing.

Stores Management

- Quick finalisation of tenders.
- Economy in purchase of quality materials.
- Early elimination of Material at Site Account (MASA).
- Minimizing inventory level.

General Administration

- Speedy action on Employees' representation, holding Grievance Committee meetings regularly, finalizing and circulating seniority lists of all cadres.
- Backlog clearance for S.C., S.T., DT/NT and updating of roster registers.

Civil

- Maintaining updated list of all Civil Assets (Buildings, lands, etc.)—Record of rights, costs, usage etc.
- Timely completion of construction, maintenance, finalization and closure of contracts.

Vigilance and Security

- Building up of sources and collect information about corruption and other malpractices.
- Conducting special drives to detect theft of energy and prompt action into complaints of theft of energy.

FOURTEENTH WORLD ENERGY CONGRESS HELD AT MONTREAL, CANADA

The Fourteenth World Energy Congress was held in the first week of May 1989 at Montreal, Canada. It was held once in every three years and is recognized as the World's premiere multi-energy event, often attracting more than 5,000 delegates from all over the world, representing the energy industry, government, international organizations, academicians and others interested in sustainable energy development. The Congress featured a major energy exhibition, addresses by several recognized experts and round table conferences on major energy themes and issues. It was the first opportunity for me to attend such an International Conference. S Rajgopal, Secretary, Ministry of Power, Government of India led a big delegation representing various SEBs and private sector representatives, including the Tatas. I participated actively in the deliberations of the Congress at various sessions, which was organized on a huge exhibition ground in several multi-storied exhibition halls, in which exhibits from reputed manufacturing firms were displayed. Among many other things, I saw the giant screens for the first time in the conference halls. While I was addressing the gathering, I could see myself on giant screens all across the entire conference room, which made it a memorable experience. LCD presentation on huge screens have now become quite a common thing which was then a novelty.

VISIT TO EAST BERLIN THROUGH THE "ALLIED CHECKPOINT CHARLIE"

While I was working as the Chairman, Maharashtra State Electricity Board, I had an opportunity to visit Berlin for the first time during May 1989. The West Berlin and the East Berlin were separated by the famous Berlin Wall, an impregnable fortress with tight security. Obviously, I was keen to visit East Berlin too. All the visitors to East Berlin have necessarily pass through the "Allied Checkpoint Charlie" which was under the control of the United States. The sign board at the Checkpoint Charlie read as "visitors to the East Berlin should go with the permission of United States Forces". When I passed through "Checkpoint Charlie" the security checks were very strict and it was almost like an iron curtain as nobody knew what was happening on the other side of the wall as East Berlin was under the control of East Germany. When I crossed the checkpost and went to East Berlin on 18/05/1989. I thought that in the modern age, one cannot have a wall prohibiting the people from communicating with each other, even though they once belonged to the same country. When I returned to the West Berlin after a few hours visit to the East Berlin and after visiting all the beautiful historical monuments, I told my friends that the Berlin Wall would not last long in modern times and its fall was eminent. I did not realize at that time that the Berlin Wall would collapse in the next few months itself. I had another opportunity to visit Berlin immediately after the wall collapsed and had the opportunity of breaking the wall myself and brought a few rocks of the wall as souvenirs and exhibited in my drawing room.

During my first visit to Berlin, I was lucky to watch the German Open Tennis tournament, when Steffi Graf and Gabriel Sabatini, played the doubles tournament. Steffi Graf, subsequently, ruled the world as no. 1 tennis player for several years. I was also amazed to see a huge tennis court for the first time with sitting arrangement for thousands of spectators.

OUR FRIENDS IN BOMBAY

We stayed in Bombay for several years. We had very close friends with whom we spent memorable time. Notable among them are Upasanis, Jadhavs, Modis, Padmanabhans, Bhagwats, Makhijas, Balaramans, Bongirwars, Srinivasans, Padmanabhaiahs, Subrahmanyams, Gopalakrishnans, Vijay Paparaos etc. Their friendship made all the difference to our stay in Bombay.

GOVERNMENT OF INDIA SEEKS MY SERVICES FOR APPOINTMENT AS ADDITIONAL SECRETARY

In early January 1991, K.B. Sreenivasan, IAS (1956), Chief Secretary mentioned to me that a call was received from the Cabinet Secretary,

Government of India enquiring whether my services could be spared for appointment as Additional Secretary, Government of India. The Chief Secretary asked me to discuss the matter with the Chief Minister, as I was holding a very crucial position as Chairman, MSEB. When I broached the subject with Sharad Pawar, Chief Minister, he congratulated me on my empanelment as Additional Secretary and stated that he would be happy to spare me after the Lok Sabha Elections in May 1991, as major complaints during the election period were about the break downs, interruptions and shortages of power. I had no alternative but to continue as Chairman, MSEB during the critical period of the General Elections.

In the Elections to the Lok Sabha held during May 1991, the Congress party won with a thumping majority by winning 39 out of 42 MP seats in Maharashtra. The overwhelming success of the Congress Party in Maharashtra spurred Sharad Pawar to stake his claim to the post of the Prime Minister. Eventually, he became the Union Defence Minister in June 1991. He was succeeded by Sudhakarrao Naik, who was earlier Minister (Energy) as Chief Minister. Sudhakarrao Naik was, however, reluctant to spare my services to Government of India, as he knew me well, as Chairman, MSEB when he was the Minister (Energy).

I visited Delhi after Sharad Pawar became the Defence Minister and called on him and reminded him about his promise to send me to Delhi after the Lok Sabha Elections, while he himself landed in Delhi before me! He burst into a loud laughter and promised to speak to Sudhakarrao Naik to spare my services on deputation to the Government of India.

In the meanwhile, the Chief Secretary had conveyed to the Government of India that my services would be available for being considered as Additional Secretary after the Lok Sabha elections. After a few days, I received a surprise call from none other than Sharad Pawar himself. He asked me if I would like to work with him in Defence Ministry. I was quite surprised at such a query and replied that it would be an honour to continue to work with him. Sharad Pawar mentioned to me that my name had been proposed by the Cabinet Secretary for appointment as Additional Secretary in the Ministry of Defence, although he had never asked for me for that post and he was approving the proposal. I subsequently learnt that R.M. Narayanan (Kerala—1962), Additional Secretary, Ministry of Defence, my own batch mate was reverting back to Kerala Cadre, as the newly elected Chief Minister of Kerala, K. Karunakaran wanted his services as Chairman, Kerala State Electricity Board. As the only vacant post at that time was that of Additional Secretary (Defence) and I was the only officer on the panel overdue for posting, my name was duly recommended by the Cabinet Secretary, in a routine way, to the Defense Ministry for appointment as Additional Secretary. Hence the surprise call from Sharad Pawar, Defence Minister, himself who obviously could not believe that my name had come for posting in his own Ministry without being asked! Many in Maharashtra felt that as I was close to Sharad Pawar as Chairman, MSEB, he took me to Delhi for being posted as his Additional Secretary in the Government of India. Whatever it may be, my stock in Maharashtra had shot up sky high!

This period of six years, from 1986 to 1991, in the State Power Sector was highly satisfying experience inasmuch as the State Utility saw a high trajectory of growth on multiple fronts. I was in a position to influence this growth, both from the policy level and later from the direct operational front in MSEB.

As per the provisions of the Electricity (Supply) Act, 1948, the Chairman, State Electricity Board is appointed for a fixed tenure of three years, unless he is removed on disciplinary grounds, is insolvent, is found to be of unsound mind or unless the Chairman himself resigns. It is a unique position provided in the statute and hence holding the position of such unique character was in itself a proud privilege. After a very successful and satisfying innings, I had to resign as Chairman and I was succeeded by Ajit Nimbalkar (1967), Secretary to the Chief Minister, as Chairman, MSEB.

The opportunity given to me by Sharad Pawar, Chief Minister to function as the Chairman of the biggest and the best performing State Electricity Board in the country, is certainly, a turning point in my career and I am extremely beholden to Sharad Pawar for giving me once in a life time opportunity to a civil servant.

Photo 33: Abraham, Union Power Secretary with Mr. George H.W. Bush, former President, U.S.A. in New Delhi in 1995.

Photo 34: As Union Power Secretary (right) with Shri H.D. Deve Gowda, Prime Minister inaugurating the Chief Minister's Conference on Power in 1996.

Photo 35: Shri & Smt. Abraham.

Photo 36: As Member, UPSC calling on Shri K.R. Narayanan, President of India in 1999.

Photo 37: The author along with grandson Manish in conversation with Hon'ble Speaker, Lok Sabha, Shri G.M.C. Balayogi, Shri Yerren Naidu, MP and son-in-law Sam Bob (extreme left).

Photo 38: The author with Sitar Maestro Pandit Ravi Shankar and his wife.

Photo 39: Shri & Smt. Abraham with grandchildren at Trafalgar Square, London in 1998.

Photo 40: Abraham visiting his son Rajesh in London in 1998.

Photo 41: Shri & Smt. Abraham exchanging rings on the occasion of author's 60th Birthday (Manish, grandson on the right).

Photo 42: The author's daughter Manjula Sam Bob with her family.

Photo 43: Abraham with family members at the time of son Rajesh's wedding reception.

Photo 44: The author with family members paying homage to his wife Suryakumari.

Photo 45: Abraham with his family members in 2005.

Photo 46: The author being felicitated by Krishna District Felicitation Committee as a "Prominent Achiever" from the District by Smt. Prathibha Bharati, Hon'ble Speaker, Andhra Pradesh in 2003.

Photo 47: The author with the trainees at Suryakumari Abraham Memorial Foundation (SAMF) Centre for Tailoring & Embroidery, Kondur, Andhra Pradesh.

Photo 48: Computer trainees at SAMF Centre for Computers, Kondur, Andhra Pradesh.

Photo 49: The author with family members during the inauguration of Drinking Water Tank constructed by SAMF at Hyderabad.

Photo 50: Shri A.B. Vajpayee, Prime Minister of India releasing "Ambedkar's Contribution for Economic Planning and Development - It's Relevance" written by the author (in suit) in 2002. (right to left) Shri Suresh Prabhu, Union Power Minister, Shri M. Venkaiah Naidu, Union Minister Rural Development, Shri Yerran Naidu, Leader, TDP Parliamentary Party, Shri Sushil Kumar Shinde, MP, Shri Vidyasagar Rao, Union Minister of State (Home Affairs), Shri N. Janardhana Reddy, MP & Former Chief Minister, A.P. and T. Subbarami Reddy, MP were present.

Photo 51: Shri Vilasrao Deshmukh, Chief Minister, Maharashtra receiving the Book "Ambedkar's Contribution for Economic Planning and Development - It's Relevance" written by the author.

Photo 52: Shri S. Jaipal Reddy, Union Minister for Urban Development (third from left) releasing "Dr. Ambedkar - Bharatiya Arthik Shilpakar" (Hindi) written by the author in 2005. (right to left) Shri N. Janardhana Reddy, MP, Shri Abraham, Shri Charanjit Singh Athwal, Deputy Speaker, Lok Sabha, Shri G. Venkat Swamy, Deputy Leader, Congress Parliamentary Party in Lok Sabha and Shri Y. Yerran Naidu, MP, Leader TDP Parliamentary Party were present.

Photo 53: Dr. Y.S. Rajashekhara Reddy, Chief Minister, Andhra Pradesh releasing "Bharata Arthika Roopa Silpi - Dr. Ambedkar" (Telugu) written by the author (in suit) in 2006. (right to left) Dr. Geeta Reddy, Minister (Industries), A.P. and Dr. Ravi Mallu, A.P. State Representative, New Delhi were also present.

Photo 54: Hon'ble President of India Dr. A P J Abdul Kalam receiving the first copy of the book "Power Sector Reforms - Focus on Distribution" from the author in 2003.

Photo 55: The author presenting a momento to Shri Sushilkumar Shinde, Union Power Minister

Photo 56: The author as President, Andhra Cultural and Welfare Society, New Delhi felicitating Megastar Chiranjeevi on being conferred 'Padmabhushan' Award.

Photo 57: The author's granddaughter Aishwarya performing Kuchipudi dance during her *Arangetram* in April 2007.

Photo 58: Abraham playing his favourite sport, Golf at Pebble Beach Golf Course, California, USA.

EIGHTEEN

IN THE SERVICE OF DEFENCE OF THE COUNTRY

Additional Secretary, Later Special Secretary, Ministry of Defence

I received my promotion orders as Additional Secretary, Ministry of Defence, Government of India, in the middle of July 1991, while I was still functioning as Chairman, Maharashtra State Electricity Board. By that time, Sudhakarrao Naik, former Minister (Energy), had already taken over the reigns as Chief Minister of Maharashtra, after Sharad Pawar relinquished charge to become Union Defence Minister (Raksha Mantri), following the Parliamentary Elections in 1991. Sudhakarrao Naik, under whom I had served both as Secretary (Energy) and Chairman, MSEB, was reluctant to spare my services to the Government of India, as he had just taken over as Chief Minister and did not want to have any instability in an important organisation like the MSEB so soon after becoming Chief Minister.

I made an earnest plea to him to spare my services, as not many IAS officers got empanelled as Additional Secretaries to the Government of India. It was a rare opportunity to work in the Government of India and, in any case, it would be advantageous to the state to have its own officers at the Centre. It was after much pleading that Sudhakarrao Naik, very reluctantly, agreed to spare my services to go to Delhi.

After a brief holiday during which I visited my native place in Andhra

Pradesh, I joined the Government of India on 19 August 1991 as Additional Secretary, Ministry of Defence.

I had the privilege of having access to very important and sensitive information in the Ministry, but I will mention only those matters which are already in the public domain.

SHARAD PAWAR—DEFENCE MINISTER

Sharad Pawar assumed charge as Raksha Mantri on June 26, 1991 and S. Krishna Kumar, a former IAS officer of 1963 batch from Kerala cadre, was Raksha Rajya Mantri. Sharad Pawar demitted charge on March 5, 1993 to become Chief Minister, Maharashtra, for the third time. Thereafter, PV Narasimha Rao, Prime Minister, kept the portfolio of Raksha Mantri to himself. S. Krishna Kumar relinquished charge as Raksha Rajya Mantri on 18 January, 1993 and Mallikarjun took charge in his place. I therefore had the privilege of working with PV Narasimha Rao, Prime Minister until I was transferred out of the Ministry of Defence in April 1994.

The Raksha Mantri was assisted by a number of Committees dealing with various aspects of defense activities. One of the important meetings he chaired was the weekly meeting attended by the RRM, Principal Secretary to the PM, Cabinet Secretary, the three Service Chiefs, Foreign Secretary, Secretaries in the Ministry of Defence and Financial Adviser (Defence Services). This forum considered important and urgent defense-related matters and I used to attend these meetings along with my colleague K.A. Nambiar (IAS, Tamil Nadu-1961), another Additional Secretary in the Ministry, who subsequently became the Defence Secretary.

When I joined the Ministry, the Chief of Army Staff (COAS) was Gen S.F. Rodrigues, PVSM, VSM, the Chief of Naval Staff (CNS) was Admiral L. Ramdas, PVSM, AVSM, Vrc, VSM and the Chief of Air Staff (CAS) was Air Chief Marshal N.C. Suri, PVSM, AVSM, V.M.

N.N. VOHRA—DEFENCE SECRETARY

N.N. Vohra IAS (1959-Punjab) was the Defence Secretary. He had the unique distinction of having functioned earlier in the Ministry as a Joint Secretary, Additional Secretray and Secretary, Defence Production. He was forthright and fearless while putting across his views on a vast number of Defence matters. He was very thorough and accurate on his facts and clear in his thinking. I still recollect vividly a presentation made by him on a highly sensitive issue with serious security implications to P.V. Narshima Rao, Prime Minister, when the three Service Chiefs were present. His analysis was heard in rapt attention and accepted in toto, to put in bureaucratic language without changing a comma or full stop, even though every draft note put up to Vohra comes back quite often as a new note!! I had the privelege of working with one of the finest and outstanding administrators in the service and consider him worthy of emulation. K.A. Nambiar (IAS-1961—Tamil Nadu) and myself were the two Additional Secretaries in the Ministry.

N. Raghunathan (IAS-59-Maharashtra) was Secretary, Defence Production and Supplies. Dr. V.S. Arunachalam was Secretary, Defence Research and Development Organisation and Scientific Advisor to the Defence Minister.

DR. A.P.J. ABDUAL KALAM—SECRETARY, DRDO

Dr. A.P.J. Abdul Kalam succeeded Dr. V.S. Arunachalam as Secretary, Defence Research and Development Organization and Scientific Advisor to the Defence Minister, a few months, after I joined the Ministry. It was a privilege and an honour to be associated closely with Dr. Kalam in the Ministry. I used to represent the Ministry in several meetings taken by Dr. Kalam. I was also present at the successful demonstration of the field trials of Main Battle Tank (MBT) in Rajasthan desert conducted in the presence of Sharad Pawar, *Raksha Mantri,* organized by Dr. Kalam, as Secretary, DRDO.

While several eminent people from all over the World spoke and wrote volumes on various traits of his multifaceted personality. I would, however, like to recollect a small incident which permanently etched in my memory about Dr. Kalam. I continue to be invited for various functions of the Indian Air Force and the Indian Navy. On one such occasion, I was being escorted directly to the Chief of Navy who was receiving the guests personally, while few others were proceeding in a queue. To my utter surprise, I found Dr. Kalam was also proceeding in the queue. When I spotted Dr. Kalam in the queue I requested him to directly proceed to the Chief. His reply floored me completely when he smilingly said 'why don't you also join me in the queue'. I had no alternative except to follow him. I then felt, 'Humility and Simplicity is thy name, Dr. Kalam, a 'Bharat Ratna' already, who in the later years distinguished himself as much respected President of India.

The Defence Secretary, in addition to his functions as head of the Department of Defence dealing with the Army, Navy and Air Force and Inter-Services Organisations, was also responsible for coordinating the activities of the Departments of Defence Production and Defence Research and Development Organisation (DRDO) in the Ministry.

After I gave my joining report to the Defence Secretary on 19 August 1991, I went to call on Sharad Pawar, Defence Minister (Raksha Mantri). As Sharad Pawar was about to leave for some urgent engagement, he asked me to follow him, as he was going to the war room. I could not comprehend the necessity of going to the war room, when to the best of my knowledge, there was no war going on at that time anywhere in the world, let alone in India. Till that time, I did not know that there was a permanent war room in the Ministry of Defence. It was in the war room that I came to know that Mikhail Gorbachev, President of USSR, was kept under house arrest in USSR since the night before. I could not believe that Gorbachev, all powerful President of USSR, a super power, being put under house arrest in his own country. It was indeed a historical day for the entire world as it marked the beginning of the end of USSR's reign as one of the two super powers. It was also the first time that I met all the three service Chiefs, namely, General S.F. Rodrigues, Admiral S. Ramdas and Air Chief Marshal N.C. Suri at one place.

After I received my deputation orders to the Government of India, friends in Delhi advised me to secure an application for house allotment well in advance so that I could hand it over to the Estates Officer the day I joined the Government of India, as the allotment of houses was done based on how early the application had been submitted. I came to know of a peculiar rule or convention that all applications received on or before the nineteenth of a month were considered together for allocation of accommodation. As I joined on the nineteenth, I immediately sent an application to the Estates Officer, Ministry of Urban Development. The very second day after joining, I contacted the Estates Officer and was pleasantly surprised when he told me that they had identified a suitable accommodation for me in the multi-storied building on Shahjahan Road, which would be allotted once I gave my approval. I was quite surprised that an accommodation was offered to me so promptly, while in general, it took several months to secure one. When I came to Delhi, the general security scenario was quite serious and there were armed patrol in every corner of the city, after the brutal assassination of Rajiv Gandhi in May 1991. As the flat was on the fifth floor, it fully met the security and safety concerns of my wife, who was reluctant to move to Delhi due to the prevailing security scenario, so I immediately accepted the accommodation.

FORMATION OF COMMON WEALTH OF INDEPENDENT STATES (CIS)

One of the most significant events of that period was the dismemberment of the USSR into a Commonwealth of 15 Independent Sovereign States. The final fragmentation of the USSR signaled an end to the cold war era. The political changes in the erstwhile Soviet Union brought to an end the East–West tensions which had vitiated international relations for decades. For India, the changes in the USSR held special significance in the context of our long relationship with the Soviet Union on several vital matters, including on defense matters, as India depended substantially on the Russian-made military equipment and ammunition. The Air Force depended largely on Russian or indigenously built MIG fighter aircrafts.

The splintering of the USSR and the emergence of the 15 independent sovereign States meant that the process of dialogue would have to be conducted with a number of authorities and agencies. We had initiated negotiations in right earnest with all the new successor countries.

It is the cardinal responsibility of the Central Government to ensure the country's security, which rested with the Ministry of Defence. As Additional Secretary, I was entrusted, inter alia, with all matters pertaining to the Navy, Air Force, Coast Guard, Establishment matters of the Ministry, Armed Forces Medical services, Directorate General Resettlement dealing with welfare of ex-armed forces personnel, Security of South Block and the National Cadet Corps (NCC), among other subjects. I had to spend long hours every day to cope up with the work, especially in view of the high security matters dealt with in the Ministry. The primary duties and responsibilities of the Additional Secretary entailed acting as a facilitator between the Government and the armed forces and to ensure that the armed forces were not put in a disadvantageous position in any manner. There were four joint secretaries reporting to me in the Ministry. I was very lucky to have V Tulsidas (IAS-1972), Vinod Rai (IAS-1972), Suresh Chandra (IAS-1970) and

Mala Srivastav (IAS-1971), as Joint Secretaries. All of them were very intelligent, hardworking and outstanding officers, who proved their mettle and subsequently become Secretaries to the Government of India.

NAVY

The safeguarding of the country's vast coastline, stretching over more than 7,500 km, is the primary responsibility of the Indian Navy. The Navy also plays a major role in safeguarding the country's maritime interests in the vast Exclusive Economic Zone and in protecting the offshore oil installations. The Indian Navy added more war ships, aircrafts and helicopters to its force levels during this time, to keep pace with increasing responsibility and to replace the aging fleet. A significant achievement during the year was the construction and commissioning of the first Indian built submarine, INS Shalki in Mazagaon Dock, Bombay in February 1992. With this, India joined the select band of nations capable of building their own submarines. During this period, the Naval Air Arm was further strengthened by the commissioning of a Naval Air Station at 'INS Rajali' at Arkonam in Tamil Nadu. I frequently visited the station to assess its progress for early completion. The Air Station 'INS Dega' at Vishakhapatnam, and INS Rajali provided the Navy with much needed flexibility for maritime surveillance of the coast.

Navy-to-Navy interaction provides an opportunity to establish friendly relations with maritime countries and the Navy plays a significant role in promoting confidence building measures with the Navies of other countries. This was sought to be done through 'Goodwill' visits and conducting Joint Exercises. During my tenure as Additional Secretary, Indian Naval Ships carried out Joint Naval Exercises with the French, British, American and Australian Naval Ships which were on goodwill visits. Indian Naval Ships also undertook goodwill visits to Iran, UAE, Oman, Indonesia, Australia, Malaysia, Bangladesh and Singapore.

A VISIT TO INS VIRAAT

I visited INS Viraat, the flagship of Indian Navy, within a month of joining the Ministry. It was my first visit to a Naval ship, that too, such a prestigious Aircraft Carrier. The visit gave me a very valuable exposure to the might of the modern Aircraft Carrier. Rear Admiral Kailash Kohli,

Flag Officer, Commanding Western Fleet (who retired as Vice Chief of Navy) and Captain Arun Prakash, Commanding Officer, INS Viraat (who recently retired as Chief of Naval Staff), conducted me around and explained the various capabilities of INS Viraat. I also visited other Naval Warships and Naval establishments.

A DAY AT SEA WITH THE PRIME MINISTER—7TH OCTOBER 1992

One of the major events that took place during my tenure as Additional Secretary (Defence) was that the Prime Minister, PV Narasimha Rao, came on board INS Viraat, to see for himself the awesome power of the Indian Navy during a day long exercise of the Western Fleet, off the coast of Bombay on 07 October 1992. He was accompanied, amongst others, by Sharad Pawar, Raksha Mantri; C. Subramaniam, Governor of Maharashtra and Sudhakarrao Naik, Chief Minister of Maharashtra.

The distinguished visitors were received by Admiral L Ramdas, PVSM, AVSM, Vrc, VSM, ADC, Chief of Naval Staff, Vice Admiral KASZ Raju, PVSM, AVSM, NM, Flag Officer Commanding-in-Chief, Western Naval Command, Rear Admiral A.R. Tandon, AVSM, Flag Officer Commanding Western Fleet and Captain Madanjit Singh, Commanding Officer INS Viraat. The day long exercises involved ships of the Western Fleet, prominent among them being two aircraft carriers INS Viraat and INS Vikrant, which guided missile destroyers, indigenously built frigates, patrol vessels, units of Local Flotilla, one submarine, aircrafts and helicopters. The exercises conducted included a series of naval manoeuvres, flying operations and weapon firings to demonstrate the capabilities and prowess of the modern naval ships. The final event was the traditional Fly Past and Steam Past.

PV Narasimha Rao, Prime Minister, who watched the sea and air power of the fleet lauded the role of the Indian Navy, and emphasized the importance of induction of a modernized aircraft carrier like INS Viraat. He stated that he was impressed by the might of the Western Fleet and reiterated that the Navy must be fully prepared to defend the country's territorial waters. He said that it was unfortunate that some countries were criticizing India's expenditure on defence, despite the fact that the total budgetary provisions and per capita income were comparable or less than that of many of the nations in the world, including our critics. For me, it was once in a life time experience to witness the might and fire power of Indian Navy, with which I was privileged to be so closely associated.

AIR FORCE

I was also entrusted with work relating to the Indian Air Force in the Ministry. The IAF guards the Indian skies against violation and provides air support to the Army and Navy. In addition, the IAF is responsible for air maintenance of far-flung border areas such as in Siachin and also assists the civil administration during natural calamities. The Aviation industry is a highly technologically advanced and sophisticated industry. The IAF is an equipment intensive force and obsolescence sets in early. Therefore, continuous modernization of the Air Force, although expensive, is crucial and inescapable. All possible efforts have been made to adopt and develop new technologies to suit its requirements. Efforts to indigenize various equipments, systems and spares over the years were further intensified to accelerate its pace. The establishment and optimum utilization of indigenous overhaul facilities of aircraft was given continuous encouragement. The necessity for the replacement of the MIG aircraft, which the IAF had in abundance, by Light Combat Aircraft (LCA) was anticipated and, accordingly, a project for the development of the LCA was under implementation.

In order to ensure that the aircraft held in the inventory of the IAF are put to optimum use, the possibility of extending the life of various aircraft and aero engines was under constant review with manufacturers. A wide range of training activities were undertaken at a host of IAF training institutions in the country in flying, technical and non-technical fields.

I visited several Air Force establishments and one of the major decisions taken during my tenure was to shift the Command Headquarters of South Western Command from Jodhpur to Gandhinagar.

COAST GUARD

The Coast Guard was established during 1978 as an Armed Force of the Union to assist the Navy in its non-military tasks and as an agency for protecting the country's vast maritime interests. It is responsible for keeping India's Exclusive Economic Zone (EEZ) under regular surveillance in order to prevent poaching/smuggling and other illegal activities in the EEZ. The Coast Guard had made rapid progress during the last 14 years and has developed into a full-fledged maritime service with its own ships, aircraft and helicopters. It successfully carried out several anti-poaching, anti-smuggling and search and rescue operations, resulting in the nabbing of several foreign fishing vessels and crew members.

DIRECTORATE GENERAL RESETTLEMENT

I was also dealing with all the matters pertaining to the Directorate General Resettlement (DGR), the nodal agency looking after the resettlement and welfare of ex-Servicemen and their families. Each year, about 50,000 service personnel retire or are released at a comparatively young age of 35-45 years. They required fresh employment opportunities, and the Government, therefore, provided for reservations for ex-servicemen. The present strength of ex-serviceman is estimated to be around 44 lakhs.

NATIONAL CADET CORPS

I was also looking after all matters pertaining to the Directorate General, National Cadet Corps (DGNCC), which had an enrolled cadet strength of 11 lakhs, poised for further increase every year. Having been an NCC cadet once, I was happy to initiate several measures to further strengthen the organization.

The Chief Administrative Officer (CAO), Ministry of Defence, who looked after the personnel management of about 15,000 civilian employees posted in the three Services Headquarters and 26 Inter-Services Organizations, also reported to me. In addition, I was dealing with matters pertaining to the Armed Forces Medical Services consisting of the Army Medical Corps (AMC), Army Dental Corps (ADC) and the Military Nursing Service (MNS), which provided medical cover to the members of the Armed Forces, ex-servicemen and their families.

VISIT TO FRANCE WITH THE PRIME MINISTER

I was fortunate to be a part of the Prime Minister's delegation when P.V. Narasimha Rao, made an official visit to Paris, France in November, 1992. This was my first foreign visit as a part of the Prime Minister's delegation. The Prime Minister had several rounds of meetings with leaders and also addressed several literary gatherings. Narasimha Rao's literary and oratory skills were at their best during such gatherings and he kept the audience spell bound by his statesmanlike analysis of the world situation.

VISIT TO SIACHIN

I had an opportunity to visit several important and sensitive armed forces establishments, notable among them being the visit to Siachin. There was a visit of Parliamentary Committee on Defence to Leh and other forward areas of military operations during October 1991, within a few months of my joining the Ministry. The committee was led by Sharad Pawar, Defence Minister and consisted of about 25 Members of Parliament. Leh in Ladakh is at a very high altitude and it takes considerable time for outsiders to acclimatise themselves. We had the privilege of travelling with Lt. General J.S. Aurora, M.P., hero of the Bangladesh war in 1971. When we landed in Leh, General Aurora complained of breathlessness due to high attitude and had to return back in the same aircraft to Delhi. Indeed, some of the MPs and the officers had to be given oxygen till they got acclimatised.

The entire team travelled to Thoise, the base camp on the way to Siachin, the highest battle field in the world. Several helicopters were commissioned for flying us from Thoise to Siachin and back. The flight path was quite treacherous and highly risky and indeed very scary. The helipad at Siachin was just sufficient to land and a minor error of judgment in landing could lead to fatal consequences. There was nothing but snow covered peaks and we could see our dedicated armed forces working in the most inhospitable climatic conditions. We were informed that Ms. Jayanti Natarajan, MP had the rare distinction of being the first lady to visit the Siachin glacier. The *officers and Jawans* were pleasantly surprised to see a lady representative of the people to visit them and enquire about their living conditions and the communication arrangements with their families. It was a memorable and once in a lifetime opportunity to visit our *jawans* at the highest battle field in the World.

VISIT TO ROHTANG PASS

One major advantage in the Ministry of Defence was that whenever the Parliamentary Committees visited Armed Force establishments, we could always commission armed forces planes and helicopters for the journeys. When the Consultative Committee wanted to observe the snow clearance operations by the Border Roads Organization at Rohtang Pass in the first week of November 1992, we could commission two air force aircrafts up to Kullu and four helicopters to Manali. The team was led by S. Krishnakumar, RRM, in the absence of Sharad Pawar, N.N. Vohra, Defence Secretary and I accompanied the Committee. We were supposed to visit Rohtang Pass in the early morning of next day, but to our pleasant surprise when we got up in the morning at Manali, there was totally unexpected and heavy snow fall in Manali itself and we had to commission the snow clearing equipment to come out of the Guest house, instead of watching the snow clearing operations at Rohtang Pass!!. We still managed to go a few km on the road towards Rohtang pass with the help of the Border Roads Organization. We could observe how difficult and time consuming it was for the Border Roads Organization with all the heavy equipment to clear the snow at those heights.

VISIT TO ANDAMAN AND NICOBAR ISLANDS

The Consultative Committee also visited Andaman and Nicobar islands and toured extensively various strategic locations, observed environmentally fragile nature of the islands, seen the life styles of several rare indigenous tribes, visited Indira Point, the southern most tip of India. I accompanied the Committee during its visit.

MEETING WITH SHABANA AZMI

There were some unauthorized colonies that had come up outside the compound wall of naval establishments in Colaba, Mumbai, posing a security threat to the naval establishment, as they were trespassing into the naval establishment. Several efforts were made to evict them from the area without much success, as they were staying there for some time. These slum dwellers were demanding that the basic minimum needs of water, electricity and sanitation facilities should be provided to them. At one time, these demand were raised by none other than Shabana Azmi, the famous film personality and social activist, who sat on hunger strike in support of their demands. I had to visit the venue of the fasting along with Vice Admiral H. Johnson, Flag Officer Commanding Western Fleet, Mumbai, to persuade her to give up her hunger strike.

SHOOTING OF TELUGU FILM 'MAJOR CHADRAKANT'

During this period, I had a surprise telephone call from K. Raghavendra Rao, the famous film Director from Andhra Pradesh and also a dear family friend, indicating that he would like to call on me in my office in the South Block. It was certainly an unusual request from a family friend. He was accompanied by Mohan Babu, a famous superstar of Telugu movies, who also became subsequently a Member of the Parliament. When Mohan Babu, in his trade mark white shirt and flannel with a felt hat walked into the South Block, many in the South Block watched him with great admiration. They were deputed to meet me by N.T. Ramarao, former Chief Minister, Andhra Pradesh and a super hero of Telugu screen to meet me, when N.T. Rama Rao came to know that I was working in the defense Ministry. I knew N.T. Rama Rao personally, as I had the privilege of working with him as Commissioner of Industries when he was the Chief Minister, during which period he retained industries portfolio with him. N.T. Rama Rao himself was playing the heroes role, a Major Chandrakant. Their request was to allow the shooting of the movie in the army locales to add authenticity to the movie. They requested for my intervention, as the Army Authorities denied permission to shoot in Army locations. I approached the army authorities in my personal capacity to permit the shooting of the movie, which highlighted the sacrifies made by Army Officers for the service of the nation and in which no less than the former Chief Minister of Andhra Pradesh himself was playing the leading role. Finally, the army authorities relented to my request and permitted the shooting of the movie. The movie was one of the most successful movies ever produced in Telugu and the Army locations were an added attraction in the movie.

MEETING WING COMMANDER RAKESH SHARMA, FIRST ASTRONAUT FROM INDIA

Wing Commander Rakesh Sharma, the first Astronaut from our country called on me and I was privileged to meet him and chat with him. Indeed, my son Rajesh was also quite excited to meet him. Rakesh Sharma came to request me to permit him to take pre mature retirement from the Indian Air Force. I was only too happy to oblige him.

INDUCTION OF WOMEN IN THE ARMED FORCES

The recruitment of women into the Armed Forces was confined to the Medical Corps, Dental Corps and Military Nursing Service. The credit for inducting women in the armed forces goes to Sharad Pawar as Defence Minister. It was during his tenure in 1991-92, while I was Additional Secretary, it was decided to induct women into the officer cadres in the Education, Postal, Legal, Ordinance and Service Corps of the Indian Army; Administration, Education, Logistics, Accounts, Education and Meteorological Branches of the Indian Air Force and Logistics and Education in the Navy, which was expanded to the Air traffic controllers cadres during 1993. The first batch of 12 women cadets, belonging to the Education and Administration Branches, commenced training from July, 1992 in the Air Force. Due to the overwhelming response for selection in these Branches, Government decided, in August 1992, to further extend the scheme for the induction of women to also cover the Transport, Helicopter and Navigation streams of the Flying Branch. A new chapter was added to the IAF history when the first batch of Women Short Service Commissioned Officers joined the Air Force fraternity in June 1993.

CEREMONIAL FUNCTIONS

The Ministry of Defence organizes important ceremonial functions on National days during the year, which includes the Republic Day Parade, Beating Retreat and Independence Day. The Defence Investiture Ceremonies were also organized at Rashtrapati Bhavan for the presentation of gallantry awards and distinguished service decorations to defence personnel. Organising these ceremonies required close co-ordination among various agencies concerned, and the timely completion of a large number of formalities and activities.

REPUBLIC DAY PARADES

When I watched Republic Day Parades, Independence Day Celebrations on the TV, I never realized that I would, one day in my career, be closely associated with organizing these functions which I did during 1992, 1993 and 1994. The Republic Day parades are of national and international significance and every activity had to be done in a systematic manner as it could not afford to go wrong. The function required extraordinary coordination between the various agencies, including the State Governments and educational institutions in Delhi so as to make the celebrations colourful and successful. It was quite a tension filled period before the Republic Day and we used to heave a sigh of relief, once the Republic Day festivities passed off successfully.

BEATING RETREAT CEREMONY

The Beating Retreat Ceremony, organized at Vijay Chowk, brings down the curtain on the Republic Day festivities. Bands of the three services participate in the ceremony. It is virtually a feast to view the turn out of the bands and literally and figuratively music to the ears, when different contingents play selected pieces. The conclusion of the ceremony was followed by the illumination of Rashtrapati Bhavan and the South Block and the North Block.

PEACE KEEPING FORCE TO SOMALIA

I visited Mogadishu, capital of Somalia in April 1993, as a part of the two member delegation to assess the need to send a peace-keeping force there. In 1991, after successfully ousting the government controlled by President Mohammed Said Barre which was in control of Somalia for over two decades, the so-called liberators started fighting among themselves for assuming power. Hundreds of civilians were killed. The warlords, belonging to different factions embarked on killing, looting and indiscriminately destroying public and private properties. The fight among the local war lords made the United Nations to intervene to restore peace and stability in the country and in the region, as Somalia's location made it geopolitically significant as a gateway between Africa and the Middle East. A reconnaissance Indian Naval ship was already stationed at Mogadishu, capital of Somalia. The UN requested India to send a peace-keeping force. A number of countries were already participating in the peace-keeping operations, including USA and Pakistan. A team consisting of Shri H.R. Hiramath, IFS, (Retd.) a distinguished diplomat who served earlier in Somalia and I was sent to Somalia to assess the situation and give our views about India's participation in peace-keeping operations. We were received by the United Nations representatives at Nairobi and were flown to Mogadishu by a special Executive jet of the United Nations, with a seating capacity of just 6 persons. While the journey from Nairobi to Mogadishu was quite comfortable, I was quite scared to fly in such a small Executive Jet. It was the first time I was travelling in such a small Jet. During our entire visit of 5 days, we stayed in the Indian Navy ship, stationed off Mogadishu. Every morning we flew to the airport in a Naval helicopter stationed on the ship, and visited various United Nations establishments and relief centres. Even during our visit, we witnessed several minor exchange of fire between the local militia groups and looting of rations from the relief trucks. Most of the places in Somalia appeared to have been deserted. We also met some local warlords to assess their reaction to India sending the peace-keeping forces. Most of them welcomed them, since Indian troops have a reputation of being fair, impartial and non-partisan. As some peace negotiations were being held at Adis Ababa, capital of Ethiopia, we also visited Ethiopia, and met some Somalia leaders. The matter was discussed with P.V. Narasimha Rao, Prime Minister, who was also holding the portfolio of Ministry of Defence, on our return from the visit. As India had a tradition of sending peace-keeping forces whenever such a request was received from United Nations, it was decided to send a small contingent of armed forces and also a medical team with a huge consignment of medicines as humanitarian aid.

SPECIAL SECRETARY, MINISTRY OF DEFENCE

While I was working as Additional Secretary, the 1962 batch of IAS officers had become due for empanelment as Secretaries to the Government of India. There was considerable tension among the batch mates, as we were fully aware that all of us could not make the grade, as the criteria for promotion for Secretary was quite stringent. I was quite relieved to know that I was among the 22 batch mates out of 98, who were empanelled as Secretaries to the Government of India. There was considerable discontentment among those who could not get into the panel and even court cases were filed by some who had been left out of the panel. In the meanwhile, some of my batch mates were promoted and my turn was yet to come in view of the court case. The Cabinet Secretary, Zaffar Saifullah, took the initiative and obtained orders from the Prime Minister to promote me as Special Secretary, Ministry of Defence. I therefore had the distinction of becoming the first Special Secretary, Ministry of Defence, in the annals of the Ministry of Defence. I was aware that my stint as Special Secretary in the Ministry would be purely temporary. Lo and behold, I worked as Special Secretary, Ministry of Defence, only for seven days out of which two days were holidays and one day I attended 'one day' cricket match at Delhi, before I was transferred as Special Secretary, Ministry of Power.

GOLFING AS HOBBY

While working in the Ministry of Defence, I noticed that many officers from the Ministry regularly played golf. Sharad Pawar, *Raksha Mantri* (Defence Minister) also took to golfing in a serious way and used to play golf with his counterparts from other countries and obviously many matters of importance were discussed informally during such golf sessions. It is a tradition that whenever the Defence Minister of other countries visit Delhi, they make it a point to have a round of golf. I did not take to golfing easily even though several of my friends from the services suggested, primarily as a good golf set would cost a fortune and also time consuming. However, when Malikarjun became *Raksha Rajya Mantri* (RRM), he insisted that I should take to golfing as it provides excellent exercise in old age. One day he insisted that I should accompany him to the golf course and I reluctantly followed the Ministers directions. He took me to the Air Force Golf Course on the Race Course Road and gifted me one of his golf sets. That is how I started taking interest in the golf. Similarly, N.C. Suri, Chief of Air Staff, insisted that I should become a Member of the Air Force Golf Course, while serving in the Ministry of Defence. It was very kind of him that he brought the application form and forced me to sign the application form in his presence. This good gesture of the Air Chief made me a Civilian Member of the Air Force Golf Course on the Race Course, New Delhi. I regularly play golf now.

Many golfers believe that a 'hole in one' is a fluke which may happen once in a life time. Could anyone believe that I had three times 'hole in one' in Delhi Golf Course, while many regular golfers dream of having atleast once such a fluke in their life time. The three trophies I won for 'hole in one' are very cherished memories of my life and they occupy a pride of place in my personal collections.

A RARE HONOUR TO BE GIVEN FAREWELL BY THREE CHIEFS

When I was transferred as Special Secretary, Ministry of Power,

Government of India, a farewell was organised in the Ministry which was attended, among others, by Gen B.C. Joshi, PVSM, AVSM, Chief of Army Staff; Admiral V.S. Shekhawat, PVSM, AVSM, Vrc, Chief of the Naval Staff and Air Chief Marshal S.K. Kaul, PVSM, MVC, Chief of the Air Staff. It was a rare honour to have all the three Chiefs at one's farewell, making the occasion even more memorable. As I went on record at the farewell, I made more friends in three years of my stay in Defence Ministry, than my thirty years in the IAS, which I cherish. It was also a rare opportunity to work closely with Armed Forces. God bless the Defence Services for the selfless service they render and sacrifices they make for the nation.

NINETEEN

POWERING INDIA–FOCUS ON DISTRIBUTION REFORMS

Union Power Secretary

It was 7.30 pm on 31 March 1994 and I was still in my South Block office in the Ministry of Defence when I got a call on the RAX (Restricted Auto Exchange) from Zafar Saifullah, the Cabinet Secretary, asking me to meet him if I was not very busy in the office. It was a polite way of summoning me to meet him in his office. How can any officer say that he is very busy when called by Cabinet Secretary even if it is midnight? I tried to recollect whether there was any important matter on which he wanted to have urgent discussions, but I could not recall any such issue. Not knowing what was in store for me, I rushed to the Cabinet Secretariat, which is located in the Rashtrapati Bhavan.

When I entered his chamber, the Cabinet Secretary was browsing through some papers and appeared to be in a relaxed mood. He handed over a letter which mentioned that I had been posted as Special Secretary, Ministry of Power. I was happy about the transfer, since I had already worked for 10 years in the power sector. When I took a close look at the document once again, I saw that it was dated 31st March. As the next day, 1st April, 'all fools day', was just a few hours away, I could not contain myself and asked the Cabinet Secretary, whether it was an 'April Fool joke'. He had a hearty laugh and assured me that he was serious and directed me to take over charge in the early morning of 1st April itself, as he had already spoken to Vijay Shunglu, Special Secretary (Power) to hand over charge to me and join as Secretary, Ministry of Health.

When I went to my new office in Shram Shakti Bhavan to take charge of my assignment, I found to my utter dismay that I had to walk up to the fourth floor, as there was no power supply in the building, giving a clear indication of the power situation in the capital and also in the country. It did not come as a surprise to me, since I knew the sector very closely for over a decade. I also had the unique distinction of being the first Chairman of any State Electricity Board in the country ever to become Secretary, Ministry of Power, since Independence.

MINISTRY OF ENERGY RESTRUCTURED IN 1982

Prior to July 1992, the Ministry of Power was known as the Ministry of Energy. It included the Departments of Power, Coal and Non-Conventional Energy Sources. Ideally, the Ministry should have continued as Ministry of Energy, as coal has been the mainstay of power generation and better coordination would have been possible for planning and development of coal and power. However, it had been the general experience in governance that depending on exigencies, Ministries are bifurcated, even trifurcated or reorganized. Hence, a separate Ministry of Power was created in July 1992 and we had separate Ministries for Power, Coal and Non-Conventional Energy Sources, instead of one.

The Ministry of Power is primarily responsible, *inter alia*, for the general policy and development of electrical energy in the country and for perspective planning, policy formulation, processing of projects for investment decisions, monitoring of the implementation of power projects, administration and enactment of legislation with regard to power generation, transmission and distribution, research and development, rural electrification and energy conservation. Prior to the enactment of the Electricity Act 2003, it was also responsible for the administration of the Indian Electricity Act 1910 and the Electricity (Supply) Act 1948.

The Ministry of Power is assisted by the Central Electricity Authority (CEA) in all technical and economic matters. A large number of central sector power corporations/statutory bodies are also under the administrative control of the ministry, namely, the National Thermal Power Corporation (NTPC), National Hydro-Electric Power

Corporation (NHPC), North Eastern Electric Power Corporation (NEEPCO), Power Grid Corporation of India Limited (PGCIL), Naphtha Jhakri Power Corporation (NJPC) in Himachal Pradesh, Tehri Hydro Development Corporation (THDC) in Uttaranchal, Damodar Valley Corporation (DVC), Bhakra Beas Management Board (BBMB), Rural Electrification Corporation (REC), Power Finance Corporation (PFC) Central Power Research Institute (CPRI), National Power Training Institute (NPTI) and Energy Management Centre (EMC). All matters relating to the above undertakings are under the Ministry. The senior-most officer in the Ministry is the Secretary (Power), who is assisted by a Special Secretary and six Joint Secretaries. There are very few such large Ministries in the Government of India, which have a Special Secretary and so many Joint Secretaries, assisting the Secretary, in discharging his functions.

N.K.P. SALVE—MINISTER OF POWER

I was privileged to work under a senior seasoned administrator, a legal luminary and financial wizard, an internationally acknowledged cricket administrator and, above all, a very hospitable and considerate person, N.K.P. Salve, as Minister of Power. P.V. Rangayya Naidu, IPS (Retd.), a distinguished former Director General of Police, Andhra Pradesh, who was succeeded by Urmila Ben Patel, was Minister of State in the Ministry. I was also fortunate to have, as Secretary (Power), R. Vasudevan (UP-1959), a highly respected and dynamic civil servant, who had the distinction of functioning as Joint Secretary to the Prime Minister of India, Rajiv Gandhi. He entrusted me, *inter alia*, the work of Private Sector Investment Promotion Cell. He also encouraged me to play an active role in disseminating the policies of the government. Under their supervision, the Power Ministry made tremendous strides in furthering energy development in the country.

When I became Secretary, a year later, I had an excellent team of officers who were all committed to the cause of the power sector, working tirelessly for achieving our goals. Among them were Pradip Baijal, IAS (1966-Madhya Pradesh), who was initially Joint Secretary (JS) (Investment Promotion Cell) and subsequently promoted as Additional Secretary in the Ministry; Akbar Jung, IAS (1965), JS (Transmission); Ajay Dua, IAS (1971-Maharashtra), JS (Thermal); Gayatri Ramachandran, IAS (1972-Andhra Pradesh), JS, (Planning); Sudhakar Rao, IAS (1973-Karnataka),

JS (Hydro) who was succeeded by J. Vasudevan, IAS (1968-Karnataka) and T. Sethumadhavan, IAS (1965), JS and Financial Advisor who was succeeded by Shivrain, IAS (1968). Their performance and contribution to the Power Sector can be gauged from the fact that most of them became Secretaries to Government of India. For instance, Pradip Baijal became Secretary (Disinvestment) and Chairman, Telecom Regulatory Authority of India (TRAI); Vasudevan rose to become Secretary (Small Scale Industries); Akbar Jung was elevated to the position of Secretary (Steel) and Ajay Dua became Secretary (Industrial Policy and Promotion). There were also outstanding Directors in the Ministry; notable among them were A.K. Upadhaya, IAS (1975-Bihar) and P.K. Basu, IAS (1976-Bihar). Both of them became Joint Secretaries in the Ministry during my tenure.

A.B. VAJPAYEE, PRIME MINISTER, RETAINS POWER PORTFOLIO

There was a change of government after the Lok Sabha Elections in 1996, with the Bhartiya Janata Party (BJP) forming a minority government under the leadership of A.B. Vajpayee. During the thirteen-day period, the Prime Minister retained the subject of power with himself. One major issue pertaining to the Power Ministry which came for consideration during his time was about the extension of the counter guarantee given to the Dabhol Project of ENRON, which was originally given by the previous Government. The Government extended the counter guarantee. The other was the meeting chaired by the Prime Minister about environmental issues about Tehri Hydro project raised by Sunderlal Bahuguna, who was on fast which he refused to call off even after an appeal by the Prime Minister. Subsequently, however, the BJP Government failed to prove its majority in Parliament and had to resign.

H.D. DEVE GOWDA, PRIME MINISTER, ALSO RETAINS THE POWER PORTFOLIO

The next government was formed by the United Front, with H.D. Deve Gowda as the Prime Minister. Throughout his tenure, he too retained the Power portfolio, thus giving me another opportunity to work directly under the Prime Minister. The Minister of State for Power was S. Venugopalachari, a first time MP from Andhra Pradesh who belonged to Telugu Desam Party. T.R. Satish Chandran, (IAS–1952) Principal Secretary to the Prime Minister, who had earlier functioned as Secretary, Department of Power, was of immense help to me in discharging my functions in the Power Ministry. Satish Chandran with long years of experience in the Energy Sector had the unique distinction of being the only Indian who was the President of World Energy Council.

PRIME MINISTER, I.K. GUJRAL, TOO RETAINS THE POWER PORTFOLIO

Once again there was a change of Government in April 1997 when I K Gujral became the Prime Minister. He too retained the portfolio of Power till I retired from the IAS in June 1997. Thus, for one year of my tenure as Secretary (Power), I had the privilege of directly reporting to three Prime Ministers.

While I was functioning as Special Secretary, Ministry of Power, I was sounded once by the Cabinet Secretary, whether I was interested in shifting to another Ministry as a full-fledged Secretary since some of the officers, even from the junior batches were already posted as Secretaries in some Ministries. As I had specialised experience in power, I requested the Cabinet Secretary not to consider shifting me for the time being, especially as R. Vasudevan was scheduled to retire as Power Secretary on 30 June 1995. I did not mind waiting till then to be considered for that appointment. The Cabinet Secretary told me while he had no problem to continue me as Special Secretary (Power), he could not give an assurance that I would be posted as Secretary, Ministry of Power, as postings were decided by the Prime Minister. I agreed to continue till the retirement of R. Vasudevan and if I was not considered for this appointment, I would be happy to go to any other Ministry.

ADB CONFERENCE AT NICE, FRANCE

About a month after taking over as Special Secretary, I was required to attend the Asian Development Bank (ADB) conference held at Nice, which was on the French Riviera. I had to make a presentation about new initiatives taken by the Government in promoting private sector investments in power generation. While travelling to Nice, via Frankfurt,, I was pleasantly surprised to meet Dr. A.B. Lal of the famous Lal Pathological Laboratory, New Delhi, a very old friend of mine on the Air India flight. Dr. Lal joked that a Secretary to Government of India was going all the way to French Riviera, to merely attend an official conference, without much fun and frolic for which the French Riviera was famous!

It was the first time I was addressing an Asian Development Bank (ADB) Conference. The ADB had a tradition of bringing out a news supplement every day during its Annual Conference. At the ADB reception counter at Nice airport, we were handed over the news pull out of the first day. On the front page of the first issue was a prominent and a nice photograph of N.K. Singh (Bihar—1964), Additional Secretary, Department of Economic Affairs, Ministry of Finance, with a write up of how a representative of a developing country which was the seeking loans from the ADB had checked into a luxurious suite in a hotel in Nice, a suite larger and costlier than the suite occupied by the president of ADB. True to his style, N.K. Singh, a dynamic officer, held the centre stage throughout the Conference, which included hosting a lavish dinner in his hotel suite which was also attended, among several VVIPs, by the President, ADB.

HAZEL O' LIARY, ENERGY SECRETARY, U.S.A. VISIT TO INDIA

Another important event which is worthy of recollection was the visit of Hazel O' Liary, Energy Secretary, U.S.A. Her visit was of special significance to the country, as a large number of MoUs had been signed with American companies and also since many NRIs had shown considerable interest in the power projects. A large number of MoUs were signed in her presence, including the MoU with M/s Spectrum, one of the few units established through the MoU route in Andhra Pradesh. She became very popular in the energy sector by making a Power Point presentation and freely moving in the audience and answering questions with great aplomb.

LUNCHEON MEETING WITH PRESIDENT GEORGE BUSH

George Bush, United States President (1988 – 1992) visited Delhi at the invitation of Citibank on 29th November 1995. I was one of the invitees for the Luncheon meeting. I was seated next to the President George Bush and I was introduced as Secretary, Ministry of Power. Prior to the meeting, we chatted for sometime. All persons present addressed him as Mr. President. How I wish that in India too we address our Presidents and Prime Ministers in the similar manner after they demit their offices. During the address by the President Bush, he referred to our conversation more than once in his speech. Several friends after the Luncheon enquired whether I knew him so well to be referred frequently in his speech. I replied in negative. I presumed that President Bush obviously mistook me as equivalent to Secretary Energy in the U.S.A., where all the Secretaries are the Cabinet Ministers, while in India, the Secretary is the senior most bureaucrat in the Ministry.

VISIT TO URI HYDRO POWER STATION IN J & K

I accompanied N.K.P. Salve, Minister for Power on his visit to Uri Hydro Power Station in J & K, which was then under construction. Uri was hardly about 6 kms away from the border of Pakistan. We went from Srinagar in the Indian Air Force helicopter. We certainly took more than expected time to land at Uri. After we reached Uri, we were told by the people waiting to receive us at the helipad at Uri that our helicopter had apparently intruded into Pakistan and we were lucky to come back safely, especially as we were flying in the Indian Air Force helicopter. On our return to Srinagar, some media persons queried during the press conference about the intrusion. The Minister replied that he would take up the matter suitably with the Ministry of Defence on his return to New Delhi. We did lodge a complaint with the Ministry of Defence and the Air Force flatly denied about any intrusion into Pakistan. I totally forgot this episode till I was reminded about the same during my recent visit to the Indian Embassy Beijing, China in September 2007 by Saurabh Kumar IFS (1989) Deputy Chief of Mission, who dealt with this matter while he was in the Ministry of External Affairs.

MY FIRST VISIT TO MOSCOW

The Minister for External Affairs, I K Gujral, led a delegation to Moscow in February 2006 to discuss various bilateral issues before the visit of the Prime Minister, Deve Gowda. Ronen Sen, present Indian Ambassador, was Ambassador then. I was a part of the team alongwith Salman Haider, Foreign Secretary, Government of India. This visit gave me an opportunity to visit several historical places including Kremlin in Moscow.

PRIME MINISTER DEVE GOWDA'S VISIT TO MOSCOW

I was a part of the Prime Minister Deve Gowda's High Power delegation to Moscow in March 1997. The delegation among others consisted of

P. Chidambaram, Finance Minister; K. Bulli Ramaiah, Commerce Minister; T.R. Satish Chandran, Principal Secretary to the Prime Minister and R. Chidambaram, Secretary Atomic Energy Department. Discussions were held on several bilateral issues during this visit with the Russian counterparts. An 'in principal' agreement to implement Kudankulam Nuclear Power Project was finalized between His Excellency Boris Yeltsin, President of the Russian Federation and H.D. Deve Gowda, Prime Minister of India. The Prime Minister also unveiled a statue of Mahatma Gandhi in a prominent place in Moscow. He also inaugurated a laboratory established by Dr. Reddy's Laboratories, Hyderabad, on the outskirts of Moscow, during which time I was also present.

SIXTEENTH WORLD ENERGY CONGRESS, TOKYO, 1995

I attended the World Energy Congress for the second time, but now as Secretary (Power) in Tokyo on 12th and 13th October 1995. The Indian delegation was led by N.K.P. Salve, Union Minister of Power and included several representatives both from public and private sector power utilities. It was a unique opportunity for the country to showcase before the international community the various measures being undertaken in India to encourage private sector investments in the power sector and the avenues available in there for foreign investments.

After attending the Congress, the delegation visited Seoul, South Korea from the 14th to 17th of October, which again offered a unique opportunity to see how South Korea had become one of the most progressive and developed countries in the world. During this period, we visited Daewoo's automobile factory at Inchon, Kepco's gas-based power project at Sangyong and the Hyundai projects.

INDO–U.S. ENERGY PARTNERSHIP

An MOU was signed between India and U.S. authorities during January 1996 starting an Indo – U.S. Energy Partnership Forum which provided opportunities for U.S. Energy business firms to interact with Indian authorities as well as Indian business firms on matters of mutual interest. It has functioning since then very successfully. It celebrated its existence for a decade on 22nd January 2006. I was honoured on this occasion for starting the forum while I was Secretary Power.

ELECTRICITY SCENARIO IN THE COUNTRY

Electricity is one of the most vital infrastructure inputs for economic development in a country and it is the fulcrum on which rests the future pace of growth and development. The demand for electricity in India is enormous and is growing rapidly. The vast electricity market offers one of the highest growth opportunities for private developers.

At the time of Independence, electricity seemed to be more of an urban phenomenon. There was greater emphasis on providing power to the industrial, commercial and domestic segments, which were based mostly in urban areas. The Electricity (Supply) Act, 1948, sought to rectify this imbalance by insisting that the SEBs should discharge their social obligations and extend the benefits of electricity to semi-urban and rural areas in the most efficient and economical manner. The Act also stipulated that the area of development must transcend the geographical limits of a municipality. In fulfilment of the obligations envisioned in the Electricity (Supply) Act, 1948, the State Governments had been extending the reach of electricity to ensure a more balanced development. Supply of power at heavily subsidised rates to various categories of consumers like agricultural and domestic was conceived of for socio-economic reasons. The Industrial Policy Resolution of 1956 reserved the power sector for public investments in India. Thus, for many decades, the Government had assumed the role of developer, promoter and regulator of electricity.

Since independence, development of the electricity sector was primarily the responsibility of the Government, except for a few "licensees" like Tata Electric Company (TEC), Bombay Suburban Electricity Supply Company (BSES), Calcutta Electricity Supply Company (CESC), Ahmedabad Electricity Company (AEC). In its quest for increasing the availability of electricity, the country has adopted a blend of thermal, hydel and nuclear sources and non-conventional sources like solar, wind and tidal energy. The all India installed capacity of generating stations was 76,753 MW as on 31st March, 1994. In spite of significant growth in power generation, the shortage continued mainly due to the growth in demand, far outstripping the growth in generation. The energy shortage ranged from 7 per cent to 11 per cent and peak shortage from 16 per cent to 21 per cent during the year, even though the overall generation in the country had increased by over 8 per cent in the recent years.

India's electricity needs are enormous. This is evident from the fact that the perspective plan for the power sector indicated incremental capacity requirement of 1,42,000 MW during 1992-2007 to meet the growth in demand. This implied the creation of an incremental capacity of nearly 10,000 to 12,000 MW per year. The acute shortages in power supply in the country, both energy and peak, was a matter of grave concern since the economic development of the country depended on the availability of adequate and reliable power. The broad strategy of the Government was to deal with both supply side and demand side management to meet these shortages. On the supply side, however, the emphasis was primarily on the addition of generation capacity.

The abundant energy resources of the country were not being put to optimum use, primarily due to financial constraints. In the context of paucity of resources with both the Central and State Governments, as well as PSUs and SEBs, the need was to bridge the gap between the rapidly growing demand and supply for electricity. A policy to encourage greater investments by private enterprises for capacity addition in power generation and distribution was formulated by the government in 1991. Mobilisation of resources for achieving self-sufficiency in the electricity sector assumed high priority; therefore, the role of the private sector had become very important.

NEW ENVIRONMENT FOR PRIVATE SECTOR INVESTMENTS

Private sector participation in the power sector was not a novel concept in the Indian context. The private sector was a participant in India's electricity sector for over a hundred years. Even during the period of public sector domination, some private sector companies operated as 'licensees' of the State Electricity Boards and were rated amongst the best in the country in terms of performance and profitability. Such power companies have been operating their own power generation with a total capacity of around 3,000 MW and distribution systems to around ten million consumers, before the Government decided to encourage more private sector investments.

In response to the new economic realities of liberalisation and globalisation, the Government formulated a policy in 1991 to encourage greater participation by privately owned enterprises in electricity generation, with the aim of bringing in additional resources for the capacity addition programme in the electricity sector. The Indian

Electricity Act, 1910 and the Electricity (Supply) Act, 1948, were amended to bring about a new legal, administrative and financial environment for private enterprise in the electricity sector. The new policy permitted 100 per cent foreign owned companies to set up power projects based on any fuel such as coal, lignite, gas, hydel, liquid fuels, wind or solar and repatriate profits without any export obligations. An attractive two-part tariff structure was provided which allowed recovery of full fixed charges with up to 16 per cent return on equity at specified plant load/availability factor. This was further modified from time to time to make the policy more attractive and flexible. A five-year tax holiday was also given.

Since electricity is a subject listed in the Concurrent List of the Indian Constitution, the State Governments have played a vital role in promoting electricity projects. It was significant that the policy to encourage private participation in the development of the electricity sector was welcomed by all State Governments. The response of private companies, both Indian and foreign, to the policy on private power development was very encouraging.

Response from the Private Sector

When I joined the Ministry on 1 April 1994, there was considerable euphoria in the Ministry as power generation was thrown open for private investment and more than 250 memorandums of understandings (MoUs) were signed for setting up power projects for a capacity addition of around 75,000 MW. All these proposals were at various stages of processing and obtaining clearances, including those from the FIPB. Fifty-two of these offers were from foreign private firms, including from NRIs as also joint venture proposals. A number of workshops, seminars and conferences were organised in the country to inform prospective investors about the investment opportunities in the sector.

The progress of these proposals was regularly reviewed and after further scrutiny and withdrawals, the number has come down to 194 by 31 March 1996. During 1997–98, the Ministry was monitoring about 125 private power projects for 67,200 MW capacity, all of which required techno-economic clearance (TEC) of the CEA. These included 95 proposals on the MoU/letter of intent (LoI), etc., route and 30 proposals on the competitive bidding route. In addition, there were several MoU/ LoI projects, costing up to Rs. 100 crore and projects awarded through competitive bidding, costing up to Rs. 1,000 crores, which were being set up with the approval of the state governments and which did not require the TEC of CEA.

New Policy Initiatives

As the promotion of the private sector in such a big way was a new concept, the policy encountered major roadblocks and progress was slow. Several initiatives were taken by the Government of India to facilitate early setting up of the projects. Some of the major initiatives undertaken during my tenure as Secretary (Power), which need specific mention, are as follows:

(1) *Model Power Purchase Agreements Circulated*

In August 1994, the State Electricity Boards (SEBs) were provided flexibility to negotiate the Power Purchase Agreements (PPAs). This allowed determination of tariff in deviation of the norms laid down in the two-part tariff notification, provided the tariff was less than the normative tariff. To add more clarity, the tariff notification was amended from time to time, wherein, *inter-alia*, liberalised tariff norms for hydroelectric projects were notified. Government formalised model PPAs for thermal and hydro power projects.

(2) *Competitive Bidding for Awarding Projects*

The initial batch of projects were awarded in 1992–94 on the basis of negotiations between the SEB and a single developer through the MoU route. There was considerable criticism about the MoU route on the grounds of lack of transparency, favouritism and even allegations of corrupt practices. As government was committed to a transparent system to encourage competition for finalising private power projects, it was decided in January 1995 that no private power project proposal would be considered by the CEA if the project was not awarded through competitive bidding in the selection of developers. A cut-off date of 18 February 1995 was prescribed and only the MoUs signed before this date were considered by the CEA for techno-economic clearance. The States were advised during June 1996 to follow the international competitive bidding route in the selection of equipment procurement and construction (EPC) contractors for power projects in a transparent manner. A notification for competitively bid projects was issued in May 1997, defining the manner in which tariff would be determined for such projects.

(3) *Enhancing the Capital Expenditure Limit*

The limit of capital expenditure requiring concurrence of the Central Electricity Authority was enhanced from Rs. 100 crore to Rs. 1,000 crore, in September 1995, for projects selected through competitive bidding to enable the States to plan projects for quick capacity addition from the private sector. The number of clearances required for appraisal by CEA were reduced substantially in January 1996.

(4) *Introduction of 'In Principle' Clearance by CEA*

As the private sector project developers experienced difficulties in finalising financial packages, with even the Coal Ministry insisting on 'in principle' clearance from the CEA before giving coal linkages, it was decided to issue 'in principle' clearance to facilitate tying up of coal linkages.

(5) *Policy on Automatic Approval for Foreign Direct Investment Up to 74 Per cent in Power Sector*

It was decided to accord automatic approvals for foreign equity up to 74 per cent in all types of generation projects. The model 'Request For Proposals' (RFP) and 'Request For Qualifications' (RFQ) documents were circulated to all the States. The State Governments were provided funds to engage reputed consultants to advise them on PPAs.

(6) *PFC Established Technical Assistance Project*

On the instructions of the Ministry to play the role of a developmental financial institution, the Power Finance Corporation (PFC) established the technical assistance project for private power development scheme with World Bank assistance to hire services of experienced consultants for preparation of feasibility reports, detailed project reports, bid preparation/evaluation, selection of project developers, negotiation of power purchase and other related agreements.

(7) *Promotion of Captive and Cogeneration Power Projects*

It was decided to open an alternative route where the industries themselves would meet their power requirements by setting up of captive, co-generation and small power plants and sell surplus power to the grid on mutually agreed terms. The State Governments were advised to give rational tariff and third party access for direct sale of power to the other industrial units. It was also decided on 9 January 1997 to permit setting up of captive plants, fully dedicated to an industry or group of industries by an independent power company (third party) with concessional customs duty.

(8) *Barge-Mounted Power Plants in the Private Sector*

It was felt necessary to encourage short gestation projects, including barge-mounted power stations by the coastal states, as these projects have the inherent advantage of making available power in a short period. Karnataka and Gujarat had invited proposals for capacity addition of 900 MW through barge-mounted plants.

(9) *Policy on Mega Power Projects*

When the private power policy was initiated during 1991–92, it was envisaged that the projects would be basically state projects selling power to the State grid. We were required to add more than 10,000 MW every year for the next ten years to meet the growing demand, which was an onerous task. Moreover, coal was basically available in eastern and central India, whereas the hydel power potential was concentrated in the north east and the north but a higher demand for power was in the south and the west. It was, therefore, felt that unless mega power projects were set up in the region having coal and hydel potential, we would not be able to tackle the increasing demand for power. Establishing mega power projects, based on imported coal, in the coastal regions was also considered as a feasible option.

It was also recognised that the State in which the mega project was to come up would not always be able to absorb the total power, thus requiring it to enter into power purchase agreements with more than one state. Since a number of states would be involved, it was felt desirable to have a central organisation to play a coordinating/facilitating role and provide escort services to the promoter. It was in this context that the government formulated a mega power policy on 10 November 1995, when I was the Secretary (Power). The salient features of mega power policy were as follows:

- Projects of capacity of *1000 MW and more* and *catering to more than one State* should be considered as a mega project;
- The *CEA should identify potential sites* and NTPC would prepare feasibility reports;
- The promoters should be *selected through the competitive bidding route. POWERGRID would select promoters* and provide escort services and arrange for wheeling of power; and

- Concessional import duty facilities were extended for such projects.

Based on this policy, a few sites were identified. An MoU was signed between seven States and the China Light and Power Company, Hong Kong to set up 10,000 MW project at Hirma in Orissa.

PRESENTATION TO PRIME MINISTER P.V. NARASIMHA RAO

During the later part of 1995, I felt that in spite of several initiatives, not much progress was being made in the projects promoted by the independent power producers and the power supply position was becoming quite serious and the financial condition of the SEBs was also deteriorating. I felt that it was necessary to make a presentation to the Prime Minister to apprise him of the prevailing scenario in the power sector so that an action plan could be prepared. I, therefore, requested that I should be given time to make a presentation to the Prime Minister and was very happy when I was allotted twenty minutes from his very busy schedule. Amar Nath Varma, Principal Secretary to the Prime Minister cautioned me not to exceed time by even a minute. Dr. Manmohan Singh, Finance Minister and N.K.P. Salve, Power Minister were also present. As the presentation progressed, the Prime Minister evinced keen interest and sought clarifications on several issues. The presentation lasted for nearly an hour. I was happy to place my plan of action for reforms in the power sector before the Prime Minister. It was indeed the beginning of major reform initiatives in the power sector.

COUNTER GUARANTEE

The Government of India decided to extend counter guarantee as an incentive to the first few projects that would be set up under the policy announced by the Government of India in 1991 to encourage private sector investment in the power generation. The counter guarantee was extended primarily to give comfort to the Independent Power Producers (IPP) regarding payments for supply of power to the State Electricity Boards, whose financial position was none too comfortable. It was apprehended that the financial closer of the IPP projects may not be achieved without the guarantee regarding the payments by the state governments on behalf of the State Electricity Boards and counter guarantee by the Government of India. It was therefore decided by the Government of India to extend counter guarantee for eight projects. The Dabhol Project in Maharashtra promoted by ENRON was one such project assured by the Government of India to issue counter guarantee.

ENRON SAGA—DABHOL POWER COMPANY

ENRON has been in the news for a number of reasons and has generated more heat than power. As I have no intention to generate further heat without producing power, I would make a passing mention about the project. I may add here that even though I belong to the Maharashtra cadre and had served as chairman MSEB, the entire saga unfolded after I demitted office as Chairman, MSEB. I relinquished charge in July 1991, whereas ENRON emerged on the scene in June 1992, when I was serving as Additional Secretary, Ministry of Defence. Also, the PPA between the company and the Government of Maharashtra was signed in December 1993, whereas I joined the Ministry of Power in April 1994. Thus, at no stage was I associated in promoting the project. Every time the Enron Project was discussed, I used to mention that I was *Chairman, MSEB before ENRON* and *Secretary, Ministry of Power after ENRON.*

The project had generated so much public criticism that it could be easily said that if the paper on which charges and counter charges were levelled against the project was burnt, it could have generated power without any fuel, equivalent to its installed capacity for the entire life of the project!! The project even after completion continued to generate heat, without producing any power.

Under the new policy of the Government, a MoU was signed on 20 June 1992 between Enron and MSEB. This was one of the projects promoted on the MoU route after the visit of a high power delegation to the U.S.A. After extended negotiations with the assistance of national and international consultants, a power purchase agreement for the first phase of 740 MW was signed in December 1993. Ever since the MoU was signed, the project was faulted on the grounds of lack of transparency in selecting the promoter, undue favours to the promoter, corrupt practices, high cost and high tariff due to lack of competition. It was also alleged that the PPA was one sided. One of the major controversies was that CEA issued techno-economic clearance without proper scrutiny of the cost. This resulted in unreasonably high tariff of the project. The project itself was discussed several times in the Foreign Investment Promotion Board (FIPB) meetings, chaired by Amar Nath Varma, Principal Secretary to the Prime Minister. The Finance Secretary discussed the matter pertaining to the tariff in great detail with all concerned in two meetings held on 3 November 1993. In the FIPB meeting, held on 5 November, 1993, it was recorded that "Finance Secretary (Montek Singh Ahluwalia) observed that the question of cost of power had been looked into and was found that it was more or less in line with other projects being put up in Maharashtra". Based on this observation from the Finance Secretary, further clearances followed. Financial closure was achieved in February 1995 and construction was started immediately thereafter.

The Government decided to extend counter guarantee for eight projects and one such project was Dabhol project in Maharashtra, promoted by ENRON. The Government of Maharashtra initially conceived the project in two phases, the first phase of 695 MW. There was also a mention that the ultimate capacity of the project would be increased to 2,015 MW. The second phase was to be optional, based on the completion of the first phase. The fuel for the project was naphtha initially till LNG facilities were created at the site and the entire power would be supplied to Maharashtra. Since the very beginning, the project got into a number of legal cases and various Opposition political parties also criticised the project, which only added further controversies in its implementation.

At the time of elections to the Maharashtra Assembly in February 1995, both the Shiv Sena and the BJP, the major opposition parties in Maharashtra, vowed that in case they came to power, they would "dump the project in the 'Arabian Sea', due to various irregularities and corrupt practices adopted in promoting it. A coalition government of the Shiv Sena and Bhartiya Janata Party was formed in Maharashtra after the elections and the new Government set up a Cabinet Sub-Committee to inquire into the Dabhol project. Based on the recommendations of the committee, the new Government scrapped Phase I and cancelled phase II of the project in August 1995 in fulfilment of its electoral promise of "dumping" the project in the 'Arabian Sea'. Arbitration proceedings and legal actions were initiated by both the parties. When ENRON showed its willingness to renegotiate the contract, the Maharashtra Government constituted on 8 November 1995 a re-negotiation committee of technical and economic experts notable among them were Dr. N. Tata Rao, former Chairman, APSEB and Dr. Kirit Parikh, Director General, Indira Gandhi Institute of Development Research, Bombay. The committee submitted its report on 19 November 1995. It was recommended that the entire 2,015 MW project be implemented, as against 695 MW approved by the previous government in the first phase and the optional second phase was to be pursued after implementation of the first phase. There was now to be a slightly lower power tariff of Rs. 1.86 per kWh as compared to Rs. 1.89 per kWh agreed earlier. The first stage was implemented and generated power for a few years. While the second phase was under implementation, there was a dispute between the MSEB and ENRON and the project was closed for over five years. The project, since renamed as Ratnagiri project, has been restarted. However, it is operating intermittently, based on availability of fuel. The saga of ENRON continues unabated.

PRIVATE INVESTMENT IN GENERATION FAILED TO TAKE OFF

In spite of initial euphoria and several facilitating steps taken by the government, the Government's counter guarantee to some projects in generation as well as private power generation initiatives failed to take off. There were many reasons for such failure. The financial viability of the State Electricity Boards was very poor and they were not able to make due payments to (i) Coal India for coal purchased from it, (ii) central power sector undertakings like NTPC, etc., for power purchased from them and (iii) to several firms which have supplied equipment. Under those circumstances, the SEBs were not able to inspire confidence among the investors in power generation regarding payment security. In addition, 'power' being in the 'Concurrent List' under the Constitution of India, the decisions taken by the Government of India were not binding on the State Governments. This added a new dimension in implementing the private sector policy. In addition, the government was unable to promptly issue the counter guarantees to the 'fast track projects' which created a creditability gap in the policies announced by the Government.

COUNTER GUARANTEES

At the time the private power policy was launched in 1991, the credit rating of the country as a whole and that of the Indian power sector was too low to attract any worthwhile private investment in the sector. In order to encourage the investors, the Government of India offered counter guarantee to the initial eight fast track projects. After prolonged delays, the Government issued a counter guarantee to the ENRON project at Dabhol in Maharashtra, AES Project in Orissa and the GVK Project at Jegrupadu in Andhra Pradesh.

GVK Industries

GVK Industries was one of the eight Fast Track Independent Power Projects (IPP) identified by the Government of India for issue of counter guarantee in 1993. It proposed to set up a 235 MW gas-based combined cycle power project (Phase-I) at Jegurupadu, Andhra Pradesh. It signed a Power Purchase Agreement (PPA) with Andhra Pradesh State Electricity Board (APSEB) and tied up supply of natural gas with Gas Authority of India Limited (GAIL). It was the first IPP to obtain finances from International Finance Corporation (IFC) Washington for this project.

The company obtained the counter guarantee from the Government of India (GOI) on 4th September 1996, which provided comfort to the foreign lenders by way of repayment of their debt, after protracted negotiations with APSEB, Government of Andhra Pradesh, Ministry of Power and Ministry of Finance. As the Government of India was issuing counter guarantee for the first time, the negotiations carried on endlessly, as it was a new experience to everyone concerned. However GVK relentlessly pursued and obtained the counter guarantee and implemented the project and commenced the commercial operations from June 1997. The company started making profits since inception and repaid all the loans without any difficulty and Phase I is now a debt-free project.

The counter guarantee received from GOI had immensely benefited the company, not only in stabilizing the operations but also expanding its activities. Phase-II project for 220 MW was also implemented and is awaiting gas supply for commercial operations from the Reliance Industries. GVK Power & Infrastructure Limited (now a listed company of the GVK group) is holding company of the GVK Industries Limited and also setting up a 330 MW Hydro-electric Power Project at Alaknanda and 370 MW Hydro Power Project at Gauri Ganga in Uttarakhand. GVK Power & Infrastructure Limited has got subsidiaries of different infrastructural facilities like roads, airports, aviation, power, coal and mining etc.

Thus the counter guarantee extended by the Government of India for GVK Group's first major project had enabled the group to emerge as a major infrastructure development group, recognized nationally and internationally.

GVK industries was the first major project of the GVK Group and GVK has since forayed into a wide range of infrastructure development projects. Some of the important projects implemented or under implementation by the GVK Group are India's first 6 Lane Jaipur–Kishangarh Expressway, three Deluxe Luxury Hotels in Hyderabad in strategic alliance with Taj Group, one hotel in Chandigarh and one in Chennai. The GVK Group recently secured the prestigious project of modernization and development of Chatrapati Shivaji International Airport, Mumbai against stiff international competition.

The various ventures of GVK are providing excellent employment opportunities and furthering the economic growth of the country. Last but not the least, as a socially committed corporate entity, GVK is making contributions to promote socio-economic development activities, such as establishing schools, colleges, hospitals, houses for elderly and destitute, drinking water supply, sports etc. GVK-sponsored Sania Mirza, spotted and sponsored by GVK long ago, is today the pride of India in Tennis.

The counter guarantee extended by the Government of India for GVK Group's first major project had enabled the group to emerge as a major infrastructure development group, recognized nationally and internationally.

DELAY IN ISSUE OF COUNTER GUARANTEES

While there were many reasons which contributed for the delay in issuing the guarantees, one of the major reasons for delay in issuing the counter guarantees was due to multilevel and multi-agency scrutiny adopted by the different Ministries.

DELAYS IN ISSUE OF GUARANTEES TRIGGERED REFORMS

Despite all possible efforts put in by the Ministry of power, the desired capacity addition in generation was not forthcoming. It was under these circumstances, that reforms were introduced in the distribution sector during my time which has been vigorously pursued since then, to make the sector healthy and create confidence about payment security to the investors.

NEED TO GET MORE OUT OF EXISTING ASSETS

Since the envisaged additional generation capacity could not be added, a number of measures were taken to achieve optimum utilisation of the existing thermal units. The Plant Load Factor (PLF) of the power plants, which was 61.0 per cent in 1994–95, went up to 64 per cent by 1996–97, the highest ever so far. Some SEBs and NTPC achieved PLF higher than the all India average of 64 per cent. Demand Side Management (DSM) initiatives were taken, which included rationalising energy tariffs, and creating general awareness about end use efficiency, energy audits and conservation.

RENOVATION AND MODERNISATION

In order to improve the performance of the existing thermal power stations, a massive renovation and modernisation (R & M) programme was undertaken. This resulted in substantial additional generation. Fifty-five schemes were identified for R & M with an aggregate capacity of 9,653 MW. Detailed guidelines were issued to encourage private investments indicating the possible options such as (i) lease, rehabilitate, operate and transfer, (ii) sale of plants and (iii) joint ventures. In January 1997, R & M schemes, costing up to Rs. 500 crore, were excluded from CEA approval.

ENERGY CONSERVATION

Conservation and efficient use of energy was accorded high priority, considering the need to bridge the gap between the demand and supply of power. The task of evolving and implementing a coordinated strategy in energy conservation was entrusted to the energy management centre. A draft bill on 'conservation of energy' was prepared and further necessary action was initiated to make it into an Act.

ASSESSMENT OF SMALL HYDRO POTENTIAL

Another major initiative taken during my tenure was assessment of small hydel potential. The Government undertook a systematic survey for the first time in the country, which could be harnessed by small developers.

NATIONAL POWER GRID

Emphasis was given to integrated grid operations in the country. The national power grid would eventually comprise strong regional networks with suitable high voltage direct current (HVDC) links between the regions. Already 22,740 ckt km of 400 kV lines and 6,424 ckt km of 220 kV lines were laid in the central sector. An inter-regional HVDC link connecting the Western and Northern regions was also in operation. Several inter-State and inter-regional transmission lines were planned to facilitate the integrated operation of the state systems within the region under centrally sponsored programme. The Regional Power Grids were established in the Northern, Western, Southern, Eastern and North-Eastern regions to make optimum utilisation of the unevenly distributed power resources in the country by facilitating flow of power within the region and between regions. During 1996-97, all the regional grids were operating in parallel.

AWARDS FOR REDUCTION IN TRANSMISSION AND DISTRIBUTION LOSSES

One of the major problems in the power sector has been the incidence of very high Transmission & Distribution losses, causing substantial losses to the SEBs. These losses were brought down to 20 per cent during 1996-97. However, the losses continued to be high and several measures were pursued vigorously to further bring down the losses. Under the incentive scheme, launched by the government of India, several SEBs were awarded shields and cash awards for reducing losses.

RURAL ELECTRIFICATION

Rural electrification involved electrification of villages, supply of electricity to rural areas, energisation of agricultural pumpsets and production-oriented activities like minor irrigation, rural enterprises etc. Electrification of villages had picked up during these years, bringing the cumulative figure of electrified villages to 5,02,721, accounting for more than 86 per cent villages in the country, while a total of 1,13,32,767 pumpsets were energised till 1996-97. Emphasis was continued to be laid on electrification of tribal villages and dalit basties. The kutir Jyoti Scheme also continued and about 24 lakh connections were released during 1996-97.

AGITATION AND FAST BY BAHUGUNA AGAINST TEHRI HYDRO PROJECT

Sunderlal Bahuguna, founder of the 'Chipko' Movement and reputed environmentalist, was leading the agitation against the Tehri Hydroelectric Project. However, the work on the Project continued uninterrupted since 1994. Among the important issues raised by Bahuguna were the seismic safety of the dam, the environmental consequences of the project, the rehabilitation of the project affected persons and the cultural, social and religious impact of the dam. Bahuguna was actively supported by several groups opposing the project.

Bahuguna went on fast for the first time in 1992 seeking a review of the project. P.V. Narasimha Rao, Prime Minister, had himself reviewed the project a number of times between May 1992 and June 1995. In spite of the once-in-a-year fast by Bahuguna, the Prime Minister had reiterated that while new issues would be looked into, those already examined would not be reopened and work would continue on the project.

Bahuguna started his 'maun vrat' and fast yet again on 13 April 1996, almost like an annual ritual. The then Prime Minister, Atal Behari Vajpayee, met certain eminent citizens on 25 May 1996 and requested Bahuguna to call off his fast to facilitate fresh efforts of the new Government. Bahuguna did not heed to the appeal of the Prime Minister. There was a change of Government soon after and H.D. Deve Gowda, the new Prime Minister went to great lengths to persuade Bahuguna to call off the fast, deputing S. Venugopalachari, Minister of State for Power and myself to Tehri to personally deliver the Prime Minister's letter of 4 June 1996, inviting him to Delhi to meet the PM and persuading him to withdraw his fast. Bahuguna agreed to come to Delhi to meet the Prime Minister. A helicopter was sent to bring Bahuguna to Delhi, but when he reached, instead of coming to 7, Race Course Road, the Prime Minister's Residence, he went straight to Rajghat, Mahatma Gandhi's Samadhi and continued his fast, insisting that the Prime Minister come to Rajghat to meet him. I tried my best to persuade the Prime Minister not to go to Rajghat to meet Bahuguna, but as Deve Gowda had assumed office only recently, he did not want any major problem on his hand immediately. The Prime Minister was persuaded by Bahuguna's followers to go to Rajghat and offer him 'neembu paani' (lemon water), after which Bahuguna broke his fast on 25 June 1996. I did not accompany the Prime Minister as a matter of principle although, as per protocol, I was required to be present. Fortunately for me, the Prime Minister did not take my absence seriously.

DHARNA BY MEDHA PATKAR AGAINST NARMADA DAM

Medha Patkar, founder of Narmada Bachao Andolan and a social activist, observed a day's dharna in front of Shram Shakti Bhavan, as the Government decided to increase the height of Narmada Dam which would create additional generation capacity. I was happy to receive her delegation in my chamber's. Although she was projected as a 'fire-brand', I was quite surprised that she was very well informed and pleasant while presenting her arguments opposing the project. Although I was not in agreement with her views, I was very much impressed by her commitment to the cause.

COOPERATION WITH NEIGHBOURING COUNTRIES IN HYDRO POWER

Special efforts were made to have the active cooperation of some neighbouring countries to fully exploit the potential of hydro resources for mutual benefit. The development of the water resources of the common rivers of India and the neighbouring countries of Nepal and Bhutan for mutual benefits was regularly reviewed with these countries.

Indo–Nepal Cooperation in Hydro Power Development

Nepal has three major river basins, namely, Sapta Kosi, Gandaki and Karnali. Two other rivers, the Mechi and the Mahakali form the India–Nepal border for the major portion of their length. The hydro potential of Nepal is estimated to be around 83,000 MW, of which, about 25,000 MW is expected to be economically exploitable. Nepal had exploited a capacity of about 300 MW till then. Three major water resource projects in Nepal, namely, Karnali, Pancheshwar and Saptakoshi had been under discussion. The feasibility report of Karnali Multipurpose Project (10,800 MW) was prepared in 1989. Pancheshwar Multi Purpose Project (Stage-I 2000 MW) had been examined by both countries and Detailed Project Report was under finalisation jointly. Pranab Mukherjee, Minister for External Affairs led a delegation comprising of Salman Haider, Foreign Secretary, Dr. M.S. Reddy, Secretary, Ministry of Water Resources and myself to Kathmandu, for negotiations on integrated development of Mahakali River Treaty with Pasupati Shamsher Rana, Minister for Water Resources, Nepal. I went with considerable interest to see Mount Everest, at close quarters, as this was my first visit to Nepal. However, negotiations between the delegations of both the countries went on continuously without any break till we signed the draft Treaty, with the result my trip was from Kathmandu Airport to the hotel and back except for one hour break at midnight for a visit to the casino located in the same hotel. Contrary to expectations, I won about Rs. 1,000 in the casino, which was the major talking point of the delegation in Nepal. We also called on Sher Bahadur Deuba, Prime Minister, His Majesty's Government of Nepal during the visit. It was a successful visit as the development of Pancheshwar Multi Purpose Project was covered in the treaty of integrated development of the Mahakali River, including Sarada Barrage, Tanakpur Barrage and Pancheshwar Project, signed between P.V. Narasimha Rao and Sher Bahadur Deuba, Prime Ministers of the two countries on 12 February, 1996, when I was Secretary, Ministry of Power. Dr. D. Dungal, Secretary, Water Resource Department, Government of Nepal and I exchanged signed copies of the Indo–Nepal Agreement of Hydro Electricity Generation on 18 February 1996 at Mumbai in the presence of Sher Bahadur Deuba, Prime Minister of Nepal.

Cooperation with Bhutan

India and Bhutan have close and consistently friendly ties, which enabled them to work for the economic development of Bhutan. Since all the rivers are snow fed, they offer attractive possibilities of hydroelectric development. The potential of the easily accessible sites is roughly estimated to be 10,000 MW and could be harnessed for the mutual benefit of both the countries.

Chukha Hydroelectric Project (336 MW) was implemented with Indian financial and technical assistance and is operating in an excellent manner. The surplus power from the project is being imported by India. Kurichu H.E. Project (45 MW) in eastern Bhutan is presently under implementation on turnkey basis with assistance from India. The Royal Government of Bhutan is interested in Chukha-II (Tala-1020 MW) Project. An agreement was signed in March 1996 between the two countries, when I was Secretary (Power). The Tala Project is now under implementation. The investigation of Shankosh Multi-Purpose Project (4060 MW) was completed and DPR was finalised in December 1995. Two other hydroelectric projects namely Wangchu and Bunakha, with a total installation of 1,080 MW, have been examined and their DPRs were under discussion with the Bhutanese Government.

Indo–Bangladesh Power Exchange Programme

To meet the power requirements and for optimally utilising the generating resources of India and Bangladesh, a transmission network was proposed to be executed to facilitate exchange of power between the two countries for mutual benefit. This would help towards formation of the SAARC Grid for the development of the South Asian Region. The Asian Development Bank (ADB) offered to undertake a technical assistance study covered under a grant to discuss all technical and commercial issues for such a project. ADB proposed a tripartite discussion between the two countries and ADB in Manila, Philippines between 28th and 30th May 1997 to discuss the proposal. The first tripartite meeting between the Government of India, Government of Bangladesh and ADB was held at Manila on 29 and 30th May 1997 and the team from India was led by me. Both the countries are making efforts to continue the cooperation.

POWERGRID'S DIVERSIFICATION INTO TELECOMMUNICATIONS

It was recognised that the power transmission lines, owned by POWERGRID, provided excellent connectivity throughout the country. The right of way already existed for installation of overhead optical fibre cables. POWERGRID had several strengths to provide the best telecom infrastructure for adoption of state-of-the-art technology such as fibre optic and excellent credit rating by financial institutions like the World Bank. A feasibility report was prepared to enable POWERGRID to make a foray into the telecom sector.

KUDANKULAM PROJECT

I was a part of the Prime Minister's High Power delegation to Russia in March 1997, when the matter regarding establishment of Kudankulam Project with Russian cooperation came up for extensive deliberations. The Kudankulam (KK) Project symbolises the technical and financial cooperation between The Russian Federation and India, within the framework of the inter-governmental agreement (IGA) signed with the Soviet Union in November 1988, for cooperation in the construction of a nuclear power station in India. When the two sides were about to sign the DPR contract in 1990, the activities on the project had to be halted due to developments in the USSR. Deliberations on the KK Project were revived in January 1993, during the visit of the Russian President to India and deliberations continued. An 'in principle' agreement to implement the project was finalised between His Excellency, Boris Yeltsin, President of the Russian Federation and H.D. Deve Gowda, Prime Minister of India, during his visit to Russia in March 1997.

DELHI VIDHYUT BOARD CREATED TO FACILITATE PRIVATISATION

While I was Secretary (Power), major initiatives were taken to dismantle the Delhi Electricity Supply Undertaking (DESU) and create the Delhi Vidhyut Board (DVB) to facilitate privatisation of power distribution in Delhi. DESU was unable to meet the growing requirements of power, either quantitatively or qualitatively, and had been incurring financial losses year after year due to high T & D losses, rampant theft of energy and inefficiency in performance parameters. It was observed that more than fifty per cent of the power received from generating stations was lost in transmission, sub-transmission and distribution, including theft of energy. There was also total mismanagement of revenue administration and non-recovery of dues. One of the major reasons for the poor performance of DESU was that it was under the control and supervision of the Delhi Municipal Corporation (DMC). Reportedly there was considerable interference in the day-to-day management of its functioning, resulting in malpractices and inefficiency. The Government of India had to repeatedly come to the rescue of DESU in order to bail it out of financial problems. Under these circumstances, it was decided during my tenure as Secretary, Ministry of

Power, to de-link DESU from the DMC Act and delegate powers of the State Government to the Lt. Governor, by amending the DMC Act and Electricity (Supply) Act, 1948. Accordingly, the Delhi Vidhyut Board (DVB) was created, hoping that the performance would improve, and if not, to facilitate early privatisation of DVB, as DVB was fortunate to function in a highly urbanised, compact and easily accessible area for power management, supervision and control and with the entire power being sold to commercial, domestic and industrial consumers without any agricultural load. Legal changes that were made during my time had facilitated the restructuring of DVB and private sector participation in distribution of power in Delhi.

PRIORITY OF DEVELOPMENT OF HYDROELECTRIC POWER

The hydroelectric potential of India is estimated at 84,000 MW at 60 per cent load factor, which would correspond to an installed capacity of about 1,50,000 MW. The share of hydel capacity in the total installed capacity in the country was 50 per cent in 1962-63 and thereafter it declined to about 25 per cent. In the late fifties and early sixties, the need to expand irrigation facilities led to the setting up of large but long-gestation multi-purpose projects such as Bhakra. In the 1970s, the emphasis switched to the industrial sector, necessitating speedy availability of power. Thermal Projects of shorter gestation, therefore, acquired priority. Over the years, hydel projects were confronted with problems relating to environment and forests, resettlement and rehabilitation, land acquisition and funding. Disturbed conditions in some parts of the country also led to delays in the execution of some projects. There were as many as 32 projects with a capacity of almost 4300 MW, which were held up due to inter-state disputes. During the Eighth Five Year Plan, not more than 2,600 MW could be commissioned. Even though CEA had earlier estimated that 18,783 MW may be added in the Ninth Plan, this has now been scaled down to 11,616 MW.

Government introduced enhanced incentives for hydel generation in the private sector since January 1995. A Committee under the chairmanship of M.K. Sambamurti, former Chairman, CEA, was constituted in August 1996 to suggest measures to speed up hydroelectric development in the country. The committee's recommendations were being implemented when I demitted charge as Secretary.

SPECIAL ACTION PLAN FOR EXPLOITATION OF HYDRO POTENTIAL IN J & K

Development of hydroelectric potential in J & K was one of the points included in the CMNPP adopted by the Chief Ministers in 1996. A special action plan for taking up several projects in J & K was finalised. The Dulhasti Hydro-Electric Project was being set up in Kishtwar Region of Doda District in J & K on the River Chenab, with bilateral assistance from France and was awarded for turnkey execution to a French consortium in October 1989, and was scheduled to be commissioned in July 1994. However, after only about 28 per cent of the work was completed, the French consortium suspended the work in August 1992, contending that the security environment was not conducive. Finally, a decision was taken to award the work to another contractor in March 1997 and the work resumed at the site. Further, after continuous follow up, three units of the Uri Hydro Power Project were commissioned and the project was dedicated to the nation by Prime Minister H.D. Deve Gowda on 13th February 1997, when I was Secretary Power. In order to exploit the hydro potential further, it was decided to entrust the Sawalkot and Baglihar Projects to NHPC for execution, but on the request of Government of J & K, these projects were returned to J & K Government for execution.

SPECIAL ACTION PLAN FOR NORTH EASTERN REGION

The North Eastern Region has a huge hydel potential of 31,857 MW. Out of this, barely 1 per cent of the potential has been developed and another 1 per cent is under development. Insufficient load, inadequate transmission and distribution facilities, evacuation system for transmitting power out of North East and funding constraints, R & R problems and law and order problems are some of the reasons for the slow development of power potential in the North East. The principal agency for investigation and preparation of Detailed Project Report in the North East is the Brahmaputra Board, which has been activated. In the context of new initiatives for development of north eastern region announced by the Prime Minister in November 1996, the implementation of the Doyang project (75 MW) in Nagaland, Turial Project (60 MW) in Mizoram and Loktak Downstream Project (90 MW) in Manipur was closely monitored. It was ensured that a minimum of 10 per cent of the Plan Budget in a year was earmarked for development of the North Eastern States.

COMMITTEE ON INTEGRATED COAL POLICY

The Planning Commission constituted a Committee on Integrated Coal Policy on 27 April 1995. The Committee was chaired by K S R Chari, former Secretary Coal, Government of India and I was one of the members of the Committee. The Committee recommended that an integrated coal policy, an independent agency at the central level be created to step up exploration; all new coal and lignite blocks be offered on the basis of competitive bids in which national coal companies and private sector can participate, de-regulation of coal prices in a phased manner and an autonomous regulatory body be set up. The committee submitted its report on 14 May 1996.

VISIT TO TOKYO FOR JUST A FEW HOURS

I was invited to participate in the workshop organised jointly by the World Bank and Japan Chambers of Commerce and Industry (JCCI) at Tokyo on 14 May 1997. The participants in this workshop included representatives from ADB. A Study Group of JCCI on Power Development in India, constituted in July 1996, had identified four States viz. Andhra Pradesh, Gujarat, Karnataka and Rajasthan for future investments. I made a detailed presentation about the prospects for investment in the power sector. I reached Tokyo on 13th May 1997, late in the night, and was there only for a few hours. While in Tokyo, I received a message to return to Delhi immediately to be present during the Cabinet Meeting scheduled for 15th May 1997. I left Tokyo on 14th May 1997 in the afternoon via Singapore and Madras (Chennai) only to be told on arrival at Madras (Chennai) Airport that the Cabinet Meeting, for which I was rushing back to Delhi, had been postponed!

NINTH PLAN POWER PROGRAMME PREPARED

The Working Group on Power for preparation of the Ninth Plan Power Programme was constituted by the Planning Commission in November 1995 under my chairmanship. After taking a mid-term review of the Eighth Plan in August 1995 and after taking into consideration various constraints during the plan, capacity addition was expected to be only 18,100 MW, as against a target of 30,538 MW, reflecting a likely achievement of around 60 per cent. One of the reasons for the significant shortfall was the slow execution of hydro schemes. Another important reason for slippages, particularly in the thermal projects, was that the State saw the announcement of policy for private participation in 1991 as an opportunity to cut back on their involvement in generation projects. As a result, many projects that were scheduled for commissioning through the state sector resources were transferred to the private sector, which did not materialise. Taking into consideration the relevant demand estimates, norms for utilisation of various types of generating plants and constraints, the Working Group recommended a programme of addition of 58,000 MW, with matching investment in transmission and distribution. The Group submitted its report in January 1997 to the Planning Commission.

STATE ELECTRICITY BOARDS—REFORMS: FOCUS ON DISTRIBUTION

Despite a forty-fold increase in the installed generation capacity since the beginning of the planning process, chronic power shortages continued to prevail in all the States. The critical problem area in the power sector was the poor performance of SEBs, which had been looking after generation, transmission and distribution of power, set tariffs, and collection of revenues within their respective States. It would, however, be totally unfair to blame only the SEBs for their poor performance. The State Governments were also responsible since they had fixed unviable tariffs; provided free supply of power to the agricultural sector, without fully subsidising the SEBs; gave concessional tariffs to some categories of consumers and tended to interfere in the functioning of the SEBs. To sustain the process of economic development, particularly in the wake of the liberalisation process started during the 1990s, it had become critically important to give adequate attention to the restructuring of the power sector.

Broadly, the major problems confronting the power sector were:

- *Deteriorating Financial Condition of the State Electricity Boards*: In terms of Section 59 of the Electricity (Supply) Act, 1948, SEBs were required to earn a minimum rate of return (ROR) of 3 per cent on their net fixed assets in service. While in 1992-93, 11 SEBs had a positive ROR of more than 3 per cent, in 1994-95, there were only 3 SEBs (one of which was MSEB). In turn, this situation adversely affected the future capacity addition and system improvement programmes. While SEBs did not have enough resources to finance their programmes, their ability to raise funds from other sources was limited due to poor financial and commercial performance.
- *Unviable Tariffs*: Industrial and agriculture sectors continued to be the two most important categories of consumers in terms of their relative shares, with electricity tariffs set at very high rate for industry and much below unit cost for domestic sectors and many States supplying power free of cost to the agricultural sector. The commercial losses of the SEBs were to the tune of Rs. 6,125 crore in 1994-95 and were projected to increase substantially every year.
- *Subsidies*: The subsidy for agriculture and domestic sectors, was Rs. 11,477 crore in 1994-95 and was projected to go up to Rs. 13,307 crore in 1995-96.
- *High T & D Losses*: The SEBs continued to suffer as high as 22 per cent T&D losses, and many States had much higher losses. Delhi was accounting for more than 40 per cent. The losses were due to sparsely distributed loads over a large rural area, substantial energy sold at low voltage, under investment in the power distribution, inadequate billing and, more importantly, high pilferage and theft of energy.
- *Lack of Adequate Resources*: It was estimated that a new capacity of around 1,00,000 MW was required in the next 10 years to meet the growing demand of power, with an investment of about Rs. 4,00,000 crore, for generation projects alone, with an equal amount for the matching transmission and distribution projects. It necessitated deepening and widening of the debt market. This called for mobilizing private investment.
- *Availability of fuels and their transportation*: The new capacity addition would require massive investments in coal, railways and ports for the transportation of fuel. Supply of natural gas,

even for the existing gas based stations, was totally inadequate, resulting in under-utilisation.

- *Growing Demand-Supply Gap*: The country was facing an acute energy and peaking shortages of about 9 per cent and 18 per cent, respectively.
- Operational and technical inefficiencies resulted in the under-utilisation of existing capacities.

The rationalisation of tariff, levy of a minimum agricultural tariff, reduction in T & D losses and commercialisation of operations could improve the financial health of the SEBs. Restoration of financial health of SEBs and improvement in their operational performance continued to remain the most crucial issue in the power sector.

It was in the context of these identified problems that a Conference of Chief Ministers was convened on 16th October 1996 to discuss various aspects of these problems and with specific focus on major issues such as:

(i) *Restructuring SEBs and Creation of the institution of Regulators*: In order to enable the State Electricity Boards to meet the power needs efficiently, they had to become commercially viable entities. The first step in this direction was to have sufficient autonomy and ability to take decisions on commercial considerations. It was observed that there were serious structural barriers to the implementation of such reforms within the present framework of State Electricity Boards. There was a need for early restructuring of SEBs so as to make their physical and commercial operations more viable and to set up independent Regulatory Commissions. The hitherto neglected area of power distribution needed to be accorded focussed attention since the financial health of the power sector could be substantially improved by strengthening the distribution segment.

(ii) *Short-Term and Long-Term Measures*: It was essential to improve the performance of the existing thermal plants, bring about reduction of gestation period of power projects, accord priority to the on-going sanctioned schemes, accelerate the present pace of hydro power development, ensure reduction in T & D losses; make optimum use of regional energy surpluses, demand side management, operational and financial action plan, make speedy settlement of outstanding dues to central PSUs and make the Central Power Sector Undertakings attuned to contemporary requirements.

(iii) *Private Sector Initiative of 1991 Did Not Progress*: The private initiative in the power sector to get required investments did not make much progress and many projects had encountered unforeseen hurdles, controversies and delays. One of the most important hurdles was that the SEBs were perceived as highly risky customers due to their extremely poor financial record and inability to discharge their financial obligations. The private power programme could survive only if the SEBs functioned as commercially viable entities.

REFORMS AND RESTRUCTURING OF STATE ELECTRICITY BOARDS

Major initiatives were taken under these circumstances during my tenure as Secretary by introducing reforms in the power sector and restructuring of SEBs. The credit for initiating restructuring of SEBs goes to the Government of Orissa. A series of meetings were held by me to improve the draft provisions made by the consultants, and after extensive consultations with Ministry of Law and Justice, the Orissa Electricity Reform Act 1995 was finalized. The assent of the President of India was obtained for the Act and the Orissa Electricity Reform Act came into force from 1 April 1996. In the restructured electricity set up in Orissa, the SEB was replaced by separate corporate entities for generation, transmission and grid operation and four distribution companies. An Independent State Electricity Regulatory Commission was set up in Orissa to undertake the licensing, fixation of tariffs, etc.

After the Orissa Electricity Reform Act, 1995, was implemented, I played a predominant role in persuading the other States to carry out diagnostic studies and to restructure their Electricity Boards. A number of States such as Andhra Pradesh, Haryana, Rajasthan, U.P. Bihar and Gujarat have initiated measures to reform the power section.

CHIEF MINISTERS CONFERENCE ON 16 OCTOBER 1996

It was in this context that H.D. Deve Gowda, Prime Minister of India, convened a Conference of Chief Ministers on 16 October 1996. This meeting was being held after nearly four years as there was a need to arrive at a national consensus on power reforms. *H.D. Deve Gowda, Prime Minister of India,* while addressing the Chief Ministers, discarded the prepared speech, and gave a clarion call for power reforms. I quote from his speech: "The country was facing a power famine and its primary cause was the lack of a coherent National Power Policy and, unless tackled, this famine would not allow the country to grow either in the field of industrial development or in the field of agriculture. Other causes for power famine were the vagaries of the monsoons for the hydroelectric sector, shortages/quality of coal and poor railway transportation facilities and lack of political support for the financial betterment of the power sector as a whole. The State Electricity Boards were allowed to pile up huge debts and losses because the political leaders were chary of taking hard decisions. Decisions were also not being taken by the States or the Centre for fear of invoking allegations of a nexus between the investors and the Government to promote (private) generation projects." He, therefore, called for a collective shouldering of the responsibility in resolving the power problem.

The Prime Minister also called for identification of priorities and to reach a consensus unanimously on several areas with a time-bound programme, irrespective of political affiliations. He also highlighted the decision to constitute an empowered committee to monitor the progress and stated that Government of India was ready to go a step further and delegate even greater powers to the States for clearance of projects and minimising the role of the Central Government. The Prime Minister felt that environmental activism and public interest litigation tend to delay the implementation of projects. He also stressed that the power sector policy should not be made a political issue and the States would have to take hard decisions on tariff issues. In conclusion, he urged the Chief Ministers to arrive at a unanimous solution—a National Power Policy—so that the identified goals could be achieved in a time-bound manner and without this, the nation as a whole would have to pay dearly.

During the ensuing discussion, N. Chandrababu Naidu, Chief Minister, Andhra Pradesh and Digvijay Singh, Chief Minister, Madhya Pradesh suggested that a national consensus on tariff reforms and restructuring of SEBs be evolved. All the Chief Ministers present unanimously endorsed the suggestions made by them and suggested that the Draft Common Minimum National Action Plan for Power (CMNPP) circulated for the meeting should be further improved by Secretary, Ministry of Power after discussions with State Secretaries and Chairman SEBs. The next meeting of the Chief Ministers was to be convened in three months. The basic elements suggested in the CMNPP were:

(1) Setting up of National/State Regulatory Commissions in a time-bound manner.
(2) Restructuring of SEBs
(3) Rationalising Tariff Structure
(4) Private Sector Participation in Distribution
(5) Formulation of National Energy Policy

SOME CHAIRMEN, SEBS WERE NOT IN FAVOUR OF RESTRUCTURING OF SEBs

During the discussions with representatives of the States, there were serious differences among the Chairman and Secretaries about the restructuring of SEBs. Some Chairmen expressed shock about the proposal for restructuring of SEBs emanating from me, especially since I had worked as Chairman of a premier SEB like the MSEB. It was a very difficult and unpleasant task for me to convince them as to why the electricity industry in the country needed restructuring, in spite of the excellent work done by SEBs all over the country, without whose untiring work, electricity would not have reached the nooks and corners of the country. However, there was a need for restructuring the sector, as the demand for power was growing by leaps and bounds and the SEBs were unable to meet the demand, due to inadequate investment and unviable tariff policies of the Government. There was, therefore, a need to restructure the electricity sector itself, resulting in restructuring of SEBs and to encourage private investments. I had several meetings to convince them and credit for finally agreeing to a consensus "Draft Common Minimum National Action Plan for Power" goes to all of them.

Before the agenda for the proposed Chief Ministers conference held on 3 December 1996 was finalised, I had individually called on some Chief Ministers like N. Chandrababu Naidu (Andhra Pradesh), Digvijay Singh (Madhya Pradesh), Bhairon Singh Shekhawat (Rajasthan) and Jyoti Basu (West Bengal) and had extensive discussions on the reforms and also the proposed agenda. I also discussed with P. Chidambaram, Union Finance Minister who gave several valuable suggestions. I extensively briefed H.D. Deve Gowda, Prime Minister (who was holding the Power portfolio), on my discussions with the Chief Ministers.

SECOND CHIEF MINISTERS' CONFERENCE ON 3RD DECEMBER 1996 TO FINALISE "COMMON MINIMUM NATIONAL ACTION PLAN FOR POWER"

The Chief Ministers' Conference on Power, on 3 December 1996, chaired by the Prime Minister was attended, among others, by Bhairon Singh Shekhawat (CM, Rajasthan), Lalu Prasad Yadav (CM, Bihar), Bansi Lal (CM, Haryana), Digvijay Singh (CM, Madhya Pradesh), Veerbhadra Singh (CM, Himachal Pradesh), J.B. Patnaik (CM, Orissa) and Sahib Singh Varma (CM, Delhi). The meeting was also attended by P. Chidambaram, Union Finance Minister.

The Conference discussed the draft CMNPP and recognized that the gap between demand and supply of power was widening; the financial position of SEBs was deteriorating and the future development of the power sector could not be sustained without viable SEBs; need to encourage private sector participation in generation, transmission and distribution; necessary to undertake the reforms and restructuring of SEBs and necessary to set up Electricity Regulatory Commissions.

A national consensus was thus evolved for improving the performance of the power sector in a time-bound manner and CMNPP was adopted, containing, inter alia, the following:

(i) The Government should soon finalise a *National Energy Policy*.
(ii) Each State shall set up an independent *State Electricity Regulatory Commission*.
(iii) The Union Government should set up a *Central Electricity Regulatory Commission*.
(iv) *Rationalisation of retail tariffs* to ensure a minimum overall 3 per cent rate of return and cross-subsidisation may be allowed

and no sector should pay less than 50 per cent of the average cost of supply. *Tariffs for agricultural sector* should not be less than fifty paise per kWh and it should be brought to 50 per cent of the average cost in not more than three years.

(v) The States should *restructure* their *Electricity Boards.*

(vi) The State Governments agree to a gradual programme of *private sector participation in distribution of electricity.*

(vii) North-eastern region should get equitable share in the investments in the power sector.

(viii) Development of *Mega Power Projects at Pitheads.*

On the day of Chief Ministers' Conference, which was scheduled to be held at 6.00 pm at Parliament Annexe, H.D. Deve Gowda, Prime Minister, had programmes in Bangalore and Hyderabad. He left Delhi in the morning and attended programmes in Bangalore as well as in Hyderabad and returned to Delhi at about 5:00 p.m. I met him before the Conference and briefed him about the various items on the agenda. When the meeting started, the Prime Minister, in his inaugural remarks, totally deviated from the agenda and started mentioning as to how to transmit power from surplus states to deficit states, which was not the subject matter for discussion (in any case, there was not much surplus power in the country!!) and everybody was looking astonished, as the meeting was convened to finalise draft common minimum national action plan for power. It is obvious, without meaning any offence, that the Prime Minister was perhaps under jet lag, as he had traversed the country from north to south and south to north in such a short time and had also attended several programmes during the day. Even some Chief Ministers also seemed to be at the same wavelength as the Prime Minister. One Chief Minister talked about strengthening the 33 kV sub-stations and transmission networks in his State (which was purely in the domain of the State Government), and another Chief Minister talked about serious power shortages in his State and the Centre should come to its assistance. Not a word was mentioned by many about the Draft Action Plan. I walked up to P. Chidambaram, Finance Minister, and requested his intervention to prevent the discussions getting derailed. P. Chidambaram did his best to intervene. It was almost time for dinner and the meeting was about to end. I requested the Prime Minister to permit me to summarise the consensus arrived in the meeting. I concluded by stating that most of the suggestions made by the Chief Ministers were already included in the Draft Action Plan and I presume that the Action Plan was approved with some minor changes based on the discussions, which I could be permitted to carry out and finalise the minutes of the meeting. The Prime Minister concluded that agenda items were approved and invited the Chief Ministers to join him for dinner. Thus an important national programme in the power sector to carry out the reforms was approved unanimously, although several other issues were debated at great length by the Chief Ministers without much discussion on the agenda itself. The same policy is now being implemented as 'Common Minimum National Action Plan for Power' (CMNPP), both by the Centre and the State Governments. I waited for about three weeks after the circulation of the minutes, hoping against hope that nobody will object to the minutes. As no objections were received, I commended the implementation of the decisions to all the States on 30 December 1996, thus ushering in the New Year, 1997 with power sector reforms in distribution. This is just an instance of how some major decisions sometimes pass muster without much discussion in the Government!!

CREDIT FOR USHERING IN REFORMS IN DISTRIBUTION GOES TO H.D. DEVE GOWDA

The credit, however, for ushering in the distribution reforms in the power sector clearly goes to HD Deve Gowda, who relentlessly pursued the power sector reforms, ably assisted by P. Chidambaram, Finance Minister and T R Satish Chandran, Principal Secretary to the Prime Minister, while I steered the reforms as Secretary (Power).

ELECTRICITY REGULATORY COMMISSIONS BILL, 1997

Another major initiative taken during my tenure as Secretary was related to the framing of the Electricity Regulatory Commissions Bill, 1997. The electricity industry has been regulated through the Indian Electricity Act, 1910 and Electricity (Supply) Act, 1948, supported by the Indian Electricity Rules 1956. Regulation is carried out by several agencies, namely, Central Government, State Governments, Central Electricity Authority, Regional Electricity Boards and State Electricity Boards. I sincerely believed in distancing the State Government from controlling the power sector and to make the sector autonomous and independent in the long-term interest of the sector. After approval given by the Chief Ministers to CMNPP to provide for the establishment of a Central Electricity Regulatory Commission and State Electricity Regulatory Commissions, the Central Government drafted The Electricity Regulatory Commission Bill, 1997, to establish Central and State Electricity Regulatory Commissions. Although the ERC Bill was introduced in Parliament during the Budget Session in 1997, it could not be passed, as there was a change of government in April/May 1997 and the bill was allowed to lapse.

PRIVATE SECTOR PARTICIPATION IN TRANSMISSION

Yet another initiative taken by me was to create the Central Transmission Utility and to encourage private sector participation in the transmission sector. There was an urgent need to promote investment in transmission to transfer power from generating stations to load despatch centres within the state as well as inter-state. As the Government was unable to mobilise the financial resources, a policy decision was taken to allow private participation in the transmission sector, which needed amendments to the existing electricity laws. The Electricity Laws (Amendment) Ordinance, 1997, was promulgated on 24-1-1997 by the President of India for effecting amendments to the Indian Electricity Act, 1910 and Electricity (Supply) Act, 1948, to provide for transmission as a distinct activity and to provide for issue of transmission licenses.

A Bill, titled the Electricity Laws (Amendment) Bill, 1997, was introduced in the Budget Session of Parliament, while I was Secretary. The Bill provided for setting up of Central Transmission Utility under Section 27a of the Indian Electricity Act, 1910. POWERGRID Corporation of India Limited was to be the Central Transmission Utility. However, the bill was allowed to lapse with the change of Government in May 1997.

ELEVATION AS A CONSTITUTIONAL AUTHORITY

In late May 1997, I led an Indian delegation to the bilateral discussions between the Ministry of Power, Government of India and Ministry of Energy, Government of Bangladesh at Manila, Philippines. These discussions were arranged by the Asian Development Bank (ADB) to explore the possibility of exchange of power between the two countries.

On my return on 30th May 1997, after successfully accomplishing the task, I was informed by the Cabinet Secretary, TSR Subramanian, IAS (1961-Uttar Pradesh), that the Government has sent a proposal to the President to appoint me as Member, Union Public Service Commission (UPSC), a National Constitutional Authority under the Constitution of India. He told me that I should be prepared to join the UPSC immediately, as the proposal might be approved any time by the President. Although I was happy that the Government considered me suitable for a constitutional assignment after retirement, my initial reaction was none too happy, as the nature of the task assigned to the UPSC did not square up with my specialisation in the energy sector. I consulted a few of my well-wishers who were unanimous that I should not lose an opportunity of appointment as a Constitutional Authority, as it was in recognition of my long and distinguished service to the Government and I should accept the appointment with gratitude.

Thus my service in the IAS and active association with the power sector came to an end. However, I was happy to hand over charge to a dear friend of mine, Dr. E.A.S. Sarma, IAS (Andhra Pradesh-1965), who happened to be my contemporary in Andhra University, Waltair, Andhra Pradesh, and an acknowledged energy specialist.

TWENTY

RECRUITING CIVIL SERVICES AS A NATIONAL CONSTITUTIONAL AUTHORITY

Member, Union Public Service Commission

I must be candid enough to admit that I never even dreamt that I would be an IAS officer, let alone become a Member of the Union Public Service Commission (UPSC) after retirement. It was a rare honour to select the members of the 'heaven born' service, as the IAS is generally referred to, especially since those selected by me would be at the helm of affairs in the country, shaping the destinies of the nation for decades to come. In addition to the IAS, the Commission also selects members of other civil services such as the Indian Foreign Service, Indian Police Service, Indian Forest Service, Indian Revenue Service and a large number of generalist services known as the Allied Service.

Before I joined the UPSC, I called on J.M. Qureshi, who was the Chairman of the UPSC. I was pleasantly surprised to see him sporting a P'cap, which was quite a rare sight for a high level functionary, while seated in office. I recollected the saying that 'old habits die hard', as Qureshi belonged to the Indian Police Service. He on the other hand, was surprised to see me dressed very simply and advised me, in a lighter vein, that it would be difficult for anybody to believe that I was a Hon'ble Member, UPSC. He advised me to wear a suit for a few days in spite of it being the peak of summer in Delhi, but I did not, obviously, take his advice seriously. I took oath under the Constitution of India as Member, UPSC on 5th June, 1997—a rather sultry day in Delhi.

HISTORY OF THE UPSC

The first Public Service Commission was established in India on October 1, 1926, on the basis of recommendations of the Royal Commission on the superior civil services in India, under the Chairmanship of Lord Lee. Subsequently, a Federal Public Service Commission was set up in 1937, under the Government of India Act, 1935 to replace the Public Service Commission of India. After independence, the Federal Public Service Commission, was given a constitutional status with the Constitution of India on January 26, 1950 when the Union Public Service Commission was constituted under *Article 315 of the Constitution. Article 316 of the Constitution* mandates that the Chairman and Members of the Union Public Service Commission shall be appointed by the President of India. The Chairman and Members shall hold office for a term of 6 years from the date on which they enter office or till they attain the age of 65 years, whichever is earlier. *Article 317 of the Constitution* states that the *Chairman or any other Member shall only be removed by order of the President on the ground of misbehaviour, after the Supreme Court, on a reference made by the President, after inquiry, recommends his or her removal.* The President may also remove the Chairman or any other member, if the Chairman or Member is adjudged as insolvent or engages during the term of office in any paid employment or is unfit to continue in office by reason of infirmity of mind or body. These provisions have been made to ensure that the Chairman/Members exercise their powers for merit-based selection without fear or favour and render impartial advice on matters referred to them under Article 320 of the Constitution.

CONSTITUTIONAL PROVISIONS-FUNCTIONS

Under *Article 320 of the Constitution*, the Commission is consulted

(a) on all matters relating to methods of recruitment to the civil services and for civil posts,
(b) on the principles to be followed in making appointments to civil services and posts,

(c) on all disciplinary matters affecting a person serving under the Government of India; and
(d) any other matter which the President may refer to them.

Article 323 of the Constitution specifies that it is the duty of the Commission to present annually to the President a report as to the work done by the Commission and that the President shall cause a copy of such a report, together with a memorandum explaining the reasons for non-acceptance of the advice of the Commission, if any, to be laid before each House of Parliament.

The President of India appoints ten Members in addition to the Chairman of the Commission, out of which possibly 50% of the Members should have experience as civil servants. Except for brief intervals, the Commission always had a full complement of Members. When I was in the UPSC, there were also two more Members from my batch in the IAS (1962), namely P C Hota and Mata Prasad, a rare coincidence in the UPSC.

The functions of the Commission prescribed in *Article 320* of the Constitution relate to recruitment for all civil services and civil posts by

(i) written examination with or without a viva voce examination or interview to supplement them,
(ii) interview,
(iii) promotion.

In pursuance of the mandate of the Constitution, the UPSC conducts examinations for recruitment to civil services/posts, which include Civil Services (Preliminary) Examination, Civil Services (Main) Examination, Indian Forest Service Examination, Engineering Services Examination, Indian Economic Service/Indian Statistical Service Examination, Examination for recruitment to officers grade in para-military forces of the Union as the CRPF, BSF & ITBP and Combined Medical Services Examination.

The Commission also handles work relating to

(i) promotion to Central Services,
(ii) deputation/Absorption,
(iii) promotion of State Service Officers to the All India Services viz. IAS/IPS and the Indian Forest Service governed by the Promotion

Regulations framed by the Government of India. The Selection Committees, presided over by the Chairman or a Member of UPSC, make selections of officers of various States/UTs for promotion to the three All India Services.

The Commission also conducts examinations for the National Defence Academy, the Naval Academy, the Air Force Academy and examinations for the Combined Defence Services (CDS). In respect of Defence Services, the written examination results are passed on to the Ministry of Defence for interviews, physical fitness test, etc. However, marks are not communicated to the Ministry. After receipt of interview marks, the final results are declared by the Commission after adding up marks in the written examination and the marks in the tests conducted by the Service Selection Board.

For some specified posts as per the relevant recruitment rules, direct recruitment is done through interview by the Commission. The Interview Boards consist of eminent specialists in the relevant disciplines and are presided over by a Member or Chairman, UPSC. A number of references relating to the framing/amendment of recruitment rules and for deciding the mode of recruitment are also handled by the Commission.

ENTRY INTO CIVIL SERVICES, THEN AND NOW

When I appeared for the Civil Services Examination (called the IAS Examination) in 1961, there was a clear cut distinction at the entry level in terms of recruitment between the IAS, the IPS and the Central Services, called the Allied Services. There were three compulsory papers namely English Essay, General English and General Knowledge, each of 150 marks, common for all the services. Although the candidates appearing for the IPS were required to appear for two additional papers, each of 200 marks, those, who were appearing for the Central Services, were required to appear for three additional papers of 200 marks each. In addition, all those who wanted to be considered for the IAS and the Indian Foreign Service (IFS), were required to take two advanced papers in addition to the three additional papers. Thus while the total written marks for the IPS were 850, for the Central Services, it was 1050 and for the IAS and the IFS, it was 1450 marks. Although the maximum marks in the Interview Test for the IPS and the Allied Services were 300, in the case of the IAS and the IFS, it was 400. The basis for the clear cut differentiation among the various services was to assess the cognitive, analytical and linguistic skill levels of candidates, as different services required different skills in terms of their functions. Hence, depending on the number of subjects offered and final marks obtained, including interview marks, the merit list of selected candidates were notified for the IAS/the IFS, the IPS and the Central Services separately.

In 1974, however, the Kothari Committee recommended:

(a) a preliminary examination as a screening test, followed by a Common Civil Services Examination for all services,
(b) an increase in the maximum age for selection and
(c) that all papers could be answered in any language in the Eighth Schedule of the Constitution.

Such a revised scheme of examination has totally changed the format of entry to the civil services. This revised system has been followed since the 1979 Civil Service Examination.

There could be widely divergent views on the methodology of selecting civil servants adopted since then and some of the changes introduced by the Kothari Committee could be justified on grounds of equity. I, however, feel that it is a highly retrograde step to have the Common Civil Services Examination to recruit for all the civil services ranging from the IAS, the IFS and the IPS, the Central Services as the IRS, IA & AS etc. who belong to Class I gazetted service (Group A) to Class II gazetted service (Group B) like the Armed Forces Headquarters Civil Service and section Officers in the Central Secretariat Service. While it is not my intention to denigrate any service, it is only to emphasize that the officer like qualities, dynamic leadership, decision making abilities and job requirements differ vastly from service to service. This revised selection process, in practice, has resulted in creating a plethora of administrative problems, giving rise to demands for the equality of different services, pay and promotion to mention just a few.

Another major change introduced in 1979 was that all papers could be answered by a candidate in any language in the Eighth Schedule of the Constitution. I distinctly recall that I interviewed a candidate who studied in the English medium in the highly prestigious Loyola College, Chennai and opted to write his examination in Tamil. During the interview when I told him that he could take advantage of the Tamil interpreter present, he stated that he would be more comfortable to reply in English and indeed replied only in English. When queried as to why he opted for the Tamil medium, when he studied in English medium and could reply so well in English in the interview, he had no satisfactory reply. Presumably, he answered his papers in Tamil on the assumption that they would be evaluated only by a Tamil knowing person who would be liberal in awarding marks. There were many candidates of other linguistic groups who fell into this category.

When I appeared for the Civil Service Examination in 1961, there was only one Interview Board at Delhi—called Personality Test Board—to interview the candidates for the IAS and the IFS. The interviews for the IPS and the Central Services were held in different cities such as Delhi, Calcutta. Bombay and Madras. However, at present all the candidates for all the services are interviewed in Delhi in the Commission's office at Dholpur House by as many as six to seven Interview Boards functioning simultaneously. This system of several Boards has brought in an element of subjectivity, as all the Boards cannot assess candidates on a uniform basis, although the general principles of assessment in interview followed by the UPSC are the same. It is generally said that while some boards are liberal, other boards are very conservative in terms of awarding marks in the interview.

Until 1979, the age limit for entry into the Civil Services was 21 to 24 for general candidates and 21 to 29 years for candidates of the Scheduled Castes and Scheduled Tribes. The present upper age limit for general candidates is 30 years, for the OBC's it is 33 and for the SC and ST's it is 35 years. However, while the general candidates are eligible for four chances, the OBC candidates have seven chances and the SC and the ST candidates have unlimited chances, within the prescribed age limit. The increase in the upper age limit to 30 years of general candidates and the further age concession to candidates of other categories, goes totally against the concept of ***catch them young*** and mould them to the requirements of the civil service. This has considerably eroded the value systems in service, leading to many complaints about malpractices by officers in different services, which have greatly contributed to the lowering of standards of administration.

IAS INTERVIEWS

The most interesting and satisfying job as a Member, UPSC was the annual Interviews conducted for selecting officers to the Civil Services in the country. These interviews are held for over a month without a break, except during the holidays notified earlier. Once the interview dates are announced, even if a holiday is declared subsequently by the government, the UPSC goes ahead with its scheduled interviews. The interview boards are presided over mostly by the senior most Members in the UPSC, although occasionally even the Chairman heads a few boards. These boards are assisted by eminent specialists in the country from various disciplines and geographical regions. These advisers assist the Board only for a week and every week new advisers join the board. As a policy, such advisers are not invited for the following year to ensure that they are not approached by prospective candidates coming for the interview. These advisers come from various disciplines such as management, technology, social sciences and civil services. The interviews provide an excellent opportunity for the Chairman and Members of the UPSC to see the best youngsters coming from all over the country. Most of the candidates are academically well qualified and take considerable pains in preparing for the written examinations, before they qualify for the interview.

Unlike in the past, when I appeared for the IAS examination, there are now several Institutes all over the country providing coaching for both the written examinations and also for the interview. Most of the candidates are well informed about current affairs, both national as well as international, as also the problems plaguing their respective home states and national issues. It is a pleasure interviewing the candidates to assess their suitability for various civil services of the country. There are very few candidates who qualify for the interview in the first attempt and also are successful in the first interview itself. There are not many candidates who are successful at an early age of 21–24 years, as the average age of the successful candidates is around 26–27 years.

The interviews undoubtedly are tension filled for the candidates. When one calls the candidate to the interview room, quite often, one finds them coming a couple of minutes late, as they go to the wash room to ease the tension! All the interview boards invariably try to put the candidates at ease and the interview can cover anything 'from pin to plane'. Assessment of candidates is purely on merit and without any interference from any quarters whatsoever. The Members of the Commission are not given the written marks to ensure that there is no bias in assessing the candidate. Marks once given to a candidate by the Interview Board are not altered and the same are handed over to the confidential section by the Chairman of the Interview Board after signing the final list of marks in the presence of the Board. The entire methodology has been time tested and has continued for years, even though other alternatives of interviews have been considered by the commission from time to time. I would, however, desist from going into more details to maintain the sanctity of the confidentiality of the selection process.

A MEMORABLE INTERVIEW OF A PHYSICALLY CHALLENGED PERSON

I would like to recollect the interview of a hearing impaired candidate—in the physically handicapped category—conducted by me on 17th May, 2000. I interviewed Sadasivan, who had hearing impairment. He belonged to the Other Backward Classes (OBCs) and despite his disability, Sadasivan was one among a few hundreds who qualified for the interview.

Before the commencement of the interviews, I was informed that a candidate with a hearing impairment was required to be interviewed by my Interview Board. Though I had interviewed earlier candidates with loco motor disability, visual impairment and partial deafness, it was for the first time in the UPSC that a candidate who had total hearing impairment was being interviewed for the Civil Services. The major issue I confronted was how to interview a candidate who could not hear? I discussed the matter with my four Advisors and decided to interview the candidate with the assistance of a computer and a screen, as we were informed that the candidate could see, read, write and speak but not hear.

We dictated the questions on the computer and tested them on the screen for clarity. When the candidate entered into my chamber, I found him absolutely normal. I explained the procedure for interview on the screen. After the initial exchange of pleasantries, I asked him whether he had this problem since birth. He explained that he was a normal child and had been brought up in Libya and Malaysia. After his father's death in Malaysia, his family settled down in Cochin. While he was studying in school, the family went for a holiday to Chennai. While returning from Chennai, he developed viral fever in the train and by the time he reached Cochin, he was unconscious and was hospitalized. Though he regained his consciousness later, he could neither hear nor speak. While the speech was fully restored after treatment, he did not get back his hearing.

I was amazed to find from the records that the candidate stood first at undergraduate and postgraduate examinations in Kerala and nearly completed his Ph.D. I was eager to find out how he had achieved such academic distinctions with a hearing disability. He explained that he studied at home and in libraries without any formal education. To my next query as to what were his service preferences, he revealed that his first preference was the IAS, as he wanted to be Collector and District Magistrate to serve the common man. When I explained to him that the Collector of a district is required to meet a large number of people, listen to their grievances and understand their problems, explain to them about the policies of Government and offer relief and it may be difficult for him to be an effective and successful Collector, he was quick to point out that he would take the assistance of his P.A. and a computer to redress their grievances. I found the candidate was enthusiastic, dynamic, committed and result oriented and above all, a self-made man. He had a thorough knowledge of current affairs, a good grasp of issues, clarity of thought, analytical ability, articulation and confidence and never once gave us the impression that he needed our sympathy. His overall performance could be considered as very good compared to many normal persons with access to all facilities including coaching centers. It was quite a unique experience to interview a candidate who was totally deaf.

After the interview was over, I requested the Advisors to give their overall assessment and suggest marks, which varied from average to very good. We deliberated the matter in its entirety and as Chairman of the Interview Board, I finally proposed the marks which we had awarded to candidates with a similar level of performance, regardless of his disability. This was agreed by all Advisors after a brief discussion.

I distinctly recall that I recorded a note about the candidate, stating that the Government should constitute a High Level Committee to identify those jobs which could be offered, if the candidate was finally successful. I was very clear after my four decades of experience as an IAS Officer that there were many posts in the Civil Services which could be performed very competently and successfully by Sadasivan in spite of his hearing impairment.

When the results were declared, I was very happy to find that Sadasivan secured 222 rank out of 411 successful candidates, which again shows that he secured very high percentage of marks in the written examination as well.

Sadasivan, being from OBCs, would have undoubtedly got one of the top Civil Services much sought after by almost all aspirants to the Civil Services. However, I was dismayed to hear later that government unfortunately did not find him suitable for any civil service and he was driven from pillar to post, even seeking judicial intervention. This decision of the government clearly demonstrated the general apathy towards disabled persons and the need for a change of attitude and mindset of all those dealing with the problems of the physically disabled. Although the Central Government recruits about 450 persons annually for the premier Civil Services, hardly a couple of ministries indicate a vacancy or two for physically challenged persons. Even during 2005, only four vacancies had been notified for three civil services, out of 21 Civil Services advertised. There is no basis for determination of vacancies and it is also not clear who takes such decisions in each Ministry. It is high time that an in depth and comprehensive examination of the entire matter is made by a High Powered Committee, which should consist of physically challenged persons and also dedicated NGOs with an excellent track record in the service of persons with physical disabilities, to identify Civil Services in which a physically challenged person can be accommodated. To begin with, all candidates who were recommended by the UPSC and denied allotment of service should first be offered suitable service. There are many more areas, apart from job reservations, such as access into public places, public transport, etc., where Government's active intervention can go a long way in helping the physically challenged persons to lead a dignified life. Indeed, a separate Ministry, which will look after the welfare of the disabled, which is long overdue, would be a step in the right direction.

ADVICE IN DISCIPLINARY CASES

The Commission receives several disciplinary cases against government servants under Article 320 of the Constitution of India. Since the processing of disciplinary cases is quasi-judicial in nature, the Commission has to examine all aspects of a case thoroughly and in great detail. The facts and circumstances of the case, evidence adduced during the enquiry, the deposition of witnesses and the representation of the charged officer have to be assessed before tendering its advice to the Government of India. The examination of these cases is not only taxing but also time taking. The advice given by the Commission, especially in disciplinary cases, is normally accepted by the Government. However, there are also a few cases of disagreement between the Government and the Commission. In all cases of disagreement, the Government is obliged to place such cases on the floor of the Parliament, with reasons for disagreement.

Need for Early implementation of Recommendations on Appointments

It was observed that despite repeated observations made by the Commission in its earlier Annual Reports, various Ministries/ Departments of the Government take a long time in implementing the Commission's recommendations on appointments, except in the case of appointments to the All India Services. The Commission was of the firm view that selected candidates should not be required to wait for years for the receipt of the offers of appointment from the concerned Ministries. It was also noted that in many cases candidates selected by the Commission secure placement elsewhere due to the inordinate delay, becoming unavailable for appointment under the Government, thus rendering the whole exercise of selection infructuous. The Commission has reiterated from time to time that suitable measures need to be devised to ensure that recommended candidates are issued offers of appointment as quickly as possible and that government should devise suitable mechanisms for quick police verification of selected candidates.

Assessment of Confidential Reports for Promotions

The Commission is required to assess the confidential reports of several officers while assessing their suitability for promotion to higher ranks. When there are more candidates, it is quite taxing to assess them, especially as both the Member of the Commission who presides over the Departmental Promotion Committee as well as other members of the Departmental Promotion Committees have to give their assessments. Whenever there is any disagreement in assessment, a considerable amount of time is taken to reconcile these differences. It has also its own silver lining as the confidential reports some times make very interesting reading. A few examples which I came across are given below:

- he is more honest than others
- he has improved under my able guidance—Reporting Authority. He has not improved despite Reporting Authority's able guidance—Reviewing Authority.

- He is holding a lucrative assignment—Remarks given by a Reviewing Authority.
- If only God gave him the capacity to see himself as others see him—A Reporting Authority.
- He maintains good relations unilaterally.
- He can express a sentence in two paragraphs.
- He needs a horse carriage to carry him.
- It is idle to expect a man to run when he cannot even walk.
- A *young* officer of pleasing manners—at 50 years of age
- He is *work alcoholic*—Report of an Excise Commissioner
- Outstandingly outstanding officer
- He takes *bags* of initiatives
- More than a very good officer—(after striking off outstanding)
- He is still a bachelor and quite sociable
- He is an outgoing officer—he always goes out
- An outstanding product of IAS
- She was personally of great help to me
- Decision making capacity is excellent and occasionally too willing to be persuaded
- He should get his dues in his turn (column—does he deserve out of turn promotion)
- 'Eat, drink and *be marry*' nature
- A very good officer of outstanding merit
- A civil servant in the classical mould
- He is highly contentious and dedicated officer

WORST PERSONAL TRAGEDY

While I was working as a Member, UPSC, I was staying in AB 83, Shahjahan Road, a sprawling bungalow opposite the UPSC. My son-in-law Sam Bob, IAS (1983), who came on deputation to Government of India in 1996 was working then as Secretary to the Hon'ble Speaker, Lok Sabha. In the summer of 2000, my son Rajesh, who was working in the UK, returned to India on the insistence of my wife. He got married in August, 2001 and also stayed with us, along with his wife Vineetha. We were all living like a happy family under one roof.

On 6th December, 2001, my wife Suryakumari, suddenly complained of breathlessness after lunch. All of us were at home, but she collapsed even before we could realize what was happening and before the doctor, who was just a kilometer away, could reach our home. None could really believe such a shocking death, almost instantaneous without any forewarning whatsoever. It took several months for the entire family to get reconciled to the shocking loss of the dearest member of the family.

STATUS OF CHAIRMAN AND MEMBERS

Although the Chairman and Members are Constitutional Authorities and the Government treats them with due respect and extend appropriate courtesies, the Government has not given due recognition to the role played by the Commission in meticulously selecting the right and proper personnel on merit to serve the needs of the country. The Government has, therefore, not given them appropriate status and perquisites similar to other Constitutional Authorities and even some Statutory Bodies.

The Chairman and Members of the First Public Service Commission of India, set up in 1926, enjoyed the same emoluments and status as that of the Chief Justice and Judges of High Courts, respectively. In other words, since there was no Federal Court in India in 1926, the Chairman and Members of the Commission were equated with the highest judiciary in British India. Before commencement of the Constitution in 1950, when there was no Election Commission of India, the Chairman, UPSC enjoyed the salary and status of the Comptroller & Auditor General of India. The Chairman was also higher in status than the Cabinet Secretary and the Advocate General of India (the Attorney General). However, the terms and conditions of Chairman/Members underwent a significant change after 1950. With the commencement of the Constitution, the office of Chief Election Commissioner was created in accordance with *Article 324* of the Constitution and the Chief Election Commissioner and Chairman, UPSC enjoyed the same terms and conditions of office and status from 1951 to 1991—a period of 40 years.

However, in 1986, for the first time, under the Chief Election Commissioner and other Election Commissioners (Condition of Service) Act, the Chief Election Commissioner was given the salary of a Judge of the Supreme Court. In 1991, by an executive decision, the status of the Chief Election Commissioner from entry 17 in the Warrant of Precedence along with the Chairman UPSC, was changed to entry 11 in the Warrant of Precedence. In 1994, by amending the 1991 Act, offices of two other Election Commissioners (EC) were created and the CEC & the Election Commissioners were given the same salary and perquisites as Judges of the Supreme Court, with the CEC further moving up to entry 9A in the Warrant of Precedence and the two Election commissioners being placed at entry 11 in the Warrant of Precedence, whereas there was no change in the status and position of the Chairman, UPSC, who continued at entry 17 in the Warrant of Precedence. There was also no change in the status and perquisites of Chairman and Members of UPSC.

A NEED TO REVIEW THE STATUS OF UPSC

The UPSC provides the much-needed and vital support for the functioning of the Government, both at Central and State levels, by recruiting the right and proper personnel. Every year, the UPSC conducts 12 competitive examinations for different organized services, including the three All India Services, which play a crucial role in the governance of the country. Also, every year the Commission holds interviews of about 10,000 candidates for different services/posts under Government of India and the Union Territories hold about 350 Departmental Promotion Committees (DPC) meetings to consider about 27,000 officers for promotion to different grades; hold about 180 Selection Committee meetings to recruit to various posts on deputation and hold about 80 Selection Committee Meetings to consider about 1500 officers of the State Civil Service, the State Police Service, and the State Forest Service for promotion to the three All-India Services. Apart from these interviews and selections, every year about 850 to 900 disciplinary cases are referred to the UPSC for advice. These cases, examined in depth by the Chairman/ Members of UPSC, involve a thorough scrutiny of the entire case records to decide regarding guilt or innocence of charged officials.

Under *Article 319* of the Constitution, the Chairman/Members of UPSC are made ineligible for further employment under either Government of India or under the Government of a State. No such disability is attached to the Chief Election Commissioner or Election Commissioners either under the Constitution or under any law. For removal of a Chairman/Member, a judge of the Supreme Court must enquire into the alleged misbehaviour. Only if the Judge of the Supreme Court holds the chairman/member guilty of misbehaviour, after due enquiry, the President has powers to issue an order for removal of the guilty chairman/member. This procedure is more stringent, as the matter for enquiry is entrusted to the highest court of the land, that is, the Supreme Court and the removal of Chairman/Members does not depend on the wishes of the political executive.

Apart from former civil servants, eminent academicians are appointed as Chairman/Members in the UPSC. The UPSC conducts interviews for posts/services having different academic qualifications and experience for each post/service. The tasks of the Chairman and Members are multi-disciplinary and are not confined to any particular area of specialization. It is, therefore, necessary that the Chairman and Members have a working knowledge of the broad concepts in various disciplines, as the UPSC conducts interviews for posts/services in different Ministries in a multitude of disciplines and specialties.

The Chairman/Members of UPSC are, however, not given the status of CEC & the Election Commissioners. They are also denied the perquisites of office enjoyed by Chairman/Members of the BIFR—a statutory body and the recently created Principal Information Commissioners and Information Commissioners under the Right to Information Act.

I know how different Chairmen during my tenure in the UPSC tried to get better status and perquisites for the Chairman and the Members. They met high functionaries in the Government, including the political executive, but nothing came of it. It is really unfortunate that the UPSC—started as the Public Service Commission of India in 1926—has got reduced to the status of a Constitutional midget just because the Commission does not flaunt its clout and works quietly and efficiently in accordance with its Constitutional mandate.

Finally, I learnt that from 1 May 2007, the Government have granted the same pay and perquisites of office to the Hon'ble Chairman and Members of the UPSC as admissible to the Chief Election Commissioner and the Election Commissioners of India. The issue of their higher status in the official Warrant of Precedence is, however, still under consideration of the Government of India. I fail to understand why the decision regarding the status of the Hon'ble Chairman and Members of the UPSC could not have been taken simultaneously and a composite order regarding pay, perquisites of office and status issued on the same date. The delay of several years in deciding about the higher pay and perquisites of office of the Hon'ble Chairman and the Members of the UPSC shows how important decisions are taken in the Government and how slow is the pace of the decision making.

SOME OF THE OFFICERS WHO WERE SELECTED BY ME INTO IAS AND OTHER CIVIL SERVICES

An IAS Officer Selected by me is Collector, Bhir, Where I was Collector 40 Years Back

Long after my retirement, I had to visit Bhir, where I had worked as Collector and District Magistrate during 1966 to 1969, in my capacity as Chairman, Maharashtra State Power Generation Company (MAHAGENCO), a Government of Maharashtra undertaking, which was carved out of the restructured MSEB. I was visiting the Parli Thermal Power Station in the District for 'boiler light up' programme on 21 August 2006 by Vilasrao Deshmukh, Chief Minister, Maharashtra. When I landed at Aurangabad airport, I was surprised to be received by Piyush Singh, Collector and District Magistrate, Bhir who had taken the trouble of traveling for one and half hours from District Head Quarters to receive me. I never received a VVIP away from the District, when I worked as Collector and District Magistrate, as all the VVIPs were normally received by the Collector at Bhir itself. When I asked the Collector as to why he had taken so much of trouble to receive me at Aurangabad, Piyush Singh, informed me it was an honor to receive me at Aurangabad, as he was selected by me into IAS.

I was happy to see that an IAS officer selected by me, as Member, Union Public Service Commission (UPSC), was functioning as Collector and District Magistrate, Bhir, a place where I was the Collector myself, exactly 40 years back. After the function at Parli was over, Piyush Singh, personally escorted me to the Collector's office and honored me in the presence of all the employees of the Collectorate. It was indeed a privilege and an honor to be back in Bhir under such happy circumstances.

The next person to meet was with J. Buddha Prakash IAS (2002) Sub- Collector, Vijayawada, Krishna District, Andhra Pradesh, who met me when I went on a short leave to my native place Vijayawada. When he came to know that I was in Vijayawada, he called on me and told me that he was selected by me into IAS.

Subsequently N. Gulzar IAS (1999) Commissioner, Municipal Corporation, Vijayawada, Krishna District also met me. He again happened to be another IAS Officer who was selected by me into IAS.

In my recent visit to China, Vishnu Prakash IFS, Counsel General of India, Shanghai met me and told that he was selected by me to the Indian Foreign Service.

I visited Manipur during April 2008 as Chairman, Expert Appraisal Committee for River Valley and Hydro Electric Projects. During this visit, the committee visited the site of 1500 MW Tipai Mukh Project in Manipur on 12th April 2008. I was surprised by the presence of Sumant Singh IAS (MT – 2003) Deputy Commissioner Churachandpur District, where Tipai Mukh Project was coming up. I was delighted to see him as he was selected to me into IAS. When I called on S.S. Siddhu, Governor Manipur, I was presently surprised to meet H.T. Gangte IPS (MT – 2003) ADC to the Governor, Manipur, who was again selected by me into IPS (Indian Police Service).

These and several such officers who were selected by me into the various Civil Services, would continue to service the nation for decades to come. These are some of the memorable rewards for having been the Member, Union Public Service Commission.

TWENTY ONE

THE PATH TREAD AND THE ROAD AHEAD IN THE POWER SECTOR

It is natural for me to have a fascination for the sector, due to my long innings in the realm of 'power'. No, wonder, even after my retirement from service, I have continued my association with the field which is very close to my heart. Post retirement, I have been a Member of the Committee of Experts on Restructuring of MSEB; Chairman, Committee on Accelerated Power Development and Reform Programme (APDRP) and Project Co-Director and Head of the Group of Experts for the study sponsored by the Ministry of Power on 'Impact of Restructuring of SEBs'. I am presently functioning as Chairman, Maharashtra State Power Generation Company, Mumbai (MAHAGENCO—A Government of Maharashtra Company). It would only be fair and natural for me to take stock of both what I achieved and the direction set by me for the wave of changes sweeping across the power sector in the recent times.

My initiation into the power sector started in Maharashtra. My spells of service there included Secretary, MSEB; Secretary (Energy), Government of Maharashtra and Chairman, MSEB. Even in the face of paucity of funds and a host of administrative and technological problems, it was possible to bring about phenomenal improvements in the electricity scenario in Maharashtra and maintain MSEB's pre-eminent position, as not only the biggest SEB in the country but also as one of the best performing SEBs in the country. Maharashtra's ranking as the leading industrialised State in the country has in a great measure been due to the assured and reliable power provided to the industrial and agricultural sectors, which has transformed the state completely into an economic growth hub. The State has always been conscious of the fact that electricity can indeed act as a catalyst for rapid socio-economic development. No wonder, special emphasis was laid on rural electrification, energisation of agricultural pumpsets, implementation of special component plan for dalits and Schedule Tribes and special programme of giving free domestic connections to SCs/STs/Vimukta Jatis and Nav Buddhists. I take pride in the fact that all the targets set in these programmes were not only achieved but they have been far exceeded year after year. Maharashtra was the first State to achieve electrification of all towns, that too as early as 1972. I consider it as a major milestone in my career that all villages were given electricity, according to the then prevailing definition of Government of India by 31 March 1989, when I was Chairman, MSEB and Sharad Pawar, Chief Minister. The achievements were possible since we had enlightened Chief Ministers, Finance Ministers and Power Ministers and dedicated officers in the Secretariat, officers and staff in the MSEB.

I took over my assignment as Secretary, Ministry of Power at a time when the decision was already taken at the National level for transforming the power sector through encouraging private sector investment.

The early 1990s heralded the beginning of the era of globalisation and liberalisation. The power sector could not remain untouched by the sweeping changes taking place in various spheres of commerce and industry. If the pace of growth had to be sustained, the power sector needed to grow at a commensurate pace, which was not possible in the circumstances, as existed then. There was a need for phenomenal capacity additions in generation and strengthening the transmission and distribution network. These called for massive investments, which the Governments, both Central and States, alone could not provide. Also, the SEBs, despite their yeomen role in the socio-economic transformation of the country, needed to be radically transformed so that the power sector could play a more meaningful role in sustaining the pace of economic growth. It was in this context that greater involvement of the private sector in various aspects of the power sector was conceived.

One had to contend with the phenomenal 'fear of uncertainty' since we were embarking on an untrodden path. Since this was the first time that private sector participation was being encouraged in such a big way, there were a number of hurdles. My charter included giving an impetus to the initiatives already taken and to initiate new ones so that the power sector would be able to make an even more meaningful contribution to the economic and social development of the country. To clear the roadblocks, a number of steps had to be taken and a number of measures had to be initiated to turn around the power sector to make it commercially viable. Special emphasis had to be laid on reduction of losses—both technical and commercial, including losses due to theft—so that the power sector would no longer be a drain on the exchequer.

REFORMS IN THE DISTRIBUTION SECTOR

The 'Common Minimum National Action Plan for Power' (CMNPP) finalized by the Government of India in consultation with the Chief Ministers in December 1996, while I was Secretary, Ministry of Power, envisaged restructuring of the SEBs. The SEBs had been in existence for over 50 years, with several achievements to their credit. However, they had become unviable and unprofitable, with huge accumulated losses and liabilities. They were also blamed for poor service delivery. Under the circumstances, it was felt that there was a need to restructure the SEBs into smaller, viable, functional utilities, with clearly defined jurisdictions and tasks, as part of the sector reforms. The restructuring of the distribution segment was considered essential for improving the technical and financial performance, increased consumer care, and attracting significant private participation in the electricity sector. The 'Common Minimum National Action Plan' has envisaged several significant measures such as reforms in distribution sector and restructuring of SEB's; establishment of Regulatory Commissions; mega power policy; competitive bidding route in awarding power projects; and private sector participation in distribution in Delhi. Private sector participation in transmission, etc., were initiated during my time, which are yielding rich dividends now.

REFORMS PURSUED AFTER MY TRANSFER

Though, there were changes in the Government since I relinquished the charge as Union Power Secretary, fortunately, irrespective of political affiliations, successive Union Power Ministers such as Y.K. Alagh, P.R. Kumaramangalam, Suresh Prabhu, Anant Geete and P.M. Sayeed pursued the reforms with great vigour and enthusiasm. Sushilkumar

Shinde, the present Union Power Minister is sparing no efforts to carry the reforms further resulting in considerable improvement in the Power Sector. The Policy of '*Power for All*' by 2012 is in consonance with the over all reforms strategy of the power sector.

BENEFITS ACCRUING FROM RESTRUCTURING OF STATE ELECTRICITY BOARDS

The distribution segment was considered essential for improving the technical and financial performance, increased consumer care, and attracting significant private participation in the electricity sector. Starting with Orissa, 12 more States (including NCR of Delhi) have restructured their SEBs. The remaining SEBs are legally obliged to do so at the earliest, under the Electricity Act, 2003. Orissa and Delhi even ushered in private sector participation in distribution. Other SEBs have been restructured into state-owned generation, transmission and one or more distribution companies. In most of the restructured entities, states have adopted an urban–rural mix as the basis.

There are considerable improvements in the performance of the Utilities after the restructuring. One of the major gains of the process of restructuring is the improved commercial performance, which have brought down the losses of the utilities from Rs. 29,252 crore in 2001–02 to Rs. 21,998 crore in 2004–05, a major chunk of the loss reduction was achieved by the restructured States which is a noteworthy achievement. Closely linked to the loss reduction efforts by the DISCOMs (distribution companies), the collection efficiency by these Utilities showed significant improvement. The metering, billing and collection efficiency have shown perceptible improvement. Similarly, most of the States, which have restructured have registered profits (with subsidy), after 2003-04. The percentage of subsidy as a ratio of respective revenues has also come down in some restructured states, which is again an encouraging sign. This is also reflected in the overall reduction of AT & C (aggregate technical and commercial) losses from 38.18 per cent in 2000-01 to 33.82 per cent in 2004-05. The trend towards reducing AT & C losses; increased private investments; improved customer care; progress in metering, billing and collection etc. continues. A review of the percentage of losses to revenue reveals that the majority of the restructured Utilities have done reasonably well. The all India ratio of subsidy booked by Utilities to the total revenue for the year 2001-02 was 20.75 per cent, which has come down to around 11 per cent in

2004-05. This clearly indicates that the Utilities are becoming less dependent on State Governments for financial support. It is pertinent to note that the privatised Utilities of Orissa have saved the State Government a subsidy burden of Rs. 300 crore per year for the last ten years. It can be concluded that, by and large, the overall impact of restructuring has been positive and in the right direction.

ELECTRICITY REGULATORY COMMISSIONS BILL, 1997

After approval given by the Chief Ministers to the CMNPP to provide for the establishment of a Central Electricity Regulatory Commission and State Electricity Regulatory Commissions, the Central Government drafted. The Electricity Regulatory Commission Bill, 1997, to establish Central and State Electricity Regulatory Commissions. Although the ERC Bill was introduced in Parliament during the Budget Session in 1997, it could not be passed, as there was a change of government in April/May 1997 and the Bill was allowed to lapse. Subsequently, the same Bill with minor modifications was enacted as Electricity Regulatory Commissions Act, 1998. The CERC was constituted on 24 July 1998, in accordance with the provisions of the Act. Some States have established Commissions under State Electricity Reforms Act, namely, Haryana (1998), Andhra Pradesh (1998), Uttar Pradesh (1999), Karnataka (1999), Rajasthan (1999), Delhi (2000) and Madhya Pradesh (2000). Some States also have established State Electricity Regulatory Commissions under the ERC Act, 1998. The Electricity Act, 2003 made it mandatory to establish SERC in the remaining States.

The establishment of Electricity Regulatory Commissions, initiated during my period, has contributed substantially to improving the commercial viability of SEBs. Setting up of the Electricity Regulatory Commissions has made tariff determination more rational and brought issues of efficiencies into the public domain in a transparent manner. Due to the strict energy audit measures put in place by the Regulators, a greater degree of transparency, accountability and discipline is now prevailing in the electricity sector. Establishment of the Regulatory mechanism has also insulated the power sector from the populist tilts of the changing Governments to some extent. The Regulatory Commissions have brought a refreshing change in the working of the power sector all over the country. The impact has been positive and encouraging.

The transparency in tariff fixation and related issues by introducing public hearings, fixing efficiency standards, introducing several new initiatives like Open Access, multi-year tariffs, encourage competition, etc., implemented by the Regulatory Commissions have brought a refreshing change in the working of the power sector all over the country. The impact has been positive and encouraging. The role played by the Commissions in safeguarding the interest of the restructured companies and the consumers is commendable.

INTEGRATED NATIONAL ENERGY POLICY

While the nodal Ministry for promoting power projects has necessarily to be the Ministry of Power, it has to depend largely on the other Ministries such as Coal, Petroleum & Natural Gas, Railways, Surface Transport, Environment and Finance. Perhaps the performance of no other infrastructure sector depends so heavily on the cooperation of other Ministries. One of the reasons for the results not being commensurate with the efforts made in the power sector is that, quite often, the perception of each Ministry differs and there are considerable delays in decision-making on inter-related matters. I often used to frankly remark, "What the Power Secretary proposes, other Secretaries dispose!!" Hence there was a dire need to have a comprehensive National Energy Policy. This was included in the Common National Action Plan for Power (CMNPP). In furtherance of this policy, the Planning Commission appointed a Committee under the chairmanship of Kirit Parikh, Member, Planning Commission to prepare an Integrated National Energy Policy. The Kirit Parikh Committee Report is now being implemented by the Government.

MEGA POWER POLICY

The Mega Power Policy, initiated during my time, has now been designated as Ultra Mega Power Policy by raising the limit of the capacity to 4,000 MW (which was included in ***1,000 MW or more*** formulated in my time). The Ultra Mega Power Policy of 4,000 MW being pursued presently by the Government is the continuation of this policy. All other conditions being the same except instead of POWERGRID Corporation being the nodal agency which would provide essential transmission network, it is now being implemented by the Power Finance Corporation. As transmission is an essential part of generation, finance is no more a problem, POWERGRID should have been the catalyst to provide escort services even now. However, the fact that the Government of India has already identified about seven sites for setting up these projects is a recognition of the policy formulated by me more than a decade back (1995). Bids have already been invited and finalised for Sasan project in Madhya Pradesh and Mundra in Gujarat and bids for other projects are likely to be invited soon. The policy initiatives taken during my time are thus bearing fruit eventually.

COMPETITIVE BIDDING

The competitive bidding process initiated during my period has taken strong roots in the system and all the Thermal projects offered to the private sector in power are now being offered only on the tariff-based competitive bidding. The advantages of such bidding are seen in the offers recently finalised/received under Ultra Mega Power Project scheme, where the tariff quoted was extremely low and competitive. Such lowest tariffs are bound to offer great relief to the consumers and also would set a benchmark for future projects.

RURAL ELECTRIFICATION

Intensive efforts continued to be made to provide electricity to rural households. Rural electrification is today viewed as a step towards ensuring 'inclusive justice' and providing for a more balanced development of the country. The Rajiv Gandhi Gramin Vidyutikaran Yojana, (RGGVY) launched by the Government of India, in 2005, is a continuation of the initiatives initiated towards meeting the power needs of the rural segment of our society.

DVB WAS CREATED TO INITIATE THE PROCESS OF PRIVATE SECTOR PARTICIPATION

Delhi Vidyut Board (DVB) was created by abolishing the Delhi Electricity Supply Undertaking (DESU), hoping that the performance of power utility would improve and if not, to facilitate early privatization of the DVB. Legal changes that were made during my time finally culminated in restructuring of the DVB and private sector participation in distribution of power in Delhi, which is showing positive signs in improving the overall power supply situation in the city.

ENERGY CONSERVATION BILL

The task of evolving and implementing a coordinated strategy in energy conservation was entrusted to the Energy Management Centre. A draft bill on 'Conservation of Energy' was prepared during my tenure. This was finally enacted as 'The Energy Conservation Act, 2001'. Since electricity is very important to India's future, there is a need to find ways to use it most efficiently.

PRIVATE SECTOR PARTICIPATION IN TRANSMISSION

A Bill, titled The Electricity Laws (Amendment) Bill, 1997, was introduced in the Budget Session of Parliament, while I was Secretary. The bill provided for setting up of Central Transmission Utility under Section 27a of the Indian Electricity Act, 1910. POWERGRID Corporation of India Limited was to be the Central Transmission Utility. However, the Bill was allowed to lapse, with the change of Government in May 1997. These provisions were incorporated in Electricity Act, 2003, based on which, several transmission projects are now being offered to public private partnership mode.

POWER GRID'S DIVERSIFICATION INTO TELECOMMUNICATIONS

A feasibility report was prepared to enable Power grid to make a foray into the telecom sector. The Power grid has now taken a big stride in the sector, which will be very crucial for the development of telecom industry in future.

THE WAY AHEAD

It is essential to provide reliable, affordable, secure and sustainable energy, to cater to the needs of economy growing at the average rate of about 9 per cent. The possible options, include, maximizing domestic production, diversifying the fuel mix and the source of supply and maintaining sufficient reserves. In the long-term perspective for fuelling the likely installed capacity of 8,00,000 MW by 2031-32, coal will continue to be the mainstay in the overall fuel mix for power generation in the country.

We have already embarked on the journey of making the power sector the catalyst for social and economic development of the country.

As one who has been closely observing the power scenario for close to two decades, I find a sea change in a number of areas. There is clear recognition of the need for greater professionalism, more transparency and significant improvements in several performance parameters. Several measures have been initiated which are yielding results. We cannot, however, afford to rest on our laurels. We need to take stock of what we have achieved and, if necessary, carry out a mid-course correction in areas where we have not performed to expectations. Based on my long association with the sector, I would like to make a few suggestions to make the restructuring exercise of power sector and reforms in the sector more focussed.

Restructuring is a necessary but not a sufficient condition for bringing about improvements in the power sector. It is necessary to recognise that restructuring is only the beginning and not the end of the process. It must be accompanied by continuous complementary efforts to enhance efficiency and quality of service. Success of the entire exercise would entail the active cooperation and support of all the stakeholders.

SUSTAINED POLITICAL SUPPORT FOR REFORMS

Strong and sustained political support during all phases of restructuring is the key for success of power sector reforms. It has been seen that the restructuring exercise has been more successful in States where the political leadership has given a high degree of autonomy to the restructured Utilities. Likewise, the willing support and cooperation of the employees is most essential. The states which took the employees into confidence and removed their misgivings have been more successful in ensuring a smoother transition. The level of consumer satisfaction is significantly higher in these States.

Restructuring has brought in the required accountability in the power sector, triggering improved performance. Most of the GENCOs, TRANSCOs and some of the DISCOMs have now become vibrant and viable. They have become distinct cost and profit centres with transparency and accountability guiding their operations. This is a very positive sign and needs to be sustained. It should be ensured that persons with adequate knowledge in various aspects of the power sector are inducted into the Boards of these Utilities. There is a need for more professionalism in the management system.

Public support is equally important for the restructuring exercise to be on course. Consumer redressal forums need to be strengthened. Public awareness needs to be increased about issues like checking electricity thefts. A positive atmosphere needs to be created, whereby the consumers pay for their electricity consumption, just as they pay in advance for other commodities and services.

An industry structure should be evolved which would promote competition, provide a consistent and transparent pricing regime and efficient generation, transmission, distribution and end-use efficiency. Energy conservation measures through Demand Side Management (DSM), such as time of the day (TOD), metering and differential pricing, reduction in the energy intensity of the large consumers, need to be promoted in a big way. Simultaneously, Energy Audit should be made compulsory and suitable incentives need to be provided.

After restructuring, several independent entities have come into existence. As the single carriage of power in the State, the transmission companies will undoubtedly be the most appropriate and suitable agency to undertake all functions related to statewide planning and coordination. It is essential to induct experienced and competent planners into these companies.

The Regulatory mechanism has been among the most important component of power sector reforms. This needs to be strengthened even more by persuading all States to honour the directives of the Regulatory Commissions and resolve disagreements through a consultative process.

The Electricity Act, 2003, has set a direction for the pace of reforms in the electricity sector. The reforms agenda was steered by Governments of various hues, all of whom are convinced that the power sector needs to be reformed in a substantial way to realise our national goal of becoming a developed country.

TWENTY TWO

RESTORING THE PAST GLORY OF THE MSEB

MSEB has been one of the best managed SEB's, if not the best, based on several physical and financial performance parameters until recently. However, the MSEB's preeminent position began to decline in the late nineties owing to various factors. The liberalization and globalization policy of the Government of India in early 90's generated enormous hopes in the resourccs starved states that all the investments needed would be made by the private sector and paved the way for private sector investment in the power generation which made many states including Maharashtra to systematically withdraw its share of investment in power sector.

MSEB followed the Memorandum of Understanding (MoU) route as per the Government of India Policy in the controversial Dabhol project, promoted by Enron. From 1992 to 1998, the Enron project negotiations, re-negotiations controversies, arbitrations, court cases and media hype occupied the centre stage in the energy scenario not only in the State and the MSEB but also in the country.

The entire top management of MSEB including the Government was highly preoccupied with Dabhol matters, which naturally took its toll on the other areas of operation and performance of MSEB.

The surplus of the MSEB was around Rs. 280 crores in 1991, when I left as Chairman. However, gradually the surplus draft to double figures from 1997 onwards and worsened to a level of around Rs. 1700 crs deficit during 2000, touched all time low of Rs. 3200 crs in 2001. The deficit prevailed around Rs. 500 crs on an average thereafter right up to 2005. Consequently the morale of the employees also suffered greatly. Thus one of the best SEB's in the country, earlier referred as the ' best SEB', ' only profit making SEB', 'technically sound utility' has unfortunately came to be known as 'loss making', ' moribund SEB', 'cash strapped SEB' etc. It was particularly painful for me to see this metamorphosis of a giant organization with a glorious past, an efficient, technically sound and the biggest electricity utility in the country, gradually slide into financial crunch in late 90's.

To add misery to the situation, the Energy Review Committee under the Chairmanship of Madhav Godbole concluded that the State appears to be surplus in base load supply and recommended that the State should go in for intermediate or peak load only and all the prospective PPAs on base load are ill-suited for the State. This led to the abandonment of projects of Independent Power producers. Since generation from Dabhol had also stopped by then the State found itself totally unprepared to deal with the increase in demand resulting in serious shortages and substantial load shedding. The technical and distribution loses went upto around 39%. There was also a decline in revenue collection and increase in receivables. Due to the poor financial health coupled with reduction in the State plan allocation, MSEB could neither invest in its own power projects, nor could make much needed investment in improving the T&D network.

While in the eighties, a total of 3552 MW was added in the MSEB grid, the nineties saw a capacity addition of 1740 MW only, including 500 MW added between 1996 and 2000. Even this addition was the result of projects planned in the early nineties. It was quite evident that the State had not planned any new projects in the last ten years. The State was totally unprepared to deal with the increase in demand.

Due to the deterioration in its functioning, the MSEB was unable to achieve the targets set in respect of the covenants stipulated by the World Bank for Chandrapur unit-7 and the World Bank suspended the loans in October 1996. My best efforts even as Union Power Secretary, could not save the situation for the Board of which was the best in the country, when I was the Chairman, just a few years back. Thus MSEB was forced to complete the project by diverting its internal resources, which led to further deterioration in the financial position. The credibility of the organization had received a severe beating.

DELAYED REFORMS

Meanwhile, the Government of India has taken several initiatives to evolve a national consensus for reforms in the power sector especially in the distribution sector. The MSEB's operations needed immediate structural changes. A vertically integrated MSEB catering to the diverse needs of a customer base of 140 Lakhs, increasing the consumer base on a daily bases had inherent limitations. It became almost inevitable for the various segments in the power business to be run by smaller, more manageable and commercially oriented entities, for the power sector in Maharasthra to be brought on the road to recovery. The Government of Maharashtra began to appreciate the larger national consensus which had emerged that instead of one monolithic MSEB in the sector, small entities with closure supervision, more efficiency and better consumer service are needed. In addition, unbundling was necessary to make the sector more amenable for competition. The Government of Maharashtra and the MSEB realized that internal reforms would not adequately galvanize the MSEB. Although many States like Andhra Pradesh, Orissa, UP, Rajasthan, Gujarat, Delhi, Karanataka went ahead with reforms, Maharashtra spent considerable time confabulating on the modality and dillydallied on the actions, which gave the Unions more time to exert pressure to further delay the reforms, thinking that the political will is lacking to implement the reforms.

Under these circumstances, Government after considerable delay finally restructured the MSEB into four companies namely Mahagenco, Mahatransco and Mahavitaran and MSEB Holding Company under the Electricity Act 2003. Has transferred the properties, interests, liabilities, obligations and personnel of MSEB to these four companies. The main objectives of reforms were to (i) to promote the development of an efficient, commercially viable and competitive power sector, (ii) to provide reliable quality and uninterrupted supply at reasonable prices to all consumer categories and (iii) to ensure that the social and environmental aspects are fully taken into consideration.

The primary objective of the reforms was to restructure the distribution segment of SEB, by creating small companies, who can focus on improvement of the various ills of the distribution sector. However, by retaining the entire distribution segment as a single company, the expected improvements have not been seen fully in the performance of the power sector in the State. It is not too late even now for the

Government to see the improvements achieved by some of the states like Andhra Pradesh, due to small distribution companies and further re-structure the Mahavitaran into a few distribution companies. It is also necessary to do the financial restructuring of these companies. The newly created companies should be allowed to function independently without any interference and without any Government functionaries heading these companies.

IMPORTANT INITIATIVES OF THE STATE GOVERNMENT TO RESTORE PAST GLORY

Generation

In view of the perennial shortages in power and serious power crisis, including imposing power cuts in Mumbai which has been the pride of the country in terms of power supply, various measures were taken by the Government to augment generation capacity in the State.

The Government of Maharasthra as fully taken the Electricity Plan at the national level which envisions energy demand to be fully met by 2012. It aims for electricity to be accessible to all households in the next five years.

Mahagenco after being carved out of the erstwhile MSEB in June 2005 was quick to dovetail its own vision with the above national objective viz endeavour to be the best and most efficient 'State – of – the – Art' generating utility in the country producing reliable and adequate power at the competitive and affordable rates. Mahagenco has embarked on huge capacity addition plans to augment its already highest installed capacity of 9626 MW comprising of 6425 MW thermal 2349 MW hydro and 852 MW of gas based power stations amongst all the state power generation utilities in the country. The plant load factor (PLF) of its thermal generation stations stood presently at 77% which makes it one of the few sates that have higher PLF than the average of the state utilities. The availability factor of these plants, presently stands at 86%. Nevertheless, the State is presently facing a power deficit of about 5,500 MW which is expected to further increase in the coming years Realizing that the onus of increasing capacity lies primarily with the State sector, Mahagenco is targeting to not only successfully meet the deficit in the state by taking several majors to improve the performance parameters but also be able to generate surplus power as was in the past.

Mahagenco, commissioned recently a new Parli unit (250 MW) and Paras unit (250 MW). It has also planned capacity addition for the Eleventh Plan in two phases. The first phase expansion projects add up a total capacity of 2000 MW, comprising Parli Unit to (250 MW), Paras Unit to (250 MW), Khaperkheda (500 MW) and Bhusaval (100 MW). The synchronization of all this projects are targeted in 2009–2010. The next set of projects in the phase II add up to a total capacity of 5800 MW. These are Koradi Expansion (3 × 660 MW) Chandrapur expansion (2 × 500 MW), uran expansion (1220 MW) and Dophave (2 × 800 MW). In addition the company plans to replace the existing smaller size plants ranging from 20 MW to 120 MW with larger ones. The company also plans to undertake a renovation and modernization (R & M) programme for five 210 MW. The biggest challenge to the company today is in terms of huge capacity addition required to bridge the deficit in power in the state. Thus it has commenced implementation of 7800 MW capacity addition and all these projects are set for commissioning by 2012. This would require various timely inputs like environmental clearances, land and water tie up, long term fuel linkage, financial resources etc. The Mahagenco is fully geared up to meet these challenges. In order to meet the fuel requirements for its ambitious plans, two coal mine blocks, Machhakata and Mahanadi, have been allotted for joint development by Maharashtra and Gujarat.

Transmission

Post un-bundling, MSETCL (Mahatransco) the transmission company has been strengthened to discharge three fold role as State Transmission Utility (STU), State Load Dispatch Centre (SLDC) and Transmission Licensee. Since restructuring, MSETCL was quick to add about 25 new EHV sub stations and around 995 circuit kms of EHV lines in the State. Mahatransco has devised an ambitious infrastructure plan to be executed for the next 5 years. At the end of 2012, the total transmission system of 610 sub-stations, 56217 ckt-km transmission lines and transformation capacity of 114255 MVA is envisaged to handle 30,000 to 50,000 MW demand, maintaining its lead as a premier state transmission utility.

Distribution

MahaVitaran, the state utility in the distribution business has embarked on several initiatives to turn around the distribution sector which is considered the most difficult function in the energy business. Continuing with the efforts started by MSEB, the successor entity has given greater phillip to demand side management. MahaVitaran has chalked out a comprehensive infrastructure improvement plan for next 5 years which is a micro level plan of the distribution infrastructure required in each sub-division throughout the State. The estimated investment is to the tune of Rs 15000 Crs to be spent in next 3 to 4 years, with the help of funding form Rural Electrification Corporation (REC) and Power Finance Corporation (PFC). The company is also making investments in system improvements through the Accelerated Power Distribution and Reforms Programmes (APDRP) scheme sponsored by the Ministry of Power. With the investment in infrastructure, the AT&C losses which was hovering around 39% during 2004–05 has been brought down to a level of 29% in a span of two years. This has been possible also through policy level intervention. Anti-theft legislation have been enacted in the State paving way for making energy theft a cognizable offence which has in turn helped in effective curbing of theft of power. Special Police Stations have been set up at various Districts to handle cases of power theft. This has helped the reduction in AT&C losses to a significant extent. For better service to the consumers, call centers have been set up in major cities/ towns to handle consumer complaints and ensure quick and effective redressal. The company has introduced electronic bill presentation and payment option though its website for greater consumer convenience.

MahaVitaran has embarked on 'Akshay-Prakash Yojana' scheme under which a village can avoid load shedding by reducing the load voluntarily to 20% of the existing load. Similarly, voluntary load reduction scheme in small cities is also under vogue and when the load decreases to less than 33% , load shedding in the city is removed in the evenings. Single phase supply to villages is introduced whereby at least basic light is available in the households. The other major focus areas include encouragement to CFL, introduction of capacitors on agricultural pumps, training of employees, use of latest technological tools like e-tendering, SCADA and energy accounting through transformer metering have been taken as thrust areas by the successor entities of MSEB.

Distribution franchisee model initiated by MahaVitaran at Bhivandi town is a unique public-private partnership and is a role model for distribution reforms in the country. MSEDCL entered into a distribution franchisee agreement in December 2006 valid for 10 years with Torrent group for Bhiwandi Circle having a customer base of 1.6 lakhs in an area spread over 721 square kilometers The company would undertake all activities relating to distribution of power in the franchise area as an agent of MSEDCL. The private player is expected to leverage its expertise in distribution for providing highly efficient and reliable distribution services coupled with innovative customer services at Bhiwandi. The Distribution Franchisee Scheme is extended recently to Nagpur area. MSEDL is planning to replicate this experience in other major towns of Maharastra.

Thus, the power sector is once again poised to reach the commanding heights it maintained for several decades in the past. I am privileged to be associated with the Maharashtra power sector once again as Chairman, Mahagenco and I have no doubt, sooner than latter, Maharashtra will become once again a power surplus state, contributing substantially for not only the states all round economic growth but also contribute substantially for the nation building.

TWENTY THREE

POST RETIREMENT: CONTINUED ASSOCIATION WITH POWER SECTOR

It is natural for me to have commitment for the power sector due to my long innings in the realm of 'power'. No wonder, even after my retirement from the IAS, I have continued my association with this sector, which is very close to my heart.

During my tenure as Member, Union Public Service Commission, I continued to write articles to various premier national and international dailies and journals on vital matters related to the Power Sector and participated in national and international seminars on the subject. I continue to be active in this circuit even now.

AUTHORED TWO BOOKS RELATED TO POWER DEVELOPMENT

While I was Member, Union Public Service Commission, I wrote my first book on '*Dr. Ambedkar's Contribution for Economic Planning and Development—Its Relevance*' which primarily dealt about Ambedkar's contribution to irrigation and electricity sectors while he was the Member, Labour, Irrigation and Electric Power Development in the Executive Council of the Viceroy of India during 1942–46. The essence of the book is that the foundations laid by him in these sectors even now are furthering the growth of the water resources development and power sector development in the country. This book was released by Atal Bihari Vajpayee, Prime Minister, India in February 2002.

I also wrote another book titled '*Power Sector Reforms—Focus on Distribution*' during the time I was Member, Union Public Service Commission. The book focused on the development of power sector in the country since Independence, the present status, the need for reforms, steps taken by the government to formulate '*The Common Minimum National Action Plan for Power*' (*CMNPP*), while I was Union Power Secretary, the present status of the reforms in the various states and the Plan of Action for future development of the power sector. This book was the culmination of my own experience in the sector for over a period of 15 years including as Chairman, Maharashtra State Electricity Board. While the first copy of the book was presented to Dr. A.P.J. Abdul Kalam, President of India, the book was formally released by Anant Gite, Minister of Power, Government of India, in March 2003. This book was widely appreciated.

CHAIRMAN, EXPERT COMMITTEE ON ENERGY

After complication of my tenure as Member, Union Public Service Commission, I was appointed as Chairman, Expert Committee on Energy by the Government of Maharashtra to advice the government about the action required to be taken on the implementation of various provisions of the Electricity Act, 2003 and restructuring of the MSEB.

CHAIRMAN, MAHAGENCO

I am presently functioning as Chairman, Maharashtra State Power Generation Company, Mumbai (MAHAGENCO), one of the restructured companies carved out the erstwhile MSEB. The company, apart from operating the existing power stations, is also entrusted with the task of planning and development of new generation projects to meet the ever increasing demand for power in Maharashtra. I am also an Independent Director on the boards of several Infrastructure and Power Sector Companies.

CHAIRMAN, COUNCIL OF POWER UTILITIES

While I was working as Chairman, Maharashtra State Electricity Board, during 1989–91, I was also Chairman of the Council of Power Utilities, where Chairmen of other State Electricity Boards/Utilities and representatives of Private Power Utilities in the country were also the members. The Council renders valuable advice to the Government on various policy matters pertaining to the development of the power sector in the country. I continue to be associated with its activities even now. I am a Member, Governing Council, India Energy Forum, which has been playing an active role in development of energy sector in the country.

CHAIRMAN, EXPERT APPRAISAL COMMITTEE FOR RIVER VALLEY AND HYDRO ELECTRIC PROJECTS

I was recently appointed as Chairman, Expert Appraisal Committee for River Valley and Hydro Electric Projects by the Ministry of Environment and Forests which gave me an opportunity for my continued association with the power sector. The Committee scrutinizes the environmental impact of River Valley and Hydro Electric Projects and environmental management plans prepared by the project authorities, suggests safeguards including installation of pollution control devices, choice of appropriate technology to mitigate the adverse environmental impacts in respect of projects recommended for approval and recommend clearance or rejection of the project from environmental angle. Several Hydro Power Projects, mostly coming up in J and K, Himachal Pradesh, Uttarakhand, Sikkim, Meghalaya & Arunachal Pradesh have been given the 'Terms of Reference' (TOR) for preparation of 'Environmental Impact Assessment' (EIA) and 'Environmental Management Plan' (EMP). A few Hydro Projects were recommended for issuing Environmental Clearance to the Ministry of Environment.

CHAIRMAN, TASK FORCE FOR ACCELERATED POWER DEVELOPMENT AND REFORMS PROGRAMME (APDRP)

The Ministry of Power, Government of India appointed me in March 2006 as Chairman, Task Force for examining the issues related to the Accelerated Power Development and Reforms Programme (APDRP). The Task Force consisted of several Chairmen of State Electricity Boards/ Power Utilities, former Chairman, State Electricity Regularity Commissions, among others.

The APDRP, which was launched in the year 2000–01 to speed up the reforms and improve the overall performance of the power sector, was restructured during the Tenth Plan in 2002–03, with the objective to reduce Aggregate Technical and Commercial (AT&C) losses; to bring about commercial viability; to reduce outages and to increase consumer satisfaction, based on the recommendations of Deepak Parekh Committee set up in March 2002. Under the APDRP, along with the allocation of funds under the Investment Component, Reform-Linked Incentive Component was also added for incentivising States for cash loss reduction.

The Task Force was constituted in 2006 to examine the issues related to APDRP including the achievements, the shortcomings, problems of implementation and to make suggestions for effective implementation to achieve the desired goals.

The Task Force considered the views of the Planning Commission, Advisor-cum-Consultants, Central Electricity Authority, Ministry of Power and Ministry of Finance regarding their experience and suggestions for improvement for making the programme more effective. Views of some Utilities were also taken into consideration.

It was observed that the major bottlenecks for effective implementation were poor response of states on reforms, delay in transfer of funds by the states to the utilities, unrealistic Detailed Projects Reports (DPRs), increase in price of materials/equipments, poor response to turnkey offers, employee's resistance to outsourcing and delay in finalizing IT road map for the Utilities. After detailed examination of all relevant factors and after taking the views of all stakeholders, the Task Force recommended that

- APDRP should be continued with investment and incentive component beyond the Xth Plan.
- The conditions for eligibility of APDRP assistance should be made more stringent with an objective to make States/Utilities to adopt reforms.

  The *primary conditions* of eligibility should be

  - Restructuring of SEBs;
  - Constitution and operationalisation of SERC;
  - Establishment and operationalisation of special courts and police stations under anti-theft provisions of the Electricity Act, 2003.

The *secondary conditions* are that the states should commit timeliness on

  - Finalization of Roadmap/Financial Restructuring Plan;
  - Adoption of Multi-Year Tariff;
  - 100% system metering up to 11 kV feeders;
  - Energy accounting and auditing;
  - 100% metering of consumers including agriculture consumers;
- The APDRP assistance, both investment and incentive component, should be extended to the Private Distribution Utilities also.
- Graded targets fixed for reduction in AT&C losses by the Utilities.
- Under the investment component, the grant should be increased to 50% of the project cost for the general category states.
- The APDRP should be converted into a Central scheme for speedy implementation.
- Execution of all the schemes should be on 'turnkey' basis only by adopting standard specifications.

The Task Force recently submitted its report which is under consideration of the government.

PROJECT DIRECTOR—IMPACT OF RESTRUCTURING OF SEBS

Power sector reforms were necessitated due to the uninspiring financial position of the vertically integrated monolithic SEBs, beset with unsustainable inefficiencies, unviable tariffs, high T&D losses, mounting subsidies, lack of adequate attention to the distribution sector, sub-optimal performance, and wasteful practices resulting in failure to attract the much-needed investments in the sector.

Orissa was the first State to restructure its SEB and thereafter, 12 more States followed suit. The enactment of the Electricity Act, 2003, was a distinct watershed in the Indian power sector. The Act made it mandatory for all the States to restructure their SEBs. Since, sufficient experience was available to gauge the performance of the restructured Utilities, the Ministry of Power entrusted the task of undertaking a comprehensive study on *'Impact of Restructuring of SEBs'* to the Indian Institute of Public Administration (IIPA). To undertake this study, a *Group of Experts* with rich domain knowledge of the operational dynamics of the power sector was constituted by the IIPA with me as Project Director. The group included Director, IIPA, former Secretaries to the Government of India, former Chairman SEBs, former Chairman

NTPC, former Technical Members of SEBs, among others. After wide consultations with all the stakeholders, including the Trade Union representatives, the Report was finalized.

Some of the key findings of the Study were:

- Restructuring is a necessary but not a sufficient condition for turnaround of the power sector. The restructuring is only the beginning and not the end of the process. It must be accompanied by continuous complementary efforts.
- Strong and sustained political support during all phases of restructuring is the key. Reform efforts in the politically sensitive power sector would succeed only with the strong backing and support of the political hierarchy. All efforts should be consolidated through a national level political commitment.
- Taking the employees into confidence and enlisting their willing support and strengthening the institution of Electricity Regulators are critical factors for success and sustainability of power sector reforms.
- Most of the restructured GENCOs, TRANSCOs and some of the DISCOMs have now become financially viable. Consequently, they are able to attract additional investments and better technological and managerial interventions.
- The level of consumer satisfaction in these States is also significantly higher.
- Restructuring has brought in the required accountability triggering improved performance in parameters.
- Restructuring should not be misconstrued as privatisation. It requires aggressive education, to promote the essence of restructuring.
- State Governments should appoint suitable competent officers to hold the post of the CMD in each of the new companies and give them a fixed tenure at least of three years.
- The States should grant full autonomy and should enforce corporate accountability.
- A Financial Restructuring Plan (FRP) should be formulated to achieve financial turnaround.
- Ministry of Power should not grant any further extensions of time to States for completing the restructuring process.
- State Governments should bring out a Detailed Policy Statement (DPS) about the restructuring of the remaining SEBs.

- The State Governments should establish plans to target a gradual reduction and eventual elimination of the subsidy (except for life-line support for clearly defined categories like BPL families, etc.) over a defined period.
- The model adopted by the Government of Andhra Pradesh for managing the reform may be followed after customisation, by other States.
- Multi Year Tariff (MYT) frameworks should be adopted by all the ERCs within the next two years.
- The orders and directions issued by the ERCs should be invariably honoured. Wherever there is a difference of views, consultations with the Regulator should be held to iron out the differences.
- In addition to acting as quasi-judicial bodies, the Regulatory Commissions should play a more proactive role in implementing the provisions relating to Open Access, MYTs and standards of performance (SOP).
- The Forum of Regulators (FOR) and Forum of Indian Regulators (FOIR) should become effective consultative platforms for bringing better understanding through sharing of information and experience.
- The Commissions should have full autonomy in pattern, organizational structure and adequate powers to recruit staff.
- In order to professionalise the Board of Directors, at least 50% of the Directors should be Independent Directors, drawn from a panel of experts.
- No political personnel including the Ministers should hold any position on the Boards of the restructured companies.
- The utilities should implement the Universal Metering Programme, to be completed within a definite time period, (including agricultural).
- It is necessary to conduct proper energy accounting.
- Resource Planning (ERP) based Information Technology (IT) solution would be beneficial.
- The Transmission companies should be the most appropriate agency to undertake all functions related to State-wide planning and coordination.

The Group of Experts hoped that this Report would positively facilitate a heightened appreciation of the issues and challenges confronting the power sector. The findings would trigger a rejuvenated power sector regime, enjoying fullest support of all the stakeholders.

The Report was recently presented to Sushilkumar Shinde, Minister of Power, Government of India and the same is under active consideration of the government.

CHAIRMAN, ADVISORY BOARD, URJAVARAN FOUNDATION

I have been associated as Chairman, Advisory, Board Urjavaran Foundation, ever since its inception in 2007. Urjavaran Foundation is a voluntary non-profit NGO playing the role of a catalyst in bringing together various agencies on a common platform to achieve energy conservation and sustainability of environment. It creates awareness among all sections of society and industry about the environmental degradation and endeavours to impress upon the people about energy conservation and environmental preservation. It highlights provisions of the Energy Conservation Act of 2001 and hold interactive sessions with various Industries, Associations and Chambers. It disseminates information for efficient use of energy and its conservation. It uses various channels of communications to mould public opinion, through seminars, conferences, workshops and exhibitions. It publishes bimonthly Journal highlighting the sectorwise issues on energy conservation and environmental protection.

My active association with the power sector continues.

TWENTY FOUR

AN AUTHOR

I was thinking about writing a book on Power Sector Reforms in view of my association with this very crucial sector for nearly 15 years. Even though I had conceptualized the contents of the book and had also collected some valuable material, I could not commence dictation as my work in the UPSC kept me quite busy. In the meanwhile, the earliest inspiration for writing the first book came from Prof. P. Ramarao, Vice-Chancellor, Central University, Hyderabad who had requested me, while travelling once on a flight from Hyderabad to Delhi in 2001 to deliver Dr. Ambedkar Memorial lecture at the University. So much had been written on Dr. Ambedkar by so many eminent persons that there was hardly anything new left for me to contribute. While pondering about what I could say about Dr. Ambedkar, I recollected that several persons associated with the power sector used to mention Dr. Ambedkar's contribution to the power sector without giving any details. I, therefore, decided to write about Dr. Ambedkar's contribution to the power sector. This gave me an opportunity to make an in-depth study on the various aspects of Dr. Ambedkar's contributions in the field of Economics. I also referred extensively to the 16 volumes of Dr. Ambedkar's speeches brought out by the Government of Maharashtra and the literature available on the subject in the various libraries. Eminent professors' who were present when I delivered the lecture were so impressed by the contents of my talk, that they suggested that I expand my lecture into a book by undertaking some more in-depth study on the subject. However, I was keen to first attempt a book on the Power

Sector, as I had considerable knowledge on the subject. Subsequently, if possible, I would do a book on Dr. Ambedkar's contribution to the economic planning of the country.

In the meanwhile, I suddenly lost my wife, Suryakumari on 6th December, 2001, which totally shattered me. In spite of my best efforts, I was not able to reconcile to the tragedy. It was during this time of mourning, that I decided to take up writing the book on Dr. Ambedkar, to divert my attention from my personal tragedy. I kept myself occupied by visiting Universities and Libraries to collect the necessary information. Thus the book on "Ambedkar's Contribution for Economic Planning and Development—Its Relevance" was born.

"AMBEDKAR'S CONTRIBUTION TO ECONOMIC PLANNING AND DEVELOPMENT—ITS RELEVANCE"

Most people remember Dr. Ambedkar, or "Babasaheb", as the architect of the Indian Constitution and as an emancipator of the poor and deprived who fought for social justice. One important aspect of Dr. Ambedkar's multifaceted personality, which was not widely known, was that as an eminent economist he had contributed substantially to the formulation of the post war Economic Development Plan of India in general, and water resources and electric power development in particular.

Dr. Ambedkar had distinct views on many aspects of our economy—agriculture, land reforms, industrialization and the role of labour and the poor in planning the country's growth. It is not common knowledge that the Central Government's water resources and power planning and development policy was formulated for the first time on an all-India basis during 1942–46, when Dr. Ambedkar was Member, Labour, Irrigation and Electric Power Department in the Executive Council of the Viceroy during 1942–46. He established two technical organizations, namely the Central Waterways, Irrigation and Navigation Commission—the precursor of the present day's Central Water Commission and the Central Technical Power Board, the precursor to the Central Electricity Authority. Dr. Ambedkar advocated, for the first time, the concept of 'River Valley Authority' to manage the Inter-state river valley projects. He was instrumental in promoting the Damodar Valley Project, the *first multi-purpose project* providing for irrigation, hydro-power, navigation and flood control, which later set in motion several multi-purpose projects, such as Bhakra Nangal, Damodar Valley, Mahanadi, Sone and Tungabhadra river projects. These projects have undoubtedly transformed the face of India and the Draft National Water Policy (2001) reiterated the inter basin transfer of water advocated by Dr. Ambedkar more that five decades ago.

The Department of Power was created for the first time at the national level by Dr. Ambedkar, who advocated that India should not only produce abundant power but also the cheapest power. He stressed the need for inter-connection of transmission network between the States, which laid the foundations for today's National Power Grid.

The impact of Economic Planning and Development by Dr. Ambedkar on India's planning has been substantial and he was indeed an architect of Economic Planning and Development of the country.

PRIME MINISTER RELEASED THE BOOK

The book was released by Atal Bihari Vajpayee, Prime Minister of India in the Parliament in 2002 in the august presence of Suresh Prabhu, Minister of Power, M. Venkaiah Naidu, Minister of Rural Development, and several other prominent Members of Parliament inter alia including N. Janardhana Reddy, former Chief Minister, Andhra Pradesh, Yerran Naidu, Leader, Telugu Desam Parliamentary Party, Sushilkumar Shinde and T. Subbarami Reddy.

The book "Ambedkar's Contribution to Economic Planning and Development—Its Relevance" was translated into Hindi as '*Bhartiya Arthik Shilpakar*' and was released by S. Jaipal Reddy, Minister for Urban Development, Government of India in the Parliament House in august presence of several prominent Members of Parliament which included N. Janardhana Reddy, former Chief Minister, Andhra Pradesh and G. Venkat Swamy, Deputy Leader, Congress Parliamentary Party in Lok Sabha and the function was presided over by Sardar Charanjeet Singh Atwal, Deputy Speaker, Lok Sabha.

The book was also translated into Telugu as "*Bharat Arthika Roopa Shilpi-Dr. Ambedkar*" and was released by Y.S. Rajasekhara Reddy, Chief Minister of Andhra Pradesh and attended by several dignitaries including Dr. Geetha Reddy, Minister of Industries, Government of Andhra Pradesh.

PRESIDENT OF INDIA RECEIVED FIRST COPY OF THE BOOK

The first copy of the book 'Power Sector Reforms—Focus On Distribution' was presented to Dr. A.P.J. Abdul Kalam, President of India.

The book was formally released by Anant Gite, Minister of Power, Government of India under the banner of Suryakumari Abraham Memorial Foundation, in the presence of several dignitaries in March 2003.

"POWER SECTOR REFORMS—FOCUS ON DISTRIBUTION"

Of my 35 years in the IAS, I spent 15 years working in the power sector. My first stint in this sector was from May 1969 to May 1972 (Fourth Five Year Plan of the country), when I was Secretary, Maharashtra State Electricity Board, 1969. The period coincided with all the State Electricity Boards undertaking the expansion of power generation capacities, transmission and distribution networks, massive programmes of rural electrification, electrification of villages and energisation of agricultural pump sets, in order to fulfil the objective of extending electricity beyond the urban areas. At that time, there was keen competition among the State Governments and SEBs to win national awards annually for extending electricity to the maximum number of villages, and for energisation of the largest number of pump sets. There was considerable pressure on the SEBs and their finances to ensure the supply of electricity to more and more villages and pumps. Targets, especially in energisation of pumps, used to go beyond a lakh of connections for most of the States. A substantial portion of the budgets of the States, sometimes even more than 50%, were allocated to the power sector. Although these efforts contributed substantially to ushering in an era of widespread use of electricity for the growth of industry, commerce and agriculture, there was very little realization that one day the enthusiasm of the SEBs and the State Governments would land the SEBs in considerable financial distress, bringing them to the brink of financial disaster. This would happen because rural electrification and energisation of agricultural pumps programmes, although they contributed to economic growth, was totally unremunerative.

My next phase of association with the power sector was from May 1986 to January 1989, first as Secretary, Energy Department, Government of Maharashtra. and then as Chairman, Maharashtra State Electricity Board from February 1989 to July 1991. (entire Seventh Five Year Plan and Two yearly plans). This period coincided with the growth of this sector in physical, financial and commercial performance. Although the budgetary provisions from the State Governments were getting reduced, the gap between demand and supply was increasing; T

& D losses, theft of energy, receivables and payables were on the rise; subsidies were increasing and the gap between cost of supply and tariff was widening. The extension of electricity to far-flung areas had also brought in its wake managerial problems of lack of proper supervision and control over the activities of the SEBs, as the area of control had enlarged. The deficiencies in the system, therefore, became increasingly more prominent, but still under control and manageable.

By the time I became Power Secretary, Government of India a few years later (1994–97), (Eighth Five Year Plan), the problems in the power sector had become much more pronounced and the overall deterioration in the functioning of the sector was easily palpable, with a large number of SEBs unable to earn the statutory return of not less than 3 per cent; the gap between demand and supply further widened; T & D losses had skyrocketed; theft of energy had become rampant, and the quality of power supply had deteriorated. It was under these circumstances that the 'Common Minimum National Action Plan for Power' (CMNPP) 1996 was approved in the Chief Ministers' Conference, ushering in comprehensive power sector reforms, including distribution, which has since become the national agenda. The CMNPP, *inter alia*, comprised the following:

(a) restructuring the State Electricity Boards,
(b) creation of Central Electricity Regulatory Commission (CERC) and State Electricity Regulatory Commissions (SERCs),
(c) finalisation of the Integrated National Energy Policy,
(d) Metering of all electrical connections,
(e) Reduction in T & D losses, and
(f) fixation of tariffs for agriculture.

In spite of several initiatives taken by the Government of India and the State Governments to reform the sector, the overall situation continued to be far from satisfactory. Having been instrumental in initiating reforms in the Power Sector in 1996, I had a chance to assess the performance of this sector after 6 years of reforms.

My book on the power sector was a sincere attempt to give a comprehensive view of the present status of the power industry, the need for accelerated reforms, the experience of power sector reforms at the international level, the various alternative models of reforms, status of the reforms in various states in India, especially Orissa, Delhi,

Haryana, Andhra Pradesh and Maharashtra and the lessons to be learnt from this valuable experience by the other States embarking upon similar reforms. I also analyzed the prerequisites required for carrying out such reforms as well as privatization and the road map ahead for bringing these reforms to a logical conclusion, so that a healthy and viable power sector could be created to contribute substantially to the all-round growth of our economy.

This book had provided an opportunity to those states undertaking reforms to evaluate their own strategies in terms of the Government support for reforms, including support during the transition period, organizational and financial restructuring and all other issues, which are necessary for reforms.

PRESIDENT OF INDIA RECEIVED FIRST COPY OF THE BOOK

The first copy of the 'Power Sector Reforms—Focus on Distribution' was presented to Dr. A.P.J. Abdul Kalam, President of India. The book was formally released by Anant Gite, Minister of Power, Government of India under the banner of Suryakumari Abraham Memorial Foundation, in the presence of several dignitaries in March 2003

It is natural for me to have a commitment for the sector due to my long innings in the realm of 'power'. No, wonder, even after my retirement from service, I have continued my association with this sector, which is very close to my heart. I continue to write articles to various premier national and international dailies and journals on vital matters related to the Power Sector and also participate in national and international seminars on the subject.

Post retirement, I was the Chairman of the 'Committee of Experts on Restructuring of MSEB'; Chairman of the 'Committee on Accelerated Power Development and Reform Programme (APDRP)' and Project Director and Head of the 'Group of Experts' for the study sponsored by the Ministry of Power on 'Impact of Restructuring of SEBs'. I am presently functioning as Chairman, Maharashtra State Power Generation Company, Mumbai, (MAHAGENCO—a Government of Maharashtra Company), apart from being an Independent Director on the boards of several Power Sector Companies.

TWENTY FIVE

A TRIBUTE TO MY BELOVED WIFE– SURYAKUMARI

It is quite often said that 'behind every successful man, there is always a woman'. While I do not know about the 'success' part, in my career, there is in my case, none other than my beloved wife, Suryakumari, fondly called by many as 'Suri', while for me it was always 'Bujji', during thick and thin ever since, she came into my life as my beloved life partner.

OUR MARRIAGE

Ever since I was allotted to the State of Maharashtra, after I got into the IAS, at the young age of twenty two, my parents Sundaram and Deevenamma were quite concerned about my health and well being. They were very keen that I should get married to an Andhra girl and settle down early in life, as they were afraid that by staying in Maharashtra for long as a bachelor, I would get married to a Maharashtrian girl and thus be permanently separated from them, as they would not be comfortable with a daughter in law with whom they would not be able to converse. They were, therefore, making frantic efforts to identify a suitable girl and finally chose Suryakumari, who came from the illustrious Vejendla family from Guntur. Her father Vejendla Moses was an educationist of repute and was working as Additional Director in the Directorate of Public Instructions, Government of Andhra Pradesh, at the time our marriage. During this tenure, he worked very closely with Kenneth Galbraith, US

Ambassador to India, who was closely monitoring the 'mid-day meal' programmes in Andhra Pradesh. Prior to this, he was District Education Officer, Nellore and Visakhapatnam Districts. All her uncles, aunts and cousins are in education, engineering and medical professions. Similarly, her mother Irene, a medico by profession, came from a highly educated family of engineers and doctors. Suri was the only child to her parents. She was studying for her graduation in Reddys college, Hyderabad at the time of her marriage. When the proposal came from her parents, my parents, I was informed, accompanied by a big team of my uncles and aunts went to see her at Bapatla, in Guntur District where her eldest uncle was staying. They were totally bowled over by the family and more importantly by Suryakumari herself by her beauty and brains during the marriage interview. The south Indian marriage interview for an IAS groom could be tougher than getting into the IAS itself !!. They were so impressed by her, they simply informed me that I had only to convey a suitable date for marriage and there was simply no need for me to even see her, and marry her in accordance, with our family custom of arranged marriages. When I went on a short leave, before I was posted as Assistant Collector and Sub-Divisional Magistrate, Panvel, I saw Suryakumari at Hyderabad and instantly agreed for the marriage. The marriage was celebrated on 11th July 1964 with a short notice at Vijayawada, Krishna District. One particular greetings telegram which came from 'Innocent Ramachandran and Nuts Padmanabhan' from Jalgaon, attracted the maximum attention, as none could understand the funny greeting, till I explained to them that the greeting was from the Collector whose name was Innocent, the Superintendent of Police whose name was Ramachandran, the Assistant Collector Natarajan, (whom we used to refer in private conversation as 'Nuts') and the Assistant Superintendent of Police Padmanabhan and thus it became 'Innocent Ramachandran and Nuts Padmanabhan'!!

While I was still on leave after my marriage, I received my transfer orders, as Assistant Collector and Sub-Divisional Magistrate, Panvel Sub Division, Kolaba District (present Raighad district). I went thereafter to Jalgaon and took leave of John Innocent, District Collector, D. Ramachandran, District Superintendent of Police, other colleagues and friends and joined at Panvel, in the first week of August 1964.

DISTRICT LIFE IN MAHARASHTRA

My wife, Suryakumari, also joined me at Panvel soon thereafter. As there was no assigned bungalow for the Assistant Collector at Panvel, we initially stayed in the government inspection bungalow, till we secured a private house. Thus began my family life as well as holding the first independent charge in the district. Soon after she joined me, we had to celebrate the Independence Day. She was present at the Government function to celebrate Independence Day on 15th August 1964. It was her first official function as the wife of an IAS officer. I took the salute wearing a Gandhi cap, (a white cap was usually referred as such). The function was a grand success.

We could quickly set up our rented house and she started accompanying me on tours, as I was required to tour twenty one days in a month, which included several night halts. She was quite used to traveling in the Government jeeps as the daughter of a District Education Officer. However, she was shocked that the Assistant Collector had to travel by State transport bus from place to place as they were not provided with official transport. She could adjust well to walk up to the bus stand which was fortunately very close to my rented private house. She enjoyed tours to different places in he district inspite of inconvenience in travelling by State transport buses, until I purchased a 'Morris Minor' car.

While my wife used to accompany me regularly on tours in the initial stages, later she preferred to stay behind in the bungalow, as she was expecting a baby. It was during this period I officiated twice as District Magistrate for short durations during leave periods of the District Collector, Kolaba. The Collector's bungalow was very big and as she was scared to stay alone, she used to sometimes read all night, even though there were security guards who patrolled the house. As our stay in the bungalow was only for a short while, since I was holding the additional charge of Collector, she did not mind enjoying the loneliness with a book, while I was away on tours.

Our first child Manjula was born at Hyderabad while I was working as Assistant Collector, Panvel. I had taken a short leave to be with Suri at the time of her delivery. Manjula was born on 17th September 1965 at a time when Indo Pakistan war was at its peak. My friends used to joke after my daughter's birth that they would kill me if I had another child lest it may result in another Indo Pak war !!

After over a years stay at Panvel I was transferred to Nasik and Suri joined me at Nasik with our one month old daughter, Manjula. She soon realized as the wife of an IAS Officer that bringing up the children is entirely her responsibility and duty, as I was mostly busy with tours, night halts and tent camps, which were compulsory. I was putting in hard work and tirelessly working to prove myself in my budding career. In any case, with a few month's old child, one would not like to take the risk of touring with a young child for lack of proper arrangements in Government Inspection Bungalows and due to lack of proper medical facilities in the head quarters of Tehsils. Suri was mostly busy bringing up my daughter and also taking care of her medical needs.

S.N.A. Razvi, District Collector Nasik and his wife used to treat my wife and, our daughter Manjula, with lot of affection and kindness. They still appreciatively recollected even in November 2007, the lavish party given by Suri on my daughter's first birthday !

FIRST LADY OF THE DISTRICT AS THE COLLECTOR'S WIFE

After about a year's stint, I was transferred to Bhir, as Collector and District Magistrate. Bhir being a very small and backward place, my wife was really concerned about the medical facilities for our 1 year old daughter, Manjula. There was only one hospital that too only a Government Civil hospital and hardly there was any Pediatrician. We also found that the Collector's bungalow was a very old and dingy Dak Bungalow, converted into Collector's Bungalow not hygienically good for a child. My daughter used to fall ill quite often. I had to finally opt for a newly constructed small bungalow as Collector's bungalow. Luckily, there was a very good civil surgeon Dr. Wagle, who was readily available to look after our medical needs. There was an Officer's Club of which the Collector was the Chairman and the Collector's wife was the Chairman of Wife's Association of the Club. Suri took active interest in organizing several social get together's. Suri had several friends like mrs Milan Bahadur, mrs GangaKhedkar, mrs Abhange, mrs Mahajan etc., as most of us were staying in the newly built Officer's colony. She used to accompany me on tours whenever possible. My in-laws used to visit us regularly both at Nasik and Bhir and my wife was quite happy whenever they stayed with us. It is obvious that she was missing them, being the only child.

LIFE IN BOMBAY

After a stint of 2 and half years, I was transferred to Bombay as Secretary, Maharashtra state Electricity Board. It suited us fine as my daughter was growing up and she needed a good education. To get admission for a child in a good Convent in a Metropolis like Bombay is an experience by itself. After waiting several times outside the first floor room of the Principal of the Breach Candy Convent, Warden Road, Suri finally managed to get admission in the Kindergarten class. The Convent was luckily not far away from the MSEB officer's quarters (present Soudamini), Haji Ali.

Suri very quickly adjusted to life in Bombay and made several life long friends in Soudamini building itself, prominent among them being mrs. Meena Bhagwat, Mrs. Y.S. Das, Mrs. Anil Sood, Mrs. S.N. Misra to name a few. It was for the first time that we met K. Padmanabhaiah, IAS (1961) and Satyawati Padmanabhaiah. K. Padmanabhaiah hailed from Krishna District from where I also came from and he was my senior in Andhra University. Padmabhaiah's children Gnyandeep and Manni and my children Manjula and Rajesh literally grew up together from childhood. My batchmate P. Subrahmanyam IAS (1962) and Satyabhama Subrahmanyam were the other family, whom we met frequently.

There were many important people from Andhra Pradesh in Bombay with whom we could make a lasting friendship, they included L.V. Prasad, a renowned producer and director and a well known icon of the film industry in the country and who had several national award winning movies in Hindi, Telugu and Tamil to his credit ; Ramesh Prasads, M.V. Subbaraos, Janardhana Raos, Krishna Raos, Mallikharjuna Raos etc. Having come to know a large number of film celebrities, we were frequently invited for many film premiers and film shootings. Our favourate picnic spot was Aerey Milk Colony's picturesque gardens.

BABY SITTING FOR RACE-GOING COLLEAGUES

The Soudamini building where I was allotted a flat on the seventh floor as Secretary, MSEB, was located opposite Haji Ali, a famous landmark of Bombay. It had a panoramic view of the sea. It also had a race course boundary on the other side, with a vantage view of the entire race course. We often used to go to the race course for morning walks. I rarely went for the races and also rarely watched them, although I could have watched the entire race from start to finish from my balcony. Some of my friends,.

however, used to come to our flat to watch the races on the race days. Some of my colleagues who were regular race goers, used to leave their young children with us, so that we could look after them while they were busy betting and enjoying the races. Although baby sitting was fun in the initial stages, we lost all the holidays, as we could not move out of the house, leaving the friends children behind. Suri, an excellent hostess, not only took good care of the children but also used to lay out a big spread, by the time my colleagues came to pick up their children. Even though it was inconvenient for us, this gave us an excellent opportunity to make lasting friendships with our colleagues and for my daughter, Manjula, a good number of her age group children to play. Manjula had her education in Bombay and Hyderabad.

While I was working in Mumbai, we were blessed with our second child Rajesh on 2nd November 1972. As my family could not reach in time from Vijayawada, it goes to the credit of Mrs Misra, wife of S N Misra, Chief Engineer, MSEB, who subsequently became the Chairman, MSEB to stay in Dr. B N Purandhare's hospital, Marine drive Bombay till the confinement. Suri was fortunate to have such friends. Rajesh grew up in Bombay and had his education in Bombay, Hyderabad and Delhi. After completion of his graduation from St. Stephen's College, Delhi, he acquired his MBA degree from London. He is an entrepreneur in different fields.

During our entire stay in Bombay from 1969 to 1977 we never had any problem of accommodation, even though I had three postings – from Soudamini (7th Floor) to Meher Dad (10th Floor) in Cuffe Parade and to Buena Vista (11th Floor) opposite Mantralaya. We had very good week ends socially during our entire stay in Bombay, primarily because of a lively and cohesive group of friends and colleagues, mainly comprising of Padmanabhans, Srinavasans, Gopalakrishnans, Bhagwats, Bongirwars, Borwankars Parameshwarans, Varadarajans, Nagarajans, (mostly from the services) popularly known as 'Rummy group'. We used to assemble at a predetermined residence in the evenings in the week ends on the potlock basis. All ladies used to decide among themselves who should bring what food. There was more of fun and jokes and less of cards and they were really memorable and unforgettable evenings. Whenever we meet even now, we never miss to reminiscence those good old days.

POSTING IN HYDERABAD

Although I was functioning as Joint Secretary (Industries), the

Government of India issued a circular about the vacancy of the post of Regional Iron and Steel Controller, Hyderabad under the Ministry of Steel. This circular was sent to all the states requesting for sponsoring officers to be spared on deputation.

Though I found the post of Joint Secretary (Industries) very challenging and highly valuable in terms of gaining experience, I was quite inclined to take up this assignment due to my domestic problems. Both my father-in-law and mother-in-law, were keeping very indifferent health in Andhra Pradesh and my wife, being their only child, was under considerable stress as she had to be away from her parents during their difficult days. In addition, a posting in Hyderabad would also give me an opportunity to be nearer to my parents, who were staying in Gaddamanugu, my native place near Vijayawada. Though they visited Bombay, they were not at all comfortable with the life style of Bombay. We thought that it was a God sent opportunity to apply for this assignment. Though there were many contenders for this post, especially from IAS officers hailing from Andhra Pradesh and allotted to other states like me, I was finally selected by the Ministry of Steel, perhaps due to my industrial experience in Maharashtra and the promotion of Iron and Steel Industries was being one of the primary responsibilities entrusted to the Iron and Steel Controller.

MAJOR BEREAVEMENTS IN THE FAMILY

We shifted to Hyderabad in September 1977 and moved into a private flat at Himayatnagar. Though, the objective in accepting an assignment in Hyderabad was to be with the family, unfortunately, within a few months of my posting there, my father-in-law, Vejendla Moses who had been ailing for some time, passed away in January 1978. After a year, my mother-in-law Irene also passed away. Suri could not get out of these shocks, for a long time, being the only child. However, while the loss was irreparable, we had the satisfaction of having been with them during their last days.

OUR FOREIGN TOUR

After 4 years stint as Iron and Steel Controller, I opted for deputation to the Government of Andhra Pradesh and we stayed in Hyderabad till April 1986. This gave an opportunity to spend some time with our families and relatives in Andhra Pradesh.

I undertook an extensive tour during November–December 1981, lasting for about forty days to UK, USA and Canada, as Vice-Chairman and Managing Director, Andhra Pradesh State Non-Resident Indian Investment Corporation Limited (ANRICH), to promote investments from non-resident Indians in Andhra Pradesh. Suri accompanied me during this tour which happened to be her first tour abroad. She was quite excited at the prospect of not only to make a around the world trip, visiting several countries but also to get an opportunity of meeting some of her family members who had migrated to the USA and whom she had not seen for several years. She loaded herself with several gifts to be distributed to them.

The first country of our visit was Italy and as our visit coincided with a Sunday, we were fortunate to see the Venerable Highness Pope and hear his message and receive His Blessing at Vatican, Rome. Other landmarks which fascinated her immensely *inter alia*, were the Eiffel Tower, Paris and Buckingham Palace, London. She was also thrilled at being at the top of the world at World Trade Centre, New York ; a picturesque and breath taking view of Niagara Falls ; Canada ; C & N Towers, Toronto ; Universal Studios and Disney Land, Los Angeles ; Golden Gate Bridge, San Francisco ; Hot Springs and Waikiki Beach, Honolulu (Hawai Islands) ; Emperor's Palace, Tokyo ; Thai Village, Bang kok ; Hong Kong and Singapore. She was very found of collecting crystal and porcelain figurines from various countries, an interest she continued till the end. I would be dishonest if I did not mention about her buying little bit of gold jewelry at New York and plenty of Saris at Little India, Singapore. Her complaint was that I intentionally did not allow her adequate time and money in order to make more purchases.

In New York we met Ramamurthys — Ramamurthy a Ph.D professor and Mrs Varalakshmi, a medico. They have become our life long friends and every time we visited New York or Ramamurthys visited India, we make it a point to meet.

MEETING OUR RELATIVES

Our first major meeting with our relatives was in Detroit. Suri was very happy to be received by four of her cousins at Detroit airport. She was thrilled to meet her '*maama*' (mother's brother) Rudolph and Phoebe Aunty and all their children, who migrated to the USA in mid sixties. Our visit to Detroit coincided with the 'Thanksgiving' day-a-day of celebration in USA. Her '*maama*' ensured that the entire family consisting of three daughters and their husbands and two sons were present. He also invited several guests to meet us. When her '*maama*' offered Suri some wine during the 'Thanksgiving Day' she refused to taste wine and her '*maama*' teased her about it..

She was also happy to meet another Uncle, Philip who migrated to the USA long back and his Philippino wife and their children at Los Angeles. Similarly, she was happy to meet her first cousin Vejendla Rajkumar, who also migrated to the US with his wife and their new born son, Deepak, at San Fransisco, California. The entire trip starting from Bombay – Italy – Germany – France – UK – USA – Canada – Japan – Hong kong – Thailand – Singapore and back to Bombay was a very memorable for us.

MARRIAGE OF MY DAUGHTER

While I was functioning as the Commissioner of Industries, Andhra Pradesh, we started receiving marriage proposals for my daughter Manjula. As she was only 19 years old and in the final year of B.Sc, we were not keen about her marriage. However, we received a proposal from a very highly respected and educated family of Busi's from Guntur. Busi Sam Bob, son of Mrs. Busi Jayamani and Mr. Busi Peter, got into the IAS in 1983, while pursuing his Ph.D at Andhra University, Waltair. He was undergoing training at the Lal Bahadur Shashtri Academy of Administration, Mussoorie. As it was a very good proposal, we had to convince ourselves first and then our daughter for an early marriage. Sam Bob assured us that she could continue her studies even after marriage. The marriage was celebrated on 15th May 1986 at Vijayawada, which was very well attended. N. Janardhana Reddy MP, who subsequently became the Chief Minister A.P., was among various VIPs who attended the marriage. We were honoured by the presence of N.T. Rama Rao, Chief Minister, Andhra Pradesh at the reception at Hyderabad. Suri was thrilled at becoming a young mother-in-law. Thus Sam became a new member of our family. My daughter not only completed her post graduation in English Literature but also a Bachelor of Education (B Ed), after marriage.

GRANDCHILDREN

Manish Priyank our first grandchild was born at Vellore on 4th March

1988, while Sam Bob was working as Joint Collector, Chittoor District, Suri was quite thrilled to be a grandmother at a young age. Manish had his entire early education from Delhi Public School, RK Puram. He is presently doing his final Engineering Degree in Electronics and Instrumentation at Birla Institute of Technology and Science (BITS) Pilani, Dubai Campus. Our second grandchild Aishwarya was born at Madras on 15th July 1992, when Sam was working as Collector Prakasam District, Ongole. It called for grand celebrations and the same was done with considerable fanfare.

When Sam had an opportunity for post graduate studies on Commonwealth scholarship at Manchester University, UK, he was keen to take his entire family—Manju, Manish and Aishwarya with him. Suri, however, insisted to leave Aishwarya with us as they would not be able to give the comforts abroad a two year old child deserved. She brought up Aishwarya in such a way that, Aishwarya hardly remembered her parents during her entire stay of 1 year with us. Suri used to send Aishwarya's photographs to her parents regularly to show how she was growing up. She maintained regular contact on phone and made Aishwarya to talk to her parents. She used to dress her up like a doll, take her regularly to a play school near by and waited till the class was over. Suri celebrated Aishwarya's birthday on a grand scale in the absence of her parents. Aishwarya was also a student of Delhi Public School, RK Puram since her childhood. It was Suri who initiated Aishwarya into Kuchipudi dance with Internationally renowned Padmabhushan's Raja, Radha and Kaushalya Reddy. Aishwarya had her 'Arangethram' at the young age of fourteen, on 12th April 2007 at Delhi and she is now an accomplished dancer, giving solo performances under the guidance of her 'gurus'. She is presently studying in Junior College in Hyderabad.

ANDHRA CM'S VISIT TO OUR HOUSE

N. Janardhana Reddy, Chief Minister, Andhra Pradesh once visited Bombay, for a meeting with Sharad Pawar, Chief Minister, Maharashtra at Taj Hotel, Bombay. After the meeting, when Sharad Pawar asked Janardhana Reddy whether he was going to the airport directly, he was surprised to hear from Janardhana Reddy that he will be proceeding to the airport after coming to my flat 315, Shalaka, Bombay. I was working then as Chairman, MSEB. Sharad Pawar was quite surprised that I knew his counter-spart from Andhra Pradesh so well that Janardhana Reddy took special trouble to visit us and share our hospitality. These were very special moments in our life, especially as Janardhana Reddy knew Suri from her childhood days, as her father worked as District Education Officer, Nellore in early 60's. We are ever grateful to Janardhana Reddy for this gesture.

GRACIOUS HOSTESS

Suri was a gracious hostess with plenty of warmth and grace. 'Suri, thy name is hospitality' was what her friends used to say. She was always very meticulously dressed, so much so a large portion of our savings went for making up her wardrobe. Her Kanjeevaram saree collection was the envy of her many friends. Whenever there were parties at home, they were always meticulously planned and choicest food was served. There was invariably an Andhra speciality dish known as 'Gongoora' (a leafy vegetable) mutton. Everytime, I went on tour to Hyderabad, I had to invariably bring plenty of 'Gongoora'. She used to make this curry so well, friends invariably asked for the curry, the minute they land up for the get-togethers. If there were ten guests, food would be cooked for at least double the number, even at the cost of considerable wastage. True to her nature, any visitor who comes home was never allowed to leave the house without a meal irrespective of the time of the visit and her insistence quite often bordered on embarrassment to the guests. She insisted on Rajgopal, then Chairman Lanco Group of Industries, presently MP, who used to call her 'aunty', having dinner with us just two days before her demise. The night before her death our friend, Trilok Jhalani who had come from Mumbai joined us for a last minute dinner.

Ajit Jogi prior to becoming the Chief Minister of Chattisgarh was our neighbour, at AB 79, Shah Jahan Road. He was also fond of long walks. He quite often used to drop in at our home unannounced for his favourite Idli and Dosa after morning walks and Suri never disappointed him from having his favourite breakfast ready.

OUR FOREIGN VISIT ONCE AGAIN

After I retired from the IAS and was working as Member, Union Public Service Commission, we went on a holiday for a month to London, during July–August 1997, where our son Rajesh was studying for MBA. We also visited Scotland, Wales and Switzerland during this holiday. In

Wales, we met Kondru Nooka Raju, brother of K.S.R. Murthy, an IAS officer from Andhra Pradesh. Though this was our first visit to Wales and also our first meeting with Raju's, Suri adjusted herself with the family so well, which made the visit to Wales a memorable one. Since then, whenever we visited U.K., we made it a point to visit Wales and spend as much time as possible with Raju and his family.

Her last visit abroad was in the summer of 1998 alongwith our daughter Manjula and two grandchildren Manish and Aishwarya. Rajesh was still in London. Suri enjoyed our holiday with our children and grandchildren. Suri loved playing with grandchildren in Kensington and Hyde Park gardens and visiting important places in London, Wales and Scotland, that time too. While visiting Scotland we had a stop over at Manchester and spent some time with Sucharita and Jayachandra Reddy. Reddys have been in UK for over three decades. Although Jayachandra Reddy was a very renowned doctor, Sucharita Reddy was a well reputed social activist and President of Andhra Association of Europe. Although my daughter took us to the place where she stayed in Manchester during 1994–1995, Manish took us to the school where he studied. Both my daughter and my grandson met all their friends during their stay in Manchester.

FAVOURITE PAST TIME—MATCH MAKING

Her favorite past time was 'match making'. Several people used to be in touch with her because of her wide contacts not only in Andhra Pradesh but also in Bombay and Delhi. She was only too happy to help them in these matters.

SAM TRANSFERRED TO DELHI

While I was working as a Member, UPSC, I was staying in AB 83, Shahjahan Road. My son- in-law Sam Bob, IAS, came on deputation to the Government of India in 1996 and was working then as Secretary to the Hon'ble Speaker, Lok Sabha, G.M.C. Balayogi.

MARRIAGE OF MY SON

In the summer of 2000, my son Rajesh, who was working in London, U.K., with Barclay Bank, after completion of his MBA at London returned to India on the insistence of my wife. Presently he is an entrepreneur in several sectors including I.T. She was also very keen for my son's early marriage and settle down. Vineetha, our daugher-in-law is the second daughter of Mrs. Vimala Nehamiah and Mr. Nehemiah, both of whom are in the medical profession and were working in Kenya. Vineetha had her early education in Kenya and persued her Engineering degree and MBA in Andhra Pradesh. He was married on 31st August, 2001. The reception at Hyderabad was attended by several 'who is who' of Hyderabad. We were honoured by the presence of GMC Balayogi, Hon'ble Speaker, Lok Sabha both at Hyderabad and New Delhi receptions. We had a reception at Mumbai too. Suri was at her gorgeous best. For the reception at Delhi, Ajit Jogi, Chief Minister, Chattisgarh came alongwith his entire family just to attend the reception. We were also honoured by the presence of Mrs. Sheila Dixit, Chief Minister, Delhi at the reception at Delhi. Rajesh also stayed with us, along with his wife Vineetha. We were all living like a happy family under one roof. One could not have asked for more from the God Almighty.

WORST PERSONAL TRAGEDY

On 6th December, 2001, my wife Bujji, suddenly complained of breathlessness after lunch. Inspite of each one's busy schedule, it so happened that the entire family was at home for lunch including our grandchildren. All of us were at home, but she collapsed even before we could realize what was happening and before the doctor, who was just a kilometer away, could reach our home. None could really believe such a shocking death, almost instantaneous without any forewarning whatsoever. It took several months for the entire family to get reconciled to the shocking loss of the dearest member of the family. As soon as the news of her sudden death spread, G.M.C. Balayogi Hon'ble speaker Lok Sabha, Yerran Naidu, Leader of Parliamentary party, Telugu Desam Party and N. Janardhana Reddy, M.P. and former Chief Minister of Andhra Pradesh rushed to the hospital. N. Chandrababu Naidu Chief Minister of Andhra Pradesh visited our house and paid a floral tribute before the body was taken for cremation. Several VVIPS followed her funeral procession including Mohan Babu, the superstar of Telugu cinema. The memorial service was attended by several well wishers.

She used to take long walks both in the morning and evenings. As we were staying in AB 83, Shahjahan Road, where Shrimati Rama Devi then Secretary General, Rajya Sabha was also residing in the same colony also used to have long walks together. Rama Devi, who had become subsequently the Governor of Himachal Pradesh and Karnataka, paid glowing tributes to Bujji during the memorial service. Similar tributes were also paid by G. Venkat Swami, N. Janardhan Reddy, G.M.C. Balayogi, Yerran Naidu etc.

Although, it has been 6 and half years since my wife's death she is very fondly remembered by her friends and relatives alike. Our family is really touched whenever people talk about how genuine a human being she was. She was always ready to help people, especially the poor. As a family, each one of us in our own way tries to fill the vacuum she has left but it has been next to impossible.

At times, I wonder due to my pre-occupation to excel in my career whether, I neglected to take care of her health, which led to her early demise. This lingering thought will remain with me forever though I try to convince myself otherwise.

TWENTY SIX

BACK TO THE ROOTS

SURYAKUMARI ABRAHAM MEMORIAL FOUNDATION

My wife Suryakumari and I were quite keen to start some socio economic activity in and around the area, where I had grown up and had my early education, even though we were able to contribute from time to time for the development of my village and the surrounding areas. My efforts resulted in getting electricity to my unelectrified village, which contributed for the overall development of the village, including getting electricity to the agricultural pump sets. I could personally take a young IAS colleague, S. Banerjee, IAS (1971), Sub Collector, Vijaywada to my village in early seventies appreciate the problems of the poor villagers and he was able to redress their grievances primarily relating to land matters and in particular, granting *pattas* (land rights) to the poor. He was the first IAS officer ever to visit my village, in early seventies, besides the village having produced an IAS Officer in me. We had also facilitated improving the sanitary facilities, construction of village roads and community centre. Due to my efforts, a gas filling station was established at my village by Gas Authority of India (GAIL), providing employment opportunities to the local population. Through my efforts, an Industrial Estate was established at Kondapalli in eighties, which helped considerably for the industrial development of the area, providing employment to the local people.

However, in spite of our best efforts, we could not establish any organization to undertake the socio economic activities on a continuous basis in the area, primarily because I was working most of the time in Maharashtra and New Delhi and my jobs kept me so busy that there was no spare time. In the meanwhile, unfortunately, my wife Suryakumari suddenly passed away on 6 December 2001, plunging the entire family in shock and utter disbelief. As one of her earnest desires during her life time was to undertake major socioeconomic activities work which would be useful to society, I could not delay the starting of a formal organization any longer. I, therefore, started the Suryakumari Abraham Memorial Foundation in 2002, in her memory, of which I am the Chairman.

Aims and Objectives

- To uplift the downtrodden, and illiterate villagers irrespective of caste and creed.
- To provide education for the poor and the needy through establishment of schools and vocational training courses.
- To facilitate self-help programmes and provide technical and computer education in rural areas.
- To provide medical aid through mobile medical vans, dispensaries and medical camps in rural areas.
- To undertake other humanitarian programmes to improve the socio-economic conditions of the rural poor.
- To work for welfare of beggars and street children.
- To promote schemes for the welfare, employment and empowerment of women and children in rural areas.

It is a socio-economic Voluntary Organization, a non profit service organization, with the sole objective of working in the rural areas for the upliftment of poor and villagers, with an emphasis on children and empowerment of women irrespective of caste and creed. The Corpus for the Foundation has primarily come from the contributions made by my family and well wishers. All the sale proceeds of the four books written by me have gone towards Corpus of the Foundation.

The activities so far undertaken by the Foundation are as follows:

1. *A Centre for Tailoring and Embroidery* was started in August 2005 in our family house, dedicated to the Foundation at our village

at Gaddamanugu Kondur in Krishna District, Andhra Pradesh. The first batch of 50 women, 25 each in the morning and evening sessions, were trained in tailoring and embroidery for a year by highly qualified teachers. All the 50 women were presented Sewing Machines free of cost by the Foundation at a largely attended public function at G Kondur on 24th October 2006. The sewing machines gifted by the Foundation helped the women to become self reliant through self employment, while making a useful addition to their family income. The second batch of 50 women are presently undergoing training at the Centre. It is proposed to make substantial investments to purchase more modern sewing machines and high speed embroidery machines for giving better training, so that they could be better equipped to embark on their own self employment programmes. The Foundation intends to make the Centre a model organisation by forming self help groups and tying up with markets for the products made by them, so that, they can generate additional income to the family on a regular and permanent basis.

2. The Foundation has started giving *scholarships to meritorious boys and girls of* 7th Standard who secure high grades in public examination from *Elementary School at Gaddamanugu and meritorious boys and girls* who secure high grades in the 10th Standard examination from Jilla Parishad *High School at Kondur,* where I had my early schooling. These scholarships are being given annually since 2002.

3. The Foundation had also conducted a *Medical Camp at G. Kondur,* where a team of 30 specialist doctors and paramedical staff, from Vijayawada, attended to a large number of villagers in 2004. Free Medical check ups, including lab facilities were provided in the Camp and free medicines were also distributed to the needy. The Foundation also supplied spectacles to about 30 patients free of cost. The camp was a tremendous success. The Foundation proposes to organize more such Free Medical Camps on annual basis in the future to provide relief, to the otherwise medically neglected rural people.

The Foundation has been extensively propagating AIDS prevention practices through dissemination of information in rural areas.

4. The Foundation has started Computer Training courses from November 2007 for unemployed educated rural women, using qualified teachers. It is proposed to substantially expand the computer training facilities at Kondur.

I have been visiting my village very frequently and my last visit was as late as 21st July 2008. It is my cherished wish to spend as much time as possible to make the Foundation a role model in creating self help groups and help the poor and contribute for the socio economic development of the rural area, in which I grew up to return something to the society which gave me so much to cherish in my life.

Index